COMPUTER AIDED GEOMETRIC DESIGN

ACADEMIC PRESS RAPID MANUSCRIPT REPRODUCTION

Proceedings of a Conference
Held at The University of Utah
Salt Lake City, Utah
March 18-21, 1974

COMPUTER AIDED GEOMETRIC DESIGN

EDITED BY

ROBERT E. BARNHILL

Department of Mathematics
University of Utah
Salt Lake City, Utah

RICHARD F. RIESENFELD

Department of Computer Science
University of Utah
Salt Lake City, Utah

ACADEMIC PRESS *New York San Francisco London 1974*

A Subsidiary of Harcourt Brace Jovanovich, Inc.

ACADEMIC PRESS, INC.
111 Fifth Avenue, New York, New York 10003

United Kingdom Edition published by
ACADEMIC PRESS, INC. (LONDON) LTD.
24/28 Oval Road, London NW1

Library of Congress Catalog Card Number: 74-25196

ISBN 0-12-079050-5

PRINTED IN THE UNITED STATES OF AMERICA

CONTENTS

CONTENTS

CONTRIBUTORS

Robert E. Barnhill, (45), Department of Mathematics, University of Utah, Salt Lake City, Utah 84112.

P. Bézier, (127), Regie Renault, Billancourt Seine, Paris, France.

Edwin Catmull, (317), Department of Computer Science, University of Utah, Salt Lake City, Utah 84112.

S. A. Coons, (1), Systems and Information Science, Syracuse University, Syracuse, New York 13210.

A. R. Forrest, (17), Computer Laboratory, Cambridge University, Cambridge, England.

William J. Gordon, (95), Department of Mathematics, General Motors Research Laboratories, Warren, Michigan 48090.

John A. Gregory, (71), Department of Mathematics, Brunel University, Uxbridge, Middlesex, England (Visitor at The University of Utah, 1974).

Robert J. McDermott, (89), Department of Computer Science, University of Utah, Salt Lake City, Utah 84112.

Even Mehlum, (173), Central Institute for Industrial Research, Forskningsvn. 1, Blindern-Oslo 3, Norway.

CONTRIBUTORS

Martin E. Newell, (303), Department of Computer Science, University of Utah, Salt Lake City, Utah 84112.

Gregory M. Nielson, (209), Department of Mathematics, Arizona State University, Tempe, Arizona 85281.

George J. Peters, (259), Systems Programming, CAD/CAM, Department K692, McDonnell-Douglas Automation Company, St. Louis, Missouri 63166.

David T. Pilcher, (237), Hercules Inc., P. O. Box 98, Magna, Utah 84044.

Ronald D. Resch, (255), Department of Computer Science, University of Utah, Salt Lake City, Utah 84112.

Richard F. Riesenfeld, (95), Department of Computer Science, University of Utah, Salt Lake City, Utah 84112.

Raphael Rom, (317), Department of Computer Science, University of Utah, Salt Lake City, Utah 84112.

R. F. Wielinga, (153), Philips Research Laboratories, Eindhoven, Netherlands.

PREFACE

The first International Conference on Computer Aided Geometric Design (CAGD) was held at The University of Utah March 18-21, 1974, for the purpose of displaying the latest advances in CAGD. The word *geometric* distinguishes this field from computer aided *logical* design. This book is the edited Proceedings of the Conference.

At the conclusion of the Navy Workshop at Annapolis in 1971, Philip J. Davis proposed that there be a conference on "graphics and mathematics", a project that Leila Bram of the Office of Naval Research encouraged. Distinguished representatives in Europe and North America from universities, industry, and government laboratories were sought. Both researchers and users of the research were invited. The conference had an informal tone and ample time for discussion, with about 120 participants. There were talks and computer graphics demonstrations at The University of Utah and at Evans and Sutherland Corporation.

P. Bézier and S. A. Coons have played fundamental roles in CAGD, as was evidenced by the fact that most of the speakers referred to their pioneering work. The principal topics covered in the Proceedings are Coons patches, Bézier curves, and splines, with their applications to CAGD.

The editors express their sincere appreciation to the contributing authors, and to A. R. Forrest, W. J. Gordon, J. A. Gregory, and R. J. McDermott for their help. Proofreading and presentations of most of the papers were carried out by graduate students in Mathematics and Computer Science. The editors also thank C. Jensen, L. Merrell, and M. Holbrook for their typing and layout work, and A. R. Barnhill and L. Williams for artwork in the Proceedings.

PREFACE

The Conference and the Proceedings were sponsored by the Office of Naval Research and the Dean of Science at The University of Utah. Support was provided by the Departments of Mathematics and Computer Science at The University of Utah.

ROBERT E. BARNHILL

SURFACE PATCHES AND B-SPLINE CURVES

S.A. Coons
Syracuse University

Introduction.

This paper begins with a review of the surface patch equation, which may or may not be familiar to the reader. The properties of surface patches are described, but without proof. However, it is relatively simple to verify them by actual algebraic calculations.

Following this, the notion of "uniform cubic B-spline curves" is introduced, again without either derivation or verification of the B-spline formula. Such matters are dealt with elsewhere (see for instance Riesenfeld, deBoor, and others). These (compound) curves are then used to define the boundary conditions of surface patches, and also to describe the "blending functions" which appear in the surface patch equation. An interesting consequence of B-spline curves as boundaries of a patch is that boundaries with slope discontinuities (cusps) can be introduced, without inducing sharp folds or creases in the interior of the patch. This is an interesting, seemingly paradoxical result.

Surface Patches.

A surface "patch" is a segment of a surface, and it is expedient to represent it as the locus of a point $[x\ y\ z]$ moving in space with two degrees of freedom, u and w. We say that the point is a vector function of two independent parametric variables.

We can write

$$P(u,w) = [P_x(u,w)\ P_y(u,w)\ P_z(u,w)]$$

where the P_x, P_y, P_z are arbitrary functions. We can restrict the variables u and w to take on values between zero and one, simply to make the arithmetic more tractable. The vector quantities P(0,w) and P(1,w) then, are point loci with a single degree of freedom, represented by w, and are thus curves.

Similarly P(u,0) and P(u,1) are curves. These four curves define the boundaries of a surface segment or patch. Now we agree upon the following simplified notation:

$$\begin{aligned} P(u,w) &= uw \\ P(0,w) &= 0w \\ P(1,w) &= 1w \\ P(u,0) &= u0 \\ P(u,1) &= u1 \end{aligned}$$

We introduce some univariate functions and <u>their</u> special notation: we show it for u, but it also applied to the variable w:

$$\begin{aligned} F_0(u) &= F_0u \\ F_1(u) &= F_1u \\ G_0(u) &= G_0u \\ G_1(u) &= G_1u. \end{aligned}$$

Here we simply eliminate the parentheses. These have come to be known in the trade as "blending functions", because loosely speaking they "mix" or "blend" the shapes of boundary curves, to produce internal curves that define, or delineate, the surface.

A particular surface can now be defined as follows:

$$uw = [\,F_0u\;\, F_1u\;\, G_0u\;\, G_1u\,]\begin{bmatrix} 0w \\ 1w \\ 0w_u \\ 1w_u \end{bmatrix} + [\,u0\;\, u1\;\, u0_w\;\, u1_w\,]\begin{bmatrix} F_0w \\ F_1w \\ G_0w \\ G_1w \end{bmatrix}$$

$$-\,[\,F_0u\;\, F_1u\;\, G_0u\;\, G_1u\,]\begin{bmatrix} 00 & 01 & 00_w & 01_w \\ 10 & 11 & 10_w & 11_w \\ 00_u & 01_u & 00_{uw} & 01_{uw} \\ 10_u & 11_u & 10_{uw} & 11_{uw} \end{bmatrix}\begin{bmatrix} F_0w \\ F_1w \\ G_0w \\ G_1w \end{bmatrix}.$$

Gordon calls it a "Boolean sum surface" and he also calls it a "transfinite Lagrangian interpolant in two variables". He has extended it to interpolate curve networks.

In the equation, $u0$ $u1$ $0w$ and $1w$ are simply the vector functions that define the boundary curves. $u0_w$ $u1_w$ $0w_u$ and $1w_u$ are the normal vectors "across" these boundaries. Thus in particular, for example,

$$u0_w = \left.\frac{\partial(uw)}{\partial w}\right|_{w=0} .$$

The quantities in the square matrix (actually a tensor, since every element is a 3 component vector) are constants, obtainable from the boundary curve functions and the derivative functions. The partition in the lower right hand corner contains elements that are cross derivatives of the vectors. Thus, for instance

$$00_{uw} = \left.\frac{\partial^2(uw)}{\partial u \partial w}\right|_{\substack{u=0\\w=0}} .$$

We have come to call such quantities the "twists" of the surface at the corners, because it rather well describes the geometric implications. We call this lower right hand partition of the matrix the "twist partition". It consists of four vectors, obtainable by differentiating, for instance, $0w_u$ with respect to w, and then subsequently setting w = 0 (or 1, of course) in the result. This would give 00_{uw} (or 01_{uw}).

It's clear that in some sense the square matrix (tensor) is redundant, since the boundary conditions already contain sufficient information to specify the corner conditions. We need to know something (but not very much) about the blending functions F_0 F_1 G_0 and G_1. Accordingly, we will make some rather weak stipulations on these functions. Consider $F_i j$, a symbol that means $F_0 0$, or $F_0 1$, or $F_1 0$, or $F_1 1$. Similarly, consider $G_i j$, i = 0,1, and again with j = 0,1. Then

$$\begin{bmatrix} F_i j & F'_i j & F''_i j \\ G_i j & G'_i j & G''_i j \end{bmatrix} = \begin{bmatrix} \delta_{ij} & 0 & 0 \\ 0 & \delta_{ij} & 0 \end{bmatrix} .$$

δ_{ij} is of course the Kronecker delta symbol. The prime marks indicate differentiation with respect to the independent variable. We can draw pictures of F and G functions that satisfy these conditions, as in Figure 1.

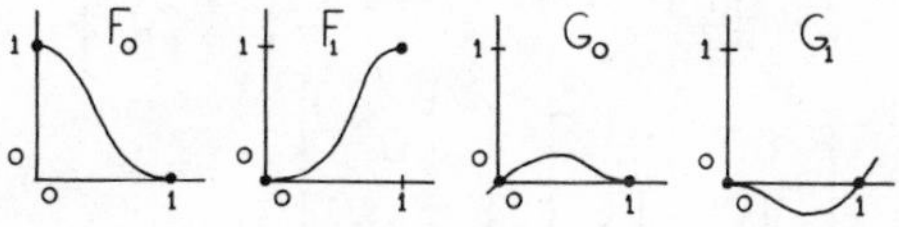

Figure 1

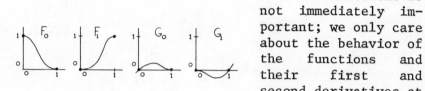

The "internal" shape of these functions is not immediately important; we only care about the behavior of the functions and their first and second derivatives at 0 and 1.

When the F and G functions obey the Kronecker delta conditions, it turns out that the resulting surface has the benign property of "containing" or passing through the boundary curves; with tangent vector functions "containing" the boundary derivative functions $u0_w$ $u1_w$ $0w_u$ and $1w_u$, and with <u>second</u> derivatives on the boundaries which are blended (or weighted) combinations of the second derivatives at the 0 and 1 ends of the boundary. We call such second derivative boundary vectors "intrinsic" to the surface. The implied consequence is that we can adjoin two such surfaces, and guarantee that they will be C^2 continuous (curvature continuous) across their mutually shared boundary. Two such patches, or an array, a mosaic, of such patches, thus provides a compound surface that is everywhere at least curvature continuous, provided only that the boundary curves are themselves everywhere curvature continuous.

A Special Default Condition.

If we do not want to specify the boundary tangent vectors, but wish to specify the corner twists, so as to avoid the pseudoflats that a null twist partition will yield, the surface patch equation becomes

$$uw = [F_0u \quad F_1u] \begin{bmatrix} 0w \\ 1w \end{bmatrix} + [u0 \quad u1] \begin{bmatrix} F_0w \\ F_1w \end{bmatrix}$$

$$- [F_0u \quad F_1u] \begin{bmatrix} 00 & 01 \\ 10 & 11 \end{bmatrix} \begin{bmatrix} F_0w \\ F_1w \end{bmatrix}$$

$$+ [G_0u \quad G_1u] \begin{bmatrix} 00_{uw} & 01_{uw} \\ 10_{uw} & 11_{uw} \end{bmatrix} \begin{bmatrix} G_0w \\ G_1w \end{bmatrix} .$$

The four vectors in the square tensor of the last term can be adjusted so as to remove the pseudo-flats.

B-Splines

Now it turns out that an extremely attractive curve form can define the $u0$ $u1$ $0w$ $1w$ $u0_w$ $u1_w$ $0w_u$ $1w_u$ boundary vector quantities. Since we plan to describe these curves in a somewhat simplistic way, we present the following formula to describe what we call "uniform cubic B-splines".

A point vector for a B-spline curve is:

$$P(u) = [s^3 \quad s^2 \quad s \quad 1] \; \frac{1}{6} \begin{bmatrix} -1 & 3 & -3 & 1 \\ 3 & -6 & 3 & 0 \\ -3 & 0 & 3 & 0 \\ 1 & 4 & 1 & 0 \end{bmatrix} \begin{bmatrix} v_i \\ v_{i+1} \\ v_{i+2} \\ v_{i+3} \end{bmatrix}$$

with $s = FR(n\ u)$, $i = INT(n\ u)$, the fractional part and the integer part of the product $n\ u$, respectively. Here, n = the number of cubic segments that, piecewise, are joined together to make the compound curve. The $v_i \ldots v_{i+k}$ represent vertices, we can think, very analogous to the vertices of a Bézier polygon. Since four vertices define a single cubic segment, n = NUMBER OF VERTICES MINUS 3 = number of cubic segments. (4-3=1, for a start.)

There are some interesting geometric considerations of these cubic piecewise compound curves. They lie everywhere within the convex hull of the polygon of vertices. At $s = 0$ or $s = 1$, the curve passes through a point p that we can call the $\frac{1}{3}$ point of the median of the triangle formed by 3 sequential vertices. Figure 2 makes this clear. The first derivative vector at p is $p' = \frac{v_{i+2} - v_i}{2}$ and the second derivative vector at p is $p'' = (v_i - v_{i+1}) + (v_{i+2} - v_{i+1})$.

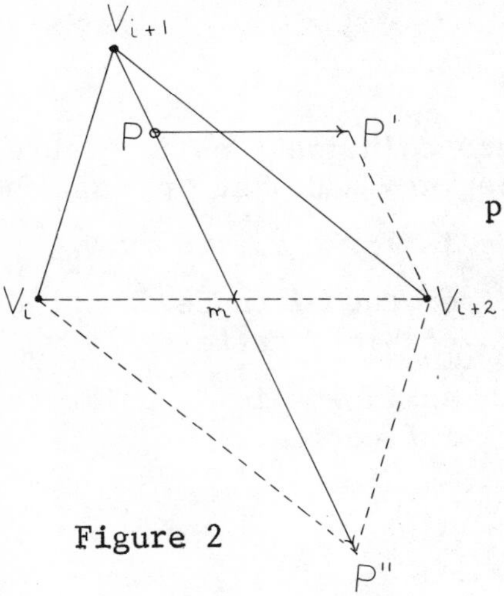

Figure 2

These extraordinarily simple geometric relations permit us to deduce some special things about B-splines. For instance, when the three vertices v_0, v_1, v_2 are collinear as in Figure 3, then the triangle is degenerate, with p on the median v_1 to m (at the $\frac{1}{3}$ point) with a tangent vector along $v_0v_1v_2$, and with a second derivative vector also concurrent with the line $v_0v_1v_2$.

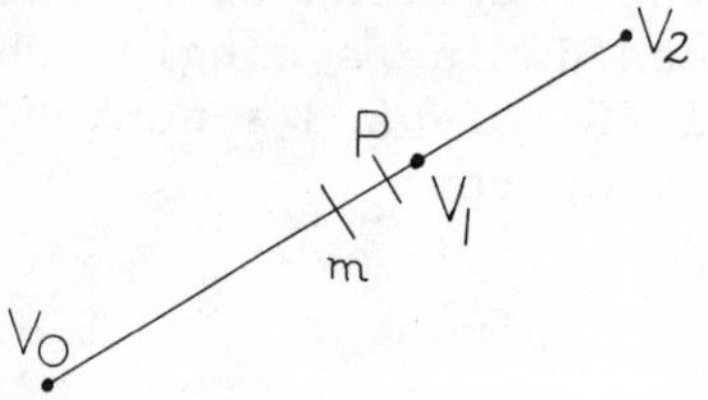

Figure 3

Now the determinant $\begin{vmatrix} x' & y' \\ x'' & y'' \end{vmatrix} = 0$ implies a point of inflection, so when $v_0v_1v_2$ are three collinear vertices, the curve begins (or ends) with a point of inflection.

Now when two vertices are coincident as in Figure 4, the cubic curve segment begins (ends) at p, which is on v_0 to v_1v_2, $\frac{1}{6}$ of the distance from the double vertex v_1v_2. Again it is a point of inflection.

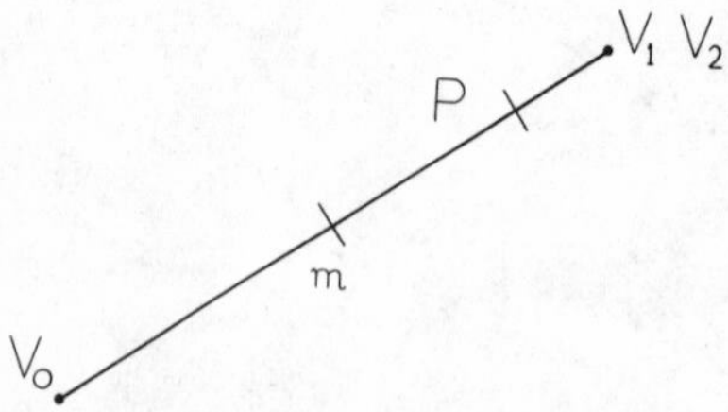

Figure 4

Finally, when three vertices are coincident as in Figure 4, we have the following: There are seven vertices, and consequently four curve segments. In Figure 5, the junctions (we say the "knots") of the cubic segments have been circled. At these knots, the curve segments are C^2 continuous.

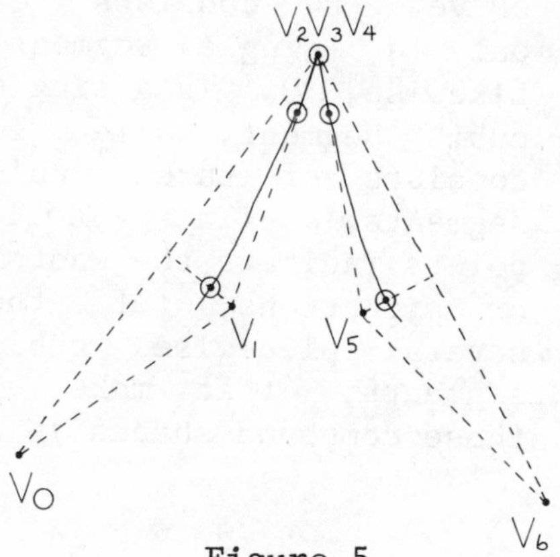

Figure 5

What's striking here is that at the triple vertex $v_2v_3v_4$ the compound curve is slope discontinuous (the slope is double valued.) But curiously, the compound curve is tangent-vector and second derivative-vector continuous there. Both the first and second derivatives simultaneously vanish at such a point, but never-the-less the compound curve is everywhere C^2 continuous.

All of this last consideration shows that, (a paradox) we can represent a cuspidal curve as a continuous, twice differentiable, parametric vector function.

Surfaces with B-spline Boundaries

Now we can use these B-spline curves as boundaries for a surface. For instance:

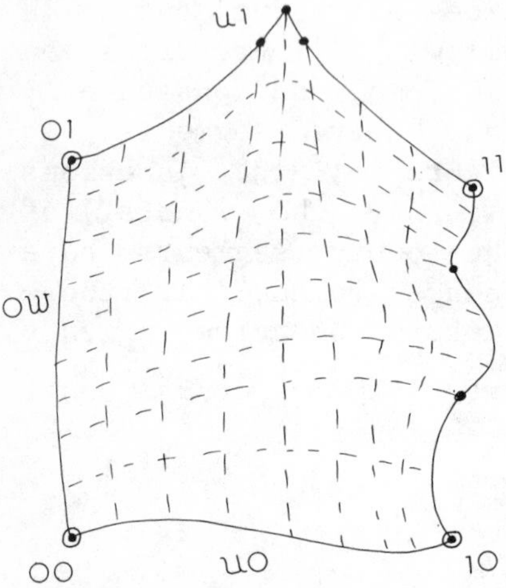

Figure 6

The curve u1 has a cusp, and consists of four segments. The opposite curve u0 consists of only a single segment. Likewise, 0w is a single cubic segment, while 1w consists of three cubic segments. (The solid points indicate the knots, or junctions, of the several piecewise cubic segments, that make up these compound shapes.)

The surface equation now generates a surface that is everywhere at least C^2 continuous. This is rather startling, since the boundary u1 has a cusp, and superficially we might think that it is neither C^1 nor C^2 continuous. But we must remember that we are using vector functions of a parameter, and their derivatives.

When we look at the characteristics of the four boundary curves,

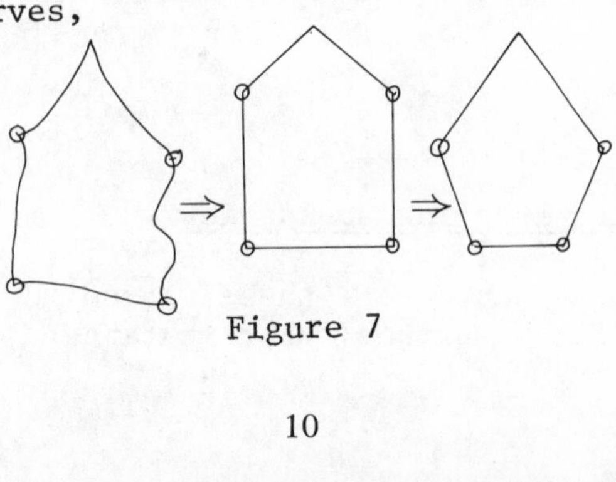

Figure 7

we observe that we have generated a C^2 continuous surface from a "five sided" boundary. Obviously this can be extended to any n-sided boundary.

Blending Functions.

Now to return to a more precise definition of the ubiquitous blending functions, F and G. We already have the Kronecker delta stipulations:

$$\begin{bmatrix} F_i j & F'_i j & F''_i j \\ G_i j & G'_i j & G''_i j \end{bmatrix} = \begin{bmatrix} \delta_{ij} & 0 & 0 \\ 0 & \delta_{ij} & 0 \end{bmatrix} .$$

We plan to use cubic segments to define the boundary curves and derivative vectors of the boundaries. It would be nice to represent the F and G blending functions also as strings of cubic segments, so that the surface equation will depend only upon cubic polynomials.

Consider F_0, which has the explicit stipulations

$$[F_0 0 \quad F_0 1 \quad F'_0 0 \quad F'_0 1 \quad F''_0 0 \quad F''_0 1]$$
$$= [1 \quad 0 \quad 0 \quad 0 \quad 0 \quad 0] .$$

There are six constraints on F_0, and this requires a sixth order polynomial (fifth degree polynomial) to satisfy the constraints. But we can construct F_0 as a piecewise cubic compound function, C^2 continuous at its joints to the second derivative, by using the B-spline equation.

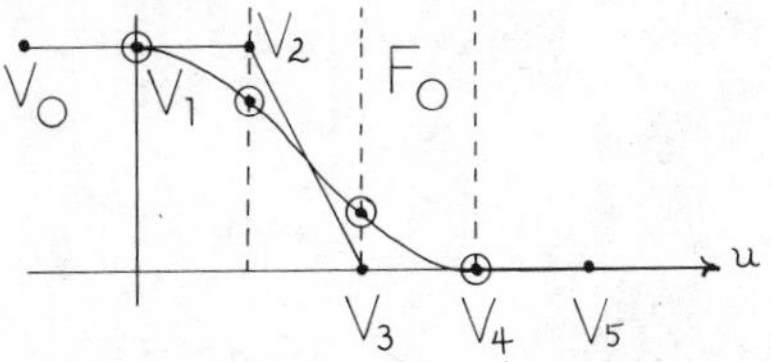

Figure 8

We choose the vertices

$$\begin{bmatrix} v_0 \\ v_1 \\ v_2 \\ v_3 \\ v_4 \\ v_5 \end{bmatrix} = \begin{bmatrix} 1 \\ 1 \\ 1 \\ 0 \\ 0 \\ 0 \end{bmatrix}$$

There are 3 segments (6 vertices minus 3 = 3) and the curve segments come from

$$F_0u = [s^3 \quad s^2 \quad s \quad 1] \frac{1}{6} \begin{bmatrix} -1 & 3 & -3 & 1 \\ 3 & -6 & 3 & 0 \\ -3 & 0 & 3 & 0 \\ 1 & 4 & 1 & 0 \end{bmatrix} \begin{bmatrix} 1 & 1 & 1 \\ 1 & 1 & 0 \\ 1 & 0 & 0 \\ 0 & 0 & 0 \end{bmatrix}$$

i=0 1 2

s=FR(3u)
i = INT(3u)

$$F_0u = [s^3 \quad s^2 \quad s \quad 1] \frac{1}{6} \begin{bmatrix} -1 & 2 & -1 \\ 0 & -3 & 3 \\ 0 & -3 & -3 \\ 6 & 5 & 1 \end{bmatrix}$$

i=0 1 2

Similarly,

$$F_1u = [s^3 \quad s^2 \quad s \quad 1] \frac{1}{6} \begin{bmatrix} 1 & -2 & 1 \\ 0 & 3 & -3 \\ 0 & 3 & 3 \\ 0 & 1 & 5 \end{bmatrix}$$

i=0 1 2

with the same definitions of s and i.

Again, the G functions can be represented by three cubic segments joined together. For G_0, the vertices v_0, v_1, v_2, v_3, v_4, v_5 must be chosen so that the first derivative

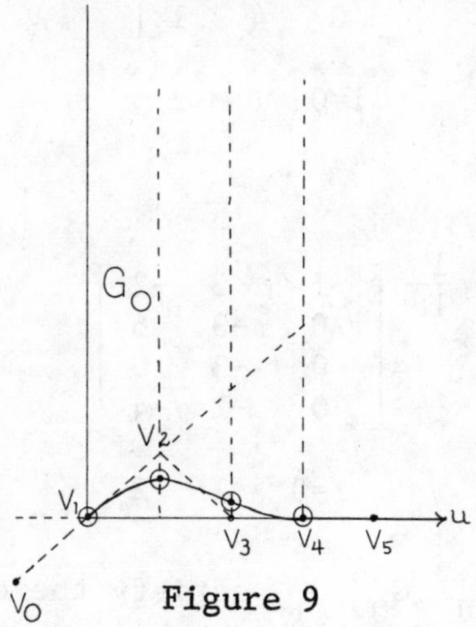

Figure 9

at u=0 is $\left.\frac{dG_0}{du}\right|_{u=0} = 1.$

But s=3u, so ds=3du,

$$\frac{dG_0}{ds} = \frac{1}{3}\frac{dG_0}{du}, \quad \frac{dG_0}{du} = 1,$$

$$\text{so} \quad \frac{dG_0}{ds} = \frac{1}{3}.$$

This implies that

$$\begin{bmatrix} v_0 \\ v_1 \\ v_2 \\ v_3 \\ v_4 \\ v_5 \end{bmatrix} = \begin{bmatrix} -\frac{1}{3} \\ 0 \\ \frac{1}{3} \\ 0 \\ 0 \\ 0 \end{bmatrix}$$

$$G_0u = [\,s^3 \quad s^2 \quad s \quad 1]\ \frac{1}{18}\begin{bmatrix} -1 & 3 & -3 & 1 \\ 3 & -6 & 3 & 0 \\ -3 & 0 & 3 & 0 \\ 1 & 4 & 1 & 0 \end{bmatrix}\begin{bmatrix} -1 & 0 & 1 \\ 0 & 1 & 0 \\ 1 & 0 & 0 \\ 0 & 0 & 0 \end{bmatrix}$$

i=0 1 2

$$G_0u = [s^3 \quad s^2 \quad s \quad 1]\ \frac{1}{18}\begin{bmatrix} -2 & 3 & -1 \\ 0 & -6 & 3 \\ 6 & 0 & -3 \\ 0 & 4 & 1 \end{bmatrix}$$

$$i=0 \quad 1 \quad 2$$

Similarly,

$$G_1u = [s^3 \quad s^2 \quad s \quad 1]\ \frac{1}{18}\begin{bmatrix} -1 & 3 & -2 \\ 0 & -3 & 6 \\ 0 & -3 & 0 \\ 0 & -1 & -4 \end{bmatrix}$$

$$i=0 \quad 1 \quad 2$$

Now these functions F_0 F_1 G_0 G_1 satisfy the end conditions of the Kronecker delta symbols and are appropriate blending functions for the surface equation.

Initial and Terminal Conditions for a B-Spline

The initial (and terminal) knots of a B-spline sequence are points where we wish to have the compound curve begin and end. Consider the beginning of a B-spline curve sequence. We want to have the curve segment begin at p_0, with a tangent vector equal to $\frac{v_2 - v_0}{2}$, and a second derivative as well. Consider the points p_0 and p_1, with p_1 on the polygon side v_1v_2. By similar triangles, it is

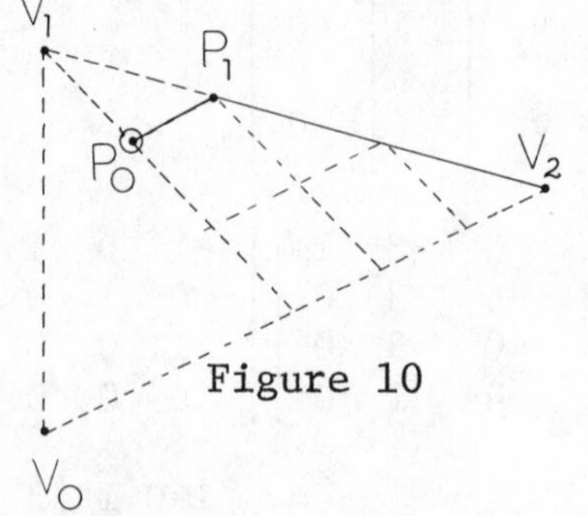

Figure 10

clear that $p_1 - p_0 = \frac{1}{3} p_0'$, the tangent vector. Likewise, $p_0 - v_1 = \frac{1}{6} p_0''$. Now given p_1 and v_2, we can find v_1: $v_1 = p_1 + (\frac{p_1 - v_2}{2}) = \frac{3p_1 - v_2}{2}$.

And again, $v_0 = v_2 + 6(p_0 - p_1)$.

We call v_0 and v_1 the "phantom" vertices to initiate a B-spline curve sequence. We furnish the points p_0 and p_1, and from these and the actual vertices v_2, v_3, ... the curve segmental sequence is defined.

Similarly, we can terminate a B-spline sequence with any desired point, first derivative vector, and second derivative vector. In the termination pattern, v_1 and v_2 (or actually v_{1+i} and v_{2+i}) are the <u>phantom terminating vertices</u>, and as before

$$v_1 = p_1 + \frac{p_1 - v_0}{2} \quad \text{or}$$

$$v_1 = \frac{3p_1 - v_0}{2}, \quad \text{and}$$

$$v_2 = v_0 + 6(p_2 - p_1).$$

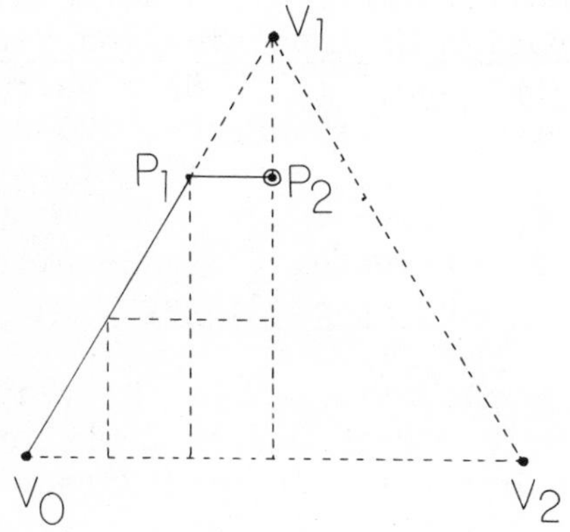

Figure 11

<u>Conclusion</u>.

The "uniform" B-spline furnishes an extremely attractive way to define boundary curves for a surface patch. Of course boundary curves can be defined parametrically in <u>any</u> way, so that the univariate functions that define boundary curves (and indeed boundary conditions) can be "mixed", so to speak, and even then the surface segment, or patch, will, in some sense, reflect these curve shapes.

References

[1] C. deBoor, "On Calculating with B-splines," J. Approx. Th., Vol. 6, 50-62 (1972).

[2] S. A. Coons, Surfaces for Computer-Aided Design of Space Forms, MIT Project MAC TR-41, (June 1967).

[3] W. J. Gordon, "Distributive Lattices and the Approximation of Multivariate Functions," Proceeding of the Symposium on Approximation with Special Emphasis on Splines, (I.J. Schoenberg, editor), University of Wisconsin Press, 223-277 (1969).

[4] W. J. Gordon and R. F. Riesenfeld, "B-spline Curves and Surfaces," These Proceedings.

[5] R. F. Riesenfeld, "Applications of B-spline Approximation to Geometric Problems of Computer-Aided Design", Ph.D. Thesis at Syracuse University (1972). Published as University of Utah, UTEC-CSc-73-126.

COMPUTATIONAL GEOMETRY - ACHIEVEMENTS AND PROBLEMS

A.R. Forrest
University of Cambridge
Cambridge, England

Summary

Considerable advances have been made in recent years in the use of computers in geometrical design, but there remain many unsolved problems. Most work has been concentrated on three particular aspects of computer aided geometric design: graphical input/output, the designer interface, and the mathematical representation. The paper surveys some of the achievements and indicates areas where more research and practical experience is required.

I. Introduction

Computational Geometry[14] is concerned with all aspects of the representation in computers and manipulation by computers of shape information. It includes such fields as pattern recognition and computer cartography as well as the subject of this paper: *Computer Aided Geometric Design*. Computational geometry, as we shall see, involves a blend of many disciplines associated, in many cases, in novel ways. Recent years have seen the recognition of the subject as a valid field of study, research and practical implementation.

A survey of the nature of this paper cannot claim to be exhaustive or unbiased. However by taking a broad overview and attempting to structure the subject area[41] the writer was able to identify not only where significant successes had been realized but also problems which seemed to have been overlooked. Indeed the gaps rapidly became more interesting than the successes. I have outlined some of the more important problems remaining and have suggested some tentative approaches to their solution. I have also mentioned in passing several topics, particularly matters relating to implementation, which properly belong to the theme of the conference, but which are not well-represented in these Proceedings.

In computer aided geometric design we wish to create, in a computer, a model which will adequately describe the particular class or classes of two- or three-dimensional shapes which are to be designed. Immediately we encounter a serious difficulty: we live in a real three-dimensional world but to use computers in geometric design we have to map the real world onto a one-dimensional computer store, perform meaningful geometric computations using a linear, sequential machine, and then generate output for the three-dimensional world. This mismatch between the real world and the computer is perhaps the most fundamental problem of computational geometry.

The computer model must have several important properties which have been discussed at length elsewhere[14,23]. Two of these are worth repeating briefly. Firstly, it should be easy to construct and modify the model, implying a good, natural interface between man, computer and model. Secondly, the creation of a model is a means to an end, and in the case of computer aided design the end is the output not merely of drawings but of analytical results and manufacturing data. Clearly the model must be such that subsequent analysis[43] and output is as simple as possible.

In the past many computer aided geometric design systems have been ad hoc; a computer model has been created which works after a fashion but which does not necessarily offer scope for extension. The correct way to regard a computer model is as a *particular implementation* of a *mathematical model*. It is the mathematical model which provides the discipline and the logical framework by means of which a well-thought-out system can be constructed. For example, in digital computers all functions are computed, in the final analysis, as truncated polynomials. Thus no matter how we design, say, surface patches, they will end up being computed as bipolynomials or rational bipolynomials. Why then should we not use bipolynomials, for the sake of convenience, right from the start? There are many reasons why we should not do so; but in summary we would lose in terms of mathematical structure and designer interface all that we would gain in implementational convenience.

It can be argued that industry has been guilty of a rush to implement, often ignoring the mathematical framework, whilst the universities and research establishments have concentrated on the mathematical model to the detriment of the study of real implemenattional problems. This has tended to lead, on the part of the former, to an adherence to outmoded methods such as the particular mathematical representations used by APT and the retention of features more relevant to previous manual techniques, or, on the part of the latter to an overemphasis on the mathematics of sculptured surfaces, and on computer graphics.

The paper will first consider the logical basis for computer aided geometric design. We shall then discuss computer implementation from the point of view of system externals and system internals. Figure 1 indicates the flow of information in a typical computer aided geometric design system.

II. The Mathematical Basis

It is instructive to consider the various types of artifacts which we might wish to represent mathematically. To a layman, some objects are more "complex" than others. To the implementor, some seemingly simple objects are difficult to handle but all "complex" objects are difficult to represent. It is not easy to define what we mean by complexity unless

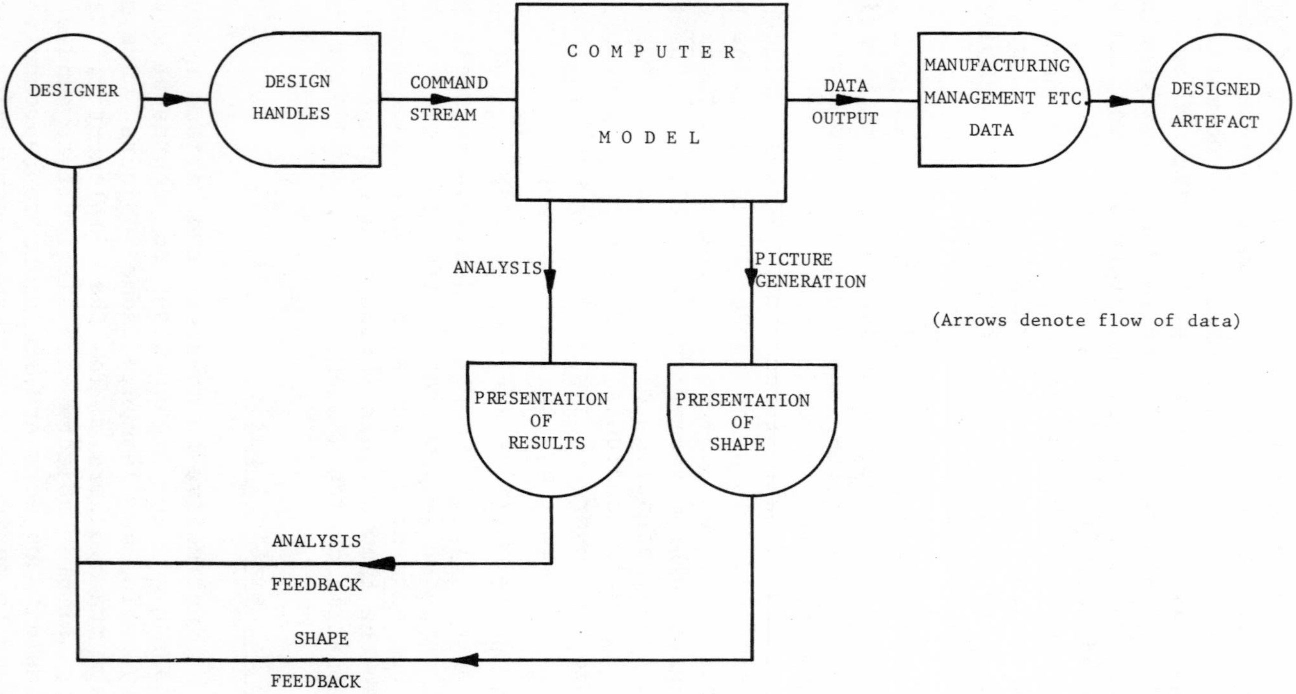

Figure 1

A TYPICAL COMPUTER-AIDED GEOMETRIC DESIGN SYSTEM

we realize that overall complexity is a blend of three different factors. The first and most obvious is the dimension of the Euclidean space which an object occupies, whether it be two-dimensional, three-dimensional or the halfway house, $2\frac{1}{2}$ D, where objects have continuous variations in two spatial dimensions and relatively few discrete steps in the third dimension. Objects of revolution which are generated by the rotation of a plane curve can be thought of as being somewhere between two- and three-dimensional in the scale of *embedding complexity*. It is rarely possible to describe an entire object in terms of a single equation; rather we regard an object as an *assembly* of *components*. Thus we have two further kinds of complexity: *component complexity* and *combinatorial complexity*. For example a bicubic surface patch is clearly more complex as a component than a planar polygon, and a typewriter is more complex as a combination than a teaspoon. Figure 2 shows the hierarchy of *representational complexity* or *total complexity* in a lattice - like form. Items lower in the hierarchy are special cases of items higher up. For convenience we assign values in the range [0,1] for each type of complexity, and use arrows to indicate the direction of increasing total complexity. As an illustration, Figure 3 shows how an aircraft and its components fit into this classification.

We can now make some rather general observations on computer aided geometric design, and in particular on mathematical modelling. Clearly we must be able to describe components geometrically. A great deal of work has been done in this area and there is now a substantial body of mathematical theory 2,9,13,16,19,26,33,36. (Referring to Figure 2, we are now discussing the lower left portion of the hierarchy $\boxed{a \mid 0 \mid c}$ where $0 \leq a,c \leq 1$.) To use a linguistic analogy, Gordon has supplied the syntax (the mathematical structure), in his paper on distributive lattices[18]. The semantics come from the particular methods of curve and surface interpolation and approximation which might be used

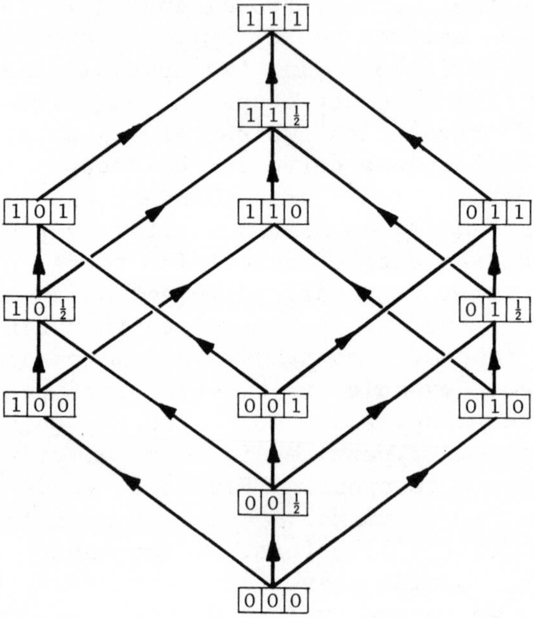

component complexity	combinatorial complexity	embedding complexity

Arrows indicate directions of increasing total complexity.

HIERARCHY OF REPRESENTATIONAL COMPLEXITY.

Figure 2

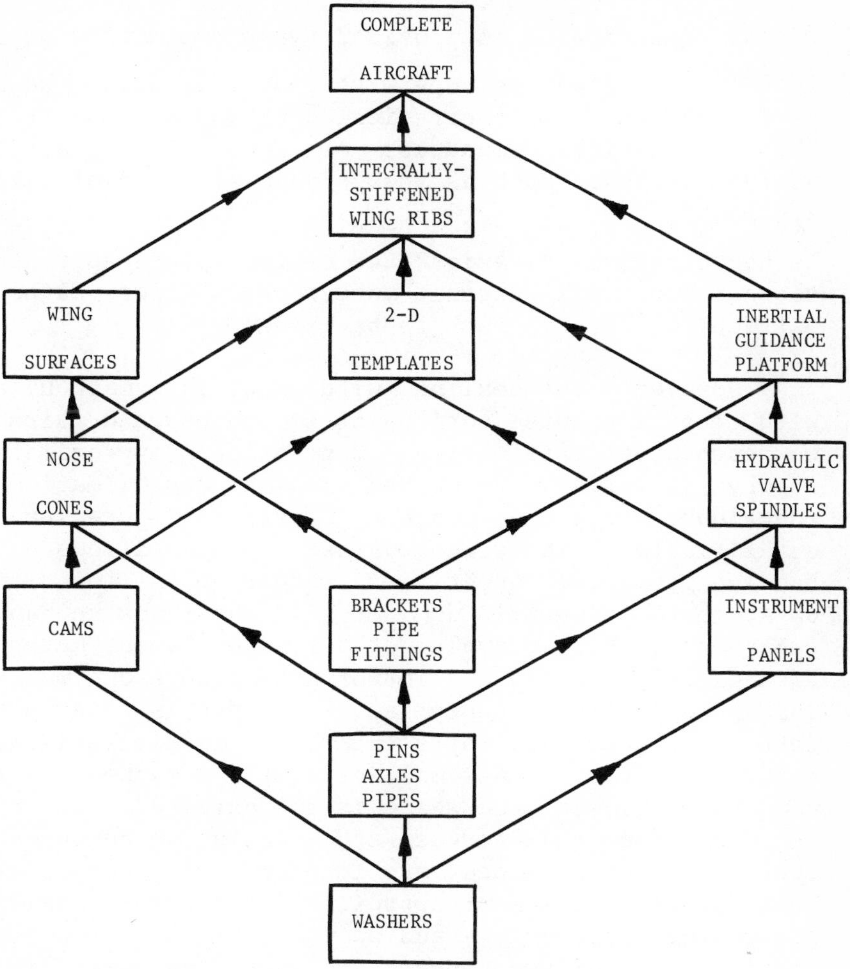

EXAMPLE OF A HIERARCHY

Figure 3

[4,8,10,15,29,30,34,42]. The mathematical theory of *component* description is provided by *approximation theory* [18,24], modified to cope with geometric data. We are beginning to see theoretical work which demonstrates the mathematical soundness of some very practical design methods such as the polynomial forms of Bézier [2,4,15] and Riesenfeld's B-splines [33,34,35]. It is to be hoped that multivariate and vector-valued approximations theory will attract more workers[24] for, although difficult, there is much to be gained.

However, in dealing with shape information, and with the imprecise notions of smoothness and fairness we encounter difficulties. Conventional approximation theory is largely concerned with the approximation of functions where the concept of error is precise and quantifiable. The vector-valued approach allows us to handle geometric quantities rather than functional data, but we still do not have the means to handle smoothness. For example, the finite element method[43] has recently attracted a lot of attention among workers in approximation theory and this area is clearly related to geometric representation. In discretising a structure into an assembly of simple components which can be analysed the shape is approximated. In order to determine the forces etc. acting on components, continuity constraints are imposed on the components. Thus in finite element approximation great emphasis is placed on continuity and compatibility. However continuity and smoothness are not the same: if we interpolate a polynomial to a set of points we obtain a completely continuous curve, but one which is not necessarily smooth in the sense of being free from unwanted oscillations. Smoothness seems to be related to simultaneous approximation of both position and derivatives; thus geometric representation poses somewhat different problems from finite element analysis.

To quote Zadeh[22]: "in our quest for precision we have attempted to fit the real world to mathematical models which make no provision for *fuzziness*" (author's italics). What we might develop as an alternative to the conventional approach, is a *fuzzy approximation theory* and *fuzzy geometry*, and I shall return to this theme later. Fuzzy mathematics[22] appears to offer a valid alternative way of looking at the problem of smoothness and geometric representation. For example, I offer the following rather trivial illustration of how fuzzy mathematics might be used in approximation theory.

A Bernstein-Bézier curve is defined by (n + 1) vertices $\overline{V}_i$ $(0 \leq i \leq n)$ which are point vectors, and the (n + 1) Bernstein polynomials:

$$B_{n,i}(u) = \binom{n}{i} u^i (1-u)^{n-i}$$

The generic point on the resulting curve is given by:

$$\overline{P}_j = \sum_{i=0}^{n} \overline{V}_i . B_{n,i}(u_j) = \sum_{i=0}^{n} \overline{V}_i . \binom{n}{i} u_j^i (1-u_j)^{n-i}$$

where $u_j \varepsilon [0,1]$.

Consider the set of vertices which *characterises* the curve:

$$\overline{C} = \{\overline{V}_0, \overline{V}_1, \overline{V}_2, \ldots \overline{V}_n\} = \{\overline{V}_i\}$$

then in conventional set theory a subset $\overline{c}$ of $\overline{C}$ may be denoted: $c \subset C$ where for example

$\overline{c} = \{(\overline{V}_0|1), (\overline{V}_1|0), (\overline{V}_2|0), (\overline{V}_3|1), \ldots (\overline{V}_n|1)\}$ or more succinctly $\overline{c} = \{\overline{V}_i|\mu_i\}$

where μ_i is a Boolean function denoting the inclusion $(\mu_i{=}1)$ or exclusion $(\mu_i{=}0)$ of a vertex $\overline{V}_i$ in the subset $\overline{c}$. In fuzzy set theory[22], the characteristic functions of inclusion, μ_i, are no longer Boolean; instead $0 \leq \mu_i \leq 1$. If we now replace μ_i by the Bernstein polynomial $B_{n,i}$ we have a fuzzy subset:

$$\bar{\underset{\sim}{c}}_j \subset \bar{C}$$

such that

$$\bar{\underset{\sim}{c}}_j = \{\bar{V}_i | B_{n,i}(u_j)\}$$

and the generic point on the curve is seen to be the vector sum of the elements of the fuzzy subset $\bar{\underset{\sim}{c}}_j$. Hence we can characterize a point on the curve by means of a fuzzy subset of the defining polygon vertices. As n increases, the maximum values of the Bernstein polynomials for $u \in [0,1]$ decrease (with the exception of $B_{n,0}$ and $B_{n,n}$). Thus the degree of inclusion of each vertex in the fuzzy subset $\bar{\underset{\sim}{c}}_j$ decreases as n increases which is just another way of saying that as n increases, the similarity between the curve and the defining polygon decreases. A Bernstein-Bézier curve can be regarded as a fuzzy manifestation (i.e., an abstraction) of the defining polygon. We can examine other methods of interpolation and approximation in a similar light. Figure 4 shows a family of B-spline curves defined by a polygon, demonstrating how the character of the polygon is lost with increase in order of the B-spline basis and corresponding reductions of the maxima of the basis functions.

Much effort has been expended, in interactive design, on the design of patches at an individual level. Joining patches together has always been a awkward procedure, and consequently designers have tended to use rather fewer patches than might be desirable. On the other side of the coin, where data are derived from non-computer sources (such as clay models) algorithms for fitting patches have tended to

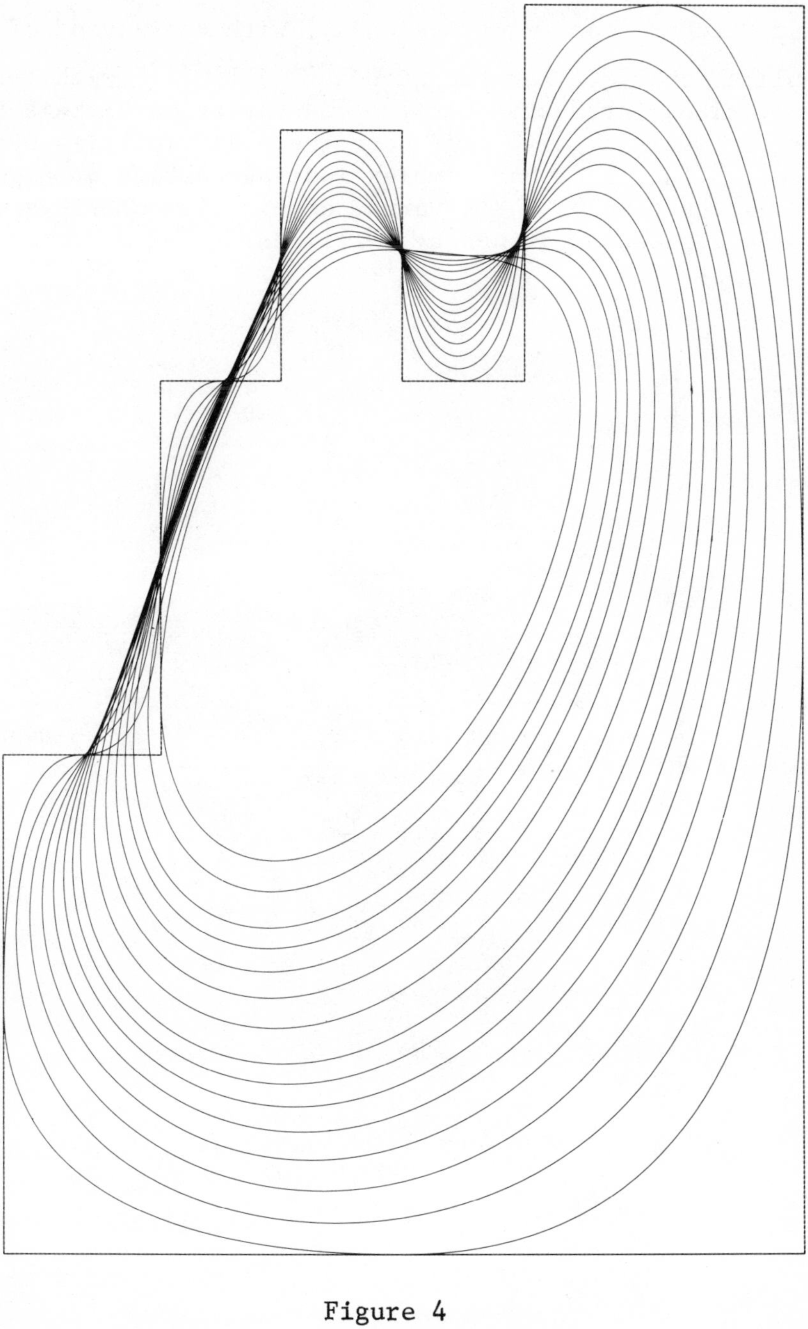

Figure 4

use rather too many patches. With the advent of B-spline and similar techniques[8,10,33,34,42] with their convenient geometric handles and variation diminishing properties we may find both these difficulties overcome. The somewhat complex looking surface of Figure 5 is a simple 9×7 array of bicubic vector-valued surface patches defined by B-splines.

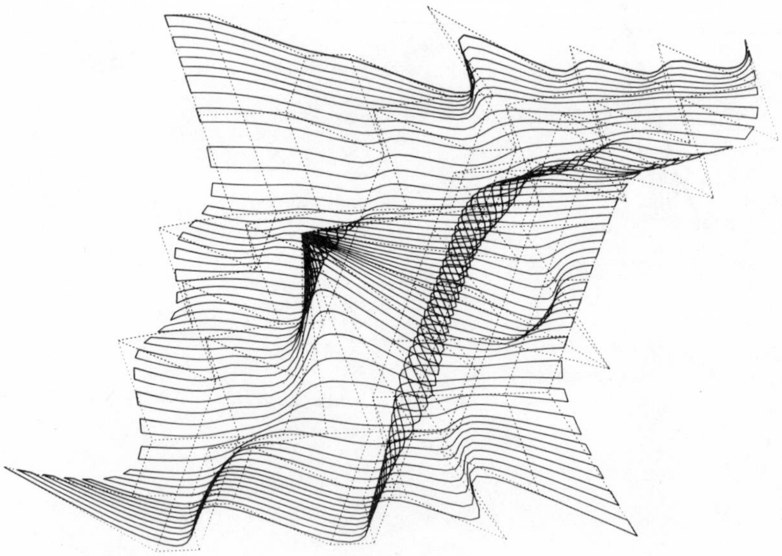

Figure 5

Whilst there remain many unsolved problems in the component area (and here I include large regular arrays of surface patches as in Figure 5 as single components), we have neglected other branches of the "lattice" of Figure 2. As Lady Bracknell says in "The Importance of Being Earnest:" "We live, I regret to say, in an age of surfaces". We know a lot about how to handle simple and complex components in 2-D and 3-D, and we have the requisite mathematical theory; but we have little experience in handling complex assemblies of simple components, far less complex assemblies of complex components. At Cambridge we have been exploring the former for several years; Braid's system [5,6] in which complex objects (as in Figure 6) are

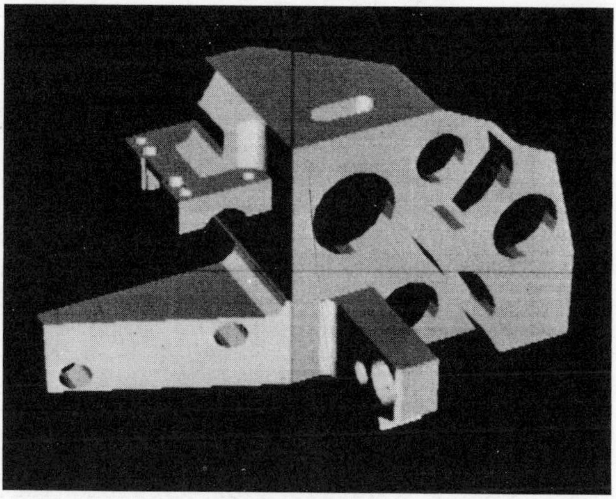

Figure 6

synthesized by assembling simple volume primitives, has pinpointed many problems. For example, it might be thought that the central problem in handling complex assemblies is one of implementation; but there is a definite need for a mathematical theory for assemblies

[12] which will provide a consistent logical framework. That is to say we need a mathematical structure for the portion of Figure 2 where [0 | b | c], $0 \leq b,c \leq 1$. In previous systems for designing complex assemblies of simple components, set theory and Boolean combination has had a "seductive appeal". However Braid found that conventional set theory led to difficulties with closure and completeness and also could not handle in a consistent manner the many special cases which arise (e.g. when combined objects share a common vertex or edge rather than a portion of a common face). Instead he has adopted[6], successfully, a simple form of fuzzy set theory[22] which enabled him to overcome these difficulties. Clearly we are only scratching the surface in this area. If we can devise an adequate mathematical theory, the way will be open to the solution of other difficult problems. For example, it is possible, using Braid's system and other systems[12], to arrive at the final design of a given object by a variety of routes. For manufacture there will be a similar choice, but a canonical representation could lead to the development of algorithms which would optimize analysis and machining operations. As the majority of manufactured objects fall into the category currently being discussed there is considerable scope and economic payoff in this area. Perhaps too much attention has been focussed on car body exteriors and aircraft external surfaces to the detriment of work on handling the multitudinous components hidden beneath.

The crucial question in handling complex assemblies of complex components ([1 | 1 | c], $0 \leq c \leq 1$) is the question of partitioning. We have to describe such assemblies piecewise, but how do we define where component boundaries lie? If there are definite discontinuities of slope, clearly we make use of these. However we do not always have such convenient indications of boundaries. Sabin[39] has pointed out that by convention sculptured surfaces tend to be represented by vector-valued mappings of regular rectangular grids in the parameter plane, but that we may well consider mappings of other differentiable manifolds, such as the sphere. For example, it is well-known that a sphere cannot be partitioned into rectangular patches, and that triangular patches [1,20,25] are required. (Of course, one could use degenerate rectangles to produce triangles, but the point is that some special action has then been taken.) Attempts to define complex objects solely in terms of regular arrays of rectangular or even triangular patches lead to difficulties which manifest themselves, typically, as regions which are unintentionally flattened, lacking fairness. If partitioning were merely a question of topology, matters would be simple, but this is not the case.

Consider, as a particular example, the case of cubes. At most, eight cubes can meet at a single vertex, but in order for there to be visible faces at a vertex, we consider all possibilities involving seven or fewer cubes which share a common vertex and are attached to each other on common faces. Suppose we now smooth off the edges, Figure 7. In the bottom row, where 2,4 or 6 faces meet simply at a vertex, rectangular partitioning is appropriate for both faces and edges. In the row second from the bottom, where we have three edges and faces meeting at a vertex, smoothing off the edges induces a triangular region which is embedded in three regions which can be partitioned rectangularly. Such a situation arises at the front of a car where the wing (fender) merges with the bonnet (hood) and the grill surfaces, and Bézier indicates that this situation has been identified by Renault[3]. The solution can take the form of a triangular patch or three rectangular patches (rather than four) meeting at a point, or a degenerate patch. Once again, we must emphasize that some non-standard action has to be taken to cope with this situation, and that the situation has to be identified a priori. In this particular instance we are dealing with a box with rounded corners (interior or exterior); notice that it leads naturally to a partitioning of the sphere into triangles and rectangles, or triangles alone.

Looking at the second row from the top in Figure 7 we have the case of, on the left, a hole in a flat surface, or on the right, a boss on a flat surface. Here the smoothing-off of edges induces a five-sided region, or five edges meeting at a point. We have two faces which can be partitioned by rectangles, and an L-shaped region which can be similarly partitioned[7].

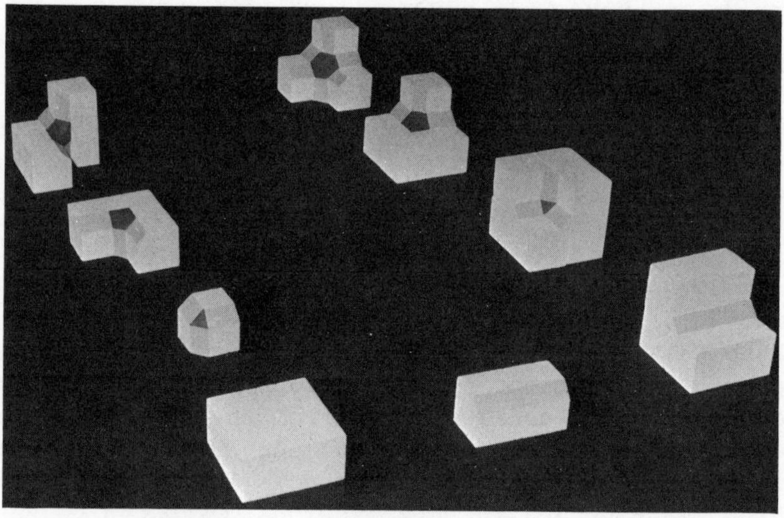

Figure 7

If we allow the faces to become arrays of sculptured surfaces, then we can identify these configurations with real problems. For example, the left-hand model is equivalent to the intersection of a wing and a fuselage, or, on a car, the meeting of the driver's window, door, bonnet (hood), windshield and wing (fender). Sabin developed a five-sided patch[37] to deal with the former and Bézier indicates that special actions are taken at Renault to deal with the latter[3].

The top row indicates the two other possible cases (barring symmetry and anti-symmetry) and demonstrates that 6-sided regions can also arise naturally. Now all the models in Figure 7 are topologically equivalent (to the sphere); what distinguishes the different cases is the number of "edges" and "faces" meeting at a given region. The problem is geometrical, not topological. It is significant that some of these cases have been identified in practical situations where special actions have had to be taken; partitioning is a non-trivial practical problem.

Clearly, Figure 7 is not an exhaustive exploration of possible configurations which could arise and would have to be recognized. One possible approach might be to regard complex assemblies of complex components as being fuzzy, rounded-off, assemblies of polyhedra. Planes become regular arrays of surface patches, edges become curves where normal slope is discontinuous *or* regions where one principal curvature changes rapidly in one direction, and vertices become regions where there is high total curvature with rapid variation.

We can envisage a scheme which partitions objects on such a basis. Just as one can design curves by polygons where the curves are smoothed-off abstractions of the polygon[4,10,33], so one might construct complex assemblies of complex objects by first constructing complex assemblies of simple objects of "similar" shape, and then by smoothing off the edges and corners. Alternatively where we are given an object such as a clay model which we are required to fit, a crude blocking-out of the model in terms of volumes distributed with regard to the model's curvature could provide the basis for a good partitioning of the surface into assemblies of arrays of patches. Thus using some form of fuzzy geometry we may be able to provide a logical mathematical framework for handling the most complex of shapes.

III. Implementation

Whilst the mathematical basis provides the logical framework for the construction of a computer aided geometric design system, the success of such a system will depend to a very large extent on the interface between the computer, the designer and the real world[23,40]. Of course, internal organization will affect the size of the computer required, the economics, and the analytical facilities offered, but the system's external appearance is of prime importance. We shall discuss first this aspect of system implementation.

There have been impressive advances in recent years in the geometric interface. Depending on the data available to the designer there are a variety of techniques which enable curves and surfaces to be created by interpolation[8,29,31] or approximation[4,26,33]. These techniques provide convenient geometric design handles so that shape can be controlled in a predictable manner. It is difficult to envisage radical improvements in this area; rather there will be an increase in the number of interchangeable special techniques for special situations providing different methods for constructing vector-valued polynomials and splines.

When dealing with the class of objects which can be handled by Braid's system the designer can specify each component precisely in verbal terms, in contrast to the more complex components where we rapidly run into such vague (one is tempted to say fuzzy) terms such as "bump" and "hollow". In Braid's system[5] the designer interface is more linguistic than geometric. Design proceeds by means of a stream of precise commands; here the discrete nature of commands typed on a a keyboard or pointed at by light pen contrasts with the light pen dragging techniques and repeated incremental changes used in designing curves and sculptured surfaces. Proper design of command languages pays dividends. At Cambridge we have had considerable success with a relatively simple command interpreter[23] which has been used to implement a wide variety of problem-oriented design and command languages. However such languages do not seem to have the same glamorous appeal as algorithmic languages and their design and implementation has been rather neglected. Once more, work in this area would be of great practical value. Whereas the geometric handles are essentially part of the semantics of a design dialogue, command processors supply the syntax and structure the dialogue, preventing attempts to execute dangerous, irrelevant, forbidden or unimplemented commands.

Computer graphics is often confused with computer aided geometric design. This is unfortunate since much useful geometric design can be carried out without recourse to graphics and similarly there are many uses of graphics which do not require geometry. The two fields may be thought of as overlapping. Spectacular forecasts were made for graphics, and there have been spectacular advances, but they have not entirely solved the geometric design problem which is not so much how to compute a picture as how to decide what picture we wish to compute and how to extract from the computer model the information required to compute a picture. In many cases, this takes more time, sometimes substantially more time, than picture generation, and real-time graphics becomes impossible.

Graphical input of two-dimensional geometric data is fairly well understood and works rather well; but three-dimensional input[27] is only now receiving the attention it deserves. Light pen and even sonic wands have been disappointing in this context perhaps because unconstrained motion of pen or wand can cause difficulties. There is reason to believe that a less free-form, more disciplined, form of input not only makes life much easier for the system but enables the designer to backtrack and store previous stages in the design iteration. Apparent freedom is often only apparent. Graphical output has received much attention and many suitable techniques are available, some of them as hardware. Real-time grey-scale pictures are a practical proposition for some applications, and the more sophisticated cathode-ray tubes can display complex shapes dynamically as line drawings. However there can be no universally applicable visualization method; the correct choice depends on the geometry of the object which the designer wishes to view.

At Cambridge we have identified two particular shortcomings of conventional hardware, and no doubt others could be isolated. First we have found the size of screen and poor resolution of conventional displays a severe drawback in tackling problems of a realistic complexity. We now possess a large-screen laser display developed in conjunction with the Computer Laboratory by Laser-Scan Ltd of Cambridge[45]. With a screen size of 100cm. × 70cm., addressability of 100,000 × 70,000 points, 5,000 × 3,500 resolvable lines and 2^{10} intensity levels, the HRD-1 can display drawings more complex than can be drawn by hand, and produce superb grey-scale pictures. Microfiche hard-copy from this device was used to produce Figures 4 and 5.

Secondly we have been dissatisfied with attempts to create an illusion by means of two-dimensional pictures, of three-dimensional objects. Similarly, the folded curves of Resch and Cohen[32] can best be appreciated as physical models. We have had many instances where design faults could not be or were not discovered by looking at dynamic displays, stereo projections, and other visualizations. As a result, and following Bézier's example[2,3,4] we have built a three-dimensional model making machine[23] (which produced the model, Figure 8, of the surface drawn by the laser display in Figure 5). Models reveal aspects of

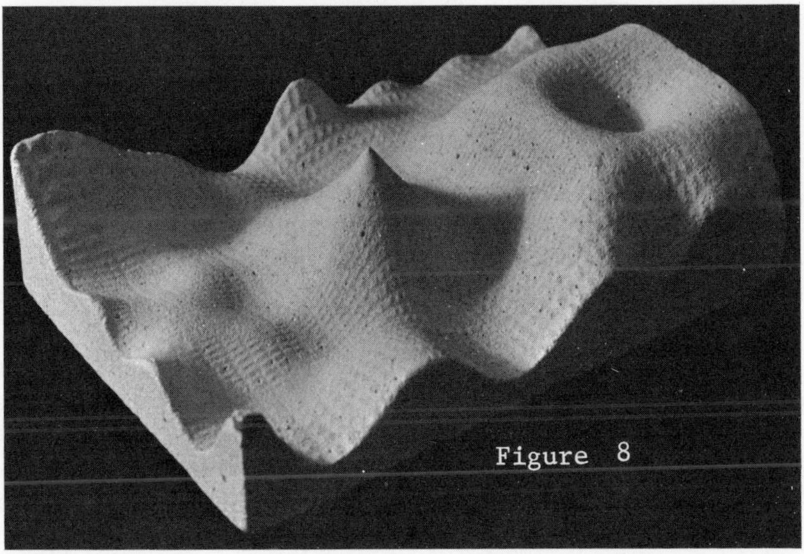

Figure 8

shape which are too subtle for other present-day visualization techniques; indeed some features can be detected only by touch. Models, moreover, make a powerful psychological impact: if a picture is worth a thousand words, as we are led to believe, then a model which embodies all possible pictures must be even more valuable. Currently we are building a second model making machine[17] which has been designed to be compact and totally enclosed: that is to say a computer peripheral which could be sited in a design or a computer room. It will be, in effect, a three-dimensional plotter of the same size as a line-printer, making models in soft plastic foam. We do not envisage design proceeding by on-line sculpture but believe a model making peripheral would be used in the design process to check shape, and to provide a visualization of the completed design. It would not replace conventional displays, but if a designer could have a model made in 5 to 10 minutes, we shall have made a useful addition to the repertoire of graphical output devices.

Computer aided geometric design leads naturally to numerical control. Indeed, we can regard numerically-controlled machine tools as slow graphical peripherals with some special properties. Unfortunately numerical control was established as a discipline before computer aided design and whereas it is possible to generate numerical control data directly from stored geometric data, the geometric description methods developed earlier are well-entrenched but not very satisfactory from several points of view. Clearly it is undesirable to design an object by computer and then redefine its geometry using an n/c language such as APT. Hopefully the two areas will be reconciled before too long.

Finally, with regard to system externals, there are many advantages from the user's point of view of device independent input and output. At Cambridge we have reaped the benefit of device independent[23] (and now machine independent[44]) graphical output through the GINO system and find it extremely convenient to switch output from storage tube to plotter to dynamic display to model making machine and so on. Device independent input is much more difficult to achieve but would be equally desirable from the user's point of view.

Turning now to internal aspects of systems implementation, we shall not discuss data structures but merely observe that once more there is no universal solution and that particular structures must be implemented for particular applications. There is a need for a high-level implementation language - an algorithmic language - which has facilities for construction and manipulation of data structures and for programming geometric algorithms. Vector manipulation would be one obvious facility to include. Quite what flavour such a language should have is a matter for discussion but nothing suitable appears to be available.

As part of computer aided geometric design we require analyses of a geometric nature[30] to be carried out in the computer. Sabin has termed some of these computations *interrogations*[38]. Once more we are in an unfashionable area, and one which is bedevilled by the one-dimensional nature of both computer processors and computer memory. With the reduction in cost of hardware we may well see the development of computer hardware more suited to two- and three-dimensional problems.

Considerable success has been achieved in the related area of hidden surface computation[28,41] which has been heavily picture oriented, using relatively simple geometric models. With the exception of the Newell, Newell and Sancha algorithm[28] the faster algorithms tend to ignore much of the geometrical structure. I mention this as hidden surface computation can be thought of as one manifestation of a more general problem: the *interference* problem. For example, given two volumes do they intersect[11]? Which components in a complex object are cut by a given plane? Do two polygons overlap, and if not, what is the shortest distance between them? Solutions to these problems exist but tend to be extremely costly in both space and time. There is considerable benefit to be gained by the use of good heuristics which take the geometry into account.

Geometric computation is affected both by the combinatorial explosion, determining the number of tests to be performed, and the number of special cases; and by the nature of these tests. There are gains to be made both by breaking the problems down into smaller problems, using the geometry in this process, and by simplifying the initial tests. For example, we might test for the intersection of two B-spline curves by first testing whether their convex hulls overlap. If there is an overlap, then we have a good starting point for a second, more sophisticated, test. In order to be able to handle realistic practical problems in a reasonable time scale we must be able to perform such geometric calculations quickly and with sufficient accuracy.

Where the number of tests to be performed is large, we may well find that some of the recently developed results in stochastic geometry[21] will lead to useful practical algorithms. Geometric computation has not received the attention it deserves, but the success of a practical system can depend to a large extent on the utility and richness of the iterrogations provided[30].

IV. Conclusions

The paper has surveyed computer aided geometric design from a general standpoint and has divided the problem into two main areas: the mathematical model and the computer implementation. In discussing mathematical models, which were classified according to complexity of embedding space, complexity of components and complexity of combination, attention has been drawn to areas where little work has been carried out. The need for a mathematical theory for combination of components and for partitioning into components has been explored. It is suggested that the techniques of fuzzy mathematics may provide a suitable framework for several mathematical aspects of computer aided geometric design.

In computer implementation the paper suggests that whilst there have been considerable advances in the techniques of geometric input and graphical output including novel graphical peripherals, other areas will reward further research. In particular more work is needed in the design of command languages, algorithmic languages for geometric problems, and in the development of fast geometric algorithms.

In writing this paper I have drawn heavily on the experience of other members, past and present, of the Computer Aided Design Group in Cambridge University and many colleagues in universities and industry throughout the world: without their help a survey paper of this kind would have been impossible to write. I am particularly grateful to Ian Braid for for introducing me to the seductive appeal of fuzzy set theory.

V. References

1. Barnhill, R.E., Smooth Interpolation Over Triangles. These Proceedings.

2. Bézier, P.E., Numerical Control - Mathematics and Applications. John Wiley and Sons, London, 1972.

3. Bézier, P.E., Numerical Control in Automobile Design and Manufacture of Curved Surfaces. In "Curved Surfaces in Engineering", I.P.C. Science and Technology Press, Guildford, England, 1972.

4. Bézier, P.E., Mathematical and Practical Possibilities of Unisurf. These Proceedings.

5. Braid, I.C., Designing with Volumes. Ph.D. Thesis, Cambridge University, 1973. Published by Cantab Press, 1974.

6. Braid, I.C. The Synthesis of Solids Bounded by Many Faces. Cambridge University C.A.D. Group Document 84, 1974. To appear, Comm. ACM.

7. Carlson, R.E., Hall, C.A., Bicubic Spline Interpolation in L-Shaped Domains. WAPD-T-2452, Bettis Atomic Power Laboratory. West Mifflin, PA., 1971.

8. Catmull, E., Rom, R., A Class of Local Interpolating Splines. These Proceedings.

9. Coons, S.A., Surfaces for Computer Aided Design of Space Forms, M.I.T. Project MAC TR-41, June 1967.

10. Coons, S.A., Surface Patches and B-Spline Curves. These Proceedings.

11. Eastman, C.M., Yessios, C.I., An Efficient Algorithm for Finding the Union, Intersection and Differences of Spatial Domains. Carnegie-Mellon University, Institute of Physical Planning, Research Report 31, September 1972.

12. Engeli, M.E., A Language for 3D Graphics Applications. Proc. International Computing Symposium, Davos Switzerland, 1973. North Holland, Amsterdam 1974.

13. Forrest, A.R., Curves and Surfaces for Computer Aided Design. Ph.D. Thesis, University of Cambridge, 1968.

14. Forrest, A.R., Computational Geometry, Proc. Roy. Soc. London A. 321, 187-195 (1971).

15. Forrest, A.R., Interactive Interpolation and Approximation by Bézier Polynomials. Computer Journal, Vol. 15 No. 1, 71-79 (1972).

16. Forrest, A.R., On Coons and Other Methods for the Representation of Curved Surfaces. Computer Graphics and Image Processing 1, 341-359 (1972).

17. Forrest, A.R., A Computer Peripheral for Making Three-Dimensional Models. Proc. AFCET-IRIA Journées Graphics, Rocquencourt, France, 1973.

18. Gordon, W.J., Distributive Lattices and the Approximation of Multivariate Functions. In "Approximations with Special Emphasis on Spline Functions", I.J. Schoenberg, Ed., Academic Press, New York, 1969.

19. Gordon, W.J., Computer Aided Design and the Geometric Aspects of the Finite Element Method. These Proceedings.

20. Gregory, J.A., Smooth Interpolation Without Twist Constraints. These Proceedings.

21. Harding, E.F., Kendall, D.G., Stochastic Geometry. John Wiley and Sons, London, 1974.

22. Kaufmann, A., Introduction á la Theórie des Sous-Ensembles Flous. Masson et Cie, Paris, 1973.

23. Lang, C.A., Achievements in Computer Aided Design. Proc. IFIP Congress, Stockholm, 1974.

24. Lorenz, G.G., Approximation Theory. Academic Press, New York, 1973.

25. McDermott, R.J., Graphical Representation of Surfaces over Triangles and Rectangles. These Proceedings.

26. Mehlum E., Nonlinear Splines. These Proceedings.

27. Newell, M.E., Man-Machine Communications in Three Dimensions. These Proceedings.

28. Newell, M.E., Newell, R.G., Sancha, T.L., A New Approach to the Shaded Picture Problem. Proc. ACM National Conference, 1972.

29. Nielson, G.M., Piecewise Polynomial Alternatives to Splines in Tension. These Proceedings.

30. Peters, G.J., Parametric Bicubic Surfaces. These Proceedings.

31. Pilcher, D.T., Surfaces Under Tension. These Proceedings.

32. Resch, R., Cohen, E., The Space Curve as a Folded Edge. These Proceedings.

33. Riesenfeld, R.F., Applications of B-spline Approximation to Geometric Problems of Computer Aided Design. Ph.D. Thesis, Syracuse University 1972. Published as University of Utah UTEC-CSc-73-126.

34. Riesenfeld, R.F., Gordon, W.J., B-Spline Curves and Surfaces. These Proceedings.

35. Riesenfeld, R.F., Gordon, W.J., Bernstein-Bézier Methods for the Computer Aided Design of Free-Form Curves and Surfaces. J. ACM, Vol. 21, No. 2, 293-310, (April 1974).

36. Sabin, M.A., The British Aircraft Corporation Numerical Master Geometry System. Proc. Roy. Soc. Lond. A. 321, 197-205, (1971).

37. Sabin, M.A., Parametric Surface Equations for Non-Rectangular Regions. British Aircraft Corporation, Weybridge VTO/MS/147, July 1968.

38. Sabin, M.A., Interrogation Techniques for Parametric Surfaces. In "Advanced Computer Graphics - Economics, Techniques and Applications", Eds. Parslow and Elliot Green, Plenum Press, London 1971.

39. Sabin, M.A., Trinomial Basis Functions for Interpolation in Triangular Regions. British Aircraft Corporation, Weybridge, VTO/MS/188, July 1971.

40. Sterling, M., Computer Aided Design in the Auto Industry. These Proceedings.

41. Sutherland, I.E., Sproull, R.F., Schumacker, R.A., A Characterization of Ten Hidden-Surface Algorithms. ACM Computing Surveys, Vol. 6, No. 1, 1-56, 1974.

42. Wielinga, R.F., Constrained Interpolation Using Bézier Curves as a New Tool in Computer Aided Geometric Design. These Proceedings.

43. Zienkiewicz, O.C., The Finite Element Method in Engineering Science. McGraw-Hill, London, 1971.

44. GINO-F Reference Manual. Computer Aided Design Centre, Cambridge, 1973.

45. The HRD-1 Laser Display/Plotter. Laser-Scan Limited, Cambridge, 1974.

SMOOTH INTERPOLATION OVER TRIANGLES

Robert E. Barnhill
University of Utah

1. Introduction.

The mathematics of computer aided geometric design involves the interpolation and approximation of curves and surfaces. For surfaces defined on a polygonal region one method is triangulation, followed by interpolation on the subtriangles. One purpose of this paper is to present some recently discovered methods for such representations of curved surfaces. These interpolants have the feature that they are locally defined approximations of sufficient smoothness and polynomial precision to provide visually esthetic pictures.

S.A. Coons [5] initiated the study of smooth interpolants to curves defined over the boundary of a rectangle. This was also generalized to matching derivatives on the boundary. (See equations (2.1) - (2.5) in Gregory's paper in these Proceedings.) The term "Coons patch" refers to the curved surface so formed. These patches are then fitted together over a set of rectangles to form a smooth surface. This method has been explicated and generalized by Forrest [6] and Gordon [7]. The term "Coons patch" is also sometimes used to denote a finite dimensional interpolant obtained by a special choice of the function and derivative boundary curves. In this paper we shall call a surface that interpolates to function and derivative boundary curves a *smooth* interpolant. We shall call an interpolant obtained by special choices of these boundary conditions a *finite dimensional* interpolant.

This paper is a survey of smooth interpolants over triangles and of the corresponding finite dimensional interpolants [2,3,4,8,9]. The two papers [10,11] immediately following this one in these Proceedings are also involved in this research effort. The overall goal of this research is to determine mathematical interpolants that will be useful for computer aided geometric design.

Triangles are frequently more appropriate than rectangles for interpolation because the latter can only be used in special situations, e.g., tensor product sets of points. Some surfaces have intrinsically triangular parts, as in Figure 1.

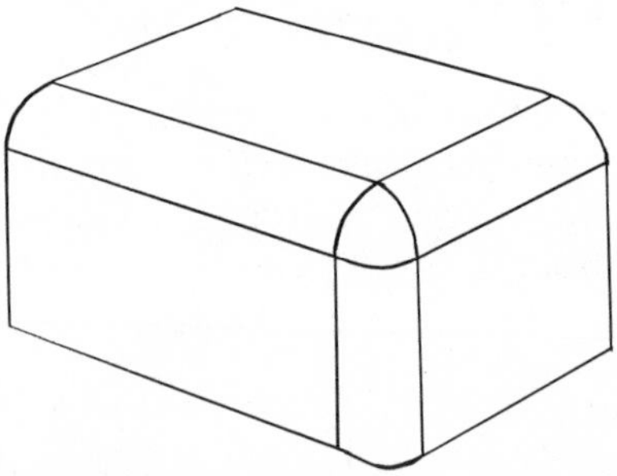

Figure 1 - Whenever a corner is rounded, a nonrectangular patch, frequently a curved triangle, is produced.

Piecewise linear interpolation (Figure 2) is an

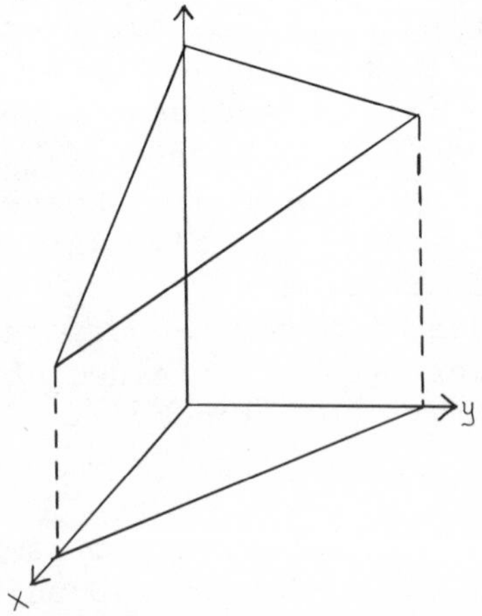

Figure 2 - The piecewise linear interpolant ax+by+c.

example of interpolation over a triangulation with the desirable properties of (1) a local basis, (2) computational ease, and (3) continuity. (This has been known since their discovery by Courant in 1943.) A continuous interpolant is insufficient in that it forms a possibly "crinkly" surface. Hence we require an interpolant which has continuous normal derivatives across the edges of the subtriangles, i.e., a C^1 interpolant. If only polynomials in two variables are considered, then the basic C^1 polynomial interpolant is the 21-parameter interpolant discovered by Zlamal, Zenisek, and others. The 21 parameters are the function value, the two first derivative values, and the three second derivative values at each vertex, and the normal derivative at the midpoint of each side, of each subtriangle (Figure 3). Ordinarily a designer

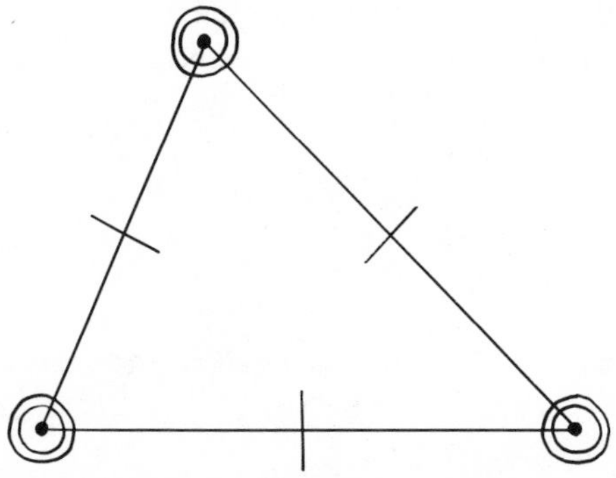

Figure 3 - The 21 parameter C^1 quintic with the data $F, F_{1,0}, F_{0,1}, F_{2,0}, F_{1,1}, F_{0,2}$ given at the vertices and the normal derivative $\frac{\partial}{\partial n}$ given at the midpoints of the three sides.

would not have all of these parameters available. In fact, a designer would probably have only the function values and the two first derivatives at each vertex and so the desired C^1 interpolant should involve only these 9 parameters per triangle, in addition to properties (1) and (2) above. This problem is solved by certain of the C^1 finite dimensional interpolants obtained from smooth interpolants over triangles. These are special cases of a more general C^N theory. The cases $N = 0,1$ seem most useful for computer aided geometric design and so only these cases are presented in this paper.

In this paper we consider functions to be of the form $F = F(x,y)$. However, in practice the parametric representation

$$x = x(s,t)$$

$$y = y(s,t)$$

$$z = z(s,t)$$

is to be used. Thus F is considered as a general coordinate and stands for x,y, and z. (See the paper by George Peters in these Proceedings for a good discussion of a general coordinate, which he denotes by $V = V(u,w)$.) Thus the identifications

$$F \leftarrow x,y,z$$

$$x \leftarrow s$$

$$y \leftarrow t$$

should be made in the formulas given in this paper, for parametric implementation.

2. Rational Boolean Interpolants.

The first smooth interpolant to boundary values of a triangle appears in the paper by Barnhill, Birkhoff, and Gordon [1]. Let T be the standard triangle with boundary ∂T and with vertices $V_1 = (1,0)$, $V_2 = (0,1)$, and $V_3 = (0,0)$. Let E_i denote the side of T opposite V_i, $i = 1,2,3$, so that E_1 is the side $x = 0$, E_2 is the side $y = 0$, and E_3 is the side $z = 0$, where $z = 1 - x - y$ (Figure 4).

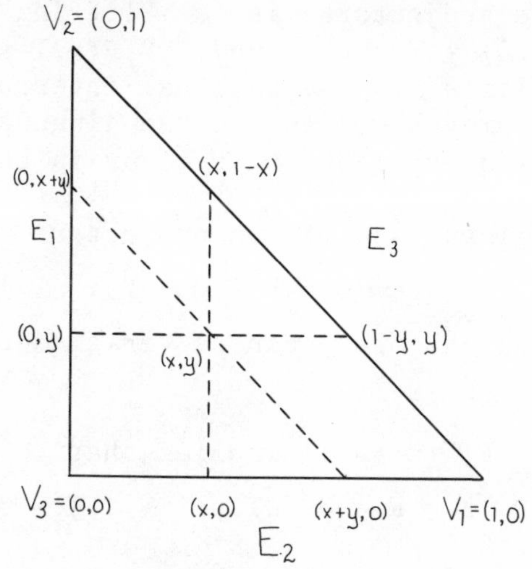

Figure 4 - The standard triangle T.

Linear Case.

Let F be a continuous function on ∂T, i.e., $F \in C(\partial T)$. We consider linear interpolation operators P_i along parallels to each side E_i of T. Figure 5 is a symbolic representation of these interpolants.

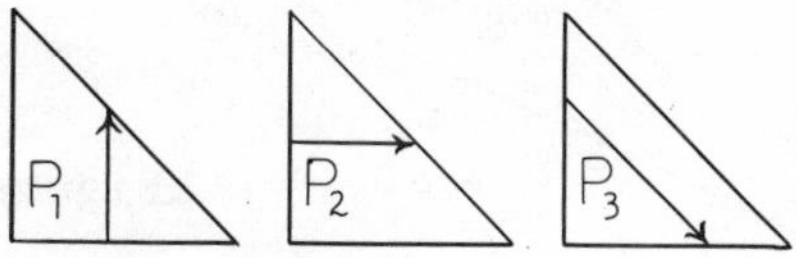

Figure 5

The formulas are the following:

$$(2.1)\quad P_1F(x,y) = \left(\frac{1-x-y}{1-x}\right) F(x,0) + \left(\frac{y}{1-x}\right) F(x,1-x)$$

$$(2.2)\quad P_2F(x,y) = \left(\frac{1-x-y}{1-y}\right) F(0,y) + \left(\frac{x}{1-y}\right) F(1-y,y)$$

$$(2.3)\quad P_3F(x,y) = \left(\frac{x}{x+y}\right) F(x+y,0) + \left(\frac{y}{x+y}\right) F(0,x+y).$$

Each of these projectors is a "lofting" interpolant, e.g., $P_1F(x,0) = F(x,0)$ and $P_1F(x,1-x) = F(x,1-x)$. The singularities in the rational interpolants (2.1) - (2.3) are removable, as are the singularities of all the rational interpolants that occur in this paper.

The Boolean sum of two projectors P and Q is

$$P \oplus Q \equiv P + Q - PQ. \tag{2.4}$$

The following theorem can be verified by direct substitution:

<u>Theorem 2.1</u> $F \in C(\partial T)$ implies that

$$(P_i \oplus P_j)F = F \quad \text{on} \quad \partial T, \quad 1 \leqslant i,j \leqslant 3, \quad i \neq j. \tag{2.5}$$

<u>Example</u>. $(P_1 \oplus P_2)F = (\frac{z}{1-x})\ [F(x,0) - (1-x)F(0,0) - xF(1,0)] + (\frac{z}{1-y})\ F(0,y) + (\frac{x}{1-y})F(1-y,y)$.

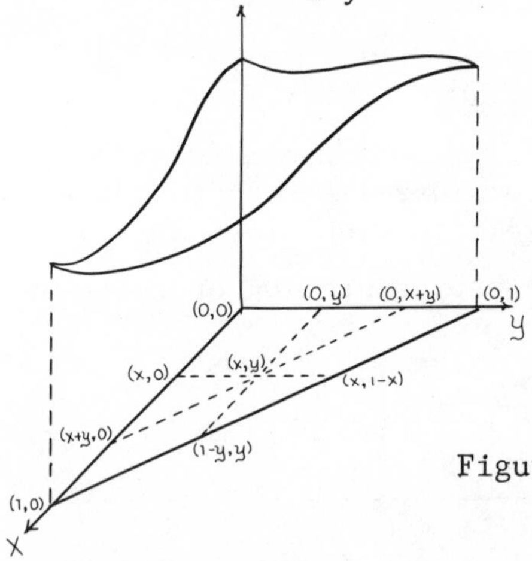

Figure 6

Symmetry can be introduced by taking averages of Boolean sums of the form (2.5). In particular,

$$\frac{1}{2}\ [(P_i \oplus P_j) + (P_i \oplus P_k)],\ 1 \leqslant i,j,k \leqslant 3, \tag{2.6}$$

$$i \neq j \neq k \neq i$$

is the same interpolant for all such i,j,k.

This is called the symmetric interpolant Q^* and it has the alternative representation

$$(2.7)\quad Q^* = \frac{1}{2}\,[P_1 + P_2 + P_3 - P_1P_2P_3], \quad \text{where}$$

$$(2.8)\quad P_1P_2P_3F = xF(1,0) + yF(0,1) + zF(0,0), \quad \text{where}$$

$z = 1-x-y$. (x,y,z) are the barycentric coordinates of the triangle T. Substitution of $z = 1-x-y$ into (2.1) - (2.3) yields formulas that look more symmetric.

$$(2.9)\quad P_1F = \left(\frac{z}{1-x}\right) F(x,0) + \left(\frac{y}{1-x}\right) F(x,1-x)$$

$$(2.10)\quad P_2F = \left(\frac{z}{1-y}\right) F(0,y) + \left(\frac{x}{1-y}\right) F(1-y,y)$$

$$(2.11)\quad P_3F = \left(\frac{x}{1-z}\right) F(1-z,0) + \left(\frac{y}{1-z}\right) F(0,1-z).$$

Terminology:

Q^* is called a "trilinear" blending interpolant in [1] because it is a combination of linearly ruled surfaces. Q^* is symmetric in its treatment of the three sides of T. The projector $P_1P_2P_3$ is the same if the product is taken in any order [1, p.118]. $P_1P_2P_3$ is called a trilinear finite dimensional interpolant because it is linear along parallels to each of the three sides of T. Note that parallels to the sides of a triangle are invariant under affine transformation.

Each of the 6 interpolants defined by (2.5) and the interpolant Q^* interpolates to the three curves $F(x,0)$, $F(0,y)$, and $F(x,1-x)$ $(F(1-y,y))$. Thus they are triangular Coons patches or "transfinite elements" (W.J. Gordon's terminology).

The polynomial precision set of $P_i \oplus P_j$ in (2.5) includes all polynomials of degree two or less. A general rule: *Boolean sums always have at least the polynomial precision of the second projector.*

Cubic Case.

The next problem is to interpolate to function and derivative values around ∂T. Analogously to (2.1) - (2.3), we define cubic interpolation projectors P_i along parallels to each side E_i of T.

$$(2.12)\quad P_1F = \sum_{i=0}^{1} \varphi_i\left(\frac{y}{1-x}\right) (1-x)^i F_{o,i}(x,0) +$$

$$\sum_{i=0}^{1} \Psi_i\left(\frac{y}{1-x}\right) (1-x)^i F_{o,i}(x,1-x)$$

$$(2.13)\quad P_2F = \sum_{i=0}^{1} \varphi_i\left(\frac{x}{1-y}\right) (1-y)^i F_{i,o}(0,y) +$$

$$\sum_{i=0}^{1} \Psi_i\left(\frac{x}{1-y}\right) (1-y)^i F_{i,o}(1-y,y)$$

$$(2.14)\quad P_3F = \sum_{i=0}^{1} \varphi_i\left(\frac{x}{x+y}\right) (x+y)^i \left(\left[\frac{\partial}{\partial x} - \frac{\partial}{\partial y}\right]^i F\right)(0,x+y)$$

$$+ \sum_{i=0}^{1} \Psi_i\left(\frac{x}{x+y}\right) (x+y)^i \left(\left[\frac{\partial}{\partial x} - \frac{\partial}{\partial y}\right]^i F\right)(x+y,0),$$

where the $\varphi_i(t)$ and $\Psi_i(t)$ are the cardinal basis functions for Hermite two point Taylor interpolation on [0,1], i.e.,

$$(2.15)\quad \varphi_0(t) = (t-1)^2 (2t+1)$$

$$\varphi_1(t) = t(t-1)^2$$

$$\Psi_i(t) = (-1)^i \varphi_i(1-t),\ i = 0,1.$$

When these formulas ((2.12) - (2.14)) were first discovered, it was thought that $F \in C^1(\partial T)$ implied that $(P_i \oplus P_j) F$, $1 \leq i, j \leq 3$, $i \neq j$, and the tricubic blending interpolant

$Q^* = P_1 + P_2 + P_3 - P_1P_2P_3$ interpolated to F and to its normal derivative on ∂T. If so, then we would have a piecewise defined smooth C^1 interpolant over a triangulation. However, $F \in C^1(\partial T)$ is not a sufficient hypothesis, a clue being that, e.g., the (1,1) derivative (the "twist" derivative) of F is contained in expressions of the form $P_i P_j F$, $i \neq j$. Lois Mansfield pointed out that a certain "compatibility condition" must be true in order to obtain a C^1 interpolant in the above cases.

Theorem 2.2 If $F \in C^1(\partial T)$ and if F satisfies the compatibility condition

$$(2.16) \qquad \left(\frac{\partial^2 F}{\partial s_i \, \partial s_j}\right)(V_k) = \left(\frac{\partial^2 F}{\partial s_j \, \partial s_i}\right)(V_k),$$

where V_k is the vertex of T with adjacent sides E_i and E_j, $\frac{\partial}{\partial s_i}$ means differentiation along parallels to the side E_i, etc., then $(P_i \oplus P_j)F$ interpolates to F and to its first derivatives on ∂T. The polynomial precision set includes all polynomials of degree five or less.

Thus, e.g., $(P_1 \oplus P_2)F$ interpolates to F and to its first derivatives on ∂T, if

$$(2.17) \qquad \left(\frac{\partial^2 F}{\partial x \partial y}\right)(0,0) = \left(\frac{\partial^2 F}{\partial y \partial x}\right)(0,0).$$

Similar results are true for Q^* and can be obtained from (2.6) and (2.16).

Compatibility conditions of the form (2.16) arise whenever one forms Boolean sums of projectors involving derivatives. This is an essential point in Section 4 of this paper on finite dimensional schemes. These incompatibilities occur for Boolean sums defined on squares, as well as on triangles. This leads to a way of excluding the twist values (e.g., $F_{1\,1}(0,0)$), from interpolants and this idea is presented in the paper by Gregory in these Proceedings.

If the compatibility condition (2.16) does not hold, then $(P_i \oplus P_j)\,F$ can be "corrected" so as to remove the incompatibility. A second general rule for interpolatory Boolean sums: *Boolean sums always have at least the interpolation properties of the first projector.** Since the projectors P_i defined by (2.12) - (2.14) interpolate to F and its first derivatives except on E_i, then $(P_i \oplus P_j)\,F$ interpolates to F and its first derivatives on at least $\partial T - E_i$. $(P_i \oplus P_j)\,F$ also interpolates to F itself on E_i, because this happened in the linear case (Theorem 2.1), which is a special case of the cubic case. Interpolation to F along the side E_i implies interpolation to the (tangential) derivative of F along E_i and so the only problem is interpolation to the normal derivative of F along E_i. This is corrected by the addition of a suitable rational function, as the following theorem states.

Theorem 2.3 If $F \in C^1(\partial T)$, then

$$(2.18)\quad (P_i \oplus P_j)\,F - \frac{\varepsilon_i\,\varepsilon_j^2\,\varepsilon_k^2}{1-\varepsilon_k}\left(\left[\frac{\partial^2 F}{\partial s_j\,\partial s_i}\right](V_k) - \left[\frac{\partial^2 F}{\partial s_i\,\partial s_j}\right](V_k)\right)$$

$$1 \leqslant i,\ j,\ k \leqslant 3,\quad i \neq j \neq k \neq i,$$

interpolates to F and to the first derivatives of F on ∂T, where $\varepsilon_1 = x$, $\varepsilon_2 = y$, and $\varepsilon_3 = z$.

---

*Thus a Boolean sum $P \oplus Q$ always has the duality property that $P \oplus Q$ *has at least the interpolation properties of* P *and the function precision of* Q.

Example $i = 1,\ j = 2,\ k = 3$:

$$(2.19)\quad (P_1 \oplus P_2)F - \frac{xy^2z^2}{1-z}\left[\left(\frac{\partial^2 F}{\partial x\partial y}\right)(0,0) - \left(\frac{\partial^2 F}{\partial y\partial x}\right)(0,0)\right].$$

3. Polynomial Boolean Interpolants.

The interpolants in Section 2 involve rational blending functions. Polynomial blending functions would be preferable. Such interpolants are developed in this Section, which also includes theorems to help find them.

Linear Case.

Let $F \in C(\partial T)$ and consider the following projector:

$$(3.1)\quad P_2F = F(0,y) + F(x,0) - F(0,0).$$

P_2 can be thought of as the Boolean sum of the two "mini-projectors" $Q_1F = F(0,y)$ and $Q_2F = F(x,0)$. P_2F interpolates to F on $E_1 \cup E_2$. The problem remaining is to define a projector P_1 such that $P_1F = F$ on E_3 and the Boolean sum $(P_1 \oplus P_2)F$ interpolates F on all of ∂T. The following theorem gives a way to find such a projector P_1:

Theorem 3.1 Let $F \in C(\partial T)$ and $\partial T = \Gamma_1 \cup \Gamma_2$. Suppose that P_1 and P_2 are interpolation projectors defined on ∂T such that $P_iF = F$ on Γ_i and P_iF is a linear combination of values of F on Γ_i only, $i = 1,2$. Then $(P_1 \oplus P_2)F$

(1) interpolates to F on Γ_1;

(2) interpolates to F on Γ_2, if P_1F on Γ_2 is a linear combination of function evaluations on $\Gamma_2 \cap \Gamma_1$.

Theorem 3.1 is a particularization of Theorem 2.1 in [3].

We apply Theorem 3.1 with P_2 defined by (3.1). Then we let $\Gamma_2 = E_1 \cup E_2$ and $\Gamma_1 = E_3$, so that $\Gamma_2 \cap \Gamma_1 = \{(0,1),(1,0)\}$, as in Figure 7. Let

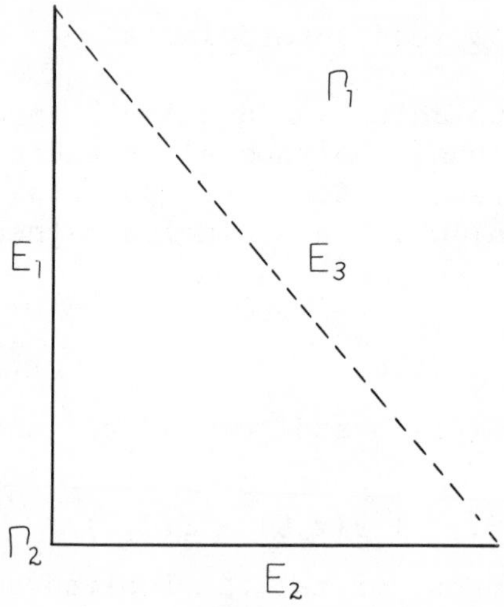

Figure 7

$$(3.2)\quad P_1 F = x\, F(1-y,y) + y\, F(x,1-x).$$

Since P_1 satisfies the hypothesis of Theorem 3.1, $(P_1 \oplus P_2)F$ interpolates to F on ∂T, where

$$(3.3)\quad \begin{aligned}(P_1 \oplus P_2)F = {} & x\, F(1-y,y) + y\, F(x,1-x) \\ & + F(0,y) + F(x,0) - F(0,0) \\ & - x[F(0,y) + F(1-y,0) - F(0,0)] \\ & - y[F(0,1-x) + F(x,0) - F(0,0)].\end{aligned}$$

This interpolant was obtained by other means by G.M. Nielson [12].

The precision set of this Boolean sum is $\{x^m y^n : m = 0 \text{ or } n = 0\}$, which includes all polynomials of degree one or less.

Cubic Case.

In order to obtain a smooth C^1 polynomial Boolean sum interpolant, we need appropriate generalizations of (3.1) and (3.2). The former is straightforward: replace (3.1) by

(3.4) $P_2F = (T_x^1 \oplus T_y^2)\ F,$ where

(3.5) $T_x^1F = F(0,y) + x\ F_{1,0}(0,y)$

(3.6) $T_y^2F = F(x,0) + y\ F_{0,1}(x,0),$ (Figure 8) so that

(3.7) $$P_2F = F(0,y) + x\ F_{1,0}(0,y) + F(x,0) + y\ F_{0,1}(x,0) - [F(0,0) + y\ F_{0,1}(0,0) + x\ F_{1,0}(0,0) + xy\ \frac{\partial^2 F}{\partial x \partial y}\ (0,0)].$$

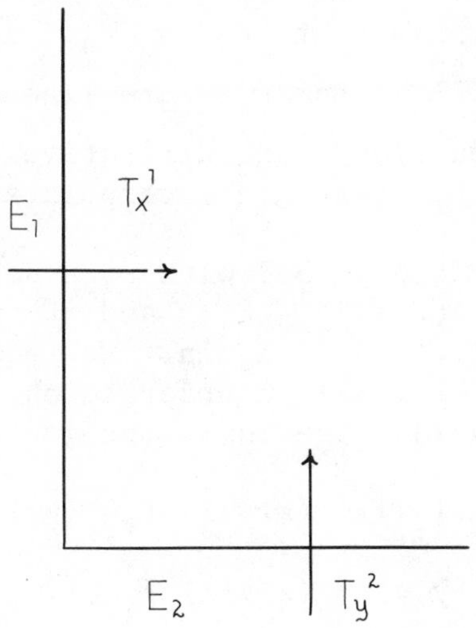

Figure 8 - Taylor Projectors.

Lemma 3.2 Let $F \in C^1(\partial T)$. Then P_2F interpolates to F and to the first derivatives of F on $x = 0$ and on $y = 0$ if compatibility condition (2.17) holds.

In order to motivate an appropriate definition of P_1, we state a generalization of Theorem 3.1 to the C^1 case [3].

Theorem 3.3 Let $F \in C^1(\partial T)$ and $\partial T = \Gamma_1 \cup \Gamma_2$. Suppose that P_1 and P_2 are interpolation projectors defined on ∂T such that P_iF interpolates to F and to the first derivatives of F on Γ_i and P_iF is a linear combination of function values and first derivatives on Γ_i only, $i = 1,2$. Then $(P_1 \oplus P_2)F$

(1) interpolates to F and to the first derivatives of F on Γ_1;

(2) interpolates to F and to the first derivatives of F on Γ_2, if P_1F, $\frac{\partial P_1 F}{\partial x}$, and $\frac{\partial P_1 F}{\partial y}$ on Γ_2 are linear combinations of function and derivative evaluations on $\Gamma_2 \cap \Gamma_1$ that are interpolated by P_2F.

We apply Theorem 3.3 with P_2 defined by (3.7). Then we let $\Gamma_2 = E_1 \cup E_2$ and $\Gamma_1 = E_3$, so that $\Gamma_2 \cap \Gamma_1 = \{(0,1),(1,0)\}$ again. We require a two-fold generalization of (3.2) in order to obtain a suitable P_1. First, consider the Taylor projectors (Figure 9)

(3.8) $T_y^3F = F(x,1-x) + (x+y-1)\ F_{0,1}(x,1-x)$

(3.9) $T_x^3F = F(1-y,y) + (x+y-1)\ F_{1,0}(1-y,y)$.

Then let

(3.10) $P_1F = \alpha(x,y)\ T_y^3F + \beta(x,y)\ T_x^3F$,

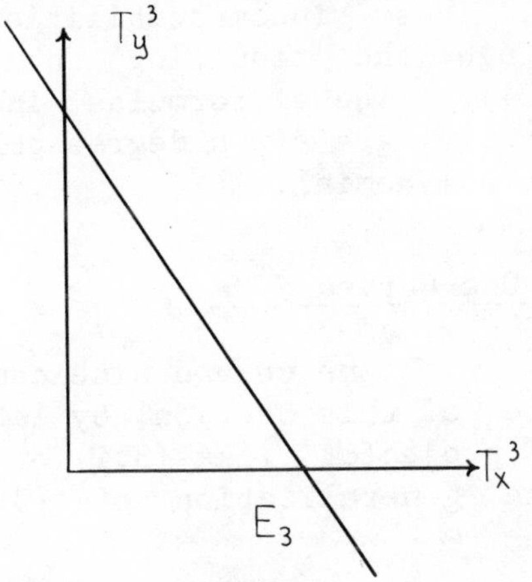

Figure 9

where α and β are certain cardinal functions for G. Birkhoff's finite dimensional tricubic interpolant. For the C° linear case, $\alpha(x,y) = y$ and $\beta(x,y) = x$, two trilinear cardinal functions. For the C^1 cubic case,

$$(3.11)\quad \alpha(x,y) = y^2[3-2y + 6x(1-x-y)]$$
$$\beta(x,y) = x^2[3-2x + 6y(1-x-y)].$$

The projector P_1 defined by (3.10) and (3.11) satisfies the hypothesis of (2) in Theorem 3.3 for P_2 defined by (3.7). E.g.,

$$P_2F(0,1) = F(0,1) \quad \text{and} \quad \frac{\partial}{\partial y} P_2F(0,1) = F_{0,1}(0,1)$$

are the conditions to be shown on side E_1.

The precision set of $P_1 \oplus P_2$ defined by P_1 in (3.7) and P_2 in (3.10) is $\{x^m y^n : 0 \leqslant m \leqslant 1 \text{ or } 0 \leqslant n \leqslant 1\}$, which includes all polynomials of degree three or less.

Incompatibilities of the form (2.16) arise at each of the three vertices of T. This happens at (0,0) because P_2 is a Boolean sum (3.7) and at the other two vertices to ensure that (2) in Theorem 3.3 is satisfied. These incompatibilities can be corrected, although the resulting formulas are rather long (see [3]). These formulas include rational corrections involving a sixth degree polynomial divided by a linear polynomial.

Triangle With One Curved Side

Triangles with one curved side can be considered by the method of this Section, by letting P_2 correspond to a projector like (3.1) or (3.4) with P_1 an appropriate generalization of (3.2) or (3.10), respectively.

Consider the curved triangle which is T except that E_3 is defined by the 1-1 functions $y = f(x)$ or $x = g(y)$, as in Figure 10. Let $F \in C^1(\partial T)$.

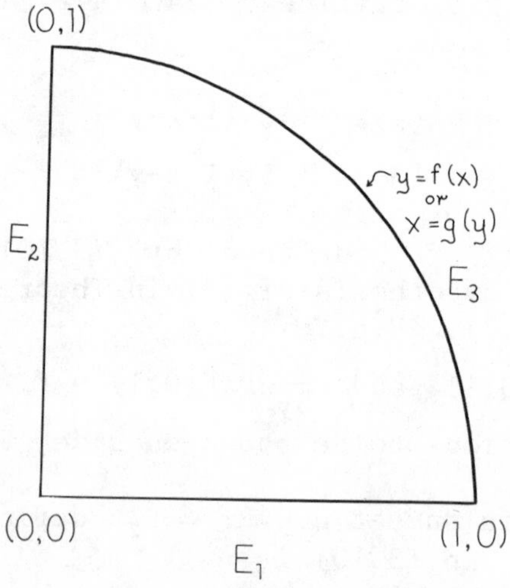

Figure 10

Suppose that P_2 is defined by (3.4) and the function $\alpha(x,y)$ and $\beta(x,y)$ are defined by (3.11). Let

(3.12) $P_1F = \alpha(1-f(x),y)T_y^3F + \beta(1-f(x),y)T_x^3F$, where

$$(3.13)\quad T_y^3F \equiv F(x,f(x)) + [y-f(x)]F_{0,1}(x,f(x))$$

$$(3.14)\quad T_x^3F \equiv F(g(y),y) + [x-g(y)]F_{1,0}(g(y),y).$$

The formula is somewhat long for the C^1 cubic case, so we state the analogue of (3.3) for the C^0 linear case. With the obvious simplifications defined into (3.12) - (3.14) above, we obtain the following:

$$\begin{aligned}(3.15)\quad (P_1 \oplus P_2)F &= [1-f(x)]\, f(g(y),y) + yF(x,f(x)) \\ &+ F(0,y) + F(x,0) - F(0,0) \\ &- [1-f(x)][F(0,y) + F(g(y),0) - F(0,0)] \\ &- y\,[F(0,f(x)) + F(x,0) - F(0,0)].\end{aligned}$$

4. Finite Dimensional Interpolants.

Smooth interpolation functions can be used to construct interpolation schemes which involve only point functionals on ∂T. This is achieved by defining the function $\tilde{F}$ and the normal derivative of $\tilde{F}$ along each side of T as polynomials which interpolate to the data functionals on that side. This ensures continuity of the function and of the normal derivative across a side common to two adjacent triangles. The polynomial precision of the final interpolant is limited by the lowest polynomial precision achieved by the boundary data interpolants. These remarks are now illustrated by a number of examples.

Example 1. Linear Rational Boolean Interpolant.

Consider Q^* defined by (2.7),

$$Q^*F = \frac{1}{2}\,[P_1+P_2+P_3-P_1P_2P_3]F,$$

where the P_i are defined by (2.1) - (2.3) and $P_1P_2P_3$ is defined by (2.8). Let

$$\begin{aligned}
(4.1)\quad \tilde{F}(x,0) &\equiv (1-x)F(0,0) + x\,F(1,0) \simeq F(x,0)\\
\tilde{F}(x,1-x) &\equiv (1-x)F(0,1) + x\,F(1,0) \simeq F(x,1-x)\\
\tilde{F}(0,y) &\equiv (1-y)F(0,0) + y\,F(0,1) \simeq F(0,y)\\
\tilde{F}(1-y,y) &\equiv (1-y)F(1,0) + y\,F(0,1) \simeq F(1-y,y)\\
\tilde{F}(x+y,0) &\equiv (1-z)F(1,0) + z\,F(0,0) \simeq F(x-y,0) =\\
&\quad F(1-z,0)\\
\tilde{F}(0,x+y) &\equiv z\,F(0,0) + (1-z)\,F(0,1) \simeq F(0,x+y) =\\
&\quad F(0,1-z)
\end{aligned}$$

where $z = 1-x-y$ and $F \equiv \tilde{F}$ at $(0,0)$, $(1,0)$ and $(0,1)$. Then

$$\begin{aligned}
(4.2)\quad Q^*\tilde{F} &= x\,F(1,0) + y\,F(0,1) + z\,F(0,0)\\
&= P_1P_2P_3F\\
&= P_1P_2P_3\tilde{F}.
\end{aligned}$$

This is a familiar kind of simplification. It is the same kind of simplification as that of Boolean sums over rectangles reducing to tensor products. (Also cf. the remarks in Section 1 about Coons patches.)

Example 2. Cubic Rational Boolean Interpolants.

Consider P_1, P_2, and P_3 defined by (2.12) - (2.14). We indicate the discretization only for P_1, the discretizations for P_2 and P_3 being dual.

$$\begin{aligned}
(4.2)\quad \tilde{F}(x,0) &= \varphi_0(x)F(0,0) + \varphi_1(x)F_{1,0}(0,0)\\
&\quad + \Psi_0(x)F(1,0) + \Psi_1(x)F_{1,0}(1,0)\\
&\simeq F(x,0)
\end{aligned}$$

$$\begin{aligned}
(4.3)\quad \tilde{F}_{0,1}(x,0) &= (1-x)F_{0,1}(0,0) + x\,F_{0,1}(1,0)\\
&\simeq F_{0,1}(x,0)
\end{aligned}$$

The functions φ_i and Ψ_i are defined by (2.15). $\tilde{F}(0,y)$ and $\tilde{F}_{1,0}(0,y)$ are defined dually to (4.2) and (4.3), respectively.

$$(4.4)\quad \tilde{F}(x,1-x) = \varphi_0(x)F(0,1) + \varphi_1(x)[F_{1,0}(0,1) - F_{0,1}(0,1)] + \Psi_0(x)F(1,0) + \Psi_1(x)[F_{1,0}(1,0) - F_{0,1}(1,0)] \simeq F(x,1-x)$$

$$(4.5)\quad \tilde{F}_{1,0}(x,1-x) + \tilde{F}_{0,1}(x,1-x) = (1-x)[F_{1,0}(0,1) + F_{0,1}(0,1)] + x[F_{1,0}(1,0) + F_{0,1}(1,0)]$$

Note that in (4.4) $\tilde{F}(x,1-x)$ is defined in terms of the tangential derivative $\frac{\partial}{\partial x} - \frac{\partial}{\partial y}$ along the side E_3. Similarly, in (4.5) the normal derivative $\frac{\partial}{\partial x} + \frac{\partial}{\partial y}$ along side E_3 is defined in terms of its values at the endpoints of E_3. Note that (4.4) and (4.5) implicitly contain the definition of all the first derivatives of F on E_3, since $\frac{d}{dx}$ of (4.4) yields $\tilde{F}_{1,0}(x,1-x) - \tilde{F}_{0,1}(x,1-x)$. The above gives a 9 parameter C^1 scheme with quadratic polynomial precision. If the normal derivatives were defined as quadratics that also interpolated to values at midpoints, then the resulting 12 parameter scheme would have cubic polynomial precision.

With reference to Theorem 2.3 and the example thereafter, is $\tilde{F}$ compatible for $P_1 \oplus P_2$?

$$(4.6)\quad \frac{\partial^2 \tilde{F}}{\partial x \partial y}(0,0) = \left.\frac{\partial \tilde{F}_{0,1}}{\partial x}(x,0)\right|_{x=0} = -F_{0,1}(0,0) + F_{0,1}(1,0)$$

$$(4.7)\quad \frac{\partial^2 \widetilde{F}}{\partial y \partial x}(0,0) = \frac{\partial}{\partial y}\widetilde{F}_{1,0}(0,y)\Big|_{y=0} =$$

$$-F_{1,0}(0,0) + F_{1,0}(0,1)$$

As is typical for discretizations, $\widetilde{F}$ is in general incompatible, e.g., at (0,0), and so a rational correction term must be added to $(P_1 \oplus P_2)\widetilde{F}$, namely,

$$-\frac{xy^2z^2}{1-z}\left[F_{0,1}(1,0) - F_{0,1}(0,0) + F_{1,0}(0,0) - F_{1,0}(0,1)\right]$$

This compatibly corrected interpolant has precision for quadratic polynomials. It had been graphically implemented by R.J. McDermott, using linear normals and also quadratic normals. (Cf. the second paper after this one in these Proceedings.)

A function with a line of singularities is presented in Figures 11 and 12.

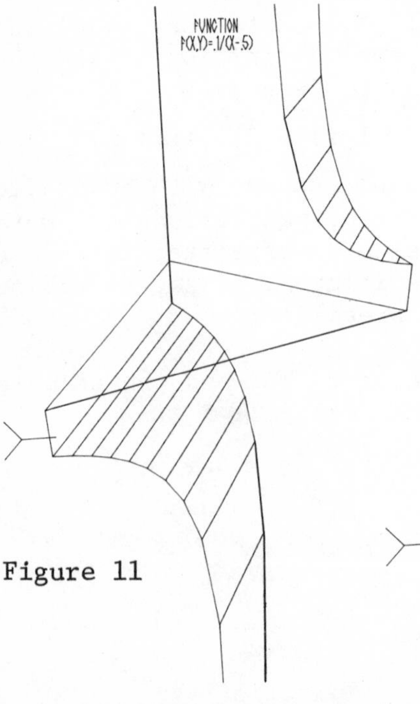

Figure 11

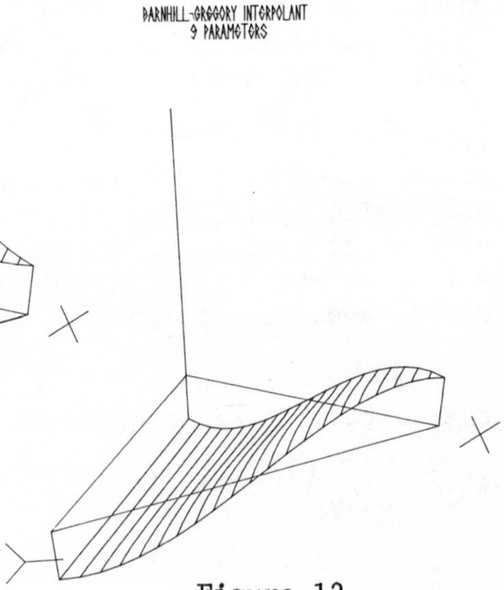

Figure 12

The function $F(x,y) = \frac{.1}{x-.5}$ on the triangle T is given in Figure 11 and its 9-parameter interpolant in Figure 12. The interpolant matches the relevant data at the vertices and produces a surface that smooths out the line of singularities at $x = \frac{1}{2}$.

Two oscillatory functions are compared in a similar way in Figures 13-16. The function $F(x,y) = \frac{\sin 4\pi xy}{2}$ is given in Figure 13 and its 9-parameter interpolant in Figure 14. The function $F(x,y) = \sin [2\pi\ x\ (1-y)]$ is given in Figure 15 and its 9-parameter interpolant in Figure 16. The interpolant "smooth out" the oscillations of these functions somewhat.

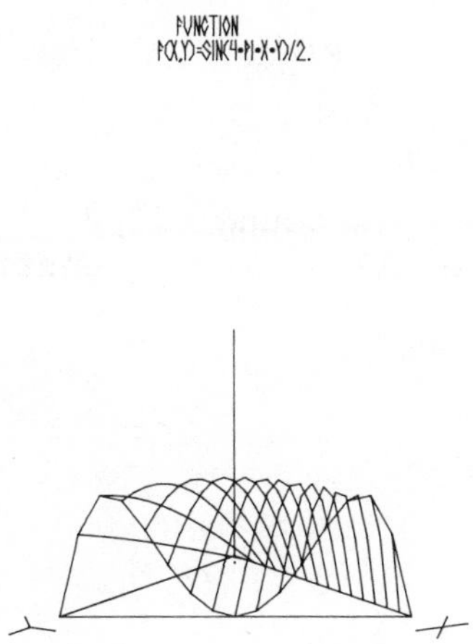

Figure 13

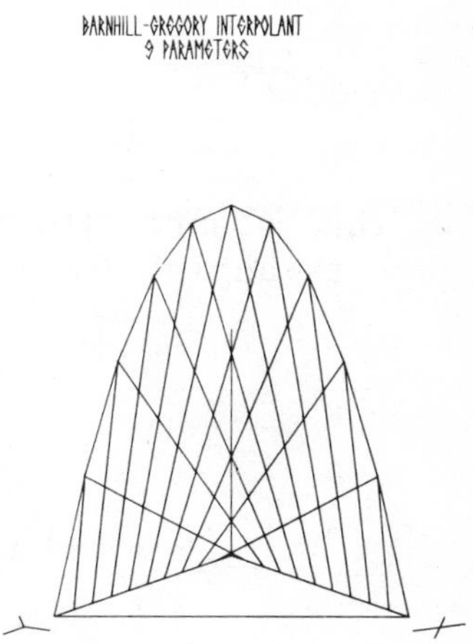

Figure 14

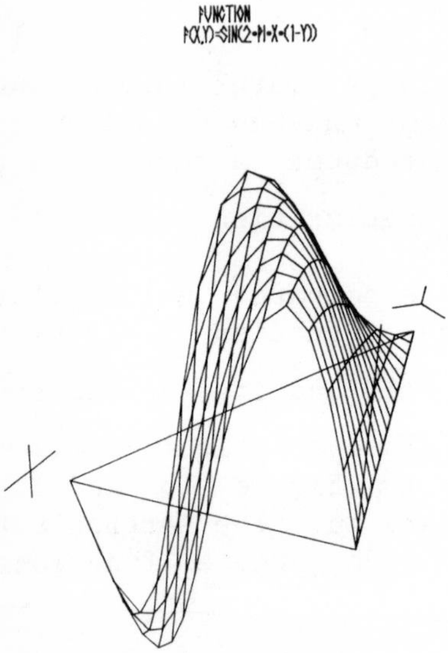

Figure 15

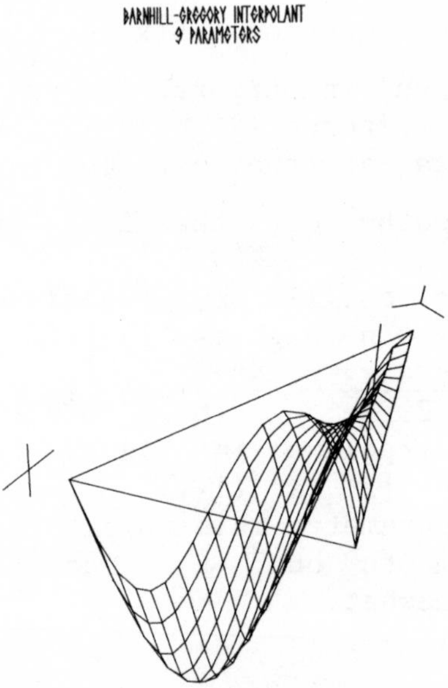

Figure 16

The square [0,2] x [0,2] is subdivided into eight triangles as in Figure 17. The function

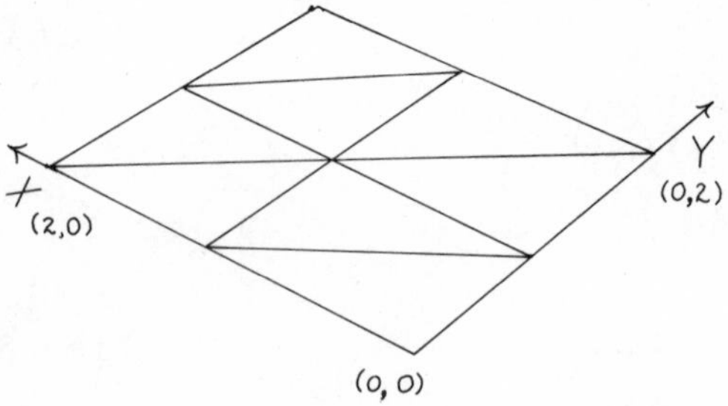

Figure 17

$F(x,y) = \dfrac{\sin 2x}{y+1}$ on $[0,2] \times [0,2]$ is given in Figure 18 and its piecewise 9-parameter interpolant over this triangulation is given in Figure 19. The

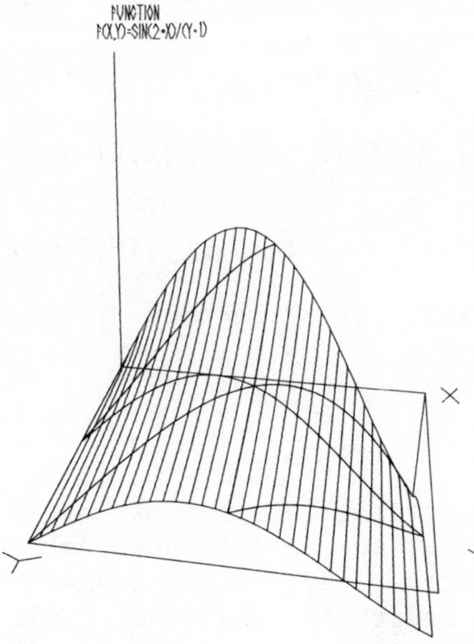

Figure 18

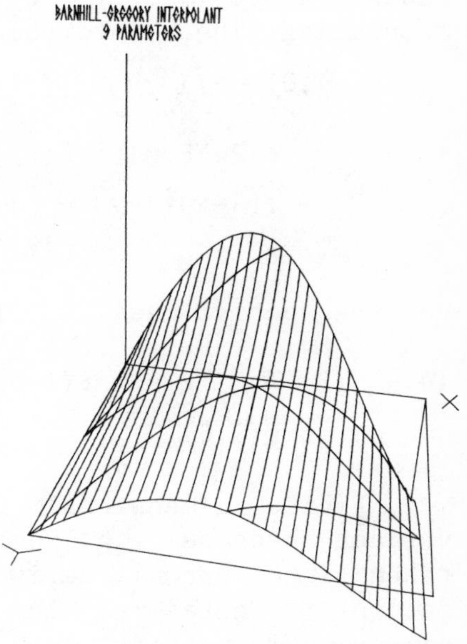

Figure 19

curved lines represent values along the edges of the triangular patches.

Example 3. Linear Polynomial Boolean Interpolant

If each univariate function in (3.3) is replaced by the corresponding linear interpolant then

(4.6) $P_1\widetilde{F} = x\ F(1,0) + y\ F(0,1)$

$P_2\widetilde{F} = z\ F(0,0) + x\ F(1,0) + y\ F(0,1)$ so that

$P_1P_2\widetilde{F} = x\ F(1,0) + y\ F(0,1)$. Hence

(4.7) $(P_1 \oplus P_2)\widetilde{F} = z\ F(0,0) + x\ F(1,0) + y\ F(0,1) = P_2\widetilde{F}$.

Example 4. Linear Polynomial Boolean Interpolant for Triangle with One Curved Side.

If each univariate function in (3.15) on the sides $x = 0$ and $y = 0$ is replaced by the corresponding linear interpolant, e.g.,

$$\widetilde{F}(g(y),0) = [1-g(y)]F(0,0) + g(y)F(1,0), \text{ then}$$

$$(4.8)\quad (P_1 \oplus P_2)\widetilde{F} = [1-f(x)]\, F(g(y),y) + y\, F(x,f(x)) + \{(1-x)(1-y) - [1-f(x)][1-g(y)]\}F(0,0) + \{x(1-y) - [1-f(x)]g(y)\}F(1,0).$$

For the special case $y = 1-x$, (4.8) becomes

$$(4.9)\quad (P_1 \oplus P_2)\widetilde{F} = x\, F(1-y,y) + y\, F(x,1-x) + z\, F(0,0).$$

Finite dimensional formulas are not affine invariant because, e.g., normal derivatives need not be taken into normal derivatives by affine transformations. Therefore, in order to use the finite dimensional methods for arbitrary triangles, the smooth interpolants should be transformed and then discretized.

Acknowledgments. This research was done jointly with Mr. John A. Gregory and was supported by The University of Utah Research Committee. The author wishes to thank Mrs. Agnes R. Barnhill for the drawings and Mr. Robert J. McDermott for the computer-generated pictures.

References

1. Barnhill, R.E., Birkhoff, G., and Gordon, W.J., Smooth Interpolation in Triangles, J. Approx. Theory 8, 1973, pp. 114-128.

2. Barnhill, R.E. and Gregory, J.A., Compatible Smooth Interpolation in Triangles, to appear in J. Approx. Theory.

3. Barnhill, R.E. and Gregory, J.A., Smooth Polynomial Interpolation to Boundary Data on Triangles TR/31, Brunel Univ., Uxbridge, England, 1973.

4. Birkhoff, G. and Mansfield, Lois, Compatible Triangular Finite Elements, to appear in J. Math. Analysis and Applications.

5. Coons, S.A., Surfaces for Computer Aided Design, Design Division, Mech. Engin. Dept., MIT, 1964, revised, 1967.

6. Forrest, A.R., On Coons and Other Methods for the Representation of Curved Surfaces, Computer Graphics and Image Processing 1, 1972, pp. 341-359.

7. Gordon, W.J., "Blending-function" Methods of Bivariate and Multivariate Interpolation and Approximation, SIAM J. Numer. Anal. 8, 1971, pp. 158-177.

8. Gregory, J.A., Symmetric Smooth Interpolation on Triangles, TR/34, Brunel Univ., Uxbridge, England, 1973.

9. Gregory, J.A. Piecewise Interpolation Theory and Finite Element Analysis, Ph.D. thesis, Brunel Univ., Uxbridge, England, 1974.

10. Gregory, J.A., Smooth Interpolation Without Twist Constraints. These Proceedings.

11. McDermott, R.J., Graphical Representation of Surfaces over Triangles and Rectangles. These Proceedings.

12. Nielson, G.M., Private communication, June, 1971.

13. Peters, G.J., Parametric Bicubic Surfaces. These Proceedings.

SMOOTH INTERPOLATION WITHOUT TWIST CONSTRAINTS

John A. Gregory
University of Utah

1. Introduction

Smooth or blending function interpolants, which match a given function and slopes on the boundary of a rectangle or a triangle, usually require that the cross derivative or twist terms be defined unambiguously at vertices. For example, the surfaces of Coons[3] over rectangles and the interpolation schemes of Barnhill, Birkhoff, and Gordon[1] over triangles require that certain cross derivatives be compatible at vertices. Smooth interpolation schemes which avoid such restrictions could be useful for the piecewise generation of surfaces in computer aided geometric design. This paper considers two such schemes, one over a rectangle and the other over a triangle.

The interpolation scheme for the rectangle is a modification of an interpolant of Coons, which was later developed through Boolean sum theory by Gordon [4]. The interpolant is modified by the addition of rational terms so that the compatibility constraints are removed.

The smooth interpolants over triangles of Barnhill, Birkhoff and Gordon can also be modified by the addition of rational terms, see for example, Barnhill and Gregory[2] or Mansfield[6]. This approach, together with a detailed discussion of smooth interpolation over triangles, is presented in the preceding paper by R.E. Barnhill. This present paper describes a new interpolation scheme for the triangle. This scheme has a relatively simple construction, it is symmetric in that each side of the triangle is treated in the same way, and it involves no compatibility constraints. Further details and generalizations of this scheme are given in Gregory[5].

For simplicity of presentation, the interpolation schemes in this paper are considered as bivariate surfaces which interpolate a function F and its slopes defined along the boundary of a rectangle or a triangle in cartesian (x,y) space. However, the interpolation schemes are immediately applicable to the construction of a bivariate vector-valued function

$$\underline{P}(s,t) = [x(s,t),\ y(s,t),\ z(s,t)],$$

where s and t are parametric variables and the rectangles or triangles are defined in the parametric (s,t) space, see R.E. Barnhill's paper.

The smooth interpolants in this paper may be pieced together to give a surface which is $C^1(\Omega)$ over a rectangular and/or triangular subdivision of a polygonal region Ω. Also, by defining the function and slopes along boundary interfaces in terms of data on that boundary, $C^1(\Omega)$ finite dimensional piecewise interpolants can be derived. For example a twelve parameter interpolant for the square, and a nine parameter interpolant for the triangle, which involve the function F and its first two partial derivatives at each vertex, can be derived by suitable choice of the boundary data. Although, for incompatible boundary data, the interpolants have discontinuous cross derivatives at the vertices, they should compare favourably with other known C^1 interpolants which impose zero second order derivative conditions at each vertex, for example the Coons patch with zero twist. (See Example 4.1.)

The interpolants considered in this paper have the property that they are able to reproduce simple polynomial surfaces. The set of polynomials which are reproduced by an interpolation scheme is defined here as the *precision set* of the interpolant and these sets are derived for each of the schemes of this paper. The precision set property gives some indication that the interpolation schemes are reasonable for design purposes.

2. Smooth C^1 Interpolation on Rectangles

The unit square S with boundary ∂S is considered with vertices at $(0,0)$, $(1,0)$, $(1,1)$ and $(0,1)$. Any arbitrary rectangle can be obtained by an affine transformation of this standard square.

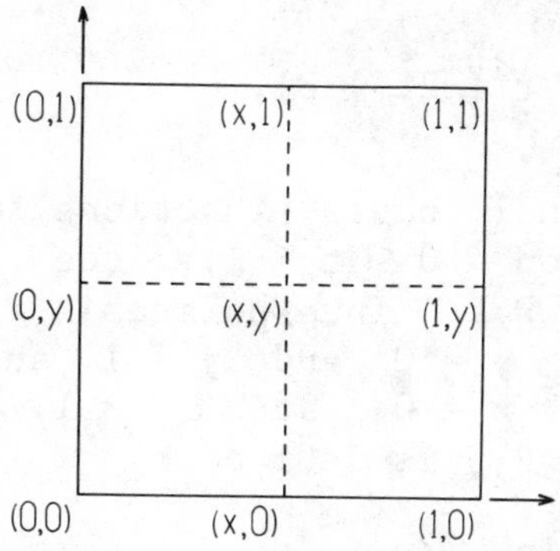

Figure 1

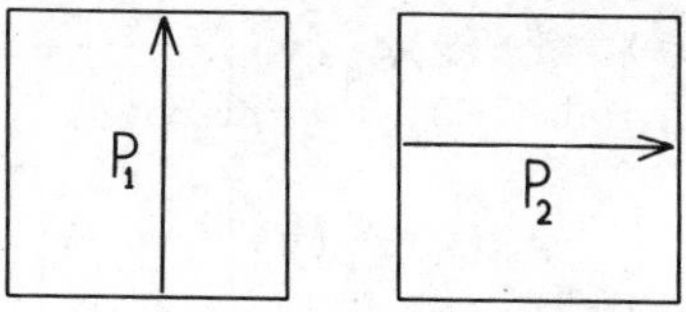

Figure 2

For $F(x,y) \in C^1(\partial S)$ and $(x,y) \in S$, cubic Hermite interpolation projectors along parallels to the sides $x = 0$ and $y = 0$ are respectively defined by

$$(2.1)\quad P_1F = \sum_{j=0}^{1} \varphi_j(y)F_{0,j}(x,0) + \sum_{j=0}^{1} \Psi_j(y)F_{0,j}(x,1),$$

$$(2.2)\quad P_2F = \sum_{i=0}^{1} \varphi_i(x)F_{i,0}(0,y) + \sum_{i=0}^{1} \Psi_i(x)F_{i,0}(1,y),$$

where

$$(2.3)\quad \begin{cases} \varphi_0(t) = (t-1)^2(2t+1), & \varphi_1(t) = (t-1)^2 t, \\ \Psi_0(t) = t^2(-2t+3), & \Psi_1(t) = t^2(t-1), \end{cases}$$

are the cardinal basis functions for cubic Hermite interpolation on $0 \leqslant t \leqslant 1$, see Figures 1 and 2. The function P_1F interpolates F and its first derivatives on $y = 0$ and $y = 1$ and P_2F has dual properties on $x = 0$ and $x = 1$. The Boolean sum projector $P_1 \oplus P_2$ is defined by

$$(2.4)\quad (P_1 \oplus P_2)F = (P_1 + P_2 - P_1P_2)F$$

where from (2.1) and (2.2) it follows that

$$(2.5)\quad \begin{aligned} P_1P_2F = &\sum_{i,j\leqslant 1} \varphi_i(x)\varphi_j(y)\left(\frac{\partial^{j+i}F}{\partial y^j \partial x^i}\right)(0,0) \\ &+ \sum_{i,j\leqslant 1} \Psi_i(x)\varphi_j(y)\left(\frac{\partial^{j+i}F}{\partial y^j \partial x^i}\right)(1,0) \\ &+ \sum_{i,j\leqslant 1} \varphi_i(x)\Psi_j(y)\left(\frac{\partial^{j+i}F}{\partial y^j \partial x^i}\right)(0,1) \\ &+ \sum_{i,j\leqslant 1} \Psi_i(x)\Psi_j(y)\left(\frac{\partial^{j+i}F}{\partial y^j \partial x^i}\right)(1,1). \end{aligned}$$

If $F \in C^1(\partial S)$ and satisfies the twist compatibility condition

$$(2.6) \qquad \left(\frac{\partial^2 F}{\partial x \partial y}\right)(V_k) = \left(\frac{\partial^2 F}{\partial y \partial x}\right)(V_k)$$

at each vertex V_k of the square, then the projectors are commutative and the Boolean sum function (2.4) interpolates F and its first derivatives on ∂S (see proof of Theorem 2.1). However, if the compatibility condition (2.6) is not satisfied at each vertex then $(P_1 \oplus P_2)F$ does not interpolate the x partial derivative on $x = 0$ and $x = 1$. The following theorem removes this discrepancy by the addition of rational terms to the Boolean sum function. It should be noted that these rational terms are zero for F satisfying (2.6), i.e. the modified interpolant reduces the standard Boolean sum interpolant when the boundary data is compatible.

<u>Theorem 2.1</u>. The function

$$\begin{aligned}(2.7) \quad PF = {} & P_1F + P_2F - P_1P_2F \\ & - \frac{x(x-1)^2 y^2 (y-1)^2}{x+y}\left[\left(\frac{\partial^2 F}{\partial x \partial y}\right)(0,0) - \left(\frac{\partial^2 F}{\partial y \partial x}\right)(0,0)\right] \\ & - \frac{x(x-1)^2 y^2 (y-1)^2}{-x+y-1}\left[\left(\frac{\partial^2 F}{\partial x \partial y}\right)(0,1) - \left(\frac{\partial^2 F}{\partial y \partial x}\right)(0,1)\right] \\ & - \frac{x^2 (x-1) y^2 (y-1)^2}{-x+1-y}\left[\left(\frac{\partial^2 F}{\partial x \partial y}\right)(1,0) - \left(\frac{\partial^2 F}{\partial y \partial x}\right)(1,0)\right] \\ & - \frac{x^2 (x-1) y^2 (y-1)^2}{x-1+y-1}\left[\left(\frac{\partial^2 F}{\partial x \partial y}\right)(1,1) - \left(\frac{\partial^2 F}{\partial y \partial x}\right)(1,1)\right],\end{aligned}$$

where P_1F, P_2F, and P_1P_2F are defined by (2.1), (2.2), and (2.5), interpolates $F \in C^1(\partial S)$ and its first derivatives on the boundary ∂S of the square S.

<u>Proof</u>. Consider the Boolean sum function which can be written as

$$(P_1 \oplus P_2)F \equiv F - (I-P_1)(I-P_2)F,$$

where I is the identity operator. Then the Boolean sum function interpolates F and its first derivatives on $y = 0$ and $y = 1$ since $I - P_1$ and its first derivatives are null on these sides. (The condition (2.6) would imply a dual result on $x = 0$ and $x = 1$ since P_1 and P_2 then commute.) Now on $x = 0$ the Boolean sum function interpolates F but

$$(2.8)\quad \left[\frac{\partial(P_1 \oplus P_2)F}{\partial x}\right]_{x=0} = F_{1,0}(0,y)$$

$$+ \varphi_1(y)\left[\left(\frac{\partial^2 F}{\partial x \partial y}\right)(0,0) - \left(\frac{\partial^2 F}{\partial y \partial x}\right)(0,0)\right]$$

$$+ \Psi_1(y)\left[\left(\frac{\partial^2 F}{\partial x \partial y}\right)(0,1) - \left(\frac{\partial^2 F}{\partial y \partial x}\right)(0,1)\right].$$

A dual result attains on $x = 1$. The discrepancy in the interpolation properties of this derivative is removed by the rational terms in (2.7). For example, the term in (2.8) which involves $\varphi_1(y) = (y-1)^2 y$ is removed by the rational term in (2.7) which involves the function

$$-\frac{x(x-1)^2 y^2 (y-1)^2}{x+y}.$$

This function has the desired properties that it and its first derivatives are zero on ∂S except on $x = 0$ where

$$\left[\frac{\partial}{\partial x}\left(-\frac{x(x-1)^2 y^2 (y-1)^2}{x+y}\right)\right]_{x=0} = -(y-1)^2 y \quad \blacksquare$$

Remark. A symmetric interpolant on the square can be obtained by taking the average of (2.7) and the dual modified interpolant for $(P_2 \oplus P_1)F$.

Corollary 2.1. Let $\tilde{F} \in C^1(\partial S)$ be defined by

$$(2.9)\quad \tilde{F}(x,0) = \varphi_0(x)F(0,0) + \varphi_1(x)F_{1,0}(0,0) + \Psi_0(x)F(1,0) + \Psi_1(x)F_{1,0}(1,0)$$

$$(2.10)\quad \tilde{F}_{0,1}(x,0) = (1-x)F_{0,1}(0,0) + x\,F_{0,1}(1,0),$$

with dual expressions for the function and normal derivatives on $(x,1)$, $(0,y)$, and $(1,y)$. Then $P\tilde{F}$ is a twelve parameter interpolant which interpolates $\tilde{F}$ and its first derivatives on the boundary ∂S of the square S.

Remark. The boundary function $\tilde{F}$ on a side is a cubic Hermite function interpolating data on that side, and the normal derivative is a linear function interpolating data on that side. (The tangential derivative is automatically defined by the boundary function.) Thus for piecewise interpolation, the function and slopes across a side common to two adjacent rectangles is maintained by the use of $P\tilde{F}$ over each rectangle.

Theorem 2.2. The set of polynomials for which (2.7) is exact is

$$(2.11)\qquad x^m y^n \begin{cases} 0 \leqslant m \leqslant 3, & \text{for all } n \\ 0 \leqslant n \leqslant 3, & \text{for all } m. \end{cases}$$

Proof. For polynomial F, (2.7) reduces to the cummutative Boolean sum function $(P_1 \oplus P_2)F$ which is precise for the union of the precision sets of P_1 and P_2, namely

$$P_1 x^m y^n = x^m P_1 y^n = x^m y^n, \quad 0 \leqslant n \leqslant 3 \quad \text{for all} \quad m$$

$$P_2 x^m y^n = y^n P_2 x^m = x^m y^n, \quad 0 \leqslant m \leqslant 3 \quad \text{for all} \quad n \; \blacksquare$$

Remark. The twelve parameter scheme defined in Corollary 2.1 has a reduced precision set.

3. Smooth C^1 Interpolation on Triangles

It is sufficient to consider the triangle T with boundary ∂T and vertices at $V_1 = (1,0)$, $V_2 = (0,1)$, and $V_3 = (0,0)$. The interpolation scheme considered below is invariant under an affine transformation which takes this "standard" triangle T onto any arbitrary triangle. The side opposite the vertex V_k is denoted by E_k and thus E_1 is the side $x = 0$, E_2 is the side $y = 0$, and E_3 is the side $z = 0$, where $z = 1 - x - y$. For

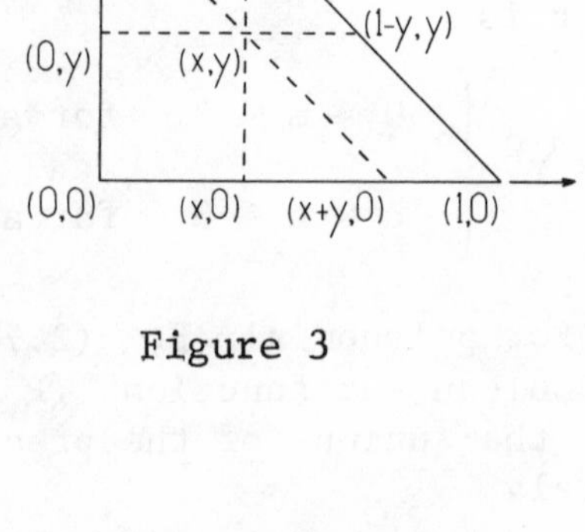

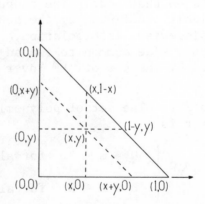

Figure 3

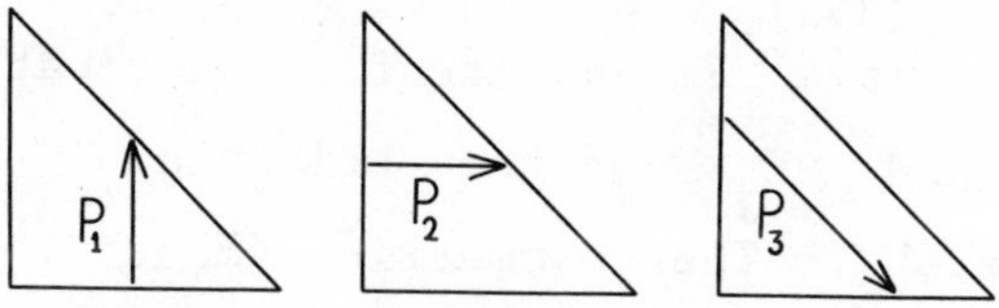

Figure 4

$F(x,y) \in C^1(\partial T)$ and $(x,y) \in T$ cubic Hermite interpolation projectors along parallels to the sides $x = 0$, $y = 0$, and $z = 0$ are respectively defined by

$$(3.1)\quad P_1F = \sum_{i=0}^{1} \varphi_i\left(\frac{y}{1-x}\right)(1-x)^i\, F_{0,i}(x,0)$$

$$+ \sum_{i=0}^{1} \Psi_i\left(\frac{y}{1-x}\right)(1-x)^i\, F_{0,i}(x,1-x),$$

$$(3.2)\quad P_2F = \sum_{i=0}^{1} \varphi_i\left(\frac{x}{1-y}\right)(1-y)^i\, F_{i,0}(0,y)$$

$$+ \sum_{i=0}^{1} \Psi_i\left(\frac{x}{1-y}\right)(1-y)^i\, F_{i,0}(1-y,y),$$

$$(3.3)\quad P_3F = \sum_{i=0}^{1} \varphi_i\left(\frac{x}{x+y}\right)(x+y)^i \left(\left[\frac{\partial}{\partial x} - \frac{\partial}{\partial y}\right]^i F\right)(0,x+y)$$

$$+ \sum_{i=0}^{1} \Psi_i\left(\frac{x}{x+y}\right)(x+y)^i \left(\left[\frac{\partial}{\partial x} - \frac{\partial}{\partial y}\right]^i F\right)(x+y,0),$$

where the $\varphi_i(t)$ and $\Psi_i(t) = (-1)^i \varphi_i(1-t)$ are defined by (2.3), see Figures 3 and 4. The function $P_k F$ interpolates F and its first derivatives on the sides E_i and E_j of the triangle T adjacent to the vertex V_k. The symmetric smooth interpolation scheme is defined in the following theorem.

Theorem 3.1. The function

$$(3.4) \quad PF = x^2(3-2x+6yz)P_1F + y^2(3-2y+6xz)P_2F + z^2(3-2z+6xy)P_3F,$$

where P_1F, P_2F, and P_3F are defined by (3.1) - (3.3), interpolates $F \in C^1(\partial T)$ and its first derivatives on the boundary ∂T of the triangle T.

Proof. By symmetry it is sufficient to consider the side $x = 0$ where

$$(P_2F)(0,y) = (P_3F)(0,y) = F(0,y),$$

$$\left(\frac{\partial P_2F}{\partial x}\right)(0,y) = \left(\frac{\partial P_3F}{\partial x}\right)(0,y) = F_{1,0}(0,y).$$

Thus from (3.4) it follows that

$$(PF)(0,y) = \left[y^2(3-2y+6xz) + z^2(3-2z+6xy)\right]_{x=0} F(0,y),$$

$$\left(\frac{\partial PF}{\partial x}\right)(0,y) = \left[\frac{\partial}{\partial x}\{y^2(3-2y+6xz)+z^2(3-2z+6xy)\}\right]_{x=0} F(0,y) + \left[y^2(3-2y+6xz)+z^2(3-2z+6xy)\right]_{x=0} F_{1,0}(0,y).$$

Now

(3.5) $x^2(3-2x+6yz) + y^2(3-2y+6xz) + z^2(3-2z+6xy) = 1$

and thus

$$\left[y^2(3-2y+6xz) + z^2(3-2z+6xy)\right]_{x=0} = 1,$$

$$\left[\frac{\partial}{\partial x}\{y^2(3-2y+6xz) + z^2(3-2z+6xy)\}\right]_{x=0} = 0.$$

Hence

$$(PF)(0,y) = F(0,y) \quad \text{and} \quad \left(\frac{\partial PF}{\partial x}\right)(0,y) = F_{1,0}(0,y)$$

Also

$$\left(\frac{\partial PF}{\partial y}\right)(0,y) = \frac{\partial}{\partial y}(PF)(0,y) = F_{0,1}(0,y),$$

or, alternatively, the dual argument to the case $\partial/\partial x$ can be applied ■

<u>Corollary 3.1</u>. Let $\tilde{F} \in C^1(\partial T)$ be defined by

(3.6) $\tilde{F}(x,0) = \varphi_0(x)F(0,0) + \varphi_1(x)F_{1,0}(0,0)$
$\qquad + \Psi_0(x)F(1,0) + \Psi_1(x)F_{1,0}(1,0)$

(3.7) $\tilde{F}_{0,1}(x,0) = (1-x)F_{0,1}(0,0) + xF_{0,1}(1,0)$

(3.8) $\tilde{F}(0,y) = \varphi_0(y)F(0,0) + \varphi_1(y)F_{0,1}(0,0)$
$\qquad + \Psi_0(y)F(0,1) + \Psi_1(y)F_{0,1}(0,1)$

(3.9) $\tilde{F}_{1,0}(0,y) = (1-y)F_{1,0}(0,0) + yF_{1,0}(0,1)$

$$(3.10)\quad \widetilde{F}(x,1-x) = \varphi_0(x)F(0,1) + \varphi_1(x)\left[F_{1,0}(0,1) - F_{0,1}(0,1)\right] + \Psi_0(x)F(1,0) + \Psi_1(x)\left[F_{1,0}(1,0) - F_{0,1}(1,0)\right]$$

$$(3.11)\quad \widetilde{F}_{1,0}(x,1-x) + \widetilde{F}_{0,1}(x,1-x) = (1-x)\left[F_{1,0}(0,1) + F_{0,1}(0,1)\right] + x\left[F_{1,0}(1,0) + F_{0,1}(1,0)\right].$$

Then $P\widetilde{F}$ is a nine parameter interpolant which interpolates $\widetilde{F}$ and its first derivatives on the boundary ∂T of the triangle T.

Remark. For piecewise interpolation, the nine parameter interpolant $P\widetilde{F}$ is restricted to a regular mesh of right angled triangles. This is because the transformation of $P\widetilde{F}$ onto an arbitrary triangle will not in general take normals into normals. However, the smooth interpolant (3.4) is invariant under affine transformation since the P_kF are defined along the invariant parallels to the sides E_k.

Theorem 3.2. The set of polynomials for which (3.4) is exact is at least τ_3, the set of polynomials of degree three or less along parallels to the three sides of T, i.e.

$$(3.12)\quad \tau_3 = \{1,x,y,x^2,xy,y^2,x^3,x^2y,xy^2,y^3,(x+y)x^2y,(x+y)xy^2\}.$$

Proof. The intersection of the precision set of P_1, P_2, and P_3 is τ_3. Thus from (3.5) it follows that for $F \in \tau_3$

$$PF = x^2(3-2x+6yz)P_1F + y^2(3-2y+6xz)P_2F + z^2(3-2z+6xy)P_3F$$

$$= \left[x^2(3-2x+6yz) + y^2(3-2y+6xz) + z^2(3-2z+6xy)\right]F$$

$$= F \blacksquare$$

4. Examples.

The examples discussed in this section have been implemented by R.J. McDermott, see the following paper of these Proceedings. The examples illustrate the twelve parameter interpolation scheme for the rectangle described in Corollary 2.1. Examples of interpolation schemes for triangles are discussed in R.E. Barnhill's paper. The data for each example is supplied by some given primitive function $F(x,y)$.

Example 4.1. $F(x,y) = xy$. The twelve parameter interpolant exactly reproduces the function $F(xy) = xy$ since it is contained in the precision set of the interpolant (see Figure 5). Figure 6 illustrates the effect of defining zero twist parameters for the Coons patch (16 parameter bicubic tensor product with zero twist conditions). Close examination reveals the "flat spot" effect at the vertices which would be more apparent in a three dimensional model.

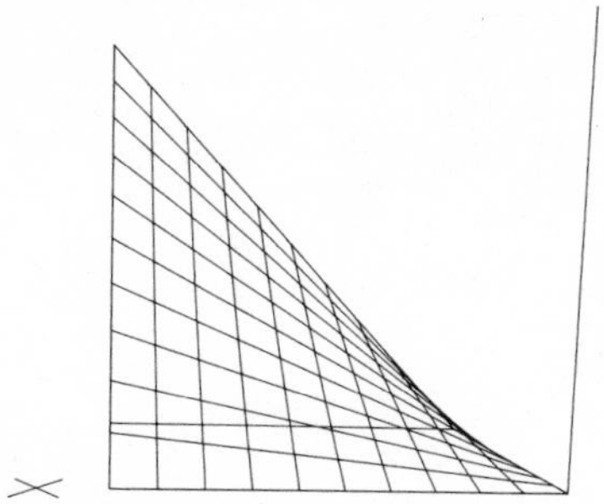

Figure 5

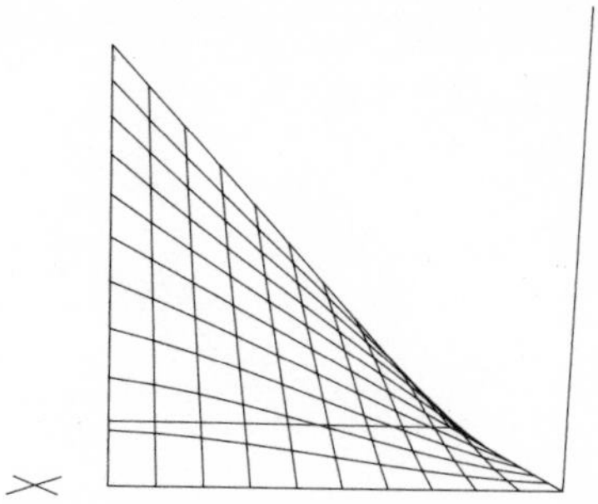

Figure 6

Example 4.2. $F(x,y) = (1-x)^2(1-y)^2$. This function (see Figure 7) is not contained in the precision set of the interpolant. However, the interpolant (see Figure 8) is a good approximation to this function.

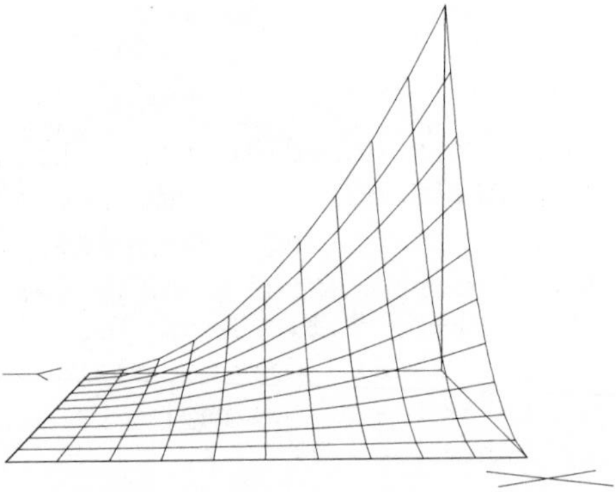

Figure 7

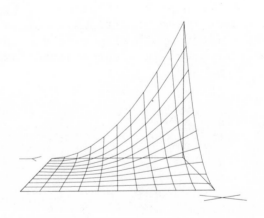

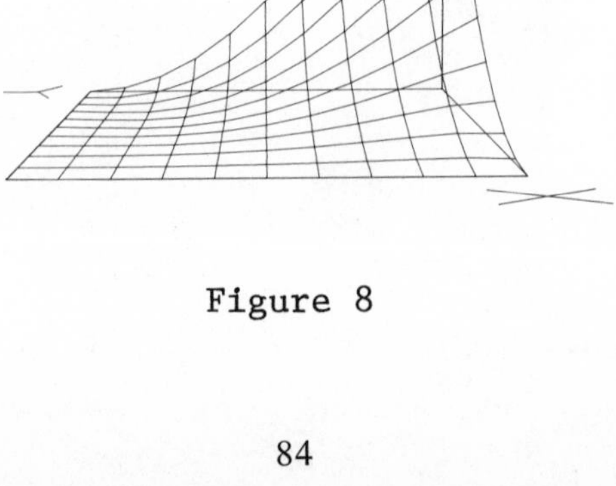

Figure 8

Example 4.3. $F(x,y) = 0.1/(x-0.5)$. The vertex data supplied by this function is well behaved although the function itself has a line singularity at $x = 0.5$ (see Figure 9). The interpolant (see Figure 10) smooths out the singularity.

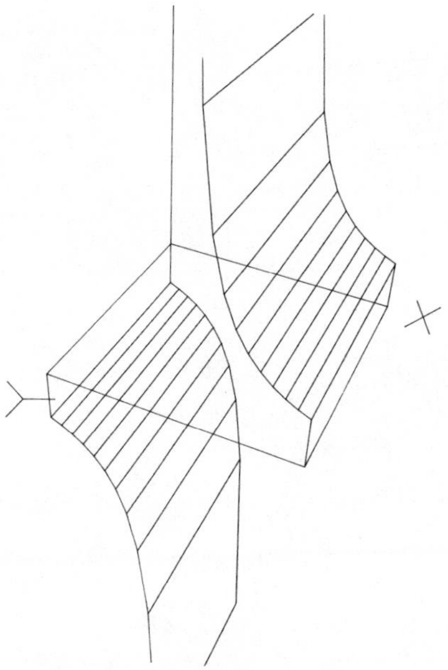

Figure 9

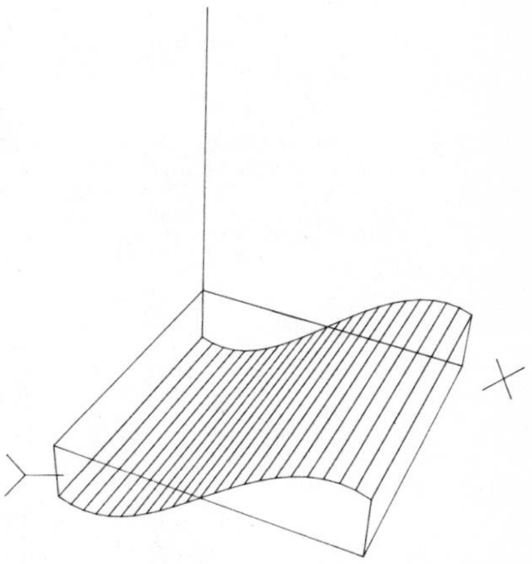

Figure 10

Example 4.4. $F(x,y) = \sin(2x)/(y+1)$. This example illustrates the join of four separate patches (see Figure 11). The function is shown in Figure 12 and the four patch interpolant is shown in Figure 13, this being a good approximation to the function.

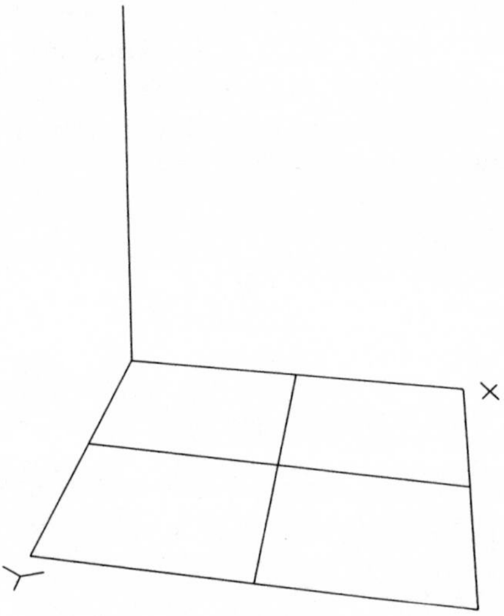

Figure 11

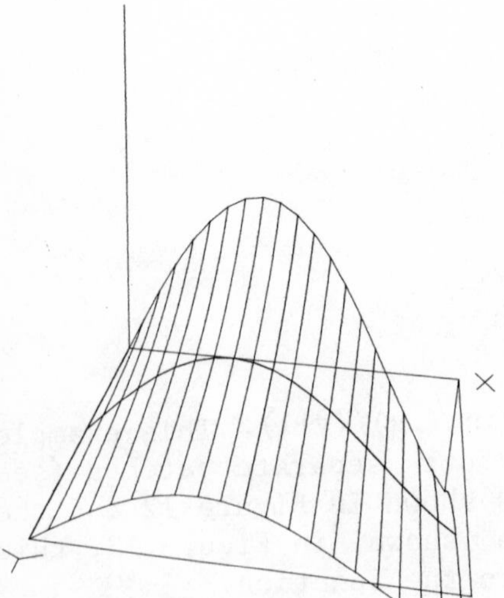

Figure 12

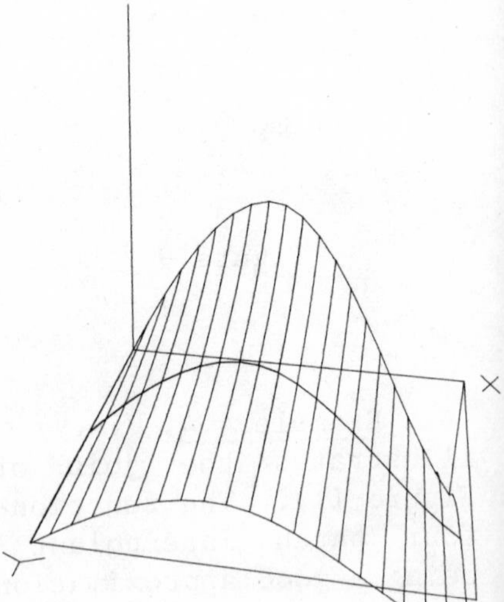

Figure 13

Acknowledgement. This paper represents a continuation and extension of joint work with R.E. Barnhill. The author also wishes to thank R.J. McDermott for the computer-generated pictures.

References

1. Barnhill, R.E., Birkhoff, G., and Gordon, W.J., Smooth Interpolation in Triangles, J. Approx. Theory 8, 1973, pp. 114-128.

2. Barnhill, R.E., and Gregory, J.A., Compatible Smooth Interpolation in Triangles, J. Approx. Theory (To appear).

3. Coons, S.A., Surfaces for Computer Aided Design, Design Division, Mech. Engin. Dept., MIT, 1964. revised, 1967.

4. Gordon, W.J., "Blending-function" Methods of Bivariate and Multivariate Interpolation and Approximation, SIAM J. Numer. Anal. 8, 1971, pp. 158-177.

5. Gregory, J.A., Symmetric Smooth Interpolation on Triangles, TR/34, Brunel Univ., Uxbridge, England, 1973.

6. Mansfield, Lois, Higher Order Compatible Triangular Finite Elements, Numer. Math. 22, pp. 89-97, 1974.

GRAPHICAL REPRESENTATION OF SURFACES OVER TRIANGLES AND RECTANGLES

R.J. McDermott
University of Utah

1. Introduction

Development of mathematical techniques for computer aided geometric design requires interdisciplinary efforts from mathematics, computer graphics, and design. Because of its evolutionary development, implementing *research* mathematics is an interactive process. A computer graphics system for the display of a function to be compared with interpolants provides common ground for interaction between mathematics and computer graphics.

This paper describes a function and interpolant display system for studying similarities between a function of two variables and finite dimensional interpolants. The interpolants are defined locally and they are smooth. The parameters of the interpolants are chosen for their geometric significance. One of these finite dimensional interpolants defines a smooth surface, interpolating the parameters provided. Thus if the parameters are function values and first derivatives at the corners of patches, the interpolant surface matches those function values and derivatives.

The software of the system consists of a file for a function and its derivatives, a file of interpolants and a display file. The display file drives the system and uses the function and derivatives file to produce values of parameters for interpolants. The display file prepares a "true perspective" view of a surface, clipping the view when necessary.

The papers of R.E. Barnhill and J.A. Gregory appearing in these Proceedings describe three finite dimensional rational interpolants implemented by this display system. Barnhill and Gregory have actively participated in working sessions of the display system. The theoretical development of their research has not been directly affected by use of this system. However, application of this research has been directly affected by the interaction of researcher and display system. This function and interpolant display system makes use of computers as an aid and companion in the process of developing new mathematics. In concluding, this could be viewed as a second more abstract level of endeavor in Computer Aided Geometric Design: computer aided mathematics for subsequent use in computer aided geometric design.

2. Implementation

From a Master's thesis produced by S. Geary [1], there was a beginning of a computer graphics system for viewing a function of two variables and an interpolant over a triangle. The triangle was somewhat nonstandard with vertices (0,0), (0,1) and (1,1) and the interpolant was from early work by R.E. Barnhill and J.A. Gregory [2]. However, the system had a sound basic structure which allowed for expansion and improvement.

At present one can view functions and interpolants over the standard triangle with vertices (0,0), (1,0) and (0,1) or over the unit square. The standard triangle and square may be transformed into mosaics of eight triangles or four rectangles to form an underlying square with vertices (0,0), (2,0), (0,2) and (2,2). The mosaics have been implemented to observe the behavior of the patches at common boundaries and surrounded vertex. In this case the patches surround a vertex above (1,1).

Instead of a single interpolant over a triangle one can now view three interpolants over a standard triangle or mosaic of triangles, or two interpolants over a standard rectangle or mosaic of rectangles. The interpolants for the triangle are comprised of 12 and 9 parameter cubic rational Boolean sum interpolants of R.E. Barnhill and J.A. Gregory [3] and a 12 parameter Lois Mansfield and G. Birkhoff [4] scheme. The rectangular interpolants include a 12 parameter smooth C^1 interpolant of J.A. Gregory [5] and the 16 parameter patch of S.A. Coons [6,7]. The Mansfield-Birkhoff scheme and the Coons patch are used as standards of interpolation.

The interpolants are implemented in a variety of forms. The Mansfield-Birkhoff interpolant is in cardinal form where each parameter is multiplied by a rational term and then there is a summation of these products. The Coons patch is in matrix form. The Barnhill-Gregory interpolants have cubic Hermite edge curves and quadratic or linear normals combined in a Boolean sum. The latter allows for the insertion of edge curves in analytic form.

3. Surface Rendering

Interaction with the system is through an IMLAC terminal with refresh scope, connected to a PDP-10 computer. This interaction includes creating files of functions and derivatives, inserting new interpolants into files and selecting views of surfaces defined by functions and interpolants. In choosing a view of a surface one can select lines parallel to the x axis, lines parallel to the y axis, or both sets of lines for crosshatching. The number of lines can be varied, depending on the visual complexity of a surface. When mosaics are produced, lines in adjacent patches can change direction to make boundaries between patches more noticeable.

Figures in the papers of R.E. Barnhill [Fig. 11-16, 18, 19] and J.A. Gregory [Fig. 5-13] of these Proceedings are Gerber Plotter drawings produced from this function and interpolant display system. These drawings use different combinations of lines to aid the understanding of a surface.

Future plans are for milling foam to view interpolants as physical surfaces. A three-axis milling machined surface would be helpful in the investigation of the applicability of interpolants.

In addition to visual rendering of surfaces, the system can produce disc files of differences between a function and interpolants. A hard copy of the residuals provide one with a tabulated look at the performance of an interpolant.

4. Direction

Improvement of this system will be made through computer supported algebraic processing. The algebraic symbolic manipulator REDUCE [8] developed at The Univ. of Utah will provide the processing power. The processing will produce various forms of the same interpolant. Shaded pictures of interpolant surfaces can be produced through the research of E. Catmull and The University of Utah research graphics equipment, if a matrix form of the interpolant can be found.

From techniques used in REDUCE a routine will be written to define functions from string input and produce derivatives of functions for parameters to interpolants. This would allow the system to make full use of analytic curves as edge curves of patches. This full use of available information would ensure a smooth transitional surface between analytic and interpolant surface.

The potential for using interpolant surfaces for design of architectural structures seems promising. Topological design schemes developed by R.D. Resch [9] at The University of Utah will use smooth interpolant surfaces to define a particular geometric configuration of a structure. The Resch schemes provide attractive possibilities with favorable prospects of structural soundness.

5. Acknowledgments

Work on this system was supported by The Univ. of Utah Res. Comm. and ARPA Contract DAHC 15-73-C-0363, at The Univ. of Utah.

References

1. Geary, S., "A Computer Graphics System to Aid The Study of Interpolants to Curved Surfaces," Masters Thesis, Comp. Sci. Div., Univ. of Utah, Aug. 1973.
2. Barnhill, R.E. and Gregory, J.A., "Blending Function Interpolation to Boundary Data on Triangles", TR/14, Dept. of Math., Brunel Univ., 1972.
3. Barnhill, R.E., "Smooth Interpolation Over Triangles", These Proceedings.
4. Mansfield, Lois, Private Communication, Fall, 1973.
5. Gregory, J.A., "Smooth Interpolation Without Twist Constraints", These Proceedings.
6. Coons, S.A., Surfaces for Computer-Aided Design of Space Forms, Project MAC MIT, MAC-TR-41, 1967.
7. Forrest, A.R., "On Coons and Other Methods for the Representation of Curved Surfaces", Computer Graphics and Image Processing 1, 1972, 341 - 359.
8. Hearn, A.C., "REDUCE 2: A System and Language for Algebraic Manipulation", Proc. 2nd Symp. on Symbolic Manipulation, Los Angeles, March 1971.
9. Resch, R., "The Topological Design of Sculptural and Architectural Systems", AFIPS - CONFERENCE PROCEEDINGS, Vol. 42, NCC, 1973, 643 - 650.

B-SPLINE CURVES AND SURFACES

William J. Gordon
General Motors Research Laboratories

and

Richard F. Riesenfeld
University of Utah

1. Introduction

In an earlier paper, the authors address the problem of interactively designing free-form curves and surfaces, i.e., it is concerned with "computational geometry" as defined by Forrest. To paraphrase Forrest [9, p.3] the essential properties of a practical computer-aided geometric design or drafting system are:

> A sufficiently general mathematical method for describing or, more appropriately, defining arbitrarily shaped curves and surfaces.

The second and perhaps even more important aspect is the interface between the underlying mathematical techniques and the designer or draftsman who may have little mathematical training. In order to be successful, a system must have appeal to the designer - it must be simple, intuitive and easy to use. Ideally, an interactive design system makes no mathematical demands on the user other than those to which he has been formerly accustomed through drafting and design experience.

One example of a highly successful computerized design system is Systéme UNISURF [3] developed by P. Bézier at Régie Renault. The essence of the success of Bézier's system is that it combines modern approximation theory and geometry in a way that provides the designer with computerized analogs of his conventional design and drafting tools. For more detailed discussions of this method of CAD see Bézier [2, 3], Forrest [8], and Gordon and Riesenfeld [11].

This paper extends Bézier's basic methods for curve and surface description by generalizing from parametric polynomials to parametric spline functions [13].

2. Spline Functions

The modern mathematical theory of spline approximation was introduced by I. J. Schoenberg in 1946 [17]. In that paper he developed splines for use in a new approach to statistical data smoothing. The first applications of splines in computer-aided design were for interpolation and approximation of existing drawings, that is, copying as opposed to design. In contrast, the present paper is concerned with the applications of spline theory in the context of *ab initio* design and drafting. However, the same interactive techniques can be adapted to the fitting and smoothing of given data.

A polynomial spline can be viewed as a generalized polynomial that has certain chosen points of derivative discontinuity.

Definition 1: Let $X = (x_0, x_1, .., x_k)$ be a vector of reals such that $x_i \leq x_{i+1}$. A function S is called a (polynomial) spline function of degree M-1 (order M) if it satisfies the following two conditions:

1. S is a polynomial of degree M-1 on each subinterval (x_i, x_{i+1}).

2. S and its derivatives of orders 1,2,...,M-2 are everywhere continuous, that is, $S \in C^{[M-2]}$.

The points x_i are called the <u>knots</u> and X is the <u>knot vector</u>. We denote the M+k-1 dimensional space of all such spline functions as S(M,X). The restriction of S to the interval (x_i, x_{i+i}) is called the <u>i-th span</u> of the spline.

3. B-spline Basis For S(M,X)

Of the several bases for S(M,X) in common use, we shall be interested in the so-called "B-spline basis" because it is the corresponding spline extension of the Bernstein basis [8, 11, 13], the mathematical underpinning of Bézier curves. Figure 1 presents a progression, ordered by degree, of B-spline basis functions having knots at the integers. Note from this figure that for degree M-1, the basis functions have finite local support of width M and are M-2 times continuously differentiable. Figure 2 displays the complete set of periodic B-spline basis functions of degree 2 for the linear space of quadratic spline functions with period 5 and with knots at the integers. It is evident from the picture that the basis functions all are cyclic translates (mod 5) of a single canonical basis function $N_{0,3}$ having the interval (0,3) for support. The set of nonperiodic quadratic B-spline basis functions in Figure 3 more closely resembles the Bernstein polynomial basis functions which are shown in Figure 4 for the linear space P_5 of polynomials of degree 5. Note, however, that at the ends of the interval [0,4], the nonperiodic B-spline basis functions are not simple translates of a canonical function.

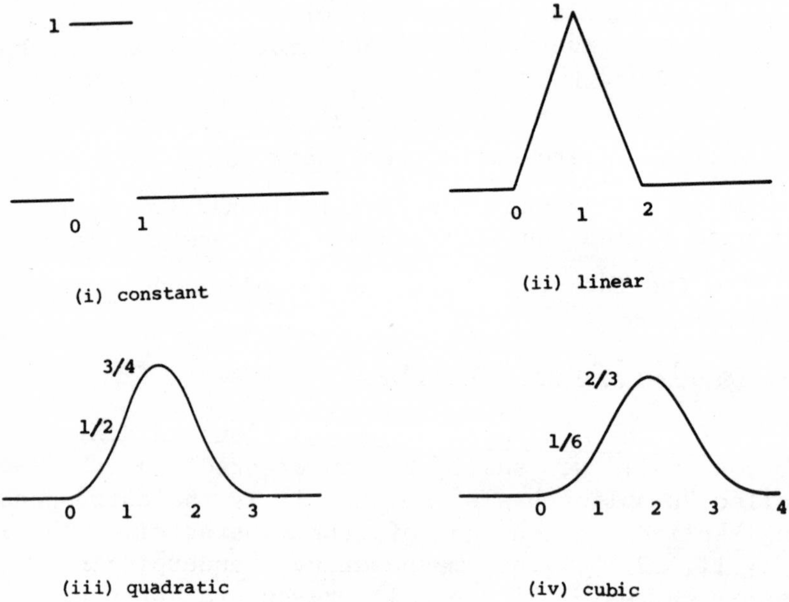

Figure 1

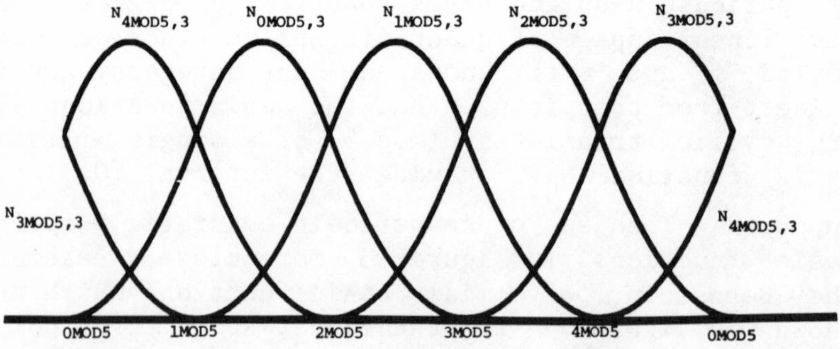

Figure 2

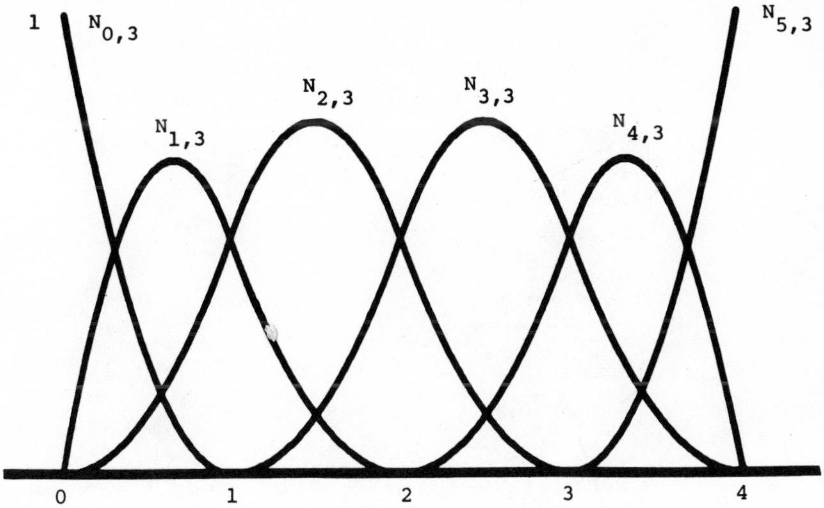

Figure 3

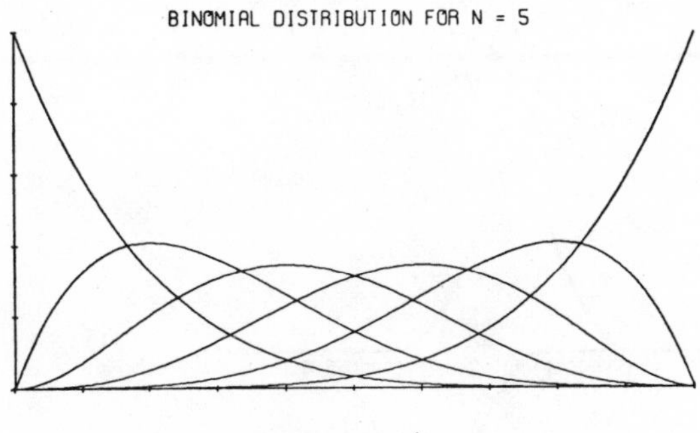

Figure 4

Although B-spline bases can be expressed in various ways (cf. Figure 5 where they are described as a sequence of integrals [13, p.30] or [5], [15]), for our purposes it is most convenient to adopt the recursive definition of deBoor and Mansfield [4] and Cox [6].

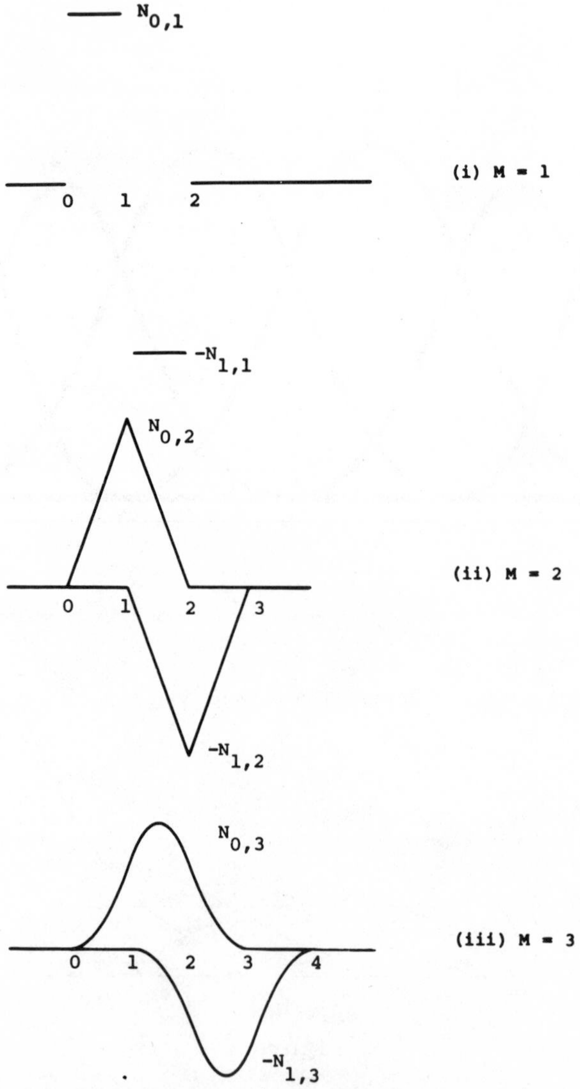

Figure 5

<u>Def. 2</u>: On $[0,n)$ the <u>B-spline basis function</u> $N_{i,M}(s)$ of degree $M-1$ having support $(x_i, x_{(i+M \bmod n)})$ is given by the following recursive procedure.

$$(3.1) \qquad N_{i,1}(s) = \begin{cases} 1 & \text{for } x_i \leq s \leq x_{i+1} \\ 0 & \text{otherwise} \end{cases}$$

$$(3.2) \qquad N_{i,M}(s) = \frac{s - x_i}{x_{i+M-1} - x_i} \cdot N_{i,M-1}(s) +$$

$$\frac{x_{i+M} - s}{x_{i+M} - x_{i+1}} \cdot N_{i+1,M-1}(s)^*, \text{ for } M > 1.$$

A knot vector X may contain identical knots up to multiplicity M. One effect on the basis of a knot x_i occurring with multiplicity k_i, that is,

$$(3.3) \qquad x_i = x_{i+1} = \ldots = x_{i+k_i-1}$$

is to decrease the degree of differentiability of basis functions $\{N_{i,M}\}$ at x_i to $C^{[M-k_i-1]}$. A basis arising from interior knots having multiplicity greater than one is sometimes called a subspline basis. Multiplicity $k_i=1$ for all i generates a full spline (or simply, spline) basis. If $k_i = 0$ for all i, the basis is a spline basis of degree M-1 and $C^{[M-1]}$ differentiability everywhere, including the knots. But, this implies that the knots are pseudo-knots so that the spline is actually just a polynomial, and the basis functions of (3.2) are the Bernstein basis functions.

The support of the B-spline basis function $N_{i,M}$ is always the interval (x_i, x_{i+M}). This implies that the width of the support of $N_{i,M}$ is equal to M spans where, as in Definition 1, the jth span is the

---

*The convention 0/0 = 0 is assumed here.

interval between x_k and x_{k+1}. Thus, multiple knots induce spans of zero length and a corresponding reduction in the width of the support of the basis functions. (See Figure 6.)

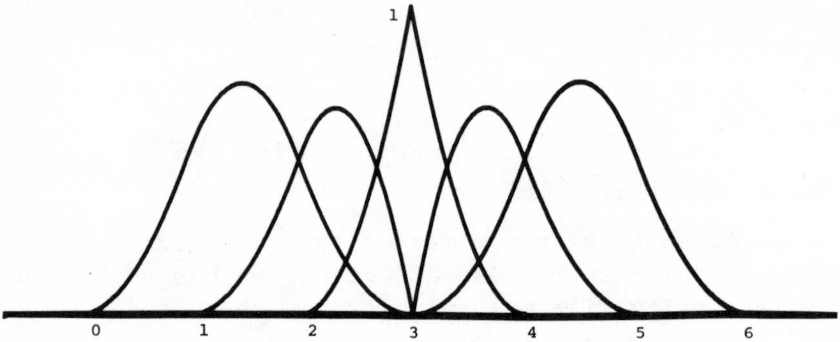

Figure 6

From Definition 2 we can generate both periodic and nonperiodic bases by appropriately specifying the knots in the vector X. For a periodic basis $\{N_{i,M}\}_{i=0}^{n-1}$ of the type illustrated in Figure 2, the knot vector is simply the string of integers

(3.4) $$X = (0,1,\ldots,n)$$

or a cyclic shift of the above. For the periodic case, indices are considered modulo n.

The nonperiodic basis $\{N_{i,M}\}_{i=0}^{M+n-2}$ with equally spaced interior knots over the interval (0,n), as in Figure 3 where n = 5, for example, has the following knot vector:

(3.6) $$X = (\underbrace{0,0,\ldots,0}_{M},1,2,\ldots,n-1,\underbrace{n,n,\ldots,n}_{M})$$

A degenerate knot vector consisting only of the end points s=0 and s=1, both with multiplicities M,

(3.7) $$X = (\underbrace{0,0,\ldots,0}_{M},\underbrace{1,1\ldots,1}_{M}),$$

results in a degenerate spline basis, namely, the Bernstein basis of Figure 4:

(3.8) $$N_{i,M}(s) = \binom{M-1}{i} s^i (1-s)^{M-1-i} \quad (i=0,1,\ldots,M-1).$$

Thus <u>B-splines are a proper spline extension of Bernstein polynomials</u>. Schoenberg provides an alternative proof of this fact [15, p.275] based on characterizing a polynomial by its zeros.

Another basic property that we can readily prove from Definition 2 by induction on the degree is

(3.9) $$\sum_i N_{i,M}(s) \equiv 1$$

In [4] deBoor gives a different proof of (3.9).

Definition 3: The <u>B-spline approximation</u> of degree M-1 (order M) to an arbitrary <u>primitive function</u> $f: [0,n]\rightarrow R$ is

(3.10) $$S_M[f;s] = \sum_i f(\xi_i)N_{i,M}(s)$$

where

(3.11) $$\xi_i = \frac{1}{M-1}(x_{i+1} + x_{i+2} + \ldots + x_{i+M-1})$$

The ξ_i's are called the <u>nodes</u> which are to be carefully distinguished from the <u>knots</u>. Formula (3.11) for the nodes first appeared in a supplement to Schoenberg's 1967 paper [15] supplied by T. N. E. Greville. Note that the nodes degenerate properly to $\xi_i = i/(M-1)$ giving Bernstein approximation for the knot vector (3.7) that generates the Bernstein basis.

In [15], Schoenberg stresses the fact that B-spline approximation enjoys the same variation diminishing property as Bernstein approximation. This property means that the approximation scheme:

1. Approximates linear functions exactly.

2. The number of intersections of the graph of the approximation with any straight line $y = a + bs$ does not exceed the number of crossings of that straight line by the primitive function.

In brief, the variation diminishing property means that the approximation is always "smoother", in the sense of undulations, than the primitive function f. While the B-spline generalization of Bernstein approximation is variation diminishing, there are other closely related schemes which do not enjoy this auspicious property.

As a consequence of the local support of a B-spline basis function, B-spline approximation is a local approximation scheme. The summation in (3.10) involves, at most, M successive nonzero terms. Therefore, a local perturbation in the primitive function produces only a local perturbation in the B-spline approximation. This stands in contrast to Bernstein aproximation which is a global approximation scheme.

The computational aspects of computing with B-splines have been considered by deBoor [4] and Cox [6], who independently developed an algorithm which overcomes the problems of numerical instability inherent in previous algorithms based upon straightforward calculations of alternate definitions of B-splines. This is the algorithm which we have adopted for the computations in this paper. For the sake of completeness, we state here the procedure for evaluating B-spline functions of the form

(3.12) $$f(s) = \sum_i a_i N_{i,M}(s)$$

and their derivatives.

<u>deBoor - Cox Recursive Algorithm</u>

<u>Step 1</u>: Find i such that $x_i \leq s < x_{i+1}$ (3.13)

<u>Step 2</u>: $F(s) = a_i^{[M-1]}(s)$ (3.14)

<u>Step 3</u>: Set $j = i$ and $k = M-1$

$$a_j^{[k]}(s) = \begin{cases} a_j & \text{for } k = 0 \\ \lambda a_j^{[k-1]} + (1-\lambda)a_{j-1}^{[k-1]} & \text{for } k > 0 \end{cases} \qquad (3.15)$$

and $$\lambda = \frac{s - x_j}{x_{j-k+M} - x_j} \quad \text{(j is the same as above)} \qquad (3.16)$$

DeBoor also gives the following formula for the jth derivative of f in (3.12):

(3.17) $$f^{(j)}(s) = (M-1)(M-2)\ldots(M-j)\sum_i b_i^{[j]} N_{i,M-j}(s)$$

where

(3.18) $$b_i^{[k]} = \begin{cases} a_i & \text{for } k = 0 \\ \dfrac{b_i^{[k-1]} - b_{i-1}^{[k-1]}}{x_{i+M-k} - x_i} & \text{otherwise} \end{cases}$$

The reader should consult the original papers [4], [6], and [14] for more details.

4. B-spline Curves

This section is concerned with the application of B-spline approximation to the problem of curve design.

Since an arbitrary <u>curve</u> in the plane or in n-dimensional euclidean space cannot generally be regarded as the graph of a single-valued scalar function, classical approximation theory *per se* is inappropriate for these and many other applications. To circumvent these difficulties, one typically uses a parametric description for curves and surfaces. Hence, to apply the results of (linear) approximation theory to the description or representation of arbitrary curves and surfaces, one treats each of the coordinates x, y and z independently.

In [11], the authors established the relationship between the Bézier methods of curve and surface design and the semi-classical theory of Bernstein approximation. In brief, a Bézier curve in R^n is simply the graph of the vector-valued function $\sum_i N_{i,M}(s)\, P_i$ where the basis functions $N_{i,M}$ are the Bernstein polynomials of (3.8) and the points P_i are an ordered collection of points in R^n. (Compare eq. (1) of [11]). Figures 7 & 8 are Bézier curves.

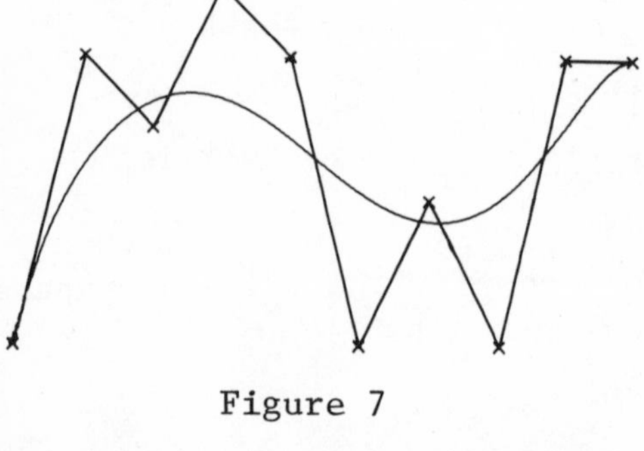

Figure 7

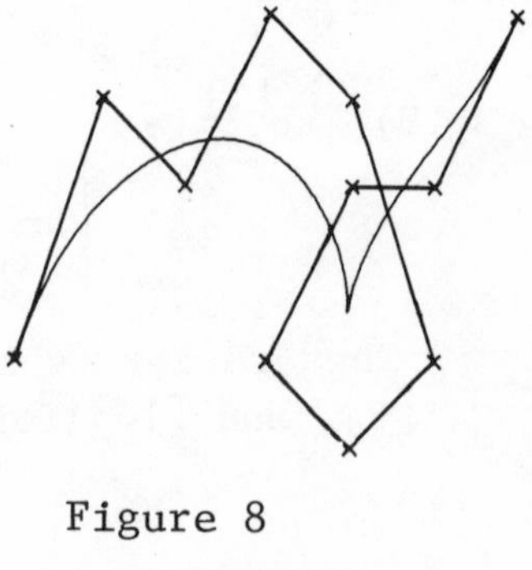

Figure 8

In the Bézier methods, the number of sides of the polygon P is equal to the degree of the Bernstein polynomial weighting functions. In the B-spline extensions, the number of sides m of the Bézier polygon $(P_0 P_1 \ldots P_m)$ is greater than (or equal to) the spline degree M-1. Let $X' = \{x_i' : x_{i-1}' < x_i'\}_{i=1}^{k}$ be the <u>set</u> of knots over which the B-splines are defined. Note that the elements of the set X' must be distinct, unlike the components of **X**, as in Definition 1 and (4.3) below.

<u>Definition 4</u>: <u>The B-spline curve of degree M-1</u> (order M) associated with the polygon P is

$$(4.1) \qquad S_M[P] = \sum_{i=0}^{m} P_i N_{i,M}(s) \qquad 0 \le s \le x_k'$$

A periodic (or closed) <u>B-spline curve</u> results when the B-spline basis functions are defined by the knot vector $X = (x_0, x_1, \ldots, x_{m+1})$ where

$$(4.2) \quad x_i = x'_{(i - M \text{ DIV } 2) \bmod x_k'} \qquad i = 0,1,\ldots,m+1$$

where DIV means integer division.

A <u>nonperiodic</u> (or open) <u>B-spline curve</u> results if $X = (x_0, x_1, \ldots, x_{m+M+1})$ where

$$(4.3) \quad x_i = x_0' \qquad i = 0,1,\ldots,M-2$$

$$x_{i+M-1} = x_i' \qquad i = 0,1,2,\ldots,m-M+2$$

$$x_{i+m+2} = x_{m-M+2}' \qquad i = 0,1,\ldots,M-2$$

Figures 11-14 are examples of the above definitions. Figures 9 & 10 are B-spline curves that correspond to Figures 7 & 8. Figures 11 & 12 are periodic B-spline curves.

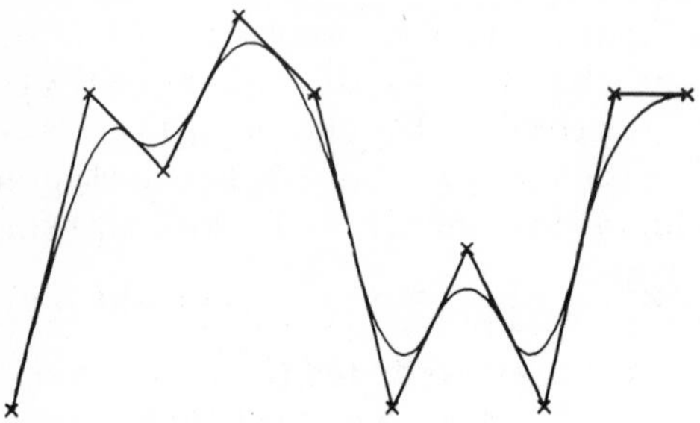

Figure 9

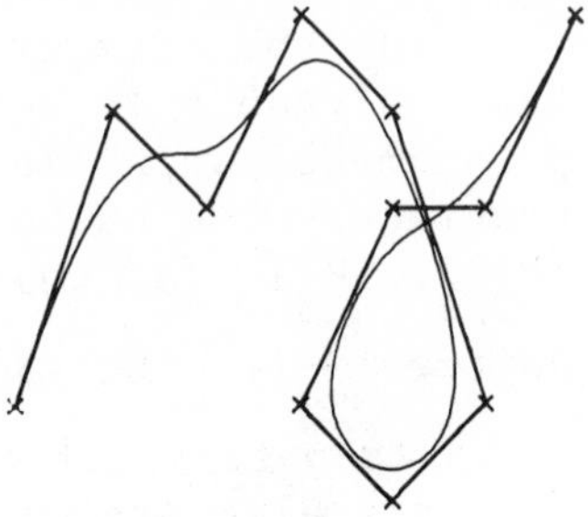

Figure 10

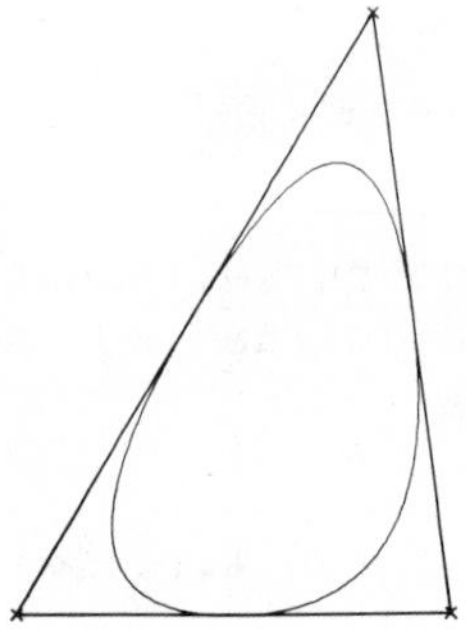

Figure 11

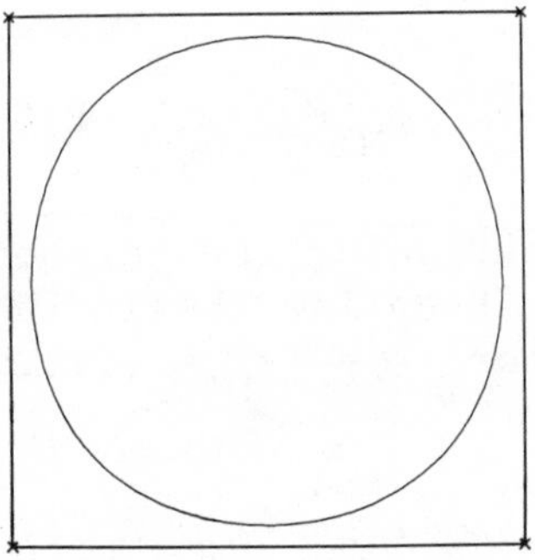

Figure 12

5. Geometric Interpretation of deBoor-Cox Algorithm

Interpreting the deBoor Algorithm geometrically leads to a constructive method for determining a point of a B-spline curve. Formula (5.1) is a vector-valued statement of (3.15) in terms of polygonal vertices P_i.

$$(5.1)\quad P_j^{[k]}(s) = \begin{cases} P_j & \begin{pmatrix}\text{for} \\ k = 0\end{pmatrix} \\ \lambda P_j^{[k-1]}(s) + (1-\lambda)P_{j-1}^{[k-1]}(s) & \begin{pmatrix}\text{for} \\ k > 0\end{pmatrix} \end{cases}$$

where

$$(5.2)\quad \lambda = \frac{s - x_j}{x_{j-k+M} - x_j} = \frac{s - x_j}{M - k} \quad \text{for the uniform periodic case.}$$

To avoid obscuring a simple procedure with unimportant generality, we furnish a specific case that illustrates matters clearly.

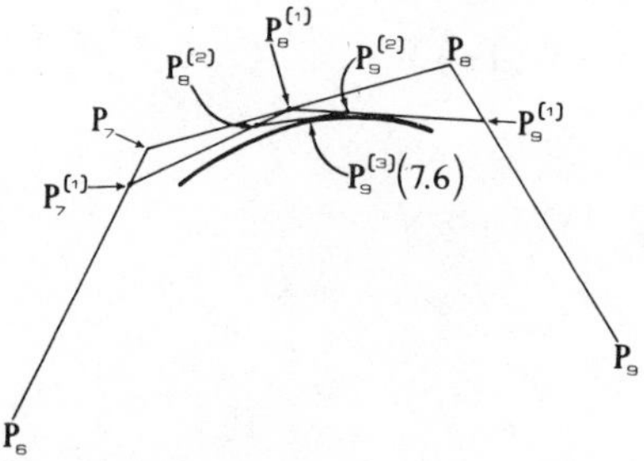

Figure 13

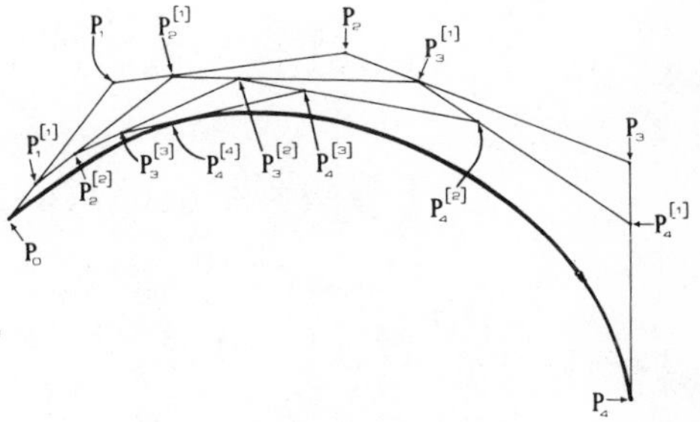

Figure 14

Example 5.1: Given the closed polygon $P_0P_1 \ldots P_{12}$, we constructively find the point on the cubic (M = 4) B-spline curve that corresponds to s = 7.6. In Figure 13 we see the relevant vertices and the geometric interpretation of the following calculation. According to (4.2) the knot vector is $X = (x_0, x_1, \ldots, x_{13})$ where

(5.3) $\quad x_i = (i - 2) \bmod 13$

Step 1 of the deBoor Algorithm requiring $x_i \leq s < x_{i+1}$ is satisfied by $x_i = 7$, or $i = 9$ according to (5.3). In the notation of (5.1) we seek the value of $P_j^{[M-1]}(s) = P_9^{[3]}(7.6)$. Recursively applying the algorithm yields:

(5.4) $\quad P_9^{[3]}(7.6) = \lambda\, P_9^{[2]}(7.6) + (1 - \lambda)\, P_8^{[2]}(7.6)$

where $\lambda = (7.6 - 7.0)/1 = 0.6$

(5.5) $P_9^{[2]}(7.6) = \lambda\ P_9^{[1]}(7.6) + (1-\lambda)\ P_8^{[1]}(7.6)$

$$\lambda = (7.6 - 7.0)/(4-2) = 0.3$$

(5.6) $P_8^{[2]}(7.6) = \lambda\ P_8^{[1]}(7.6) + (1-\lambda)\ P_7^{[1]}(7.6)$

$$\lambda = (7.6-6.0)/(4-2) = 0.8$$

(5.7) $P_9^{[1]}(7.6) = \lambda\ P_9 + (1-\lambda)\ P_8$

where $\lambda = (7.6 - 7.0)/(4-1) = 0.2$

(5.8) $P_8^{[1]}(7.6) = \lambda\ P_8 + (1-\lambda)\ P_7$

where $\lambda = (7.6 - 6.0)/(4-1) \simeq 0.53$

(5.9) $P_7^{[1]}(7.6) = \lambda\ P_7 + (1-\lambda)\ P_6$

where $\lambda = (7.6 - 5.0)/(4-1) \simeq 0.87$

Note that for the Bézier knot vector (3.7) the construction reduces to the constant proportioning scheme $\lambda = s$ in all cases and every original vertex is involved in the evaluation.

6. Geometric Properties of B-Spline Curves

The localness of B-spline approximation and the variation diminishing property are the predominant factors in analyzing the geometric behavior of B-spline curves.

Perturbing a single vertex of the polygon produces only a local perturbation of the curve in the vicinity of that vertex. It is a very desirable property for a designer to have the facility to make local alterations in the shape of a curve with the assurance that other areas of the curve will remain unaltered (Figures 15 and 16).

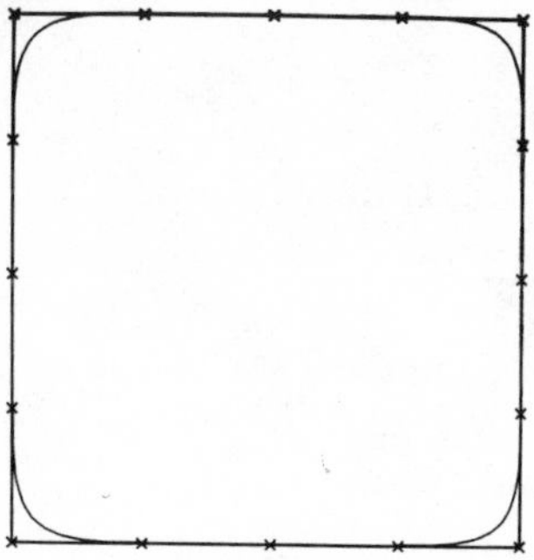

Figure 15

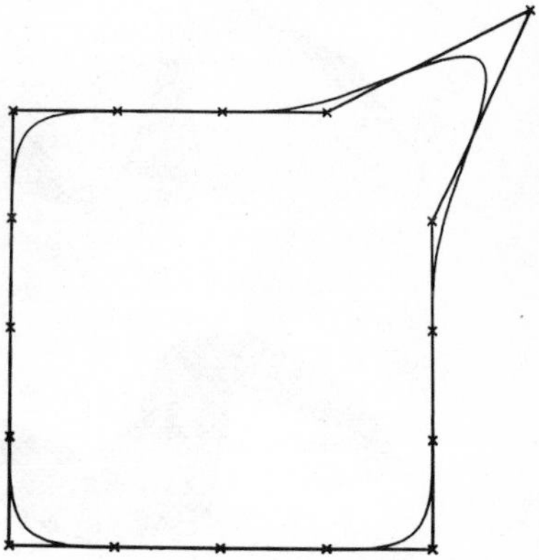

Figure 16

Since the B-spline weighting functions $N_{i,M}(s)$ in (4.1) are nonnegative and sum to 1, each point on a B-spline curve is a convex combination of polygonal vertices. Just as with Bézier curves, the weighting functions can be regarded as barycentric coordinates with respect to the base points P_i. But there are only (at most) M vertices that determine a point on the curve. This implies a much stronger convex hull property than is true for Bézier curves. Specifically, for a B-spline curve of degree M-1, a given point lies within the convex hull of the neighboring M vertices. In other words, all points on a B-spline curve must lie within the union of all such convex hulls formed by taking M successive polygonal vertices. The shaded portions in Figures 17 (i) - (v) show how this region grows from M = 2,3,4 and $M \geq 5$ (same as Bézier), respectively.

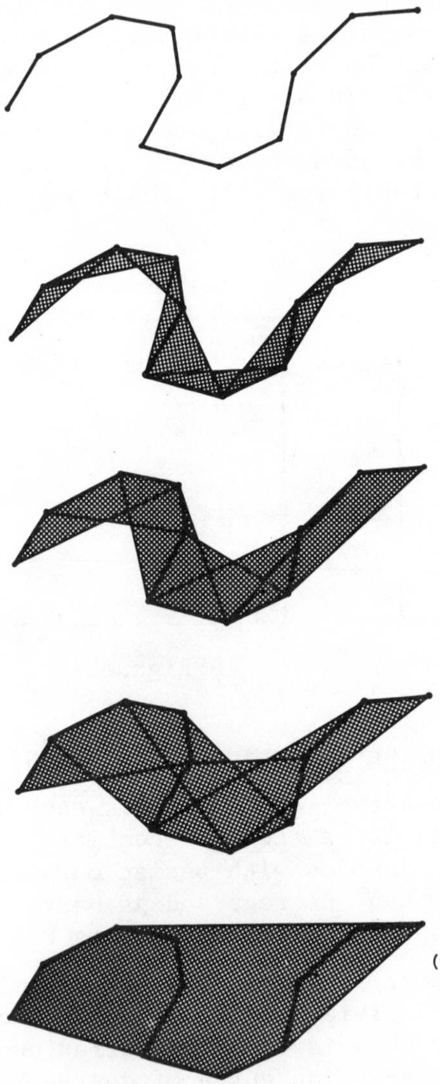

(i) $M = 2$ (linear)

(ii) $M = 3$ (quadratic)

(iii) $M = 4$ (cubic)

(iv) $M = 5$ (quartic)

(v) $5 \leq M \leq 10$ (quintic and higher)

Figure 17

An interesting special case occurs if $P_i = P_{i+1} = \dots = P_{i+M-1}$: The convex hull of that set is the point P_i itself, and so we have that the curve must pass through P_i. In fact, the entire span of the spline curve determined by these vertices is identically equal to P_i.

Another interesting special case is when the M successive vertices are all collinear. Since B-spline approximation is a local scheme, this collinear set of M points fully determines one span of the B-spline curve. We know that the variation diminishing B-spline approximation assures that it reproduces straight lines. The conjunction of these two properties is that the span determined by M collinear vertices is also linear. That is to say, B-spline curves can have locally linear segments smoothly ($C^{[M-2]}$) embedded in them. A simple example of this behavior is shown in Figures 15 and 16. Its usefulness in design is apparent when one considers the frequency of occurrence of linear segments in the engineering drawings of ordinary mechanical parts. Immediate examples where avoidance of a step change in curvature ($M \geq 4$) is desirable for dynamic reasons include cams, highways, railways, and aircraft fuselage surfaces.

7. Hodographs

Given the facility for computing B-spline curves, it is straightforward to compute the hodograph of a B-spline curve γ of degree $M - 1$

$$(7.1)\quad P_i^* = (P_i - P_{i-1})/(x_{i+M-1} - x_i)\ ,\quad i = 1,2,\ldots,m$$

Let γ^* be the B-spline curve of degree $M - 2$ determine by the derived polygon (open or closed, respectively) $P_1^*P_2^* \ldots P_m^*$. The hodograph of γ is γ^*, which differs from the tangent curve by a scale factor $M - 1$. In the uniform periodic case the scale factor cancels the denominator in (7.1), therefore simply differencing the vertices P_i gives the tangent curve exactly. By iterating this process, one can obtain hodographs of order n. The hodographs of B-spline curves are useful in the same way that the hodographs of Bézier curves are (Figure 18 and [2, pp. 128-133]. Figure 19 shows how a typical span of a uniformly spaced knot, closed cubic B-spline curve gives rise to a quadratic hodograph curve.

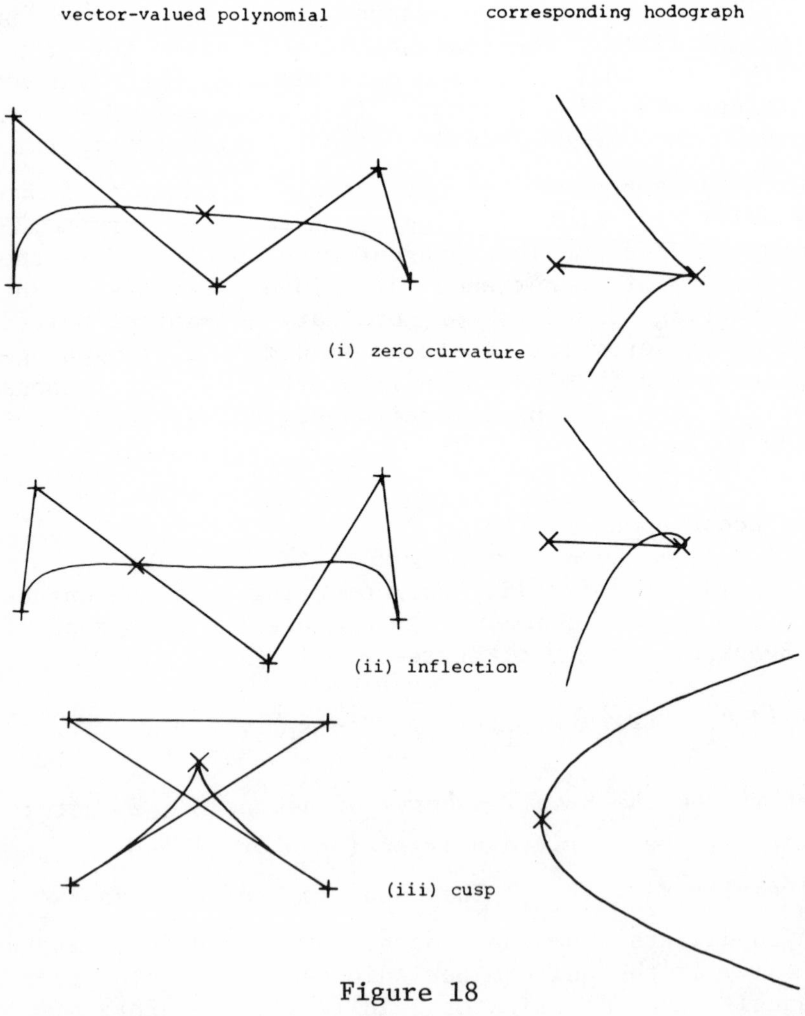

Figure 18

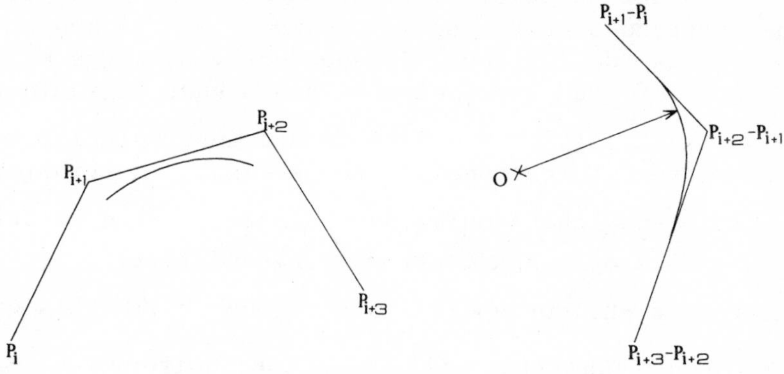

Figure 19

8. Nonuniform B-spline Curves

A further generalization of B-spline curves is available by using a nonuniform B-spline basis, one in which the knots are not restricted to integer values. The mathematical development of these curves is completely analogous to what has been done so far in this paper (cf. Supplement by Greville in [15]).

The authors experimented with a knot vector that reflected the euclidean distances of the vertices along the polygon. The relative spacing of the knots was proportional to the respective lengths of the sides. The behavior of the uniform B-spline curves does not appear to differ dramatically from the nonuniform curves unless the relative lengths of the legs of the polygon vary greatly. But, if two polygon vertices are allowed to coalesce, the effect on the nonuniform basis is to produce a multiple knot and a subsequent lowering by one of the differentiability class at the multiple knot. This loss of differentiability in the basis is inherited by the curve and this fact can be exploited to great advantage in CAD applications.

Another possible variant is a scheme that allows the user to specify the multiplicity of the knots (in the basis definition) independently of the multiplicity of the vertices. Then a knot x_j would require multiplicity M - 1 to induce interpolation at the vertex corresponding to $s = x_j$. Multiplicity M - 1 means that only one nonzero basis function $N_{j,M}$ exists at $s = x_j$. From (3.9) and (4.1) it is clear that the curve will pass through P_j in this case.

In Section 11 we will see how nonuniform bases are useful for reparametrizing a curve.

9. Cusps

Since a curve cannot interpolate smoothly to a corner vertex and still remain within the convex hull of the entire polygon, requiring interpolation and containment in the convex hull must give rise to a cusp or slope discontinuity in the curve at the corner vertex. (Constructing the hodograph affirms this conclusion.) A cusp must result if we recall that the curve is tangent to the legs on either side of an interpolated vertex.

At first glance, the notion of a cusp appears to contradict the $C^{[M-2]}$ differentiability of the uniform basis. Indeed the tangent vector varies continuously, but this condition does not preclude its vanishing and a zero tangent vector defines a cusp. Other possible generalizations can introduce cusps that lead to actual discontinuous tangent vectors. These considerations may be important for CAD systems that employ heavy machines for which inertial effects must be taken into account.

The above discussion indicates that using B-spline curves affords the designer a convenient and tractable method for introducing and controlling cusps. This behavior is illustrated in Figures 20 and 21.

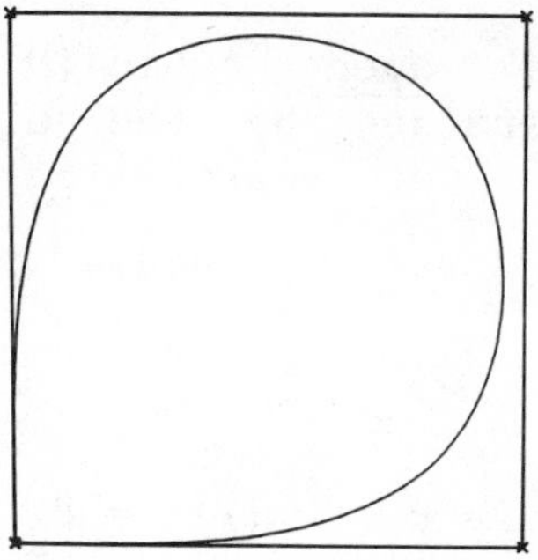

Figure 20

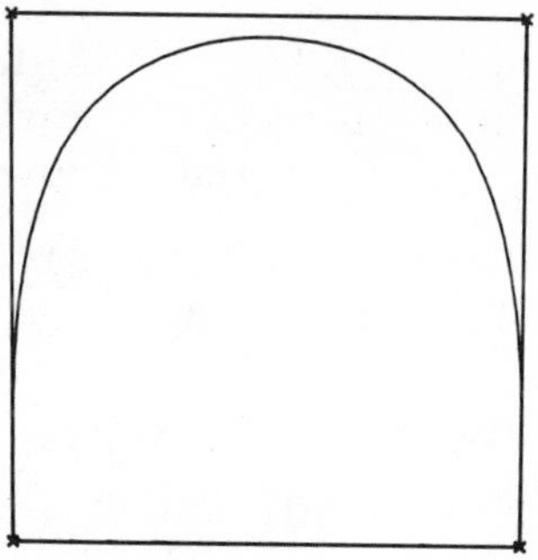

Figure 21

10. Knots, Nodes, and Vertices

If we consider the polygon P as a piecewise linear function F, where F is defined so that the B-spline curve is the parametric B-spline approximation to F, then F is characterized by

$$(10.1) \qquad F(\xi_i) = P_i \qquad i = 0,1,\ldots,m$$

where

ξ_i is given in (3.11).

Formula (10.1) relates the knots x_i, the nodes ξ_i, and the vertices P_i. We see immediately that for odd degree (M even) uniform B-splines, i.e., with knots at the integers, the nodes are also knots where the $x_{i+1}, x_{i+2}, \ldots, x_{i+M-1}$ are successive integers: $\xi_i = x_{i+M/2}$ in this case. This says that the point on an odd degree uniform B-spline curve that corresponds to the vertex P_i is the knot on the curve corresponding to the parameter value $x_{i+M/2}$. Clearly this is not the case near the ends of an open curve where the knots are not successive integers but they occur with multiplicity.

Example 10.1: Consider the open cubic ($M = 4$) uniform B-spline curve determined by the polygon $P_0 P_1 \ldots P_5$. The appropriate knot vector is $X = (0,0,0,0,1,2,3,3,3,3)$. The set of nodes is $\{0, 1/3, 1, 2, 8/3, 3\}$.

Substitution in (10.1) gives

$$
\begin{aligned}
F(0) &= P_0, & F(1/3) &= P_1, & F(1) &= P_2 \\
F(2) &= P_3, & F(8/3) &= P_4, & F(3) &= P_5
\end{aligned}
\tag{10.2}
$$

Even degree uniform B-splines, on the other hand approximate the vertices with the (parametric) mid-points between the knots, except for the special cases near the ends of the curve.

Example 10.2: Consider the closed quadratic ($M = 3$) uniform B-spline curve determined by the polygon $P_0 P_1 P_2 P_3$. The knot vector for this case is $X = (3, 4{=}0, 1, 2)$, where we indicate the modulo equivalence of 0 and 4. The nodes are $\{1/2, 3/2, 5/2, 7/2\}$. From (10.1) we see that

$$
\begin{aligned}
F(1/2) &= P_0, & F(3/2) &= P_1 \\
F(5/2) &= P_2, & F(7/2) &= P_3
\end{aligned}
\tag{10.3}
$$

11. The Inversion Problem

Suppose we pose the problem for B-spline curves of finding the unique (for the minimal number of vertices) polygon $P_0 P_1 \ldots P_m$ that corresponds to any given spline curve S. That is, can it be viewed as a B-spline curve and, if so, what is the polygon that defines it? Since we are given the spline curve S, we know the vector $X = (x_0, x_1, \ldots, x_n)$ and we can easily find the nodes by (3.11). The nodes and the knots are adequate information to calculate the Gram matrix,

(11.1) $N = (n_{ij})$, where $n_{ij} = N_{j,M}(\xi_i)$ $0 \leq i, j \leq m$

Reformulating the problem, we seek a polygon to satisfy

(11.2) $N \cdot (P_0, P_1, \ldots, P_m)^t = (S(\xi_0), S(\xi_1), \ldots S(\xi_m))^t$

The problem is solved by inverting N. The existence follows from the fact that B-splines do, indeed, form a basis for the linear space of splines with fixed knots. Viewed in this way, finding the vertices P_i is the problem of finding proper coefficients to express the given spline S as a linear combination of the B-spline basis functions $N_{i,M}$. This procedure shows how to construct <u>interpolating splines</u> from B-splines.

Another application of the inversion procedure is the problem of reparametrizing a B-spline curve. The situation can arise that the <u>shape</u> of a B-spline curve is completely satisfactory but the <u>parametrization</u> is not. In this case one may wish to specify a new nonuniform basis that has carefully chosen knot values to produce a particular parametrization. The inversion procedure determines a new polygon that defines a new curve which interpolates the nodes of the original one. Presumably the new curve would be close enough to the original curve so that only a slight adjustment of the new nodes would be necessary virtually to duplicate the shape of the original. An alternative scheme is to specify points on the original curve that are to become the nodes of the new curve with respect to the uniform B-spline basis. The applicability and the relative advantages of these techniques is a matter for further exploration.

12. Adding a New Vertex

When designing a B-spline curve S, occasionally one would like to add an extra vertex to the polygon in order to increase the potential flexibility in a certain region of the curve. Furthermore, it is desirable to add the new vertex in such a way that the shape of the curve is not altered until the new vertex is specifically repositioned. A way to accomplish this is to define a new "pseudo-knot" midway (parametrically) between two of the previously existing knots (cf. Definition 2).

From (10.1) we see that the extra knot between two original knots defines an extra node. Applying the inversion procedure of the previous section, we find a new polygon that has one more vertex than the original one. The equivalence of the curves defined by the two polygons is assured by the uniqueness of interpolating splines. As the new vertices are repositioned the pseudo-knot is free to become a *bona fide* knot bearing no more than $C^{[M-2]}$ differentiability. Note that this procedure leads to a nonuniform parametrization of the knots.

13. Designing B-spline Curves

Once a dialogue between a designer and a CAD system has begun, the effect on the curve of moving a vertex becomes immediately apparent. Altering the shape of a curve by perturbing a vertex of its associated polygon is a dynamic process. But designating an initial configuration of vertices to match either a previously sketched curve or a mental image of a curve demands an intimate familiarity with the system. Instead it seems less demanding to allow the designer initially to specify points that lie on the curve. The system responds with an interpolating spline. Then, the above inversion procedure is used to determine the unique polygon corresponding to the interpolated spline. Thereafter, the user concentrates on the polygon and uses it to perturb the initial interpolating approximation into a more satisfactory shape.

14. B-spline Surfaces

The extension of B-spline curves to B-spline surfaces is exactly analogous to the development of Bézier surfaces from Bézier curves (See Fig. 22) The B-spline equivalent of the cartesian product surface [11, eq. 16] determined by the net $P = \{P_{ij}\}$ is

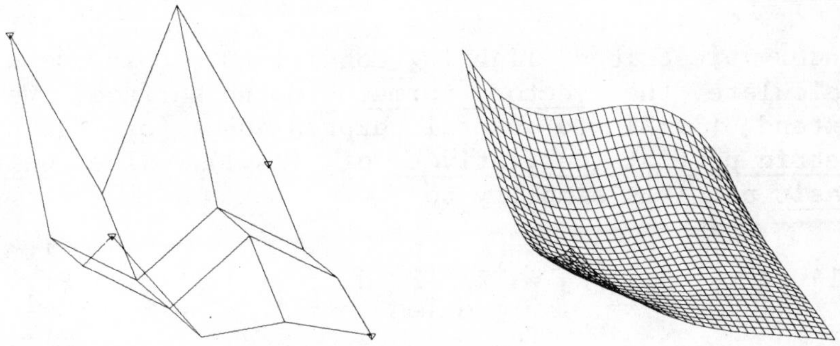

Figure 22

$$(14.1) \qquad S_{L,M}[P] = \sum_{i=0}^{m} \sum_{j=0}^{n} N_{i,L}(s)\, N_{j,M}(t)\, P_{ij}$$

Figure 23 is a half-tone picture of the biquadratic basis function given by (14.1) with L=M=3, produced at the University of Utah (Courtesy of J. Clark).

For certain purposes such as calculating offsets for milling machine cutters or presenting a smooth-shaded (half-tone) picture of a B-spline surface

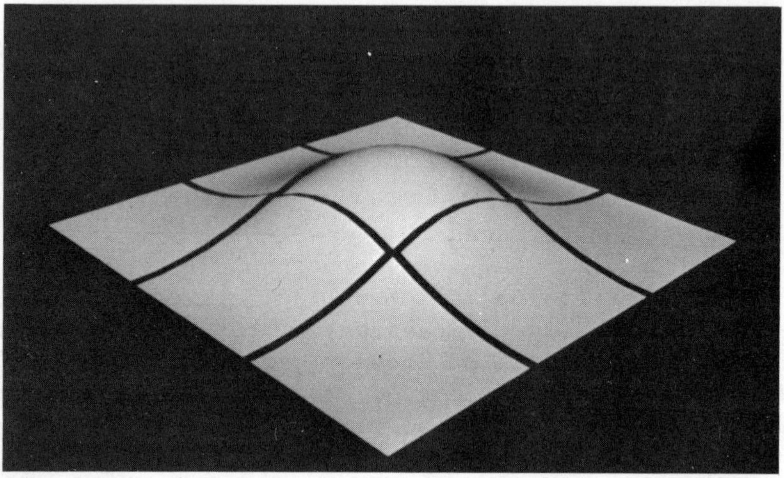

Figure 23

under prescribed lighting conditions, it is useful to calculate the vector normal to the surface. We can extend (3.17) to useful expressions for the parametric partial derivatives of (14.1). The uniform basis partials simplify to

$$(14.2)\quad \frac{\partial}{\partial s} S_{L,M}[P] = \sum_{i=0}^{m} \sum_{j=0}^{n} N_{i,L-1}(s)\, N_{j,M}(t)\, P_{ij}^{i_*}$$

where

$$P_{ij}^{i_*} = P_{ij} - P_{i-1,j}\ ,\quad i=1,2,\ldots,m;\ j=0,1,\ldots,n$$

and analogously with respect to t.

A normal to the surface results from the vector cross product of the parametric derivatives.

Figure 24 is a picture of a B-spline surface cut on the 3D plotter at the Computer Laboratory, University of Cambridge (Courtesy of A. R. Forrest).

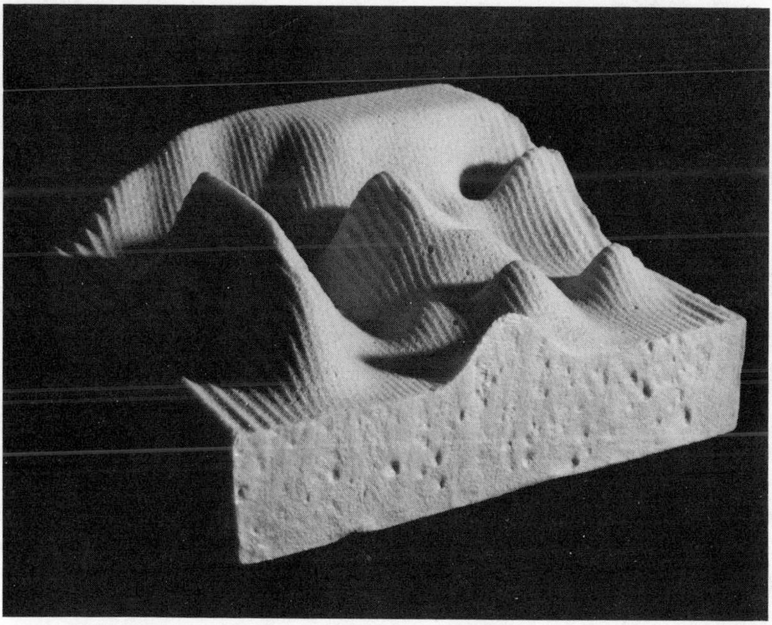

Figure 24

15. Conclusion

The B-spline approach to curve and surface design developed herein provides a generalization of Bézier's techniques that is simple to implement and computationally efficient. As we saw earlier, a simple general algorithm encompasses both the periodic and nonperiodic cases, i.e., both open and closed curves. Furthermore, the shape and complexity of the curve is easily controlled by the addition or deletion of knots.

Spline approximations afford the choice of either adding more knots or raising the degree of the polynomial in order to increase the number of parameters (degrees of freedom). By introducing more knots and keeping the degree low, they can be made to converge more quickly than Bernstein/Bézier approximations. Moreover, the "localness" and smoothness (differentiability) are properties that can be controlled. The demonstrated qualities make B-spline curves and B-spline surfaces especially attractive for computer-aided geometric design.

16. Acknowledgments

During the development of the work described in this paper the authors have especially benefitted from conversations and correspondence with P. Bézier, S. A. Coons, A. R. Forrest, L. Knapp, and M. Sabin.

R. Barnhill and R. McDermott deserve special thanks for their editorial assistant in the preparation of this manuscript. For the photographic services that the illustrations required, we thank M. Milochik. Art work by L. Williams appears in several figures. We appreciate the meticulous typing of L. Merrell.

This paper is condensed from the second author's Ph.D. thesis at Syracuse University.

The second author was supported in part by ARPA, contact DAHC15-73-C-0363.

REFERENCES

(A more extensive list of references appears in [13].)

1. Ahlberg, J. H.; Nilson, E. N.; and Walsh, J. L. The Theory of Splines and Their Applications. New York: Academic Press; (1967).

2. Bézier, P. Numerical Control-Mathematics and Applications. (translated by A. R. Forrest). London: John Wiley and Sons (1972).

3. Bézier, P. "Mathematical and Practical Possibilities of UNISURF." These Proceedings.

4. deBoor, C. "On Calculating with B-splines." J. Approx. Theory, Vol. 6 (1972), pp. 50-62.

5. Coons, S. A., "Surface Patches and B-spline Curves." These Proceedings.

6. Cox, M. G. "The Numerical Evaluation of B-splines." National Physical Laboratory (Teddington, England), DNAC 4 (August 1971).

7. Davis, P. J. Interpolation and Approximation. New York: Ginn-Blasidell (1963).

8. Forrest, A. R. "Interactive Interpolation and Approximation by Bézier Polynomials." Computer J., Vol. 15 (1972) pp. 71-79.

9. Forrest, A. R. "Computer-Aided Design of Three-Dimensional Objects: A. Survey." Proc. ACM/AICA Intern. Computing Sym., Venice (1972).

10. Gordon, W. J. "Distributive Lattices and the Approximation of Multivariate Functions." Proceedings of the Symposium on Approximation with Special Emphasis on Splines, (I. J. Schoenberg, ed.) Univ. of Wisc. Press (1969) pp.223-277.

11. Gordon, W. J. and Riesenfeld, R. F. "Bernstein-Bézier Methods for the Computer-Aided Design of Free Form Curves and Surfaces." J. of ACM, Vol. 21, No. 2 (April 1974) pp. 293-310.

12. Greville, T.N.E. "Introduction to Spline Functions." in Theory and Applications of Spline Functions. (Greville, ed.), Academic Press 1969.

13. Riesenfeld, R. F. "Applications of B-spline Approximation to Geometric Problems of Computer Aided Design." Ph.D. Thesis, Syracuse U. (1973). Available at U. of Utah, UTEC-CSc-73-126.

14. Riesenfeld, R. F., *et al* "Algorithms for B-spline Parametric Cruves." In preparation.

15. Schoenberg, I. J. "On Spline Functions." with Supplement by T.N.E. Greville, Inequalities (O. Shisha, editor), Academic Press (1967) pp. 255-291.

16. Schoenberg, I. J. "On Variation Diminishing Approximation Methods." On Numerical Approximation. (R. E. Langer, Ed.) University of Wisconsin Press 1959, pp. 249-274.

17. Schoenberg, I. J. "Contributions to the Problem of Approximation of Equidistant Data by Analytic Functions." Quart. Appl. Math, Vol 4 (1946), pp. 45-99.

MATHEMATICAL AND PRACTICAL POSSIBILITIES OF UNISURF

P. Bézier
Régie Renault
Paris, France

1. Introduction

1.1. UNISURF was intitiated in 1962. It was meant to help the process of car body design and tooling, and mainly to cut down delay and increase accuracy as well as smoothness. A prototype system equipped with one drawing and one milling machine was set up by the end of 1968. In 1972 the ASSOCIATION RENAULT-PEUGEOT started to use it, and has, by now, defined with it the skin (i.e. outer panels) of four cars to be marketed.

1.2. The mathematical properties of parametric surfaces have been investigated; the program, in its present state, takes advantage of the most useful ones; but it is intended to be expanded further.

1.3. A processor, called SURFAPT, is now partly developed and will be implemented on small computers (24 K. 16). Besides classical curves and surfaces, it includes parametric definitions.

2. Purpose

2.1. It is usual in our industry to let the drawing office translate the shape of a hand-made clay model into accurate drawings from which a master is derived. UNISURF had to help designers to perform this work.

2.2. Translation may sometimes be unfaithful, and it would be much better to use numerical control (NC) from the very start: stylists would then express their intentions by means of numbers. This method is not widely accepted yet, but we are convinced of its possibility. This was the keynote of our research.

3. Requirements

3.1. Although the system is somewhat sophisticated, mathematically, it must, first of all, be understood by nonmathematicians. Car body designers are well trained in descriptive geometry but need not know analysis and calculus.

3.2. When used for direct conception, the system must be interactive, and should be able to draw a surface within minutes and mill within one hour a few square yards of soft material such as styrofoam, plaster or resin. For that reason, and as early as 1962, we felt it compulsory to rely upon such a system generally called nowadays C.N.C.

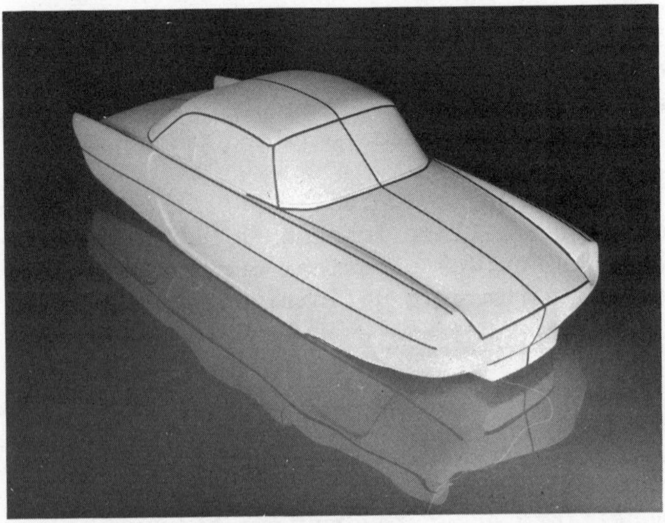

Figure 1

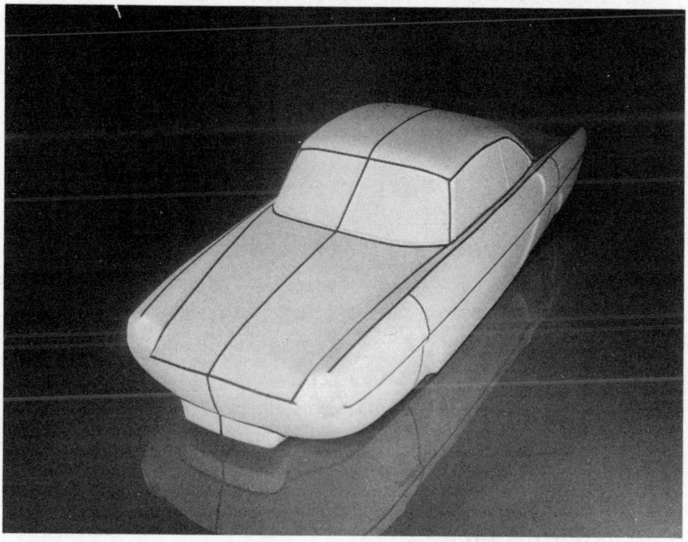

Figure 2

3.3. In order to reduce the amount of data, we felt the number of patches should be kept down to a minimum, and character lines should be used as boundary lines (Fig. 1 & 2). At the same time, the smaller the number of patches, the fewer the problems related with blending and connecting of surfaces would be.

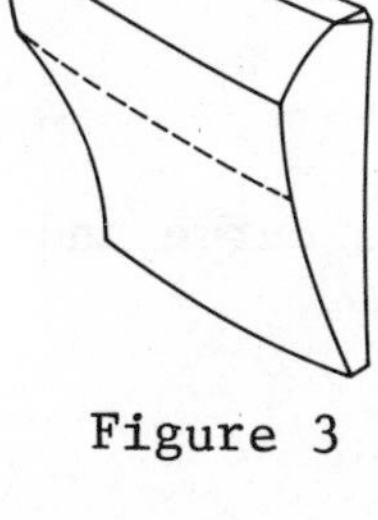

Figure 3

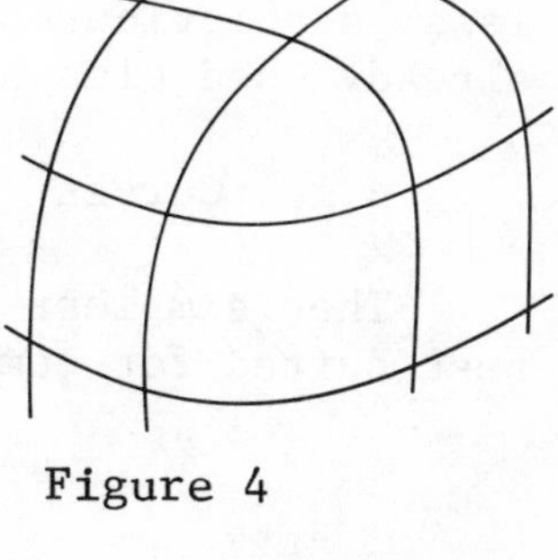

Figure 4

Limiting ourselves to collinearity and proportionality of transverse (normal) derivatives along a common boundary line seemed much too stringent (Fig. 3). The definition of degenerate patches, in this particular case, is difficult (Fig. 4) and we have had to devise a wider definition of tangency.

In practice, a car, or rather half of it, has completely been defined with less than thirty major patches; to these must be added some details such as handle recesses, gougings, windshield housing, etc., that can amount to over fifty patches although they do not cover more than 5% of the total surface.

3.4. To be available to companies the size of ours, the price of the system, as well as the capacity of the computer had to be kept within strict limits. Needless to say, it had to be highly reliable and easy to maintain or repair.

4. Solution

For evident reasons, geometric entities (curves, surfaces, slopes, normals, etc.) are expressed by polynomial parametric functions. But mechanical engineers are seldom familiar with their properties, so we have used functions that are easy to understand.

The elaboration of the program has been scheduled according to the importance of the part played by a given feature. The installment of some theoretical solutions has had to be postponed to benefit other, less sophisticated but easier to program ones, or ones already used elsewhere.

4.1. Curves

The simplest expression for a curve and the one best suited for computing is:

$$\vec{P}(u) = \sum_{i=0}^{m} \vec{b}_i u^i \qquad (u\varepsilon[0,1])$$

which is, for instance, the case for Ferguson's curves when m = 3. But a simple look of the b'_is does not tell much about the actual shape of the curve, except to highly trained specialists.

For the benefit of operators, we prefer

$$\vec{P}(u) = \sum_{0}^{m} \vec{a}_i f_{i_m}(u) \qquad (2)$$

where

$$f_{i_m} = \frac{(-u)^i}{(i-1)!} \cdot \frac{d^{i-1} \frac{(1-u)^m-1}{u}}{du^{i-1}} \qquad (3)$$

(Fig. 5)

The a_i's put end to end form a polygon from which the shape of the corresponding curve is grossly indicated (Fig. 6, 7, 8).

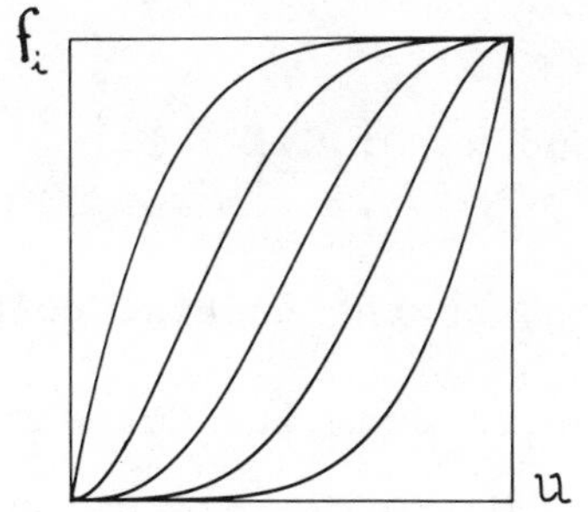

Figure 5

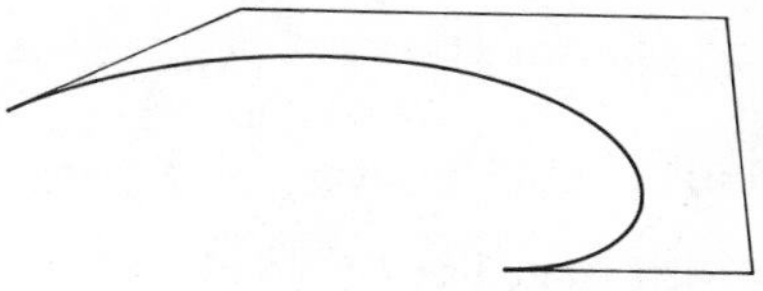

Figure 6

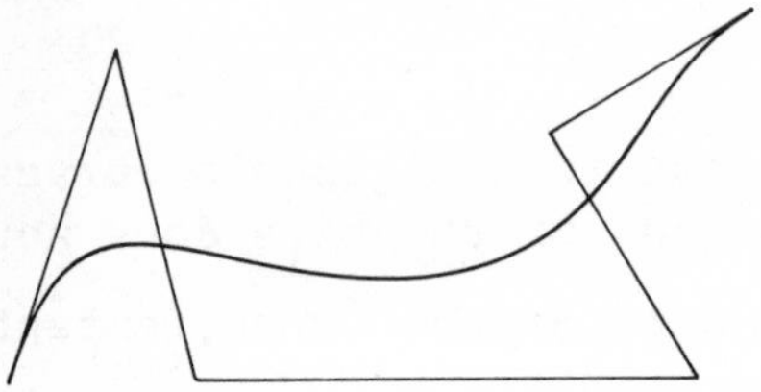

Figure 7

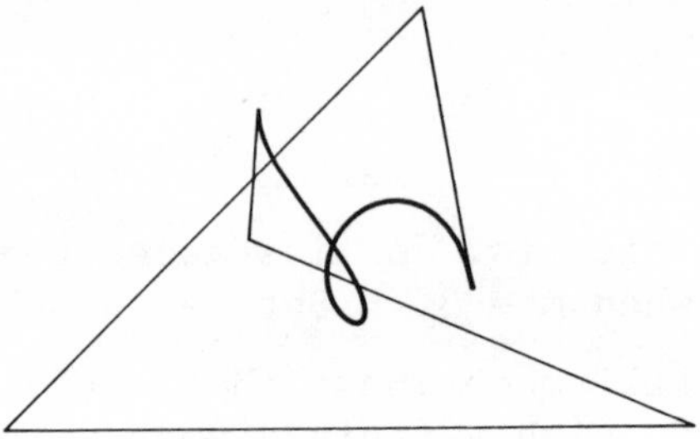

Figure 8

Once a designer has defined the polygon apexes, vectors $\vec{b}_i$ are derived from vectors $\vec{a}_i$ with the help of matrix

$$\{\vec{b}_i\} = ||M_{ab}|| \cdot \{\vec{a}_i\} \qquad (4)$$

where the matrix

$$||M_{ab}|| = ||\alpha_{\ell,c}||$$

and $$\alpha_{\ell,c} = (-1)^{\ell+c} \cdot C_{\ell-2}^{\ell-c} \cdot C_m^{\ell-1}$$

(The convention $C_y^x = \dfrac{y!}{x!(y-x)!}$ for $x \geq y$ is assumed.

Also, $C_y^x = 0$ for $x > y$, $y < 0$ and $x < 0$; $C_{-1}^0 \equiv 1$.)

Functions $f_{\frac{i}{m}}$ are such that, on the initial point ($u=0$), the curve is tangent to a_1, and its curvature is only related with a_1 and a_2. Moreover, since this family of functions $f_{\frac{i}{m}}$ is symmetric about $u = 0.5$, the same curve is obtained when reversing the order of the apexes.

If vectors a_i are translated to the same origin, the polygon connecting the terminal points defines a curve which is the hodograph H of the curve scaled by a factor of y_m (Fig. 9 & 10). From that property derives many interesting facts: for instance, P(u) being an inflexion point on curve C, the tangent to H on point Q(u) runs through O. Other features are used for determining limit lines of a surface.

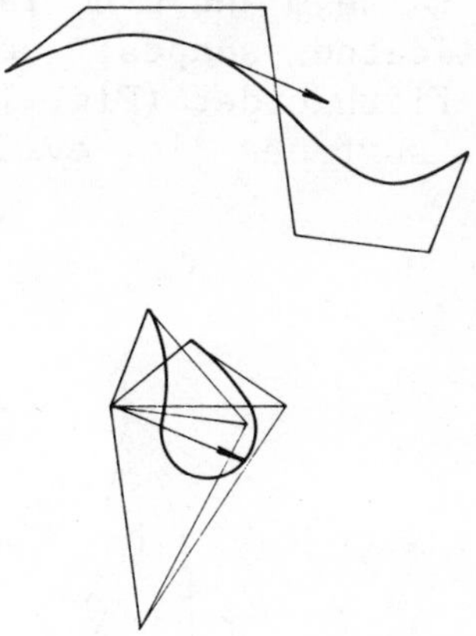

Figure 9

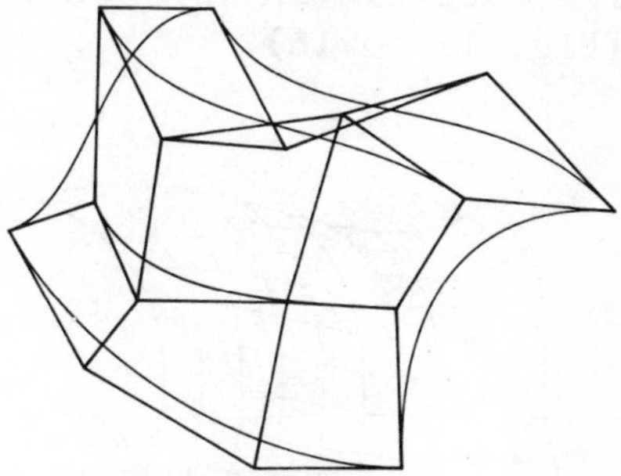

Figure 10

4.2. Surfaces

Analogous to a curve, a surface is expressed by

$$\vec{P}(u,v) = \sum_{i=0}^{m} \sum_{j=0}^{n} \vec{b}_{ij}\, u^i\, v^j, \quad (u,v)\varepsilon[0,1] \quad (5)$$

but the appearance of the b_{ij}'s tells even less than it does for curves.

In order to explain to operators how a surface can be expressed, we suppose that each apex of a curve polygon is moved along its own trajectory, which is itself defined by a polygon. The surface is looked upon as the <u>locus of the curve</u> which is at the same time moved and distorted. The connexion of apexes according to their first and to their second subscripts, respectively, gives the characteristic net of a surface (Fig. 10). Expressing P(u,v) by means of the net vectors is complicated and useless.

It is not necessary to raise m and n to large values to express very complicated shapes; so we generally limit outselves to the fifth order (Fig. 11). The definition of degenerate surfaces is evident (Fig. 12 to 16).

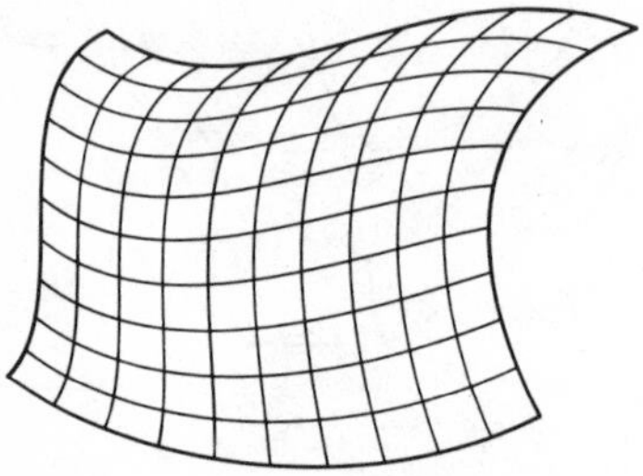

Figure 11

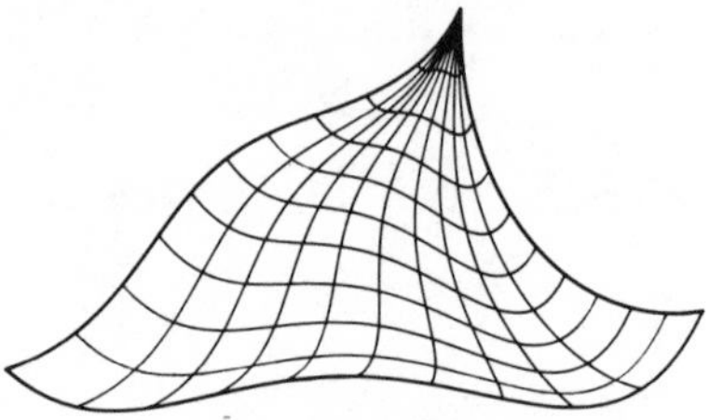

Figure 12

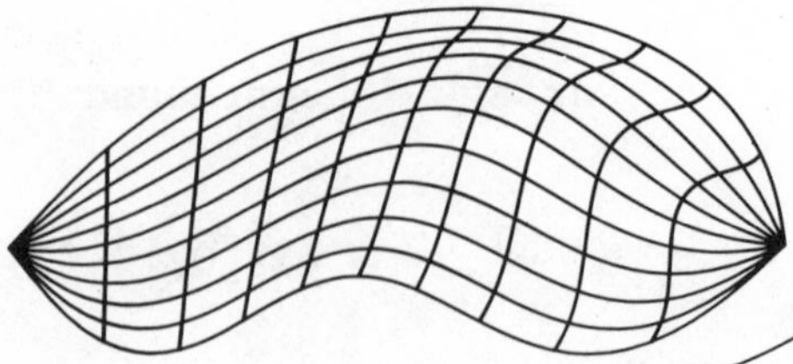

Figure 13

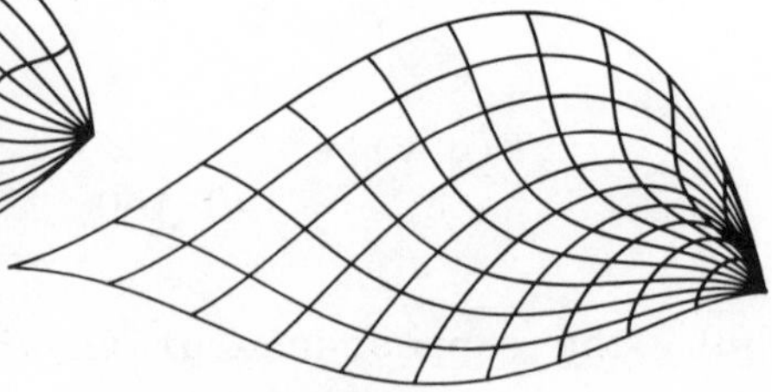

Figure 14

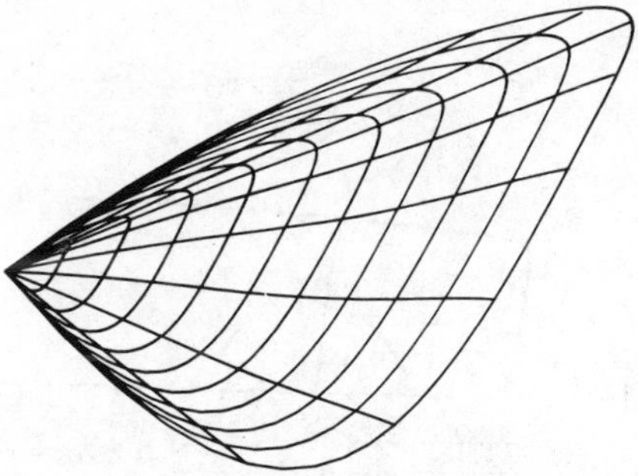

Figure 15

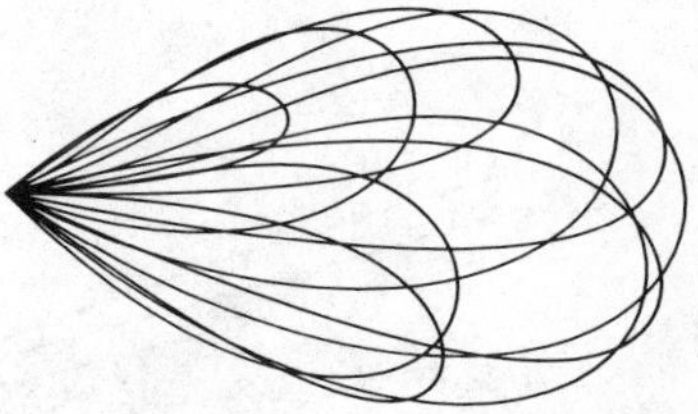

Figure 16

By similarity with the curve hodographs, we obtain successively such hodographs as:

$$\frac{1}{m} \cdot \frac{\partial \vec{P}}{\partial u}, \frac{1}{n} \cdot \frac{\partial \vec{P}}{\partial v}, \frac{1}{m.n} \cdot \frac{\partial^2 \vec{P}}{\partial u.\partial v'}, \frac{1}{m^2} \cdot \frac{\partial^2 \vec{P}}{\partial u^2} \ldots \qquad (6)$$

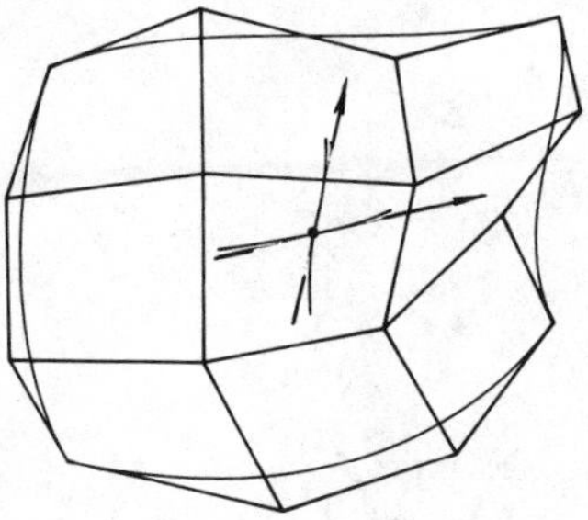

Figure 17

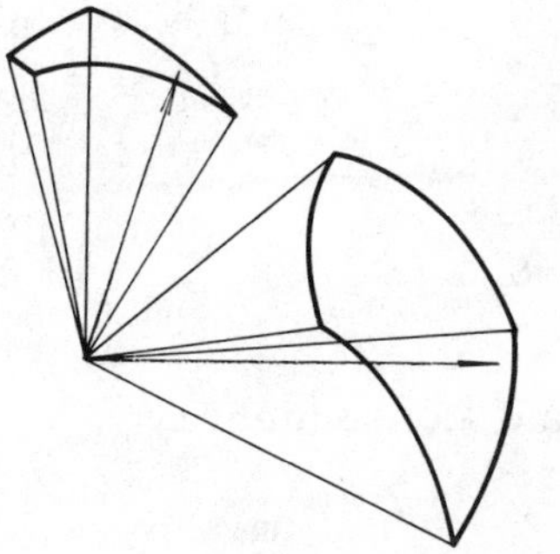

Figure 17bis

4.3. Transposants

By tradition, a line resting on a sculptured surface is defined as the intersection of the said surface with a cylinder having a plane directrix (Fig. 18). But the numerical definition of such a line needs a great amount of data. So we think it is better to define such a curve as the transposant of a parametric curve inscribed on a square patch having u and v for coordinates (Fig. 19).

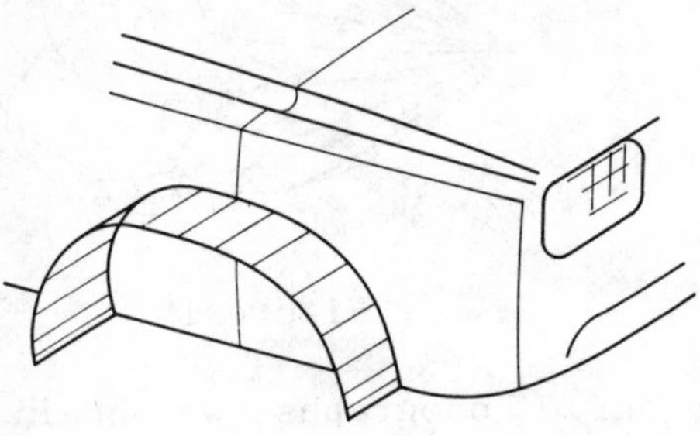

Figure 18

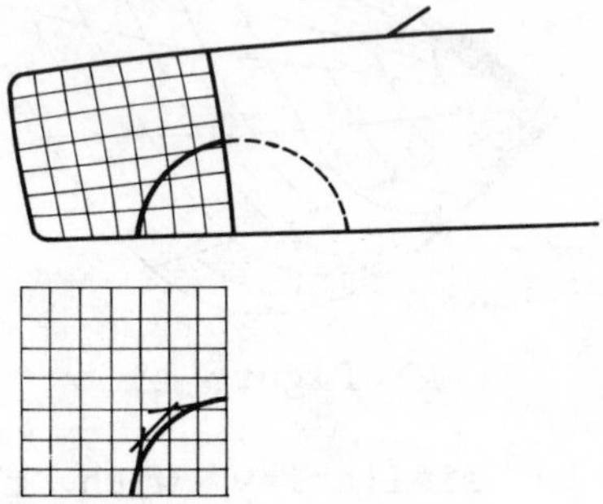

Figure 19

The transposed curve being defined by its own polygon we may state that

$$u = \sum_{0}^{p} c_k t^k$$

$$v = \sum_{0}^{p} d_k t^k$$

and consequently

$$\vec{P}(t) = \sum_{i=0}^{m} \sum_{j=0}^{n} \vec{b}_{ij} \left(\sum_{0}^{p} c_k t^k \right)^i \left(\sum_{0}^{p} d_k t^k \right)^j \qquad (8)$$

which can be brought to

$$P(t) = \sum_{0}^{(m+n)p} e_i t^i \qquad (9)$$

Although (m+n)p can reach a rather high value, definition (9) is easier to use than a great number of points.

4.4. Volumes

Expanding the notions previously stated, it is possible to describe a volume by

$$\vec{P}(u,v,w) = \sum_{i=0}^{m} \sum_{j=0}^{n} \sum_{k=0}^{p} \vec{b}_{ijk}\, u^i v^j w^k \qquad (10)$$

We shall see what use can be made of this definition later (§ 4.5.3.).

4.5 Transformations

4.5.1 Curves

When one wants to obtain a curve which is beyond the possibilities of a n-sided polygon, two possibilities arise:

i) divide the curve into segments each of which lies within the possibilities of a n-sided polygon.

or

ii) increase the number of the polygon legs.

4.5.1.1. Segmentation

Curve segmentation is compulsory to:

i) Define a panel which is included in a more general surface, (i.e. a door inscribed in a side panel)(Fig. 20).

ii) Locally alter a curve without reacting on the rest of it (Fig. 21).

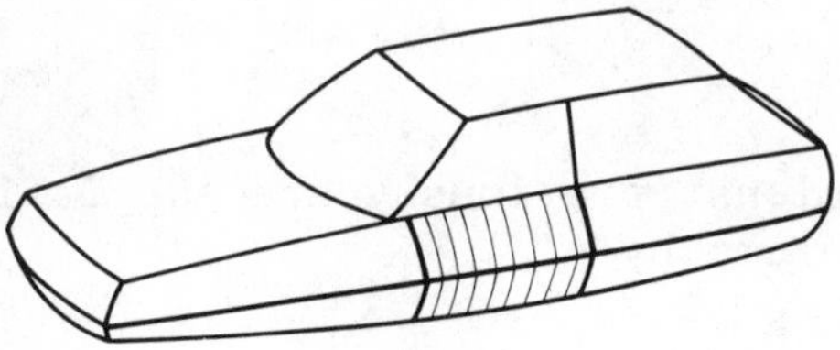

Figure 20

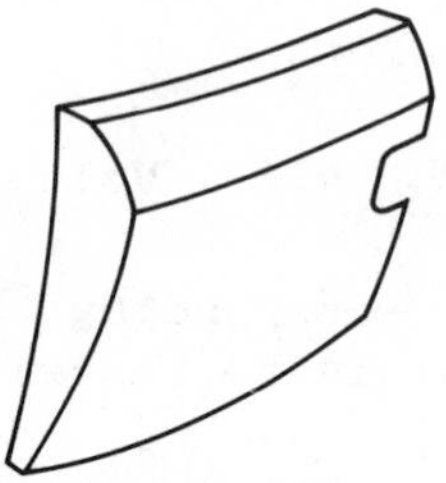

Figure 21

The solution consists in using an auxiliary parameter (w). Its value varies from 0 to 1 when the principal parameter varies from u_0 to u_1, which encompass the portion to be separately defined.

That section is expressed by

$$\vec{P}(w) = \sum_{i=0}^{m} \vec{b}_i \cdot \left[u_0 + (u_1-u_0)\, w\right]^{i} \qquad (11)$$

So, if

$$\{\vec{b}'_i\} = \left|\left| u_0^{c-1} \quad (u_1-u_0)^{\ell-1} \; C_{c-1}^{\ell-1} \right|\right| \{\vec{b}_i\} \qquad (12)$$

then:

$$\vec{P}(w) = \sum_{i=0}^{m} \vec{b}'_i \, w^{i} \qquad (13)$$

There is no limitation to the values of u_0 and u_1; if they lie out of [0,1], they define an extension of the initial curve, which is sometimes useful when designing stamping tools.

4.5.1.2. Order raising

Matrix $\|\vec{b}_i\|$ being expanded with n zero zeroes, and the operation

$$\| M_{ab} \|^{-1} \begin{Bmatrix} \{ \vec{b}_i \} \\ \{ 0 \} \end{Bmatrix} = \begin{Bmatrix} \vec{a}'_i \end{Bmatrix} \qquad (14)$$

being performed, we obtain a (m+n)-sided polygon defining the same curve, from which the operator starts to carry on the curve alteration.

4.5.1.3. Bernstein's form

Another function helps to understand the influence of apex displacements. If one considers the vectors s_i connecting an arbitrary origin to the polygon apexes (Fig. 22), the curve is expressed by

$$\vec{P}(u) = \sum_{i=0}^{m} \vec{s}_i \; \mathcal{B}_{\frac{i}{m}}(u) \qquad (15)$$

$\mathcal{B}_i$'s being Bernstein's function (Fig. 23)

$$\mathcal{B}_{\frac{i}{m}} = C_m^i \; u^i \; (1-u)^{m-i} \qquad (16)$$

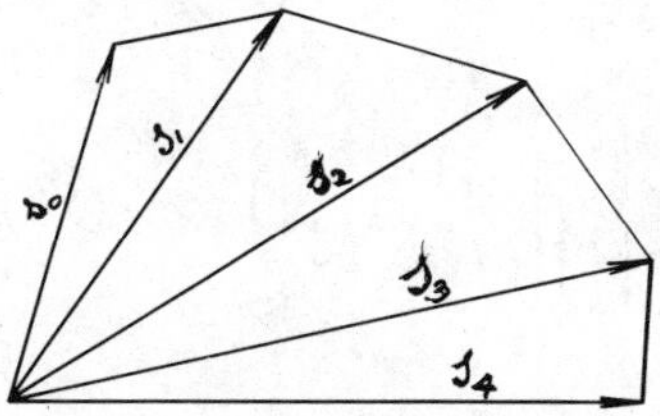

Figure 22

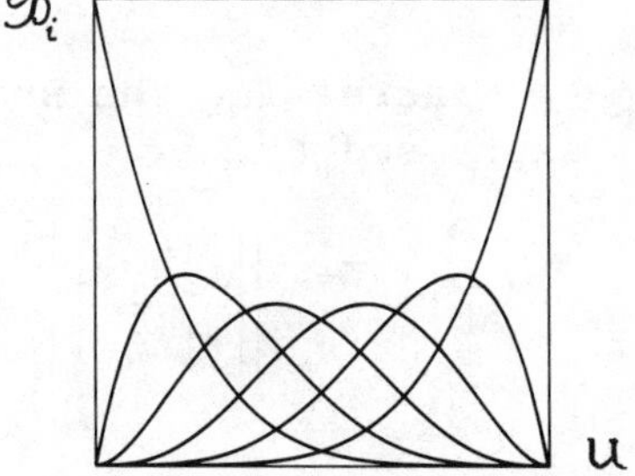

Figure 23

Considering this expression, any operator easily understands that when apex S_i is translated along a vector Δ, the curve defined by the new polygon (Fig. 24) is expressed by

$$\vec{P}'(u) = \vec{P}(u) + \vec{\Delta}\, \mathcal{B}_{\frac{i}{m}}(u) \qquad (17)$$

The maximum of the $\mathcal{B}_{\frac{i}{m}}$ function occurs for $u = \frac{i}{m}$.

4.5.2. Surfaces

4.5.2.1. Segmenting

Similarly to curves, a patch can need segmenting; the sub-patch (Fig. 25) bounded by values u_0, u_1, v_0 and v_1 is defined by:

$$\vec{P}(w,t) = \sum_{i=0}^{m} \sum_{j=0}^{n} \vec{b}_{ij} \, [u_0+(u_1-u_0)w]^i \, [v_0+(v_1-v_0)t]^j \qquad (18)$$

4.5.2.2. Order raising

Increasing the number of meshes of a net is expressed by:

$$||M_{ab}||^{-1} \left\| \begin{matrix} ||\vec{b}_{ij}|| & ||0|| \\ ||0|| & ||0|| \end{matrix} \right\| \; ||\vec{a}'_{ij}|| \qquad (19)$$

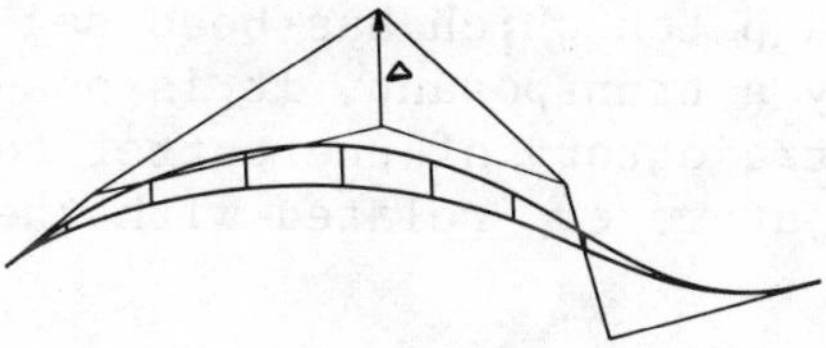

Figure 24

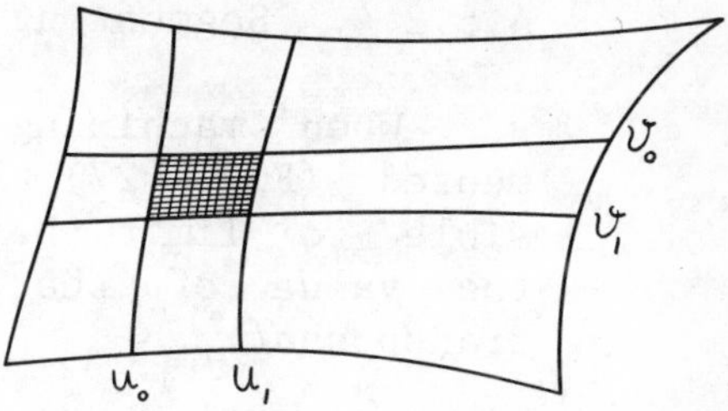

Figure 25

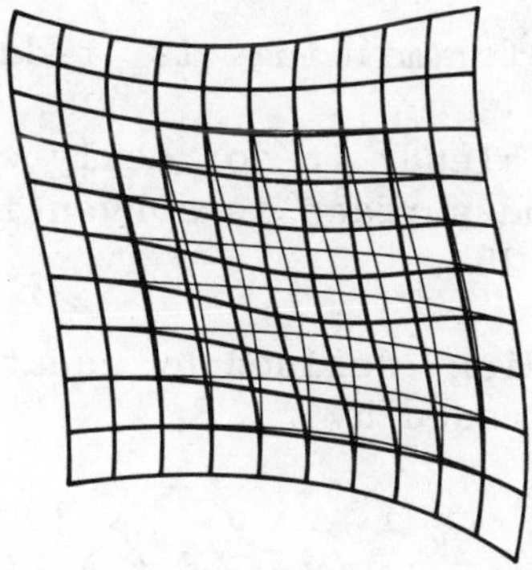

Figure 26

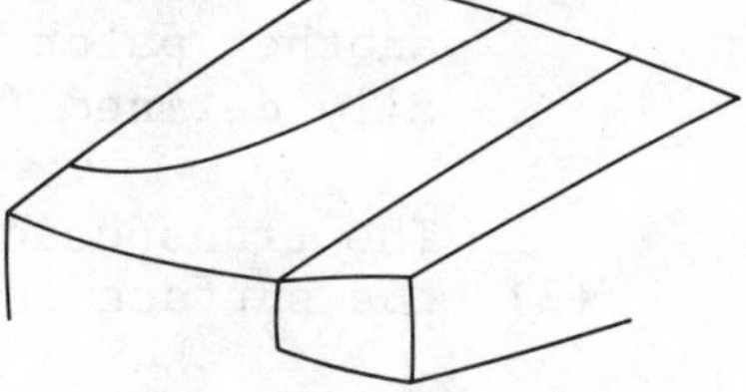

Figure 27

4.5.2.3. Bernstein's form

Expressing a surface with s_{ij} vectors gives

$$\vec{P}(u,v) = \sum_{i=0}^{m} \sum_{j=0}^{n} \vec{s}_{ij} \; \mathcal{B}_{\substack{i\\m}}(u) \, \mathcal{B}_{\substack{j\\n}}(v) \qquad (20)$$

and translating apex S_{ij} along a vector Δ yields (Fig. 26)

$$\vec{P}'(u,v) = \vec{P}(u,v) + \vec{\Delta}\mathcal{B}_{\substack{i\\m}}(u) \;.\; \mathcal{B}_{\substack{j\\n}}(v) \qquad (21)$$

for which the maximal displacement occurs at the point $P'\left(\frac{i}{m},\frac{j}{n}\right)$.

4.5.2.4. Segmenting by a transposant

When machining a patch which has been segmented (Fig. 27) by a transposant, it is possible to limit the trajectory of the cutter to the value of the parameter related with the transposant.

It would be better to express directly the portion of the patch limited by the transposant, since the benefit is two-fold:

i) The amount of data for milling is reduced

ii) It is easier to blend it correctly with another patch if the surface is conventionally defined (Fig. 28).

The transposant being defined by equation (7), the surface is expressed by

$$\vec{P}(t,v) = \sum_{i=0}^{m} \sum_{j=0}^{n} \vec{b}_{ij} \left(\sum_{k=0}^{p} c_k t^k \right)^i \left(v \sum_{\ell=0}^{p} d_\ell t^\ell \right)^j \qquad (22)$$

which can be brought to

$$\vec{P}(t,v) = \sum_{i=0}^{(m+n)p} \sum_{j=0}^{n} \vec{e}_{ij}\, t^i v^j \qquad (23)$$

4.5.3. Volumes

Suppose a group of points defining a set of patches is immersed into a space defined by relation (10), then the motion of the apexes related with this space brings a general distortion of the original surface (Fig. 29).

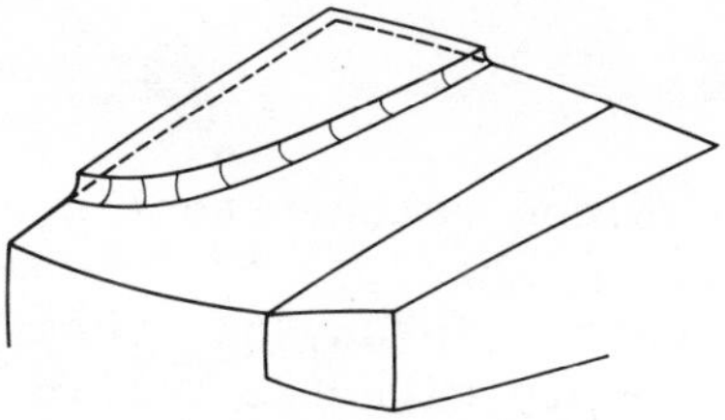

Figure 28

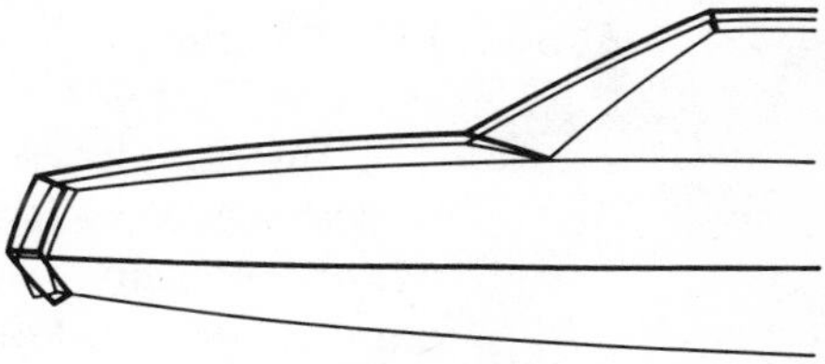

Figure 29

We feel this method is very helpful when we are faced with the task of carrying out the required minor changes of style to an already existing model.

4.6. Blending

4.6.1. Curves

There is no difficulty in blending two curves because the only requirement consists in having the first leg of a polygon collinear with the first leg of the other. Supposing the two first vectors are respectively a_1, a_2, a'_1 and a'_2, the conditions to fulfill to ensure osculation are:

$$a'_1 = g\, a_1 \qquad g < 0$$

$$a'_2 = ha_1 + ka_2 \qquad k > 0 \qquad (24)$$

$$k = \frac{n'}{n} \cdot \frac{n-1}{n'-1} \cdot g^2 \quad (*)$$

(*) n and n' being the number of the polygon legs

4.6.2. Surfaces

4.6.2.1. Tangency

We may have to blend patches that are somewhat dissimilar in shape, or whose sides are not tangent. In any of these cases, we cannot comply with the collinearity and proportionality of the transverse (normal) derivatives along the common boundary line. The most general requirement is that $\frac{\partial P}{\partial u}$, $\frac{\partial P}{\partial v}$ & $\frac{\partial P'}{\partial w}$ should be coplanar (Fig. 30).

The nullity of the mixed product is difficult to comply with so we prefer to use the relation

$$\frac{\partial \vec{P}}{\partial w} = h(u) \frac{\partial \vec{P}}{\partial v} + k(u) \frac{\partial \vec{P}}{\partial u} \qquad (25)$$

on the boundary line. In some cases, order of the second patch is above the first, but this tendency is easily controlled and its transmission to the opposite boundary of the second patch is avoided.

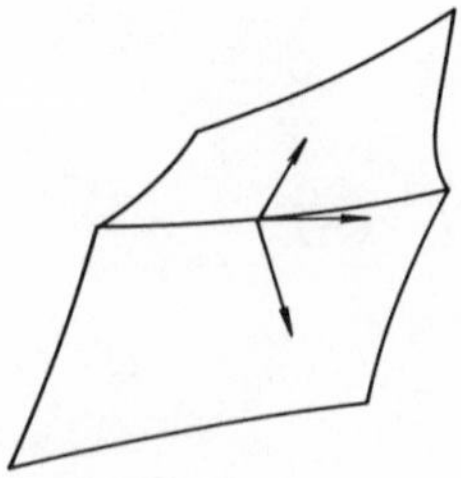

Figure 30

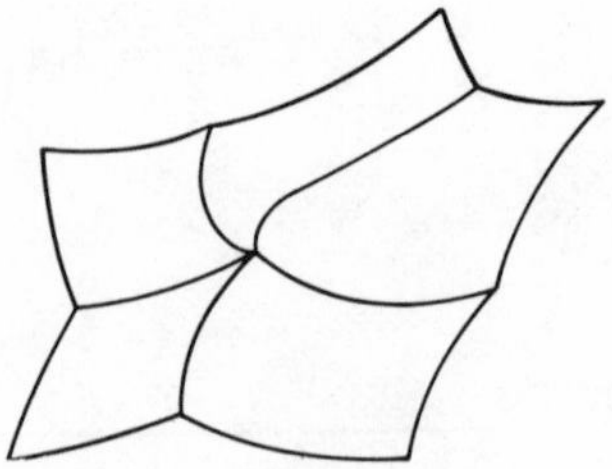

Figure 31

4.6.2.2. Multiple patches

When patches meet on one point, and when couples of boundary lines are not tangent (Fig. 31), twist vectors must be handled with great care, and the values of "h & k" functions on that point have to comply with some special requirements. But any number of patches, odd or even, can meet on a given point. This possibility is rather useful when we deal with special configurations including degenerate patches.

4.6.2.3. Intermediate patches

A stylist or a tool designer may have to define patches that intersect each other along limit lines. A fillet, large or small, constant or variable, must then be added. The patches being previously segmented by isoparametric or transposed lines, the use of "h & k" gives the definition of the fillet (Fig. 32).

When more than two patches meet on one point, the definition of these fillets leaves an empty space that must be defined separately, either as a conventional or degenerate patch, or as a group of patches (Fig. 33 and 34).

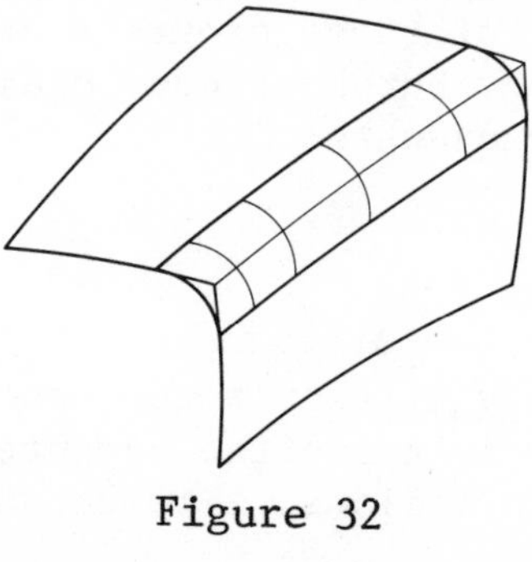

Figure 32

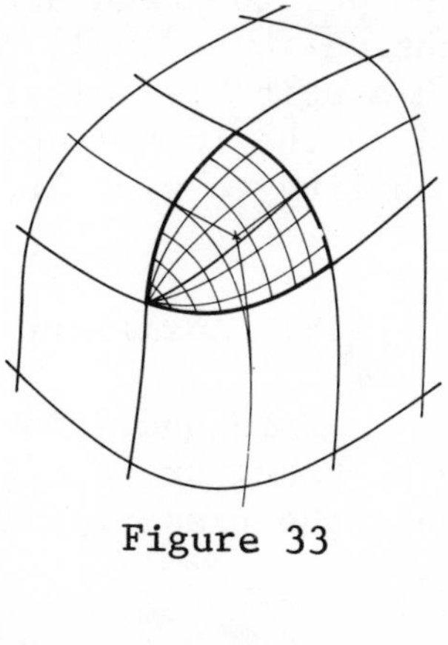

Figure 33

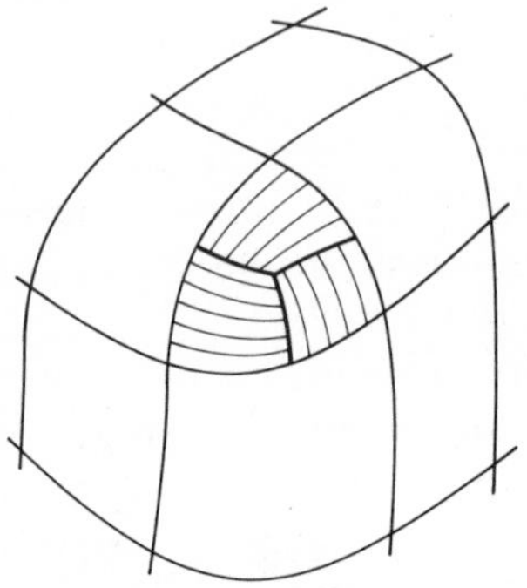

Figure 34

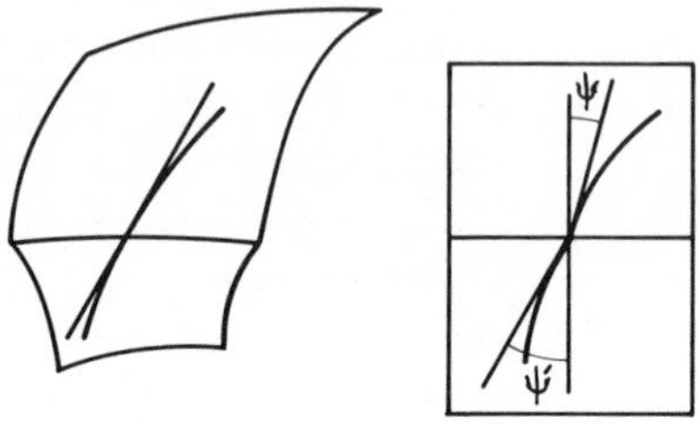

Figure 35

4.6.3. Transposant

When transposants belong to to different patches and meet on their common boundary line (Fig. 35), the tangency of the transposants is ensured by the relation

$$\text{tg } \Psi' = h(u) . \text{ tg } \Psi - k(u) \qquad (26)$$

4.7. Approximations

For curves and surfaces which have to suffer constraints such as passing through, or near, given points, or having predetermined slopes, some programs define polygons and nets. They are, so to speak, more tentative than final, but they help the designer to reach a suitable solution. Most of these programs are based on the least squares method, but none can claim the ability to give 100% optimum answers.

4.8. Auxiliary operations

Some operations, not very difficult to perform by hand, are still better left to the computer, because the traditional method is tedious, time-consuming and has a debatable accuracy.

Among them we can mention:

i) Intersections and, especially, plane sections.

ii) Rotations, which are of major importance in tool design (Fig. 36).

iii) Perspective views, mainly intended to provide stylists with an accurate sketch, completed later on with colours, chromes, details, etc. (Fig. 37).

iv) Contour lines related with one direction of sight; this helps to define the tipping angles which are best suited for stamping operations.

v) Reflection (or highlight) lines. They are the reflection, in the bright surface of the car body, of a straight line parallel to the axis of the car, as it is seen by an observer. It helps to guess whether a shape could be pleasant, the final decision relying on the sight of the tridimensional object.

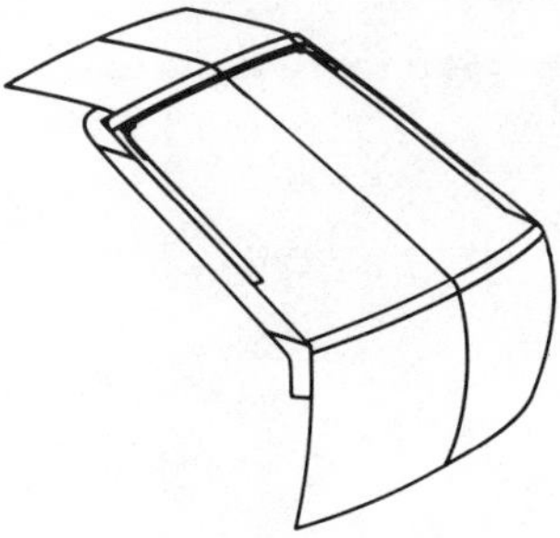

Figure 36

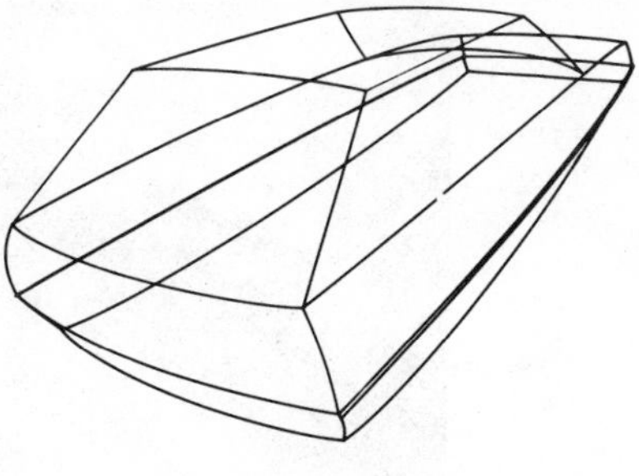

Figure 37

5. Results

5.1. Computer

A computer, not any bigger than 44 K 16, completed with a 3 M octets magdisk, controls a set of three drawing machines or one drawing machine and one milling machine. Part of the program has to be batch processed, and we would like to increase the capacity of the computer in order to speed up some operations.

Shortening the length of the tape has been a major improvement: to mill a complete clay-model or master does not require more than 80 to 100 meters (90 to 110 yds) of tape.

5.2. Facilities - Performances

Our drawing machines are controlled by a computer. Their speed is 300 mm/s (12 in/sec); their accuracy is about 0.05 mm (0.002 in) (Fig. 38).

Figure 38

As no adequate milling machine was available, we have had to design our own, its capacity is 2.2 × 1.7 × 1.2 m (7 1/2 × 5 1/2 × 4 ft) (Fig. 39). It is intended to manufacture soft materials such as styrofoam, plaster wood or plastic material. Its spindle speed ranges from 1,500 to 20,000 rpm, and its feed can reach 150 mm/s (6 in/s).

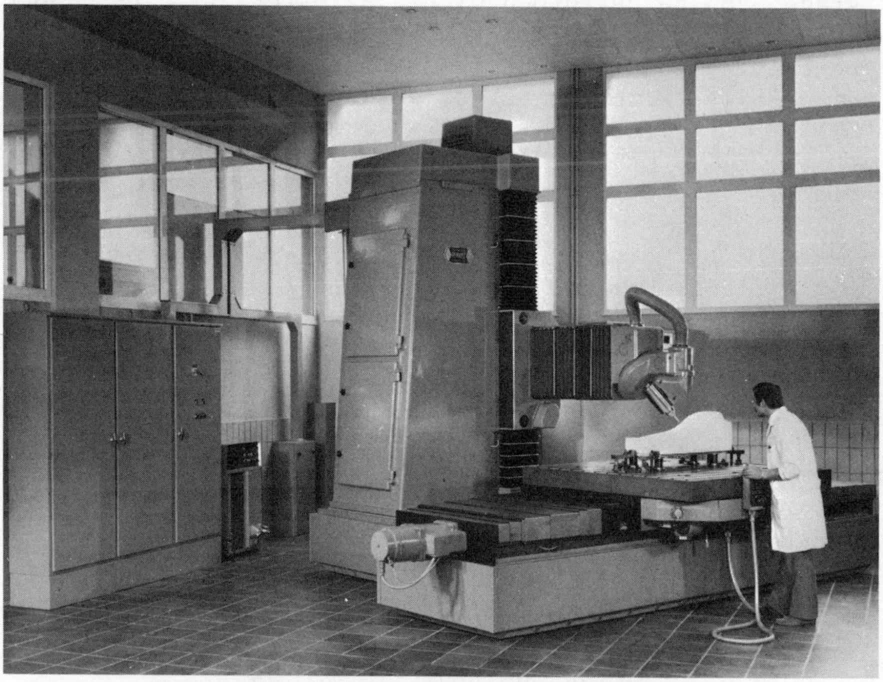

Figure 39

5.3. Acceptance

It only takes a few days for a designer to perform most tasks executed by an NC operator, but mastering all the possibilities of the system may take a few months. The task of methods men is somewhat more difficult to perform and the normal training time may exceed two months.

5.4. Applications

Although only a few experiments had been carried out to their end, and most designers only possessed a scant training, we have been able to produce within five weeks, starting from a rough full scale drawing of a "skin", the final drawing and the full scale plaster model. Subsequent minor alterations, often met at this stage, can be performed within a fortnight. The same system has been applied to the definition of objects pertaining to different industries: boat hulls, turbine foils, aircraft parts, optics, etc. (Fig. 40, 41, 42).

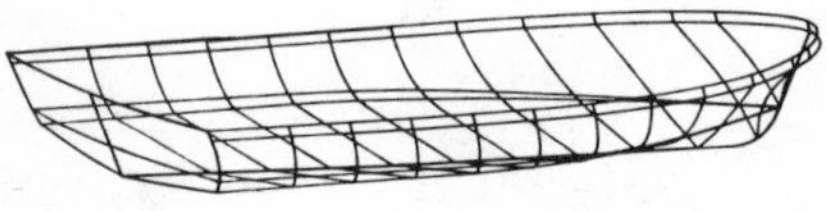

Figure 40

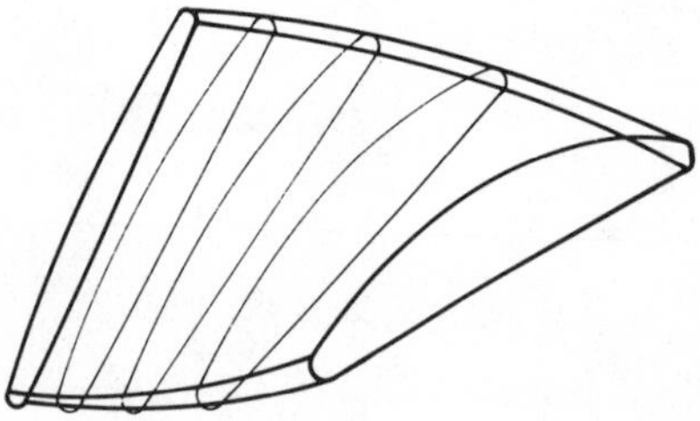

Figure 41

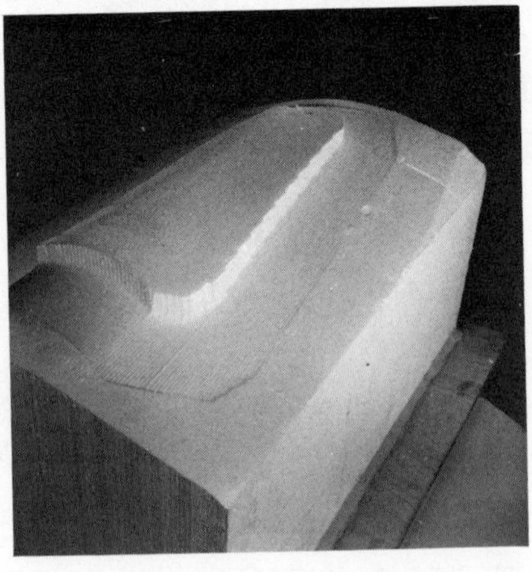

Figure 42

5.5. SURFAPT processor

For hard material manufacturing purposes, a processor is now being developed, and a good part of it is already tested. Its major features are:

i) Definitions include conventional surfaces such as planes, cylinders, tabcyls, etc., together with parametric surfaces, the order of which is only limited by the computer capacity.

ii) APT compatible.

iii) Already implemented on a 128 K 16 computer, but will be implemented on 24 K 16 computers later on.

iv) Tangent patches are scanned together, either along isoparametrics or along plane sections.

v) Tool compensation can be carried "on-line", or batch processed.

vi) Non-tangent patches are scanned, the common limit being generally non-isoparametric lines.

vii) Groups of patches limited by non-isoparametric lines can be scanned together (Fig. 43).

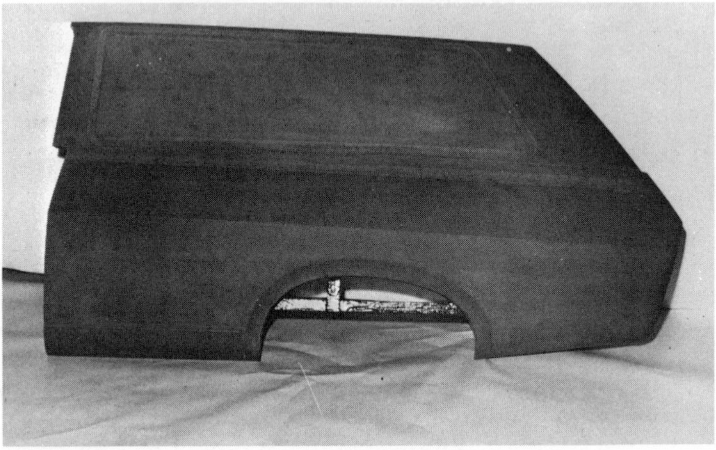

Figure 43

We think this programme will prove economical and easy to operate for ourselves as well as for our tooling sub-contractors or many other industries.

REFERENCES

1. P. E. Bézier, Numerical Control-Mathematics and Applications, John Wiley and Sons, London (1972)

2. A. R. Forrest, "Interactive Interpolation and Approximation by Bézier Polynomials," Computer J., Vol. 15, No. 1, 71-79 (1972).

3. W. J. Gordon and R. F. Riesenfeld, "Bernstein - Bézier Methods for the Computer-Aided Design of Free-Form Curves and Surfaces," J.ACM, Vol. 21, No. 2, 293-310 (April 1974).

4. ———————, "B-spline Curves and Surfaces," These Proceedings.

CONSTRAINED INTERPOLATION USING BÉZIER CURVES AS A NEW TOOL IN COMPUTER AIDED GEOMETRIC DESIGN

R.F. Wielinga
Philips Research Laboratories
Eindhoven, Netherlands

Abstract

Computer Aided Geometric Design is placed in the context of Computer Aided Design and Computer Aided Manufacture. Next the role of interpolation and approximation in geometric design is discussed. After introduction of the notation, the interpolation problem for Bézier curves is stated. The solution is given and the method is extended to surfaces. A number of basic design tools useful in a curve design package using Bézier curves is mentioned. A distinction is made between curves used for "direct" and "indirect" design, an example of each being given. A number of surfaces defined by combining Bézier curves and a contouring function are shown.

1. Introduction

The computer can play various roles in the generation of "free-form" objects. On the one side it has the possibility of unambiguous and precise definition[1] of the form and on the other side of integrating design, visualization, analysis and manufacture. While the former concerns the mathematics and implementation, the latter has to do with economics[2,3] and has social implications. An important result ensuing from computerization of the total process is a shortening of the time between initial design and product delivery.

A large number of computer programs for geometric design and manufacture using numerically controlled (NC) machines are known. They include:

a. UNISURF (Renault - Peugeot, France)[1]
b. MULTIOBJECT (Comp. Aid. Des. Centre, England)[6]
c. FMILL-APTLOFT (freely available)
d. Sculptures Surface (SSX-n, APT/IIT Research Inst., CAMI-Computer-Aided Manufacturing International)[7]
e. INCA II (General Motors Corp., USA)[8]
f. SURFACE II (Ford Motor Co., USA)[9]
h. FORMELA (Saab-Scania, Sweden)[10]
i. NMG (British Aircraft Corp., England)[11]
j. GMD (Graphic Master Dimension, Messerschmitt-Bölkow-Blohm, W. Germany)[12]
k. AUTOKON (Norway)[13].

A possible classification of these programs is based on whether the accent is mainly on design, requiring a flexible system with fast response (class 1), or on scheduling and tooling (class 2). The first two of the programs mentioned will then belong to class 1, the others to class 2.

Another division may be based on the objectives of the mathematical system[4,5]. The design may be either "ab initio" (with the information generated by the design system) (b,d), or the design specifications may originate from an external source (formulas representing the solution to some problem, data or a model) (a,c,e through k). In the latter case the mathematical system should be able to approximate and/or interpolate input by iteration (a-b) or without iteration (c-k). In practice, however, both mathematical objectives should be met. Systems (a) and (b) deal with the interpolation and approximation problem by inspecting an object produced on a fast 3D milling machine, or by drawing or working interactively using a graphical display.

A number of algorithmic interpolation- and approximation methods for computer aided geometric design are in use: univariate splines[14-17], Bézier curves[18] and various blending function methods[19-22]. An excellent survey of the methods for curved surface representation has been given by Forrest[23].

In section 3 an interpolation method is presented in which Bézier curves are used. The method can be readily extended to surfaces by analogy. It accepts various conditions, the number of which depends on the degree of the curve used. In this way design and interpolation can be combined.

In section 4 a number of other facilities are mentioned that have been implemented in a computer program for Bézier curve handling. In section 5 some applications are shown of "direct" and "indirect" design using the method of constrained interpolation discussed in section 3.

2. Notation and Formulation

For the representation of Bézier curves we choose the general notation in the form of polygon vertices as given by Forrest[18] rather than that of polygon sides used by Bézier[20], for reasons of compactness and computational accuracy.

Let $\vec{f}(t)$ denote a curve to be approximated and let $Bé_n(\vec{f};t)$ denote a (vector-valued) n^{th} degree Bézier polynomial approximation of $\vec{f}(t)$ for $t \in [0,1]$. Let the vertices of the polygon be denoted by $\vec{f}*(\frac{i}{n})$, with $i = 0(1)\ n$ (see Fig. 1). The asterisk is used to indicate that $\vec{f}*$ does not lie on the curve $\vec{f}$, except $\vec{f}^*(\frac{0}{n})$ and $\vec{f}^*(\frac{n}{n})$ which are the beginning and end points, respectively. The vector-valued Bézier curve $\vec{g}(t)$ then takes the form

$$\vec{g}(t) \equiv \text{Bé}(\vec{f};t) = \sum_{i=0}^{n} \vec{f}^*(\tfrac{i}{n})\, J_{n,i}(t), \tag{2.1}$$

with

$$J_{n,i}(t) = \binom{n}{i} t^i (1-t)^{n-i}, \quad i = 0(1)n. \tag{2.2}$$

$J_{n,i}(t)$ may be viewed as the weighting or interpolating function of the ith vertex of an n-sided polygon track.

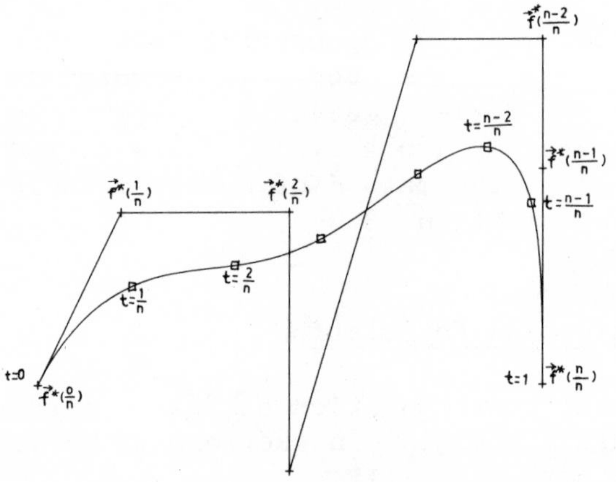

Figure 1

In ref. 20 it was shown that basis functions other than (2.2) may be chosen as a solution to the conditions posed for a Bézier curve. Forrest[18,21] has given a compact formulation of these conditions and has investigated several other sets of basis functions (of trigonometric and rational polynomial types). The choice of polynomials by Bézier is a good one, because the influence of the polygon vertices is evenly distributed and the evaluation of the interpolation functions is simple. The method of interpolation with "variable" constraints outlined in the next section is given in the notation of eqs. (2.1) and (2.2) and is therefore independent of the particular choice of basis functions $J_{n,i}(t)$.

The choice of the notation of the function on the left hand side of eq. (2.1) indicates the interpretation of eq. (2.1): the notation $\vec{g}(t)$ is chosen for ab initi o design. It is a vector-valued function resulting from a particular (initial) choice of the n polygon vertices $\vec{f}^*(\frac{i}{n})$. If the interpretation is such that a function $\vec{f}$ should be approximated, the notation $\text{Bé}(\vec{f};t)$ is chosen. The polygon vertices are then the free "parameters" that should be chosen in such a way that $\vec{f}$ is best approximated by $\text{Bé}(\vec{f};t)$.

For approximating $\vec{f}$ at specific points, $\vec{f}_i$, with $i = 1(1)k$ and k arbitrary, there are two basic methods: an algorithmic and a interactive one[21] or a combination of both. An algorithmic method yielding *interpolation* of the given points for the case $k \leqslant n + 1$ is shown in the next section.

3. Solution of the Interpolation Problem

3.1 Curves

Let an nth degree Bézier curve be given by a polygon track having $n + 1$ vertices $\vec{f}^*(\frac{i}{n})$, with $i = 0(1)\ n$ (see Fig. 1). Let a point of the curve with the free parameter value t_ℓ, where $\ell = 1(1)\ell_0$ be denoted by $\vec{g}(t_\ell)$. $\vec{g}(t_\ell)$ may be expressed as

$$\vec{g}(t_\ell) = \sum_{i=0}^{n} \vec{f}^*(\tfrac{i}{n})\ J_{n,i}(t_\ell) \tag{3.1}$$

Eq. (3.1) may be viewed in two ways. The first is that the left hand side contains the ℓth unknown $\vec{g}(t_\ell)$, which is expressed as a linear combination of the n + 1 knowns $\vec{f}^*(\frac{i}{n})$ with the "coefficients" $J_{n,i}(t_\ell)$, where t_ℓ is associated with one of the vertices i. On the other hand, if ℓ_0 points $\vec{g}_\ell$ are known to lie on the Bézier curve and if a parameter value t_ℓ is associated with the ℓth point, eq. (3.1) may be considered to represent a system of ℓ_0 simultaneous vector-valued linear equations in ℓ_0 unknown vertices. An appropriate association must be made of a known point $\vec{g}_\ell$ (with $1 \leqslant \ell \leqslant \ell_0$) with an unknown vertex i (with $0 \leqslant i \leqslant n$, while $\ell \leqslant n + 1$).

The interpretation of eq. (3.1) as a system of linear equations is simplified if the following notation is adopted:

$$\vec{\gamma}_\ell = \sum_{k_1=1}^{N} \alpha_{\ell k_1} \vec{x}_{k_1} \tag{3.2}$$

with

$$N \equiv n + 1, \tag{3.3}$$

$$\vec{\gamma}_\ell \equiv \vec{g}(t_\ell), \tag{3.4}$$

$$\vec{x}_{k_1} \equiv \vec{f}^*\left(\frac{k_1-1}{n}\right), \tag{3.5}$$

which is known or unknown, depending on the association of ℓ with k_1.

(3.6) $$\alpha_{\ell k_1} \equiv J_{N-1,\, k_1-1}(t_\ell).$$

If $\ell_0 = n + 1$ the interpolation may be considered to have no restrictions. If $t_1 > 0$ and/or $t_{n+1} < 1$, the solution of eq. (3.2) implies both interpolation and extrapolation.

An element $\alpha_{\ell k_1} x_{k_1}$ of the right-hand side of eq. (3.2) is known if vertex k_1 of the polygon track is known (eq. (3.5)) and if the parameter value t_ℓ associated with it is known (eq. (3.6)). If a known element $\alpha_{\ell k_1} x_{k_1}$ of eq. (3.2) is defined as a *constraint* for the interpolation problem, eq. (3.2) shows that the relation

$$c + \ell_0 = n + 1$$

holds, c being the number of constraints for a curve of the nth degree, points of which are interpolated.

Figures 2-4 show some examples of interpolations using evenly spaced parameters $t_{k1} = (k_1-1)/n$ for degrees 2,3 and 4, respectively. Let us take the case illustrated in fig. 4 as an example of the association of ℓ with i. The degree of the curve is 4, so i runs from 0 to 4. There are three unknown vertices, so that $\ell_0 = 3$ and ℓ runs from 1 to 3, the association being with $i = 1,2$ and 3, respectively. The fixed points γ_ℓ are denoted by circles, the vertices by a plus sign. Fig. 5 shows the effect the additional constraints of beginning and end slopes have on the form of the curve as compared to the lowest curve in Fig.4. Evenly spaced parameter values have been chosen in Fig. 5. Fig. 6 shows the

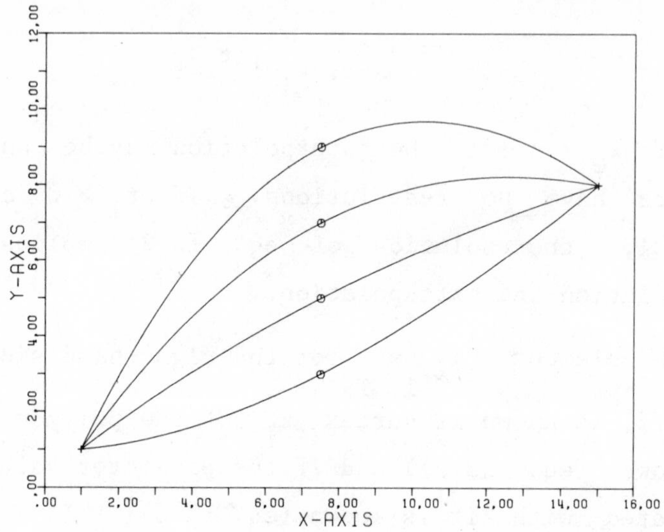

Figure 2

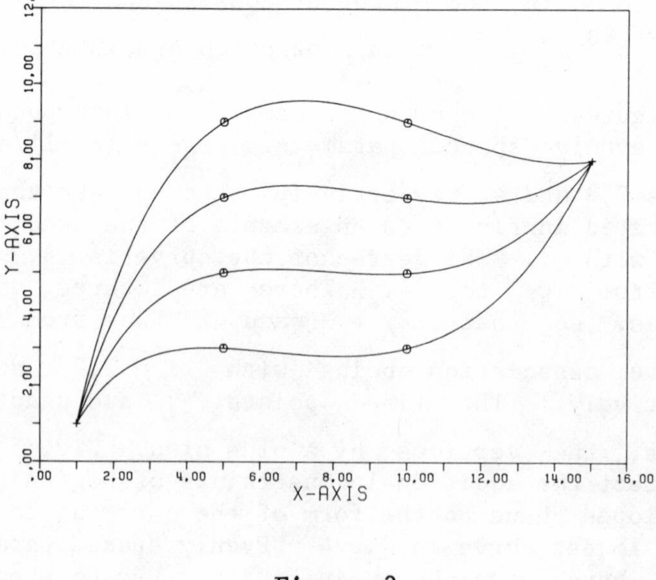

Figure 3

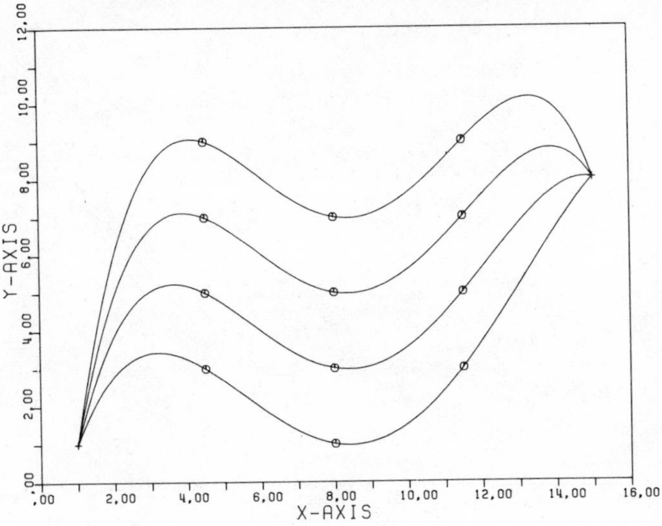

Figure 4

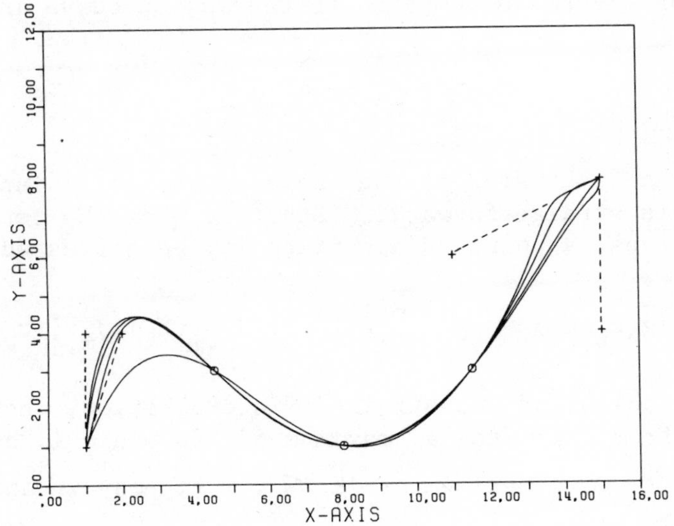

Figure 5

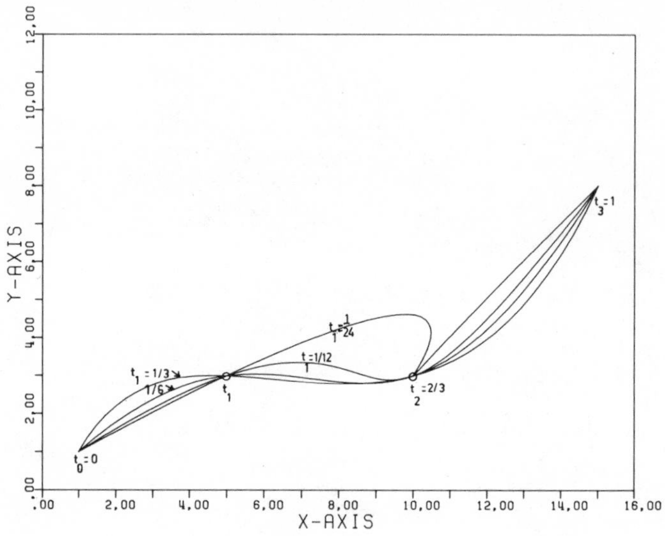

Figure 6

influence that different values of the first free parameter, t_ℓ, ($t_1 = 1/3, 1/6, 1/12, 1/24$), have on the curve form as compared to the lowest curve in Fig. 3.

3.2 Surfaces

The extension of the above method to Bézier surfaces is straightforward. Starting from the notation for curves, a point on a surface may be expressed as

$$(3.8) \quad \vec{g}(t_\ell, u_k) = \sum_{i=0}^{n} \sum_{j=0}^{m} \vec{f}^*\left(\frac{i}{n}, \frac{j}{m}\right) J_{n,i}(t_\ell)\, J_{m,j}(u_k).$$

The problem of constrained interpolation, where ℓ runs from 1 to a maximum of $\ell_0 \leqslant n + 1$ and k from 1 to a maximum of $k_0 \leqslant m + 1$, may in analogy with eq. (3.2) be expressed as

(3.9) $$\vec{\gamma}_{\ell,k} = \sum_{k_1=1}^{N} \sum_{k_2=1}^{M} \alpha_{\ell k k_1 k_2} \vec{x}_{k_1 k_2},$$

(3.10) where $N \equiv n + 1$,

(3.11) where $M \equiv m + 1$,

(3.12) $$\vec{x}_{k_1 k_2} \equiv \vec{f}*\left(\frac{k_1 - 1}{n}, \frac{k_2 - 1}{m}\right),$$ (see eq. 3.5)

and

(3.13) $$\alpha_{\ell k k_1 k_2} \equiv J_{N-1,k_1-1}(t_\ell)\ J_{M-1,k_2-1}(u_k)$$

The maximum number of equations to be solved is therefore $N \times M$. If boundary curves are specified, the number is reduced to $(N - 2) \times (M - 2)$.

4. Implementation in a Curve Handling Package

The above tool is welcome if combined design and and interpolation is required. It takes its place alongside interactive methods of approximation, which may be used to advantage if a curve has to be approximated. Even in this case, however, an interpolating method might be welcome to start with.

Other more or less conventional basic tools for Bézier curve (B-curve) manipulation available in the preliminary version of our program GTS (Geometry and Toolhandling System) are

- a routine that *reads*, interprets and stores input points defining sections of *composite curves*. A B-curve in this context is called a section. It may be joined continuously to a previous section. By adding a simple code word to the coordinates of an input point it may be interpreted as the vertex of a polygon track or a fixed point through which the curve should pass:

- a routine to *increase the degree*[21] of a B-curve without changing the curve form, to obtain more flexibility in curve design;

- a routine to calculate vertices for a full B-curve spanning only a *segment* of another B-curve;

- a routine to obtain the *distance* between a point and a B-curve;

- a routine for finding vertex points of a new B-curve so that it is *continuous* in position, slope and curvature to another B-curve (Fig. 7). By noting that in the course of finding the radius of curvature an outer product vector $\vec{a} \wedge \vec{b}$ is calculated and observing that the same vector is obtained from $\vec{a} \wedge (\vec{b} + \lambda\vec{a})$, where λ is arbitrary, the following useful expression may be derived for the third vertex point of the new curve:

$$\vec{f}^*(\tfrac{3}{n}) = \vec{f}^*(\tfrac{2}{n}) + \frac{\lambda^2 m(m-1)}{n(n-1)} \left\{ \vec{c}_1 \left(\kappa + 2\frac{\vec{c}_1 \cdot \vec{c}_2}{\vec{c}_1 \cdot \vec{c}_1}\right) - \vec{c}_2 \right\}$$

(3.14),

where $\vec{c}_1 \equiv \vec{f}^*(\tfrac{m}{m}) - \vec{f}^*(\tfrac{m-1}{m})$, $\vec{c}_2 \equiv \vec{f}^*(\tfrac{m-1}{m}) - \vec{f}^*(\tfrac{m-2}{m})$

and

(3.15) $\vec{f}^*(\tfrac{2}{n}) = \lambda \frac{m}{n} \vec{c}_1$.

λ and κ are arbitrary and m and n are the degrees of the old and new curves, respectively. Slope continuity leaves one degree of freedom λ, (see eq. (3.15)), and curvature continuity leaves two degrees of freedom, λ and κ as seen from eq. (3.4). Fig. 7 shows two families of curves in which λ and κ are varied. The curves with the end points on the upper line have $\lambda = 1$ and $\kappa = -0.5$, 0 and 1.0, respectively. The curves ending in the lower line have the same values but a different value of λ, namely $\lambda = 1.5$.

- finally a routine with which a B-curve can be *cut on an NC machine tool* within a given tolerance (segmentation into line elements).

A number of service subroutines such as a routine for rotation of B-curves and for plotting polygon track vertices and points to be interpolated completes the curve-handling facilities, so that communication with the designer is made easier.

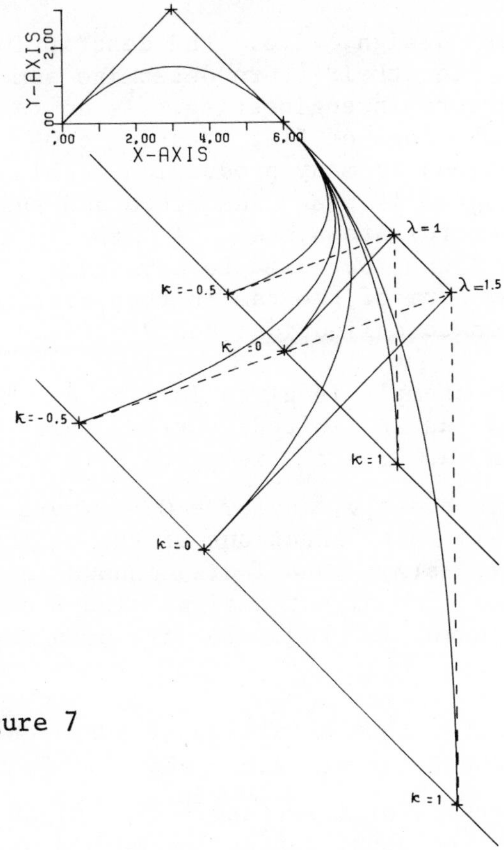

Figure 7

Visualization facilities available are routines for plotting using parallel, perspective and "global"[24] projections from arbitrary viewpoints and in arbitrary directions.

5. Applications

The B-curve has interesting properties for free-form design and may not only be used for "direct" but also for "indirect" design. Curves present in a 3D object, e.g., character lines in motor-cars, or patch boundaries may be called curves for direct design.

Indirect design, i.e. the description of functions which in their turn determine some geometric form, also occurs in engineering. As an example we may mention the form of flat rotating cams used to control functions in many production machines. The path-time diagram is best described and analysed in a Cartesian coordinate system. A two dimensional Bézier curve might be used to advantage for this purpose. The form of the cam is then obtained after transformation to cylindrical coordinates.

Another example is given in Fig. 8. The surface is described as a lofted surface whose horizontal cross-section at $z = z_0$ is given by a contour function $C(x,y,a,b,d,q,v, \text{angle}) = 0$, where a,b,d,q,v and the angle are functions of the height z. The curves a(z), b(z) and d(z) shown in Fig. 9 are B-curves used for direct design. The B-curves q(z) and v(z) shown in Fig. 10 are used for indirect design.

Figs. 11-13 show a variety of surfaces[25] defined by varying the B-curves a,b, and d. Fig. 14 shows the first version of a surface[26] that might be simply described by the above contouring method using Bézier curves. Figs. 15 and 16 show more recent designs of this type of surface.

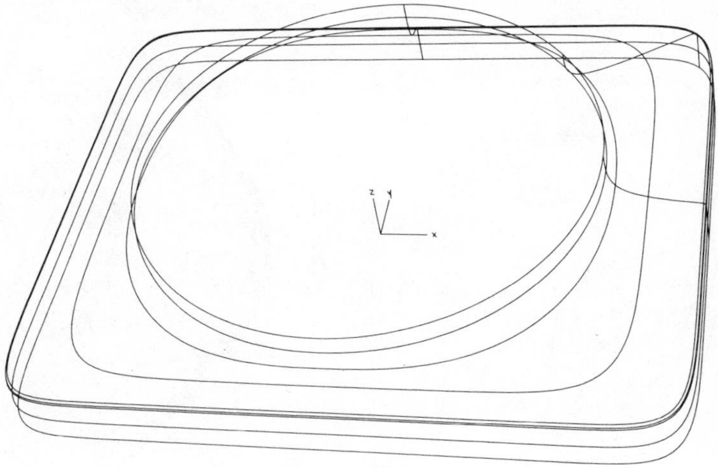

Figure 8

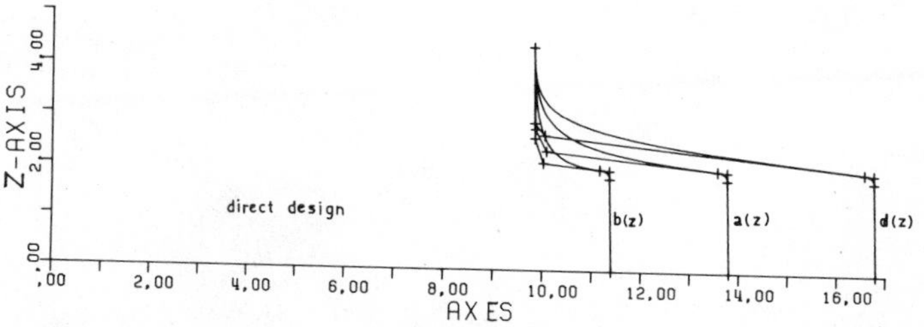

Figure 9

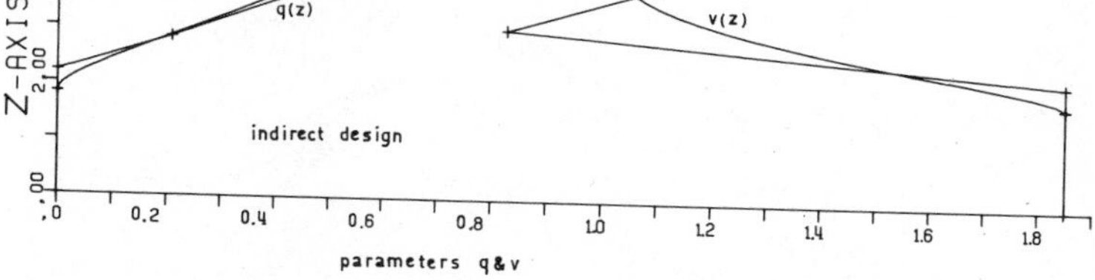

Figure 10

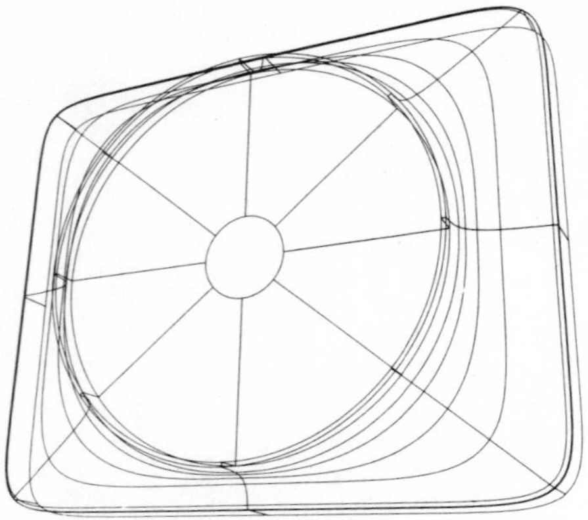

Figure 11

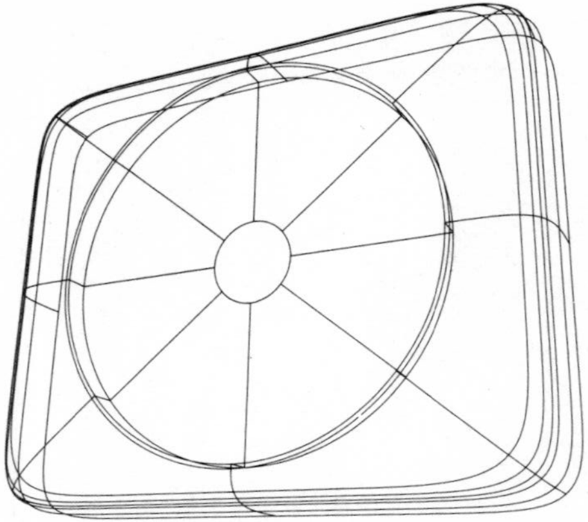

Figure 12

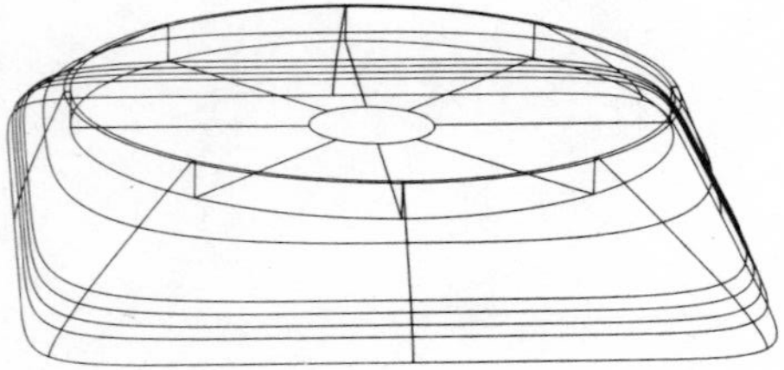

Figure 13

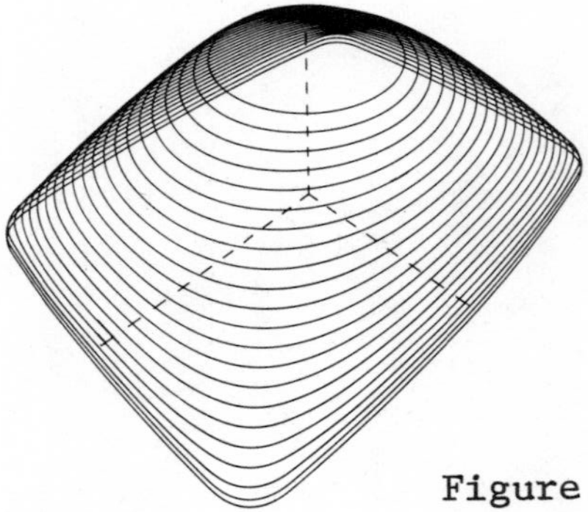

Figure 14

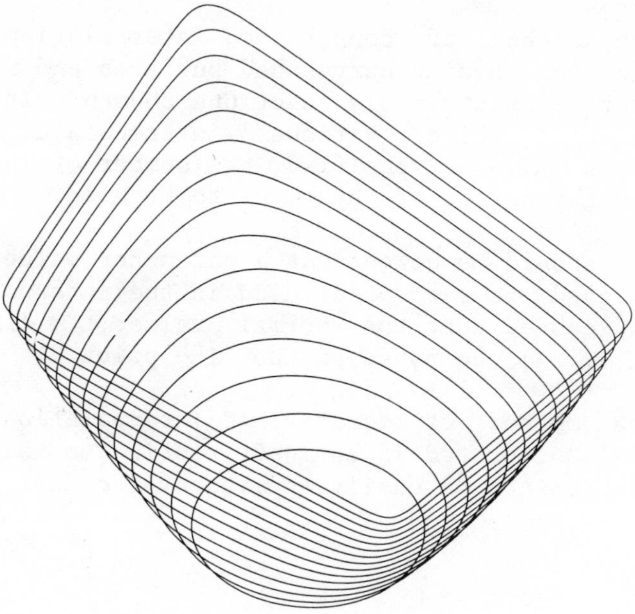

Figure 15

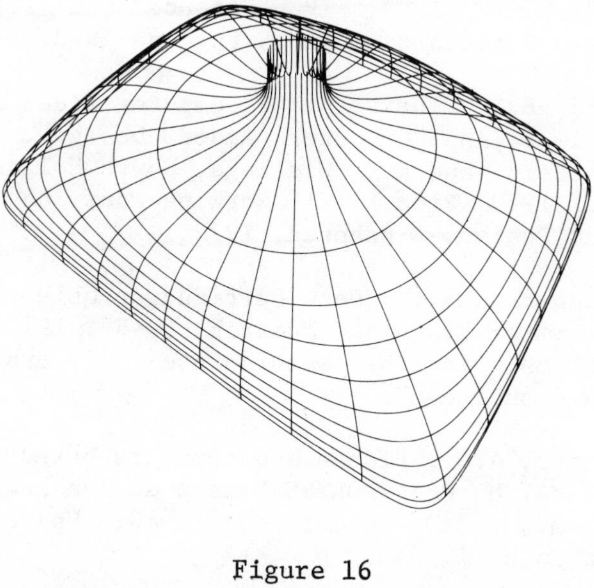

Figure 16

6. Conclusion

The method of constrained interpolation is applicable for Bézier curves and surfaces and is valid irrespective of the basis functions chosen. It allows interpolation while various intermediate or end conditions may be specified, the number of which depends on the degree of the curve to be used.

It should be noted that a parameter value has to be assigned to each point used in the interpolation. It is suggested that the "normal" value $t = i/n$ (with $i = 0,1,\dots n$) be taken to the ith point.

The method of constrained interpolation may be simply incorporated in an input routine so that curve manipulation can be easily applied by the designer.

References

1. Bézier, P.E., "NC in automobile design and manufacture of curved surfaces", pp. 44-48 of Proc. Conf. on "Curved Surfaces in Engineering", 15th - 17th March 1972, IPC Science and Technology Press, Guildford, Surrey, England 1972.

2. Gott, B., "The scope of computer aided design", p. 1-25 in "Computer Aided Design", eds. J. Vlietstra and R.F. Wielinga, North Holland Publ. Co., 1973 Proc. IFIP Working Conf. on Computer Aided Design, Eindhoven, 1972.

3. Schönherr, S., "Das Fertigungsproblem beliebig gekrümmter Flächen", Numerik, 53-57, 1973 (Engl.: Problems in the manufacture of arbitrarily curved surfaces).

4. Flutter, A.G., "Ideas and comments based on using MULTIPATCH and POLYSURF as a design and cutting system", CAD Group Doc. 40, University of Cambridge, 1970.

5. Forrest, A.R., "Current developments in the design and production of 3D curved objects: Computational Geometry: Proc. Roy. Soc. London A. 321 187-195 (1971).

6. Armit, A.P., "Interactive 3D shape design: MULTIPATCH and MULTIOBJECT" in Proc. Int. Conf. on "Curved Surfaces in Engineering" (see Ref. 1).

7. Shu, H., Hori, S., Mann, W.R. and Little, R.N., "The synthesis of sculpture surfaces" pp. 358-375 of "Numerical Control Programming Languages", ed. Lesile, W.H.P., North Holland Publ. Co., Amsterdam - London, 1970.

8. Anonymous, "Integrated System now exists: GM mechanizes body surface development", Production pp. 132-140, June 1969.

9. Pascoe, G., "NC at Ford Motor Co", Soc. for Automotive Engineers, SAE - 6600151, 19th Jan., 1966.

10. Einar, H. and Skappel, E., "FORMELA: a general design and production data system for sculptured products", Computer Aided Design, 5, p. 68-76 (1973).

11. Sabin, M.A., "An existing system in the aircraft industry: the BAC Numerical Master Geometry System", Proc. Roy. Soc. London A 321, 197-205, 1971.

12. Walter, H., "Computer aided design in the aircraft industry", p. 355-378 in "Computer Aided Design" (see Ref. 2.).

13. Mehlum, E. and Sörenson, P.F., "Example of an existing system in the shipbuilding industry: the AUTOKON System", Proc. Roy. Soc. London, A 321, 219-233 (1971).

14. Ahlberg, J.H., Nielson, E.N. and Walsh, J.L., "The theory of splines and their applications", Academic Press, N.Y., 1967.

15. Nutbourne, A.W., "A cubic spline package part 2- the mathematics", Comp. Aid. Design 5,7-13 (1973)

16. Adams, J.A., "Cubic spline curve fitting with controlled end conditions", Comp. Aid. Design 6, 1-9 (1974).

17. Reinsch, C.H., "Smoothing by spline functions", Numerical Math. 10, 177-183, 1967.

18. Forrest, A.R., "Interactive interpolation and approximation by Bézier polynomials", Comp. J. 15, 71-79 (1971).

19. Coons, S.A., "Surfaces for computer aided design of space forms", M.I.T. Mac-TR-41, 1967.

20. Bézier, P.E., "Numerical Control, Mathematics and Applications", Wiley & Sons, London, 1972.

21. Forrest, A.R., "Curves and surfaces for computer aided design", Ph.D. thesis, Cambridge University England, 1968.

22. Gordon, W.J., "Blending function methods of bivariate and multivariate interpolation and approximation", SIAM J. Numer. Anal. 8, 158-177 (1971).

23. Forrest, A.R., "On Coons' and other methods for the representation of curved surfaces", Comp. Graphics and Image Proc. 1, 341-359 (1972).

24. Wielinga, R.F., the 'global' projection allows for an unclipped plot with an angle of view of up to 360° (to be published).

25. Zabransky, F.E., is thanked for his permission to show Figs. 11-13.

26. Schoenaker, G.C.M., "Stereo drawings made with a digital computer", Philips Techn. Review 29, 102-109 (1968).

NONLINEAR SPLINES

Even Mehlum
Central Institute for Industrial Research
Oslo, Norway

Excuses and Thanks

A lot of significant work in the field of nonlinear splines is probably not mentioned in this paper. I have not followed this research very closely during the last few years because most of my work has been in a quite different field. The present ongoing research on nonlinear splines is more of a hobby than of serious work. I hope the authors in question will excuse not being mentioned.

I am also very grateful to the organizers of the present conference for pressing me to write this paper before it was definitely too late.

1. Introduction

A spline function (or a spline curve) is a piecewise analytical function. The different pieces are chained together with continuity requirements imposed on the first few derivatives at the joints. The pieces are basic curve shapes with adjustable parameters. The parameters are adjusted so that the chained curve matches the data and continuity requirements. A simple example is the cubic spline with four adjustable parameters in the basic element.

In linear splines it is customary that the basic element satisfies a certain variational criterion for smoothness to avoid extra bumps between the data points.

This paper describes a theory of nonlinear splines arising from a variational criterion of the type

$$\int (\text{curvature})^2 ds = \text{"as little as possible"}.$$

The variational criterion is subject to certain constraints such as point-wise interpolation. The general theory (Section 2) will treat space curves. Sections 3,4 and 5 treat planar curves as a special case of the general theory. In Section 6 various possibilities for design of space curve algorithms from the general theory are discussed.

For space curves, two types of curvature come into consideration. First we have the "normal" curvature

$$\mathcal{H} = |\vec{r}''(s)|$$

with r being the position vector.

Secondly, we have the "total" curvature

$$\sqrt{\mathcal{H}^2 + \tau^2}$$

with τ being the torsion.

In this paper we will use the normal curvature.

However, with methods similar to those of Section 2, the total curvature also gives interesting results.

The variational problem is solved without the often assumed "small deflection" approximation which is the origin of the cubic spline. This has two advantages:

A The results are invariant with respect to similarity transformations.

B The resulting curve can be represented in parametric form with the arc length as parameter. For that parameter only will $|\vec{r}''|$ measure curvature exactly.

Among the important related considerations not treated in this paper are:

I Smoothing of Data

Smoothing of data by cubic splines is, however, treated in ref. (7) for the "Least squares" and "Absolute value" norms.
The methods described in that reference have subsequently been refined and extended to cover nonlinear splines as well.

II Connection to Coon's patches

The restrictions imposed on the patch boundaries in the basic theory of Steven Coons and his followers are very mild. Thus the curves arising in the present paper may serve as patch boundaries for such blended surfacing methods. In fact, they are perhaps even better than the ones commonly used because the parameter can be proportional to the arc length.
We have actually studied the hook-up with the sculptured surface part of APT and the necessary modifications are very small indeed.

The theory and algorithms presented in this paper form some of the basis for the AUTOKON systems for computer aided design in the shipbuilding, aircraft and automobile industries which have been under constant development since 1958-59. This work has partly been done in parallel with hardware developments in N/C (KINGMATIC, flame-cutting, milling).

Before we dive into the analytical mess of Section 2 we collect the back-up of two authorities:

> When Newton had invented the calculus of variation he wrote:
>
> "This technique should be of value in the design of ships."

G.K. Chesterton writes in one of his poems:

> "Those bend with grace who resist the bending."

Formulating a variational criterion is what Chesterton would have done had he been a mathematician.

2. The Intrinsic Equations

To clear the stage, we start with a definition of the basic quantities to be used. To prevent excessive writing we will stick to vector notation as much as possible. First we have the position vector

> $\vec{r}(s)$ to the point (x,y,z) on the curve, where s measures the arc length.

$$\vec{t}(s) = \vec{r}\,'(s) = \frac{d\vec{r}(s)}{ds} \qquad 2.1$$

is the unit tangent vector so that

$$|\vec{t}|^2 = \vec{t}^{\,2} = t^2 \equiv 1 \qquad 2.2$$

the curvature $\mathcal{H}$ is defined by

$$\mathcal{H} = |\vec{t}\,'| = |\vec{r}\,''| \qquad 2.3$$

The torsion τ is

$$\tau = \frac{1}{\mathcal{H}^2}\,\vec{t}(\vec{t}\,' \times \vec{t}\,'') \qquad 2.4$$

The so-called "moving trihedron" has the three unit base vectors $\vec{t},\vec{n},\vec{b}$ where $\vec{n}$ and $\vec{b}$ are the unit normal and the unit binormal vectors, respectively.

$\vec{n}$ is defined by

$$\vec{n} = \frac{1}{\mathcal{H}}\vec{t}\,' \qquad 2.5$$

$\vec{b}$ is defined by

$$\vec{b} = \vec{t} \times \vec{n} \qquad 2.6$$

$\vec{t},\vec{n}$ and $\vec{b}$ are connected through the Serret-Frenet formulae:

$$\vec{t}\,' = \mathcal{H}\vec{n} \qquad 2.7$$

$$\vec{n}\,' = -\mathcal{H}\vec{t} + \tau\vec{b} \qquad 2.8$$

$$\vec{b}\,' = -\tau\vec{n} \qquad 2.9$$

The purpose of this section is to show how the intrinsic equations, i.e., $\mathcal{H}(s)$ and $\tau(s)$, can be deduced from the variational criterion for smoothness. We will also outline the analytical process in deriving the position vector from the intrinsic equations; or, in other words, to find the correct part of a geometrical shape and give it the proper position in the external world represented by points and other boundary conditions.

The smoothness criterion is

$$\int_0^L \mathcal{H}^2 ds = \int_0^L \vec{t}\,'^2 ds = \text{"as small as possible".}$$

$\vec{t}$ is constrained by the scalar equation 2.2 and the vector equation 2.1. Thus, taking the constraints into account, we arrive at the variational problem:

$$\delta \int_0^L \{\vec{t}'^2 + \lambda(s)(\vec{t}^2-1) + 2\vec{\psi}(s)(\vec{r}'-\vec{t})\} \, ds = 0 \qquad 2.10$$

It is seen that 2.10 includes a form of "spline in tension" since various values of the total arc-length L represent various degrees of tension.

The functions $\lambda(s)$ and $2\vec{\psi}(s)$ are Lagrange multipliers to be determined from the constraint equations.

Two differentiations of 2.2 and the introduction of 2.3 give

$$\vec{t}\vec{t}' = 0 \qquad\qquad 2.11$$

$$\vec{t}'^2 = \mathcal{H}^2 = -\vec{t}\vec{t}'' \qquad\qquad 2.12$$

In 2.10 the two vector functions $\vec{r}$ and $\vec{t}$ are to be varied. The Euler equations corresponding to 2.10 will therefore appear as two vector equations:

$$-\vec{t}'' + \lambda\vec{t} = \vec{\psi} \qquad\qquad 2.13$$

$$\vec{\psi}' = 0 \qquad\qquad 2.14$$

From 2.14 we immediately get the result

$$\vec{\psi} = \text{constant.} \qquad\qquad 2.15$$

We now set out to manipulate 2.13 to achieve a set of formulae which will be useful later.

Take the scalar product of 2.13 and $\vec{t}$:
$$-\vec{t}\vec{t}'' + \lambda\vec{t}^2 = \vec{\psi}\vec{t}.$$
Introducing 2.7 and 2.2 we get:
$$\mathcal{H}^2 + \lambda = \vec{\psi}\vec{t}. \qquad\qquad 2.16$$

The scalar product of 2.13 and $\vec{t}'$ is:

$$-\vec{t}'\vec{t}'' + \lambda\vec{t}'\vec{t} = \vec{\psi}\vec{t}'$$

Now using 2.11 and 2.2 we arrive at

$$-\tfrac{1}{2}\,\frac{d\vec{t}'^2}{ds} = \frac{d}{ds}\,(\vec{\Psi}\vec{t})$$

and

$$\tfrac{1}{2}\mathcal{H}^2 = D - \vec{\psi}\vec{t} \qquad 2.17$$

with D as integration constant.

Eliminate $\vec{\psi}\vec{t}$ between 2.16 and 2.17 to get:

$$\frac{3}{2}\mathcal{H}^2 + \lambda = D. \qquad 2.18$$

The vector product of 2.13 and $\vec{t}$ is:

$$\vec{t} \times \vec{t}'' = \vec{\psi} \times \vec{t}; \qquad 2.19$$

and
$$\vec{t} \times \vec{t}'' = \frac{d}{ds}\,(\vec{t} \times \vec{t}').$$

Bearing 2.1 in mind we can thus integrate to get

$$\vec{t} \times \vec{t}' = \vec{\psi} \times \vec{r} - \vec{E} \qquad 2.20$$

$\vec{E}$ - integration constant.

The scalar product of 2.19 and $\vec{t}'$ is:

$$\vec{t}'\,(\vec{t} \times \vec{t}'') = \vec{t}'\,(\vec{\psi} \times \vec{t}),$$

i.e.,

$$\vec{t}\,(\vec{t}' \times \vec{t}'') = -\,\vec{\psi}(\vec{t} \times \vec{t}').$$

Equation 2.4 is introduced on the left side and 2.20 on the right to obtain:

$$\mathcal{H}^2\tau = -\vec{\psi}(\vec{\psi} \times \vec{r}) + \vec{\psi}\vec{E},$$

i.e.,

$$\mathcal{H}^2\tau = C \qquad\qquad 2.21$$

where we have introduced the scalar constant C to denote the scalar product of the two constants $\vec{\psi}$ and $\vec{E}$.

   Relation 2.21 is an important result, which is very helpful in the design of practical algorithms.

   Qualitatively the formula says that the curve shall not have both large curvature and large torsion in the same region. If the curve is almost straight, large torsion does not hurt the esthetics of the curve and vice versa.

If $C = 0$ the curve is planar.

   Introducing 2.7 and 2.6 in 2.20 we get:

$$\mathcal{H}\vec{b} = \vec{\psi} \times \vec{r} - \vec{E} \qquad\qquad 2.22$$

The scalar product with $\vec{b}$ ($\vec{b}$ is a unit vector)

$$\mathcal{H} = (\vec{b} \times \vec{\psi}) \cdot \vec{r} - \vec{E}\vec{b}. \qquad\qquad 2.23$$

Equation 2.23 is also most helpful in the design of algorithms.

   For a plane curve $\tau = 0$ and hence from 2.9 $\vec{b}$ = constant. In that case 2.23 says that the curvature varies linearly along some fixed direction in space.

Finally, in our search for the intrinsic equations let us take the scalar product of $\vec{\psi}$ and 2.20:

$$\vec{\psi}\,(\vec{t} \times \vec{t}\,') = -\vec{\psi}\vec{E} = -C.$$

Squaring this we get:

$$\vec{\psi}^2\vec{t}^2\vec{t}\,'^2 - \vec{\psi}^2\,(\vec{t}\vec{t}\,')^2 - \vec{t}^2\,(\vec{\psi}\vec{t}\,')^2 - \vec{t}\,'^2\,(\vec{\psi}\vec{t})^2 +$$

$$2\,(\vec{\psi}\vec{t})(\vec{t}\vec{t}\,')(\vec{\psi}\vec{t}\,') = C^2.$$

Introducing 2.2, 2.3, 2.11 and 2.17 above:

$$\vec{\psi}^2\mathcal{H}^2 - (\mathcal{H}\mathcal{H}')^2 - \mathcal{H}^2\,(\tfrac{1}{2}\mathcal{H}^2 - D)^2 = C^2$$

i.e.,

$$[(\mathcal{H}^2)']^2 + \mathcal{H}^2\,[(\mathcal{H}^2 - 2D)^2 - 4\vec{\psi}^2] + 4\,C^2 = 0 \qquad 2.24$$

2.24 is a differential equation defining $\mathcal{H}^2$ as a function of arc length. We introduce the new variable η to get 2.24 into a standard form:

$$\mathcal{H}^2 = \frac{4D}{3} - 4\eta \qquad 2.25$$

and get:

$$\eta'^2 = 4\eta^3 - g_2\eta - g_3 \qquad 2.26$$

with

$$g_2 = \frac{D^2}{3} + \vec{\psi}^2 \qquad 2.27$$

$$g_3 = \frac{D^3}{27} - \frac{D\vec{\psi}^2}{3} + \frac{C^2}{4} \qquad 2.28$$

2.26 is the standard differential equation defining the elliptic "$\wp$-function" of Weierstrass, for which there exists an extensive theory. (See ref. [1] and ref. [2].)

$$\eta = \wp(s+a;\ g_2,\ g_3)$$

a - integration constant, i.e.,

$$\mathcal{H}^2 = \frac{4D}{3} - 4\wp(s+a;\ g_2,\ g_3) \qquad 2.29$$

2.29 together with 2.21 define the intrinsic equations for the curve fulfilling our smoothness criterion.

Note 1

It is seen that 2.24 also has (a) singular solution(s), namely constant(s) arising from the solution of a cubic equation.

The standard procedure to get points on the curve ($\vec{r}(s)$) from the intrinsic equations is to plug the expressions for $\mathcal{H}$ and τ into the Serret-Frenet formulae (2.7,2.8,2.9) and solve the resulting set of simultaneous differential equations to get $\vec{t},\vec{n},\vec{b}$. (See for instance ref. [3] and [4].)

Having got $\vec{t}$ and 2.1, one further quadrature gives the position vector $\vec{r}(s)$.

However, in our case there exists a simpler but equivalent way to this goal which will be outlined in the sequel.

From 2.18 and 2.29 we get:

$$\lambda = -D + 6\wp(s+a;\ g_2,g_3) \qquad 2.30$$

Taking the vector product of 2.13 and $\vec{\psi}$

$$(\vec{\psi} \times \vec{t})'' - \lambda(\vec{\psi} \times \vec{t}) = 0.$$

Defining $\vec{\psi} \times \vec{t} = \vec{A}(s)$ and introducing 2.30 we obtain

$$\vec{A}'' + [D - 6\wp(s+a;\ g_2,g_3)]\ \vec{A} = 0 \qquad 2.31$$

Each component of $\vec{A}$ thus satisfies the generic differential equation:

$$\Lambda''(t) = [q\wp(t;\ g_2,g_3) - D]\ \Lambda(t) \qquad 2.32$$

The new variable t is defined by $t = s + a$.

2.32 is another of the "classical" differential equations:

"Lamé's equation".

(See ref. [1] and ref. [2].)

Under certain conditions on D and q this equation defines the Lamé functions. In our case D does not in general fulfil any special conditions, but we are lucky with q since our q ($q = 6$) is of the form

$$q = n(n + 1)$$

In the classical literature equation 2.32 has been studied in detail for these values of q. The solution of 2.32 in terms of well known (but far from elementary) functions is therefore not treated here. Having got the general solution of 2.32 and thus of 2.31 we are in the following position.

We know the vector product $\vec{\psi} \times \vec{t}$

$$\vec{\psi} \times \vec{t} = \vec{A}. \tag{2.33}$$

We also know the scalar product (2.16):

$$\vec{\psi}\vec{t} = \mathcal{H}^2 + \lambda \tag{2.34}$$

with $\mathcal{H}^2$ given in 2.29 and λ in 2.30.

2.33 and 2.34 imply:

$$\vec{t} = \frac{\mathcal{H}^2 + \lambda}{\vec{\psi}^2}\vec{\psi} - \frac{\vec{\psi} \times \vec{A}}{\vec{\psi}^2}. \tag{2.35}$$

One further quadrature now gives $\vec{r}(s)$. $\vec{n}$ and $\vec{b}$ follow from 2.5 and 2.6.

Before we conclude this section a few words of warning should be given: During the process we have collected several integration constants, some appearing as scalars, some as components of vectors. We have also established several functions as components of vectors. There exist several implicit connections between these various quantities. We will give one example:

From 2.33 it is obvious that $\vec{A}$ is perpendicular to $\vec{\psi}$. This establishes relations between the constants arising from the solution of 2.31. A further discussion of this extremely tedious subject is dropped.

In conclusion of this section we ask the question: Why do we have to go through this analytical mess when we are going to use a digital computer anyway? The answer is of course that a thorough understanding of the exact behaviour of periodicity, singularities, asymptotic expansions, multivaluedness, etc., is of great value in the design of practical algorithms.

One example is the Weierstrass function occurring in the deductions. This function is periodic, with possible utility for closed curves. Its series expansion contains a term $\frac{1}{t^2}$, which means that the curve might get a kink, of some sort. The following question then arises: Can the data be arranged in such a way that the various constants become such that t can be zero?

The art of approximation consists in knowing as much as possible about the item which shall be approximated.

3. The Plane Curve

In the comments to 2.21 we stated that if the constant C is zero, the curve is in a plane.

$$\tau = 0$$

(We have disregarded the trivial case $\mathcal{H} = 0$, straight line.)

Section 2 gave us the intrinsic equations for an "optimum" curve type in the sense of our variational criterion. The goal of Section 3,4 and 5 is to show how one can make algorithms for curve fitting based on this information in the special case C = 0 and $\tau = 0$. This consists in selecting the proper pieces of this optimum curve, get the constants right, rotate the pieces, etc. It will be done in such a way that the resulting "chained" (splined) curve:

A Interpolates the given points.

B The slope is continuous.

C The curvature is continuous.

This work is quite analogous to the method in linearized (small deflection) splines, where the basic curve element is considerably simpler.

Two examples of such algorithms will be sketched. Many more can be devised. In Section 4 we take the results of Section 2 as they are. The only approximations will be of the "numerical analysis" type. In the limit this algorithm converges to the exact formulae of Section 2.

In Section 5 we make a "mathematical approximation" in addition to the numerical, which makes the resulting curves of Section 5 slightly different from those of Section 4. The difference is, however, not visible in practical applications.

Both algorithms (The KURGLA algorithms) have been used in the AUTOKON systems for several years.

4. Kurgla I

We start from 2.23:

$$\mathcal{H} = (\vec{b} \times \vec{\psi})\vec{r} - \vec{E}\vec{b} \qquad 4.1$$

In the comments after 2.23 we stated that the curvature varies linearly along some fixed direction in 3-space. We now have to be more specific.

First, we remember that the osculation plane is the plane through the tangent and the normal. When the curve is planar, the osculation plane is identical to the curve plane. $\vec{b}$ in 4.1 is now a constant <u>perpendicular</u> to the curve plane.

Secondly we now get the Serret-Frenet formulae 2.7 and 2.8 in the following form:

$$\vec{t}' = \mathcal{H}\,\vec{n} \qquad 4.2$$

$$\vec{n}' = -\mathcal{H}\vec{t} \qquad 4.3$$

Differentiation of 4.2 gives:

$$\vec{t}'' = \mathcal{H}'\vec{n} + \mathcal{H}\vec{n}', \qquad 4.4$$

i.e.,

$$\vec{t}'' = \mathcal{H}'\vec{n} - \mathcal{H}^2\vec{t}. \qquad 4.5$$

Both $\vec{t}$ and $\vec{t}''$ are therefore in the curve plane.

2.13 now shows that $\vec{\psi}$ is also in the curve plane.

<u>The constant vector $\vec{b} \times \vec{\psi}$ in 4.1 is therefore in the curve plane as well, so that the direction of linear curvature is in the curve plane.</u>

Without loss of generality we can now rewrite 4.1 as:

$$\mathcal{H} = \alpha x + \beta y + \gamma \qquad 4.6$$

We have introduced the coordinates x,y in the curve plane. We have also renamed the constants involved.

4.6 hides a nonlinear, second order, differential equation in the "external" coordinates x,y. The integration of this equation leads to a linear combination of elliptic integrals of the first and second kinds. This process is straightforward, and will not be treated here. We will instead introduce a numerical approximation in 4.6.

But first let us count constants and match that count with the number of conditions.

Let us number the datapoints: 1 ,..., m

We then have m-1 intervals into which to fit curves that are solutions of 4.6.

Two integrations of 4.6 give us 5 constants in each interval. We thus have 5(m-1) constants at our disposal.

The conditions are the following:

The curve segment in each interval has to interpolate the datapoints at each end of the interval. This gives rise to 2(m-1) equations.

Furthermore we require continuity of slope and curvature across all datapoints except for the two limiting ones.

This gives rise to 2(m-2) equations.

At the two end points we can specify the slopes as boundary conditions. We can instead specify the curvature equal to zero there, or specify that the curvature shall be constant in the two limiting intervals. In either case we get 2 extra conditions from the boundary points.

We have thus established

$$2(m-1) + 2(m-2) + 2 = 4(m-1)$$

equations.

Question:

Where are the missing m-1 equations hidden?

Answer:

They are hidden in the unspecified arc length L occurring as integration limit in 2.10. Since there are m-1 segments, there are m-1 unspecified L's.

The comment after 2.10 thus indicates the following question:

How much "tension" shall the spline be given in each interval?

There are several sensible answers. One is to use the classical theory for variational problems with free boundaries, where the L's will be fixed through "transversality" conditions.

Another is to use the extra freedom to get higher order continuity across the datapoints.

The author will recommend a third answer, arising from a lot of practical experience with such algorithms.

Fix each L indirectly through an extra equation between α and β in 4.6.

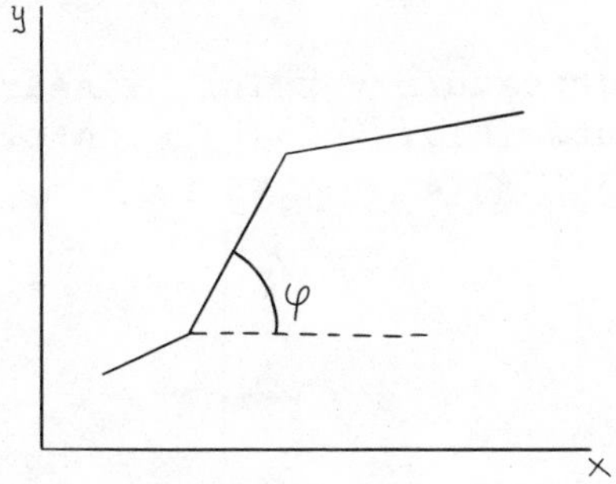

Figure 4.1

With φ being the slope angle of the chord between two consecutive datapoints let the corresponding α and β be connected through:

$$\frac{\beta}{\alpha} = \tan \varphi \qquad 4.7$$

4.7 means that the direction of linear curvature in each interval is along the chord in that interval.

Note 1

We have only matched constants to conditions for and open curve in the main text. They match for a closed curve as well.

Note 2

The problem of specifying the tension, is related to the problem of extra loops changing the topology raised in ref. [9]. The way the tension is selected in the present paper, removes the whole difficulty.

In ref. [7] there is found more detailed information on the algorithm with an iteration scheme to determine the various constants from given data. The only difference from that reference is relation 4.7.

We therefore drop a discussion of the details in the algorithm. We will just outline the type of numerical approximation used.

With the curvature varying linearly, we have the following picture (Fig. 4.2) between two datapoints:

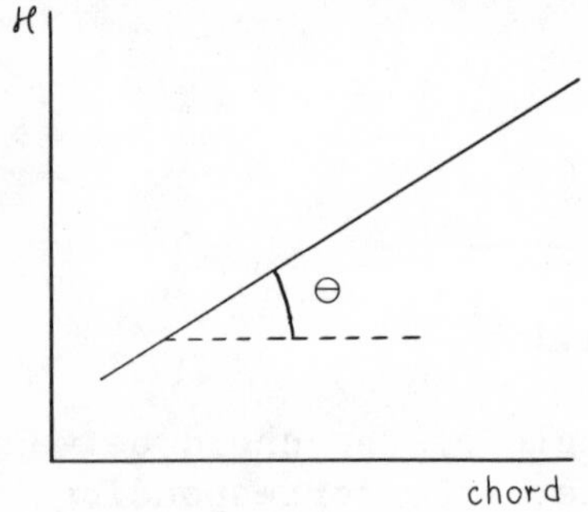

Figure 4.2

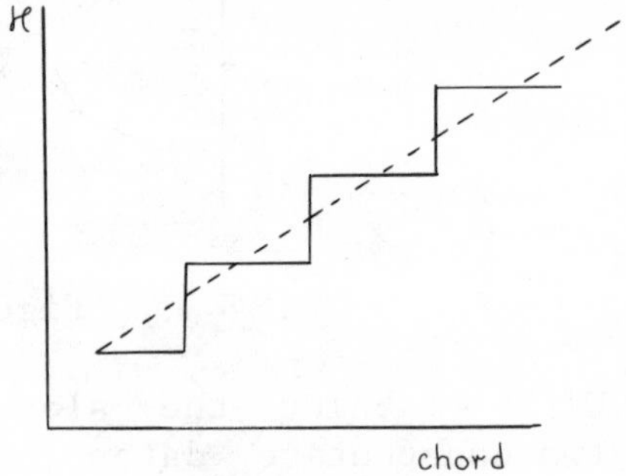

Figure 4.3

This linear curvature is approximated with a staircase (Fig. 4.3). The staircase approximation means that we approximate the curve with a sequence of circular arcs.

There are sufficiently many constants to achieve continuity of slope. The discontinuity in curvature is given from the height of the stairs in Fig. 4.3. The density of stairs must therefore be selected from the angle θ in Fig. 4.2.

In the limit, increasing number of stairs, this approximation will converge to an exact solution of our variational problem.

The present author, working in a practical environment with telephones, has never come around to actually prove this, but he sincerely hopes that somebody else will manage.

5. Kurgla II

We start from the differential equation 2.24 defining $\mathcal{H}$ as a function of arc length. With $C = 0$, $\mathcal{H} \neq 0$ this appears as:

$$\mathcal{H}'^2 + (\tfrac{1}{2}\mathcal{H}^2 - D)^2 = \vec{\psi}^2 \qquad 5.1$$

Making the "mathematical" approximation (or rather modification)

$$\tfrac{1}{2}\mathcal{H}^2 << |D|$$

we get:

$$\mathcal{H}'^2 = \vec{\psi}^2 - D^2 \qquad 5.2$$

5.2 clearly has the solution

$$\mathcal{H} = \alpha s + \beta \qquad 5.3$$

with $\alpha^2 = \vec{\psi}^2 - D^2$, β - integration constant.

We have thus obtained an intrinsic equation saying that the curvature shall vary linearly with the arc length. This is a sensible axiomatic approach to nonlinear splines in its own right, but here it appears as an approximation to the solution of a variational problem.

Note 1

Several other "mathematical" approximations are possible. One is to assume that the curvature is almost constant in 5.1 i.e.

$$\mathcal{H} = \text{constant} + \varepsilon(s)$$

where ε is small.

Introducing this $\mathcal{H}$ and skipping powers of ε higher than the second, 5.1 becomes integrable by elementary methods.

If we skip all powers of ε in the second term in 5.1, we arrive at:

$$\epsilon'^2 = \vec{\psi}^2 \quad (D - \tfrac{1}{2}\,\text{constant}^{\,2})$$

which clearly has the same effect as 5.3. 5.3 is therefore valid under the relaxed condition

$\mathcal{H} \approx$ constant.

Note 2

5.1 include singular solutions

$$\mathcal{H}^2 = \text{constant}$$

They are: $\mathcal{H}^2 = 2(D \pm |\vec{\psi}|)$

$\mathcal{H}$ = constant is included in 5.3

$(\alpha = 0)$.

This approximation has the side effect of removing the freedom we observed in section 4 in selecting the total arc length. This is so because the two constants $\vec{\psi}^2$ and D^2 coalesce into one new constant α^2.

The spiral curve resulting from the intrinsic equation 5.3 is the "CORNU" - spiral.

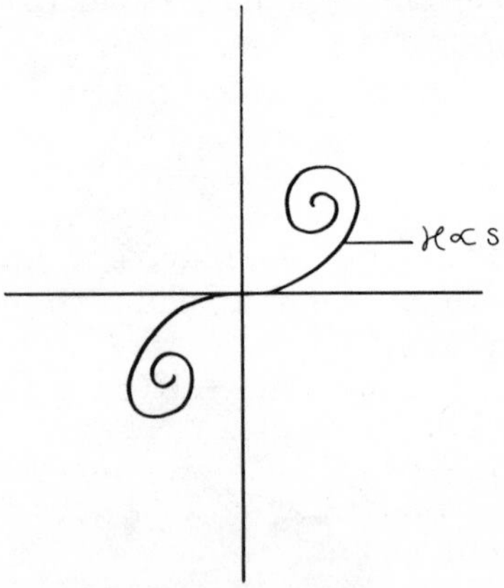

Figure 5.1

The task of the KURGLA II algorithm is to select the proper parts of the Cornu spiral, scale them and rotate them to match the requirements A,B,C and the boundary conditions of section 4. There are just the necessary constants available to perform this task.

One way to design such an algorithm is to perform the "staircase" approximation directly on 5.3 in analogy with section 4 and proceed as directed there:

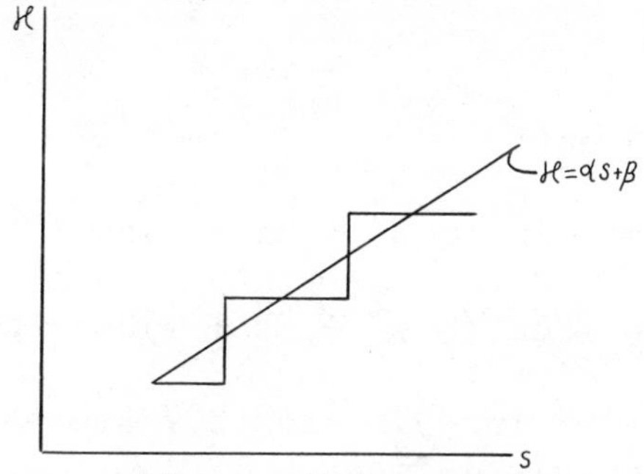

Figure 5.2

However, we have found it much cheaper on the computer to base the algorithm on known properties of the Fresnel integrals. The series and asymptotic expansion of these integrals have proved very efficient. The staircase approximation comes as a last step in the process when all constants are determined.

We finish the section by showing how the Fresnel integrals make their entrance.

Denoting the slope angle of the curve by φ, 5.3 appear as:

$$\frac{d\varphi}{ds} = \alpha s + \beta \qquad 5.4$$

Integration gives: $\varphi = \frac{1}{2}\alpha s^2 + \beta s + \gamma$,

γ - integration constant 5.5

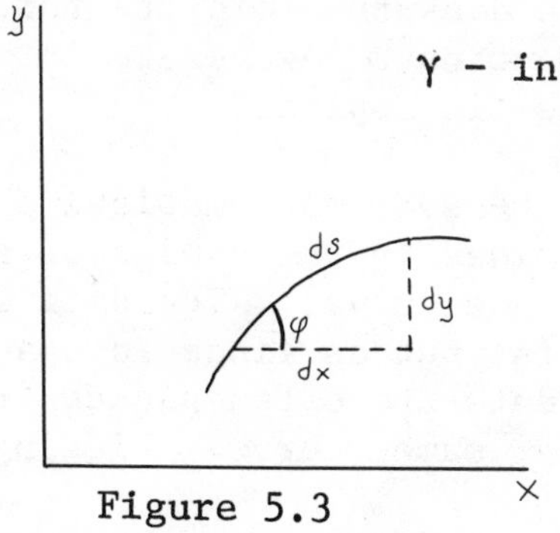

Figure 5.3

Now

$$\frac{dy}{ds} = \sin\varphi$$

$$\frac{dx}{ds} = \cos\varphi$$

We therefore get:

$$y = \int \sin(\tfrac{1}{2}\alpha s^2 + \beta s + \gamma)ds + \text{constant} \qquad 5.6$$

$$x = \int \cos(\tfrac{1}{2}\alpha s^2 + \beta s + \gamma)ds + \text{constant} \qquad 5.7$$

The integrals in 5.6 and 5.7 are easily reduced to Fresnel integrals defined by:

$$S(s) = \sqrt{\frac{2}{\pi}\int_0^s \sin t^2 dt} \qquad 5.8$$

$$C(s) = \sqrt{\frac{2}{\pi}\int_0^s \cos t^2 dt} \qquad 5.9$$

6. Space Curves

The material presented in this section must be regarded with due scepticism. The programming that has been performed around it has been done for fun and for test purposes only.

One very basic question remains to be answered:

Under which conditions does the complete three-dimensional solution of section 2 degenerate into a plane curve when the data lies in a plane?

In addition to the increased mathematical difficulties, another problem arises in the design of any practical algorithm for space curves: The data may not be presented as points, but as lines in space. This is so because the data are often picked from various projections of the same curve. Picking a point in one projection means to establish a data line perpendicular to that projection.

We now turn to a brief discussion of possible algorithms arising from the exact theory in Section 2. The discussion is based on currently ongoing research at our Institute.

First we observe that it is evidently possible to base an algorithm directly on that theory with numerical procedures for solving differential equations, evaluating Weierstrass functions, etc. This "Brute Force" approach will give erratic computing times.

We therefore seek numerical and mathematical approximations in analogy with those in Sections 4 and 5 for plane curves.

The numerical approximations will be extensions of the "staircase approximation" described earlier, converging in the limit to the exact solution of the mathematical problem. This consists in approximating the continuous intrinsic equations for the basic curve shape with staircase functions to achieve a more tractable representation of the intrinsic equations.

The mathematical approximation is analogous to that described in Section 5. It consists in actually modifying the exact mathematical formulation of the intrinsic equations before introducing the numerical approximation.

In space the requirements

A,B, and C of Section 3 have to be extended.

They now read:

A The curve shall interpolate the given data lines.

B $\vec{r}'$ shall be continuous at the joints.

C $\vec{r}''$ shall be continuous.

To achieve this goal we have a set of integration constants, appearing as a set of parameters in the description of the basic element, to adjust.

The match of constants to requirements is analogous to that described in Sections 4 and 5, when due account of the warnings in Section 2 is taken.

The author has not yet found a 3-dimensional extension to the exact planar relation 4.6.

6.1 Mathematical Approximation in Space

This approximation is the three dimensional analogue of the one done in Section 5 which gave the Cornu spiral as basic element. Again we start from the differential equation 2.24.

With $C \neq 0$, $\frac{1}{2}\mathcal{H}^2 \ll D$ this appears as

$$[(\mathcal{H}^2)'] + 4\mathcal{H}^2 (D^2 - \vec{\psi}^2) + 4C^2 = 0 \qquad 6.1.1$$

Again the two constants D^2 and $\vec{\psi}^2$ coalesce into one

$$\alpha^2 = \vec{\psi}^2 - D^2 \qquad 6.1.2$$

The solution of 6.1.1 is

$$\mathcal{H}^2 = \alpha^2(s-\sigma)^2 + \frac{C^2}{\alpha^2} \qquad 6.1.3$$

σ - integration constant

(It is observed that 6.1.3 degenerates into 5.3 when $C = 0$.)

6.1.3 together with 2.21

$$\mathcal{H}^2\tau = C \qquad 6.1.4$$

represent a simplified set of intrinsic equations.

It is of interest to look more detailed into the meaning of 6.1.3 as opposed to the corresponding equation 5.3 for the plane curve.

6.1.3 is clearly the equation of a hyberbola:

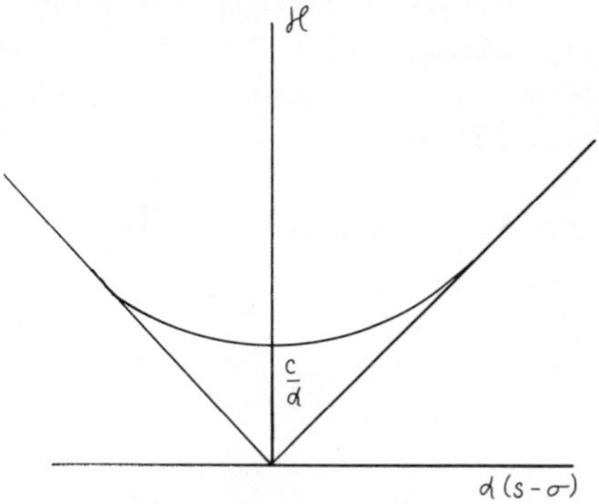

Figure 6.1.3

When C = 0 the hyperbola degenerates into its asymptotes which represent the linear behaviour encounter in Section 5.

Note

The asymptotes in Figure 6.1.1 can be combined in the equation:

$$\lim_{c \to 0} \mathcal{H} = |\alpha(s-\sigma)|$$

$\mathcal{H}$ is always positive for a space curve. The "absolute value" is missing in the corresponding equation 5.3 for the planar curve allowing $\mathcal{H}$ to be negative. This is only an apparent contradiction. For a plane curve an inflection is located at one point where the curvature is zero. For a space curve an inflection is gradual. It is taken care of by the torsion which is rotating the osculation plane. We might have treated a planar curve correspondingly saying that the rotation of the osculation plane of 180 degrees were located at the inflection point, with the curvature always being positive. For a planar curve the effect of allowing the curvature to be negative <u>without</u> rotating the osculation plane is the same.

From 6.1.3 and 6.1.4 we can branch out in two directions. One is to make the staircase approximations (Section 6.2) directly in these two equations, and start adjusting constants on this basis to meet the requirements A,B and C. This is clearly possible and leads to the goal.

The other is to look more deeply into the mathematics to find the proper generalizations to the Fresnel integrals and the Cornu spiral encountered in Section 5. Let us see what we get into, attempting to proceed in this direction.

We plug the intrinsic equations 6.1.3 and 6.1.4 into the Serret-Frenet formulae 2.7, 2.8 and 2.9 and eliminate $\vec{n}$ and $\vec{b}$.

We then obtain

$$\vec{t}''' + (\alpha^2(s-\sigma)^2 + \frac{c^2}{\alpha^2})\vec{t}' + 3\alpha^2(s-\sigma)\vec{t} = 0 \qquad 6.1.5$$

(Eisenhart (ref. [4]) reduces the solution of the Serret-Frenet equations to the solution of a Ricatti equation, but this does not seem to help much in our case.)

6.1.5 is a third order differential equation defining the components of $\vec{t}$.

The equation looks neater with the change of variable:

$$u = \sqrt{\alpha}(s-\sigma)$$

$$\frac{d^3v}{du^3} + (u^2 + \frac{c^2}{\alpha^3}) \frac{dv}{du} + 3uv = 0 \qquad 6.1.6$$

where we let v denote any component of $\vec{t}$.

Another natural variable change is

$$u^2 = 2\xi$$

Then 6.1.6 becomes:

$$2\xi \frac{d^3v}{d\xi^3} + 3 \frac{d^2v}{d\xi^2} + (2\xi + \frac{c^2}{\alpha^3}) \frac{dv}{d\xi} + 3v = 0 \qquad 6.1.7$$

which is a Laplace equation of the third order, lending itself to Laplace transformation.

Well, that is about as far as the present author has come in really understanding what the generalization of the Cornu spiral consists of. In his attempts to solve 6.1.6 he is, for the time being trying to navigate through a jungle of irregular singularities, Bateman's k-function, confluent hypergeometric functions of two variables and several other exotic trees and swamps. Maybe the exact theory of Section 2 is simpler after all.

But two things are clear:

I. The intrinsic equations 6.1.3 and 6.1.4 describe some spiral in space being a generalization of the Cornu spiral.

II. A direct staircase approximation in these equations leads to the goal.

6.2 Staircase Approximation in Space

There are two simple alternatives.

Alternative 1

We have an equation for $\mathcal{K}(s)$, exact or modified according to Section 6.1.

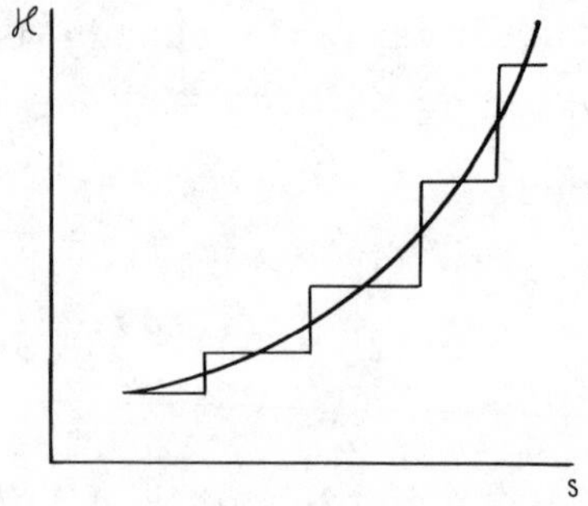

Figure 6.2.1

With the staircase approximation the curvature becomes piece-wise constant.

On the other hand the torsion $\tau(s)$ is also known. The torsion measures the rate of rotation of the osculation plane and the center of curvature around the tangent.

It thus makes sense to step the orientation of the osculation plane. The result will be a chain of circular arcs in space. The curve plane of any circle will be rotated a finite step relative to its neighbour, and the rotation is around the common tangent at the joint.

The accuracy of this approximation and the magnitude of the discontinuities in curvature and orientation of the osculation plane is kept under control with the step height.

Alternative 2

We keep the approximation shown in Fig. 6.2.1, but instead of stepping the osculation plane, we step the torsion:

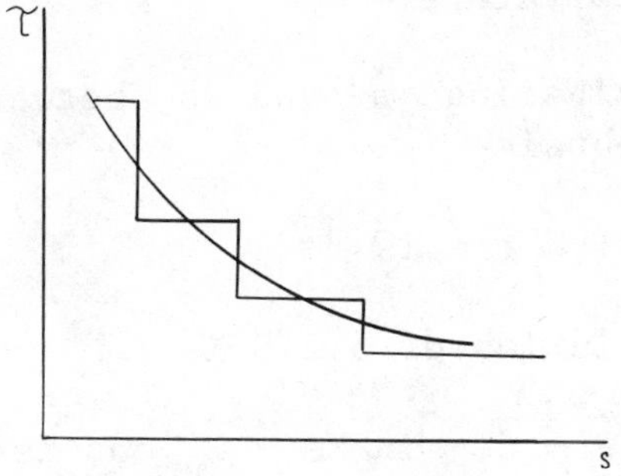

Figure 6.2.2

to get both curvature and torsion piecewise constant.

Let us investigate what this approximation leads to.

In this case the Serret-Frenet equations are easily solved for $\vec{t}$.

We have (2.7, 2.8, 2.9)

$$\vec{t}\,' = \mathcal{H}\vec{n} \qquad 6.2.1$$

$$\vec{n}\,' = \mathcal{H}\vec{t} + \tau\vec{b} \qquad 6.2.2$$

$$\vec{b}\,' = -\tau\vec{n} \qquad 6.2.3$$

with $\mathcal{H}$ = constant and τ = constant.

Eliminating $\vec{n}$ between 6.2.1 and 6.2.3 and integrating, we obtain:

$$\tau\vec{t} + \mathcal{H}\vec{b} = \text{constant} \tag{6.2.4}$$

The left hand side of 6.2.4 is known as the Darboux vector and denoted $\vec{\Omega}$. It is the vector around which the moving trihedron rotates. The quantity

$$K = |\vec{\Omega}|$$

is the total curvature.

Now, eliminating $\vec{n}$ and $\vec{b}$ between 6.2.1, 6.2.2 and 6.2.4 we obtain

$$\vec{t}'' + K^2\vec{t} = \tau\vec{\Omega} \tag{6.2.5}$$

The general solution of 6.2.5 is

$$\vec{t} = \frac{\tau}{K^2}\vec{\Omega} - \vec{C}_1 \sin Ks + \vec{C}_2 \cos Ks \tag{6.2.6}$$

$\vec{C}_1$ and $\vec{C}_2$ - integration constants

Because of the constraint 2.2 there exist five scalar equations between the vector constants. (Remember the warnings in Section 2.)

They are:

$$\frac{\tau^2}{K^2} + \vec{C}_1^{\,2} + \vec{C}_2^{\,2} = 1 \tag{6.2.7}$$

$$\vec{C}_1\,\vec{\Omega} = 0 \tag{6.2.8}$$

$$\vec{C}_2\,\vec{\Omega} = 0 \tag{6.2.9}$$

$$\vec{C}_1\,\vec{C}_2 = 0 \tag{6.2.10}$$

$$\vec{C}_1^{\,2} = \vec{C}_2^{\,2} \tag{6.2.11}$$

Integration of 6.2.6 gives:

$$\vec{r} = \frac{\tau}{K^2}\vec{\Omega}s + \frac{1}{K}\vec{C}_1 \cos Ks + \frac{1}{K}\vec{C}_2 \sin Ks + \vec{r}_0 \qquad 6.2.12$$

$\vec{r}_0$ - integration constant

6.2.12 is the parametric representation of the curve type resulting from alternative 2. When $\tau = 0$ it degenerates into a circle as it should.

7. Conclusion

In the course of this paper we have moved from the very simple:

points in space

through an analytical jungle to something very simple:

circles in space.

In conclusion we raise, and answer, the following question:

Why couldn't we instead fit the circles directly to the data to get the same results?

Well, in this paper the circles were introduced only to approximate a curve with known intrinsic equations. We therefore are on safe ground in computing their radii and center coordinates between the datapoints. From accuracy and continuity requirements we also know how many circles we need and where and how their joints shall be.

In a direct fit all this will have to be interrogated from more or less intelligent guesswork.

References

1. E.T. Whittaker and G.N. Watson, A Course of Modern Analysis, The University Press, Cambridge (1962).

2. A. Erdélyi, W. Magnus, F. Oberhettinger, and F.G. Tricomi, Higher Transcendental Functions, V. 1,2 and 3, McGraw-Hill Book Company, Inc. New York (1953).

3. T.J. Willmore, An Introduction to Differential Geometry of Curves and Surfaces, Dover Publications, Inc., New York (1909).

4. L.P. Eisenhart, A Treatise on the Differential Geometry of Curves and Surfaces, Dover Publications, Inc., New York (1909).

5. J.M. Glass, Smooth-Curve Interpolation: A Generalized Splin-Fit Procedure, BIT 6 (1966) 277-293.

6. D. Gospodnetic, Numerical Definition of Ships' Hulls by Means of Elastic Interpolation, N.R.C. No. 8383, Mechanical Engineering Report MB 258 (1965).

7. E. Mehlum, Curve and Surface Fitting based on Variational Criteriae for Smoothness, Central Institute for Industrial Research, Oslo, Norway (1969).

8. E. Mehlum, H. Melhuus, and S. Ljunggren, PROLAMAT'73, The Second IFIP-IFAC International Conference on Programming Languages for Numerically Controlled Machine Tools, Budapest April, 1973, Vol. II.

9. E.H. Lee and G.E. Forsythe, Variational Study of Nonlinear Spline Curves, Computer Science Department, Stanford University, August 1971.

10. E. Mehlum and P.F. Sorensen, Example of an existing system in the ship-building industry: the Autokon system, Proc. Roy. Soc. London A. 321, 219-233 (1971).

11. E. Mehlum, A Curve-fitting method based on a variational criterion, Nordisk Tidskrift for Informations-Behandling 4 (1964), 441-448.

Appendix

W.W. Meyer
General Motors Research Laboratories

A formal solution of the generalized Cornu spiral problem is the following: Let $z = x + iy$ be determined as a function of $\zeta = \xi + i\eta$ by

$$(1)\quad z(b,\zeta) = \gamma(b)\int_0^b \sqrt{\zeta/(2\alpha w)}\, \exp\{-\zeta w - 2\beta\cdot\tan^{-1}(w)\}dw$$

where

$$(2)\qquad \beta = C^2/(4\alpha^3)$$

and the upper limit of integration is either $b = i$ or $b = +\infty$. We restrict ζ to the strip

$$S = \{\zeta | 0 \leq \eta \leq 1\},$$

requiring also that the path of w from 0 to b lie in S. Then $\arg\sqrt{\zeta/(2\alpha w)}$ and $\mathrm{Re}[\tan^{-1}(w)]$ can be assumed both to fall in the range $[-\pi/2, \pi/2]$. The integrand is single-valued accordingly. The constant $\gamma(b)$ serves as a scale factor. Specifically

$$(3)\qquad \gamma(i) = \exp(\beta\pi/2)/\Gamma(1+i\beta)$$

whereas $\gamma(\infty)$ is real but otherwise arbitrary.

The image, in the z-plane, of the non-negative real line

$$R_+ = \{\zeta | \xi \geq 0,\ \eta = 0\}$$

is a curve $\mathcal{L}(b)$ which fulfils the main prescription of Section 6.1. With ζ as independent variable, equation 6.1.7 is satisfied by the function

$$v(b,\zeta) = \sqrt{2\alpha\zeta}\; z'(b,\zeta)$$

and v can be construed as a vector tangent to $\mathcal{L}(b)$ when $\zeta \in R_+$. We ought also to have

$$(4)\qquad |v(b,\zeta)| \equiv 1$$

since $\sqrt{2\xi/\alpha}$ is presumed to be arc length. In fact, from the integral representation one can deduce that

(5) $v(i,\xi) \sim \exp\{[\pi/4-\xi-\beta\ell n(2\xi)]i\}$ as $\xi \to \infty$,

so condition (4) obtains asymptotically. However, the integral yields as well the inequality

(6) $$|v(i,0)| \geq \sqrt{\beta\pi/\tanh(\beta\pi)},$$

which indicates that β must be small for (4) to obtain, even approximately, over the whole course of $\mathcal{L}(i)$. It is reasonable conjecture that $|v(i,\xi)| \geq 1$ always.

Incidentally, the spiriform nature of $\mathcal{L}(i)$ is evident from (5). The curve originates in $z = 0$ and, infinitely looping, approaches the point

(7) $$z(i,\infty) = \gamma(i)\sqrt{\pi/(2\alpha)}.$$

(When $\beta = 0$, we get one-half of the Cornu sprial, rotated $-45°$ so that the limit point lies on the x-axis.)

The alternative image $\mathcal{L}(\infty)$ is, of course, simply a straight line... R_+ contracted to a segment of itself. Let us consider the possibility of a space curve S, having $\mathcal{L}(i)$ as its projection onto the z-plane, $\mathcal{L}(\infty)$ as its projection onto an axis perpendicular to the z-plane, and $\sqrt{2\xi/\alpha}$ as approximate arc length. The scale factor $\gamma(\infty)$ should be chosen so that

(8) $$|v(i,\xi)|^2 + |v(\infty,\xi)|^2 \equiv 1$$

as nearly as may be, over the whole domain $\xi \in R_+$. Since, under any choice, $v(\infty,\xi) \to 0$ as $\xi \to \infty$, there is no difficulty asymptotically. But if the foregoing conjecture be true, the optimal choice is ineluctably $\gamma(\infty) = 0$.

Reference

E.L. Ince, "Ordinary Differential Equations", Dover, New York, 1956, pp. 438-441.

SOME PIECEWISE POLYNOMIAL ALTERNATIVES TO SPLINES UNDER TENSION[+]

Gregory M. Nielson
Arizona State University

1. Introduction.

Splines under tension were first introduced by Schweikert [5]. The motivation was to be able to imitate the behavior of cubic interpolating splines, yet avoid the "extraneous" inflection points (as defined by Schweikert [5]) that these functions sometimes exhibit. Extraneous inflection points are exhibited in an example given by Schweikert where all second order divided differences are negative yet the cubic interpolating spline has two inflection points. The approach taken by Schweikert is to assume the interpolant is of the form $a + bx + c \cdot \sinh(\alpha x) + d \cdot \cosh(\alpha x)$ on each subinterval $[t_i, t_{i+1}]$, $i = 1, \ldots, n-1$ and then impose continuity and interpolation conditions so as to obtain an interpolant that has a continuous second derivative. He then proves the extraneous inflection points can be removed by increasing the tension parameter α. In fact, the limiting interpolant $(\alpha \to \infty)$ is the polygonal line joining the interpolation points.

Cline [1] has also investigated the curve fitting characteristics of splines under tension. His development is somewhat different than that of

[+]This research was supported by the Office of Naval Research under Contract N00014-72-A-0070-0002, NR 044-443.

Schweikert in that he assumes that the interpolant f is a function with a continuous second derivative such that $f'' - \alpha^2 f$ is linear on each subinterval.

Both authors give systems of equations with tridiagonal coefficient matrices that will yield the spline under tension. Cline's development involves $f''(x_i)$ as unknowns and Schweikert's involves $f'(x_i)$.

In the next section, we will characterize splines under tension as having a certain minimal property. This will motivate the choice for an analogous minimization problem which will have piecewise polynomials as its solution. We will refer to these functions as ν-splines and show that many of the properties of splines under tension are shared by this class of interpolants.

2. Splines Under Tension.

Since splines under tension are piecewise solutions to the equation $f^{(iv)} - \alpha^2 f'' = 0$, we desire a pseudo-norm which will have this equation as its Euler equation. Two inner products and their associated pseudo-norms come to mind.

$$(2.1)\quad (f,g) = \int_a^b f''(t)g''(t)dt + \alpha^2\int_a^b f'(t)g'(t)dt$$

$$(2.2)\quad \langle f,g\rangle = \int_a^b [f''(t) + \alpha f'(t)][g''(t) + \alpha g'(t)]dt$$

The Euler equation for both of the functionals (f,f) and $\langle f,f\rangle$ is $f^{(iv)} - \alpha^2 f'' = 0$. Both of these inner products have been previously discussed within the context of spline functions. The first by Golomb and Weinberger [3] and the second by deBoor and Lynch [2].

We now proceed to obtain a characterization of the solution to minimizing (f,f) and $\langle f,f\rangle$ in the space $H = \{f: f'' \in L^2[a,b]$ and f' is absolutely continuous on $[a,b]\}$, subject to certain interpolation requirements. We first start by identifying a pseudo-reproducing kernel function.

<u>Lemma 2.1</u>. Let

$$K(x,y) = \int_a^b \left(\frac{1-e^{-\alpha(x-t)_+}}{\alpha}\right)\left(\frac{1-e^{-\alpha(y-t)_+}}{\alpha}\right) dt \tag{2.3}$$

where $z_+ = \min(z,0)$. Then, for $f \in H$

$$\langle f(x), K(x,y)\rangle_x = f(y) - f(a) - \left(\frac{1-e^{\alpha(a-y)}}{\alpha}\right) f'(a)$$

<u>Proof</u>: We first note that an argument using integration by parts will show that for $f \in H$

$$\begin{aligned} f(x) &= f(a) + \left(\frac{1-e^{\alpha(a-x)}}{\alpha}\right) f'(a) \\ &+ \int_a^x \left[\frac{1-e^{-\alpha(x-t)}}{\alpha}\right] [f''(t) + \alpha f'(t)]dt. \end{aligned} \tag{2.4}$$

The converse is also true in that if

$$f(x) = a_0 + \left(\frac{1-e^{\alpha(a-x)}}{\alpha}\right) a_1$$

$$+ \int_a^x \left[\frac{1-e^{-\alpha(x-t)}}{\alpha}\right] g(t)dt$$

where $g \in L^2[a,b]$, then $f \in H$ and $f(a) = a_0$, $f'(a) = a_1$ and $f'' + \alpha f' = g$, a.e. This last equation is obtained by using the differentiation formula

$$\frac{d}{dx}\int_a^x h(x,t)dt = \int_a^x \frac{\partial h}{\partial x}(x,t)dt + h(x,x).$$

If we apply this converse to (2.3) we find that

$$\frac{\partial^2 K}{\partial x^2}(t,y) + \alpha\frac{\partial K}{\partial x}(t,y) = \frac{1 - e^{-\alpha(y-t)_+}}{\alpha}.$$

Therefore,

$$<f(x),K(x,y)>_x = \int_a^b [f''(t)+\alpha f'(t)](\frac{1-e^{-\alpha(y-t)_+}}{\alpha})dt$$

from which using equation (2.4) we can conclude the desired result.■

Lemma 2.2. Let $a = t_1 < t_2 \ldots < t_n = b$ and $L_i(f) = f(t_i)$, $i = 1,\ldots,n$, and let

$$(2.5)\quad S(t) = \alpha_1+\alpha_2 t+\alpha_3 e^{-\alpha t}+\alpha_4 e^{\alpha t}+\sum_{i=2}^{n-1}\beta_i L_{i(y)}[K(t,y)].$$

Then, for $f \in H$,

$$(2.6)\quad <f,S> = \sum_{i=2}^{n-1}\beta_i L_i(f)+f(S'''-\alpha^2 S')\Big|_a^b+f'(S''+\alpha S')\Big|_a^b$$

$$(2.7)\quad (f,S) = \sum_{i=2}^{n-1}\beta_i L_i(f)+f(S'''-\alpha^2 S')\Big|_a^b+f'(S'')\Big|_a^b$$

Proof: Let h represent the first four terms of (2.5) and g the remaining portion, then we can note that

$$g''(t) + \alpha g'(t) = \sum_{i=2}^{n-1} \beta_i L_{i(y)} \left[\frac{1 - e^{-\alpha(y-t)_+}}{\alpha}\right]$$

(2.8) $$g'''(a+) - \alpha^2 g'(a) = \sum_{i=2}^{n-1} \beta_i L_i(1)$$

$$g'''(b-) - \alpha^2 g'(b) = 0.$$

Using integration by parts we have that

$$\langle f,h\rangle = f'(h'' + \alpha h')\Big|_a^b + f(h''' - \alpha^2 h')\Big|_a^b$$

since $h^{(iv)} - \alpha^2 h'' = 0$.

We can now use the previous lemma to obtain

$$\langle f,g\rangle = \sum_{i=2}^{n-1} \beta_i L_{i(y)} \left[f(y) - f(a) - \left(\frac{1-e^{\alpha(a-y)}}{\alpha}\right) f'(a)\right]$$

$$= \sum_{i=2}^{n-1} \beta_i L_i(f) - f(a)\,[g'''(a+) - \alpha^2 g'(a)]$$

$$- f'(a)\,[g''(a) + \alpha g'(a)]$$

$$= \sum_{i=2}^{n-1} \beta_i L_i(f) + f(g''' - \alpha^2 g')\Big|_a^b$$

$$+ f'(g'' + \alpha g')\Big|_a^b$$

and so these two equations can be combined to yield equation (2.6). Since it is true in general for $f, g \in H$ that

$$\langle f,g \rangle = (f,g) + \alpha(f'g')\Big|_a^b$$

then equation (2.7) follows immediately.■

Equations (2.6) and (2.7) motivate the definition of the following end conditions

i) $f'(a) = y_1'$, $\quad f'(b) = y_n'$

ii) $f''(a) + \alpha f'(a) = 0$, $\quad f''(b) + \alpha f'(b) = 0$

$\overline{\text{ii}}$) $f''(a) = 0$, $\quad f''(b) = 0$

iii) $f(a) = f(b)$, $\quad f'(a) = f'(b)$, $\quad f''(a) = f''(b)$

Theorem 2.3. The unique solution to $\min_{f \in H} \langle f, f \rangle$ (resp. $\min_{f \in H} (f,f)$) subject to $f(t_i) = y_i$, $i=1,\ldots,n$ and one of the end conditions i, ii, iii (resp. i, $\overline{\text{ii}}$, iii) is the function of form

$$(2.9) \quad S(t) = \alpha_1 + \alpha_2 t + \alpha_3 e^{-\alpha t} + \alpha_4 e^{\alpha t} + \sum_{i=2}^{n-1} \beta_i K(t,t_i)$$

satisfying the interpolation and corresponding end conditions.

Proof: For the moment, let us assume that S exists and f is an arbitrary element of H, then

$$\langle f,f \rangle - \langle S,S \rangle = \langle f-S, f-S \rangle + 2 \langle S,f-S \rangle$$

If we assume that f is any element of H satisfying the interpolation and one of the end conditions i, ii, iii then by Lemma 2.2 we have $\langle S,f-S \rangle = 0$ and so $\langle f,f\rangle \geq \langle S,S\rangle$. Consequently, S is the minimum provided we can show that it does indeed exist.

Note that the above is true for $(\cdot,\cdot)$ if one of the end conditions i, ii, iii is used.

In order to prove that S exists, we assume by way of contradiction that the homogeneous system of equations resulting from a substitution of (2.9) into the interpolation and one of the end conditions has a nontrivial solution $\bar{a}_i$, i=1,2,3,4, $\bar{\beta}_i,\ldots n-1$.

If $\bar{S}$ denotes the function of the form (2.9) corresponding to this nontrivial solution, the above argument allows us to conclude that $\langle\bar{S},\bar{S}\rangle = 0$ (resp. $(\bar{S},\bar{S}) = 0$) and since $\bar{S} \in H$, it must have the form $\bar{S}(t) = p + qe^{-\alpha t}$ (resp. $\bar{S}(t) = p$), but $\bar{S}(t_1) = 0$ and $\bar{S}(t_n) = 0$ and so $\bar{S} = 0$ in either case. Since the functions $1, t, e^{-\alpha t}, e^{\alpha t}, K(t,t_i)$, $i=2,\ldots,n-1$, are linearly independent, it must be the case that $\bar{a}_1 = \bar{a}_2 = \bar{a}_3 = \bar{a}_4 = 0 = \bar{\beta}_i$, $i=2,\ldots,n-1$, and consequently the system of equations must be nonsingular. We can note that this same argument will show that S is unique for if S_1 and S_2 were both miminizing functions than $\langle S_1 - S_2, S_1 - S_2\rangle = 0$ (resp. $(S_1 - S_2, S_1 - S_2) = 0$) and the above argument would imply that $S_1 - S_2 = 0$.■

3. Piecewise Polynomial Alternatives to Splines in Tension.

In the previous section we characterized splines in tension as functions that minimize

$$(3.1)\quad (f,f) = \int_a^b [f''(t)]^2 dt + \alpha^2 \int_a^b [f'(t)]^2 dt$$

It is this property that motivates the characterization of some functions that are piecewise polynomials and for the parametric case, have analogous properties to splines in tension. Rather than minimize (3.1), we will use

$$(3.2)\quad [f,g] = \int_a^b f''(t)g''(t)dt + \sum_{i=1}^{n} \nu_i\, f'(t_i)g'(t_i)$$

Since these functions will not have continuous second derivatives, that natural (ii) and periodic (iii) end conditions of the previous section are no longer valid. The analogous conditions are

i') $f'(a) = y_1'\ ,\quad f'(b) = y_n'$

ii') $\nu_n f'(b) + f''(b-) = 0,\quad \nu_1 f'(a) - f''(a+) = 0$

iii') $f(a) = f(b),\quad f'(a) = f'(b),$
$f''(a+) - f''(b-) = (\nu_1 + \nu_n)\, f'(a)$

<u>Theorem 3.1</u>. The unique solution to $\min_{f\varepsilon H} [f,f]$ subject to $f(t_i) = y_i$, $i=1,\ldots,n$ and i' or ii' or iii' is

$$(3.3)\quad S(t) = p + qt + \sum_{i=1}^{n-1} \alpha_i (t-t_i)_+^3 + \sum_{i=1}^{n-1} \beta_i (t-t_i)_+^2$$

such that

$$(3.4)\quad \begin{aligned} S(t_i) &= y_i,\quad i=1,\ldots,n \\ \beta_i &= \frac{\nu_i S'(t_i)}{2}\ ,\ 2,\ldots,n-1 \end{aligned}$$

and i', ii' or iii' hold.

Proof: Let f be an arbitrary element of H, then

$$[f,f] - [S,S] = [f - S, f - S] + 2[S, f - S]$$

We can note that if $g_i(t) = (t - t_i)_+^3$ then

$$\int_a^b f''(t)g''_i(t)dt = g''_i(b)f'(b) + 6[f(t_i) - f(b)]$$

and if $h_i(t) = (t - t_i)_+^2$ then

$$\int_a^b f''(t)h''_i(t)dt = 2[f'(b) - f'(t_i)].$$

Therefore

$$\int_a^b f''(t)S''(t)dt$$

$$= \sum_{i=1}^{n-1} \alpha_i \int_a^b f''(t)g_i(t)dt + \sum_{i=1}^{n-1} \beta_i \int_a^b f''(t)h_i(t)dt$$

$$= f'(b) \sum_{i=1}^{n-1} \alpha_i g''_i(b) + 6 \sum_{i=1}^{n-1} \alpha_i [f(t_i) - f(b)]$$

$$+ f'(b)\, 2 \sum_{i=1}^{n-1} \beta_i - 2 \sum_{i=1}^{n-1} \beta_i f'(t_i)$$

$$= f'(b) [\sum_{i=1}^{n-1} \alpha_i g''_i(b) + 2 \sum_{i=1}^{n-1} \beta_i] + f'(a)[-2\beta_1]$$

$$- 2 \sum_{i=2}^{n-1} \beta_i f'(t_i) + 6 \sum_{i=1}^{n-1} \alpha_i [f(t_i) - f(b)]$$

$$= f'(b)S''(b-) - f'(a)S''(a+)$$

$$+ \sum_{i=2}^{n-1} (-2\beta_i)f'(t_i) + 6 \sum_{i=1}^{n} \alpha_i [f(t_i) - f(b)].$$

Now if we assume that $f(t_i) = y_i = S(t_i)$, $i=1,\ldots,n$, then

$$[S, f - S] = \int_a^b S''(t)[f''(t) - S''(t)]dt + \sum_{i=1}^{n} \nu_i S'(t_i)[f'(t_i) - S'(t_i)]$$

$$= [f'(b) - S'(b)]\,[S''(b-) + \nu_n S'(b)]$$

$$+ [f'(a) - S'(a)]\,[-S''(a+) + \nu_1 S'(a)]$$

$$+ \sum_{i=2}^{n-2} (\nu_i S'(t_i) - 2\beta_i)(f'(t_i) - S'(t_i))$$

There if $\beta_i = \nu_i S'(t_i)/2$, $i=2,\ldots,n-1$ we have that

$$[S, f - S] = [f'(b) - S'(b)]\,[S''(b-) + \nu_n S'(b)] + [f'(a) - S'(a)]\,[-S''(a+) + \nu_1 S'(a)]$$

which becomes zero when any of the end conditions are used. Thus we have shown that if such an S exists then

$$[f, f] - [S, S] = [f - S, f - S] \geq 0$$

for all f that satisfy the interpolation conditions (and end conditions in the case of i'). An argument similar to that of Theorem 2.3 will establish the existence and uniqueness.■

We are especially interested in the case of two dimensional parameterized functions and their application to curve fitting and design. If (x_i, y_i) $i=1,\ldots,n$ represents the given data, we will denote by X_ν the function given by Theorem 3.1 coresponding to the interpolation conditions $X_\nu(t_i) = x_i$ $i=1,\ldots,n$ and one of the end conditions. We denote by Y_ν the analogous function corresponding the data Y_i, $i=1,\ldots,n$. It is then clear that the parameterized curve (X_ν, Y_ν) is the unique solution to

$$\min_{(X,Y)\varepsilon H\times H} \int_{t_1}^{t_n} [(\ddot{X})^2 + (\ddot{Y})^2] + \sum_{i=1}^{n} \nu_i[\dot{X}(t_i))^2 + \dot{Y}(t_i)^2]$$

subject to

$$X(t_i) = x_i, \quad Y(t_i) = y_i, \quad i=1,\ldots,n$$

and one of the sets of end conditions.

We recall that spline in tension of the previous section had a continuous second derivative. From (3.3) we can see that both X_ν and Y_ν may have finite jump discontinuities in their second derivatives at t_i, $i=1,\ldots,n$. Nevertheless, the parameterized curve (X_ν, Y_ν) has a similar degree of continuity as the spline in tension, which we will subsequently prove.

Lemma 3.2. For $k=2,\ldots,n-1$

$$\ddot{Y}_\nu(t_k+) - \ddot{Y}_\nu(t_k-) = \nu_k\dot{Y}_\nu(t_k)$$

$$\text{and} \quad \ddot{X}_\nu(t_k+) - \ddot{X}\,(t_k-) = \nu_k\dot{X}\,(t_k)$$

Proof: Let S be the function given by (3.3) representing either X_ν or Y_ν. Then

$$S''\,(t_k+) = 6\sum_{i=k+1}^{n-1} \alpha_i(t_k - t_i) + 2\sum_{i=k}^{n-1} \beta_i$$

$$S''(t_k-) = 6 \sum_{i=k+1}^{n-1} \alpha_i (t_k - t_i) + 2 \sum_{i=k+1}^{n-1} \beta_i .$$

Therefore,

$$S''(t_k+) - S''(t_k-) = 2\,\beta_k = \nu_k S'(t_k)$$

by equation (3.4).

Theorem 3.3. If $\dot{X}_\nu(t) \neq 0$, then $\frac{d^2Y_\nu}{dX_\nu^2}$ is continuous at $X_\nu = X_\nu(t)$. Similarly, $\frac{d^2X_\nu}{dY_\nu^2}$ is continuous whenever $\dot{Y}_\nu(t) \neq 0$.

Proof: Without loss of generality, assume that $\dot{X}_\nu(t) > 0$. Let N be a neighborhood of t such that $\dot{X}_\nu(\tau) > 0$, $\tau \in N$ and let $M = \{X_\nu(\tau) : \tau \in N\}$. Denote by g the unique inverse of X_ν on M with range in N. It is clear that g is strictly monotone increasing.

Let x be an arbitrary but fixed element of M, then for sufficiently small h, $x + h \in M$. Let $t_h = g(x + h)$ and $\overline{t} = g(x)$, then there exists $\xi \varepsilon (\overline{t}, t_h)$ such that

$$X_\nu(t_h) - X_\nu(\overline{t}) = \dot{X}_\nu(\xi)(t_h - \overline{t})$$

which implies that

$$h = \dot{X}_\nu(\xi)[g(x + h) - g(x)]. \tag{3.5}$$

If $m = \min_{\tau \in N} |\dot{X}_\nu(\tau)| > 0$ then $|g(x + h) - g(x)| \leq \frac{h}{m}$

which implies that g is continuous at x. Now returning to (3.5) and letting $\eta = \dot{X}_\nu(\xi) \in (x, x + h)$ we have

$$\frac{g(x + h) - g(x)}{h} = \frac{1}{\dot{X}_\nu(g(\eta))}$$

Allowing $h \to 0$ we observe that

$$g'(x) = \frac{1}{\dot{X}_\nu(g(x))}, \quad x \in M.$$

Thus the inverse of X_ν is a monotone, continuously differentable function on M. If $Y = Y_\nu(g(x))$ and since $x = X_\nu(g(x))$, $X \in M$ we have that

$$\frac{dY}{dx}(x) = \frac{\dot{Y}_\nu(g(x))}{\dot{X}_\nu(g(x))}$$

As long as $t \neq t_i$, $i = 1, \ldots n$ then $\ddot{X}_\nu$ and $\ddot{Y}_\nu$ are continuous at t and we have

$$\frac{d^2Y}{dx^2}(x) = \frac{\dot{X}_\nu(g(x))\ddot{Y}_\nu(g(x)) - \dot{Y}_\nu(g(x))\ddot{X}_\nu(g(x))}{[\dot{X}_\nu(g(x))]^3}$$

which is continuous on M.

If $t = t_i$, $x_i = X_\nu(t_i)$ then because g is monotone increasing we have

$$\frac{d^2Y}{dx^2}(x_i+) = \frac{\dot{X}_\nu(t_i)\ddot{Y}_\nu(t_i+) - \dot{Y}_\nu(t_i)\ddot{X}_\nu(t_i+)}{[\dot{X}_\nu(t_i)]^3}$$

and

$$\frac{d^2Y}{dx^2}(x_i-) = \frac{\dot{X}_\nu(t_i)\ddot{Y}_\nu(t_i-) - \dot{Y}_\nu(t_i)\ddot{X}_\nu(t_i-)}{[\dot{X}_\nu(t_i)]^3}$$

therefore

$$\frac{d^2Y}{dx^2}(x_i+) - \frac{d^2Y}{dx^2}(x_i-)$$

$$= \frac{\dot{X}_\nu(t_i)[\ddot{Y}_\nu(t_i+)-\ddot{Y}_\nu(t_i-)] + \dot{Y}_\nu(t_i)[\ddot{X}_\nu(t_i-)-\ddot{X}_\nu(t_i+)]}{[\dot{X}_\nu(t_i)]^3}$$

We can now use Lemma 3.2 to conclude the desired result.■

<u>Corollary 3.4</u>. If $\dot{X}_\nu(t)$ or $\dot{Y}_\nu(t)$ is not zero, then the curvature of (X_ν, Y_ν) is continuous at t.

<u>Proof</u>: This follows immediately from the previous theorem and the definition of curvature:

$$k(\tau) = \frac{|\dot{x}(\tau)\ddot{y}(\tau) - \dot{y}(\tau)\ddot{x}(\tau)|}{[ds(\tau)]^3}$$

where $ds(\tau) = \sqrt{\dot{x}(\tau)^2 + \dot{y}(\tau)^2}$.

Another important characteristic of splines in tension is the convergence to a polygonal line as the tension is increased. This property is not shared by functions characterized by Theorem 3.1 *per se*, but an analogous property holds for the parameterized curve (X_ν, Y_ν).∎

Lemma 3.4. Let $S_k' = S'(t_k)$ where S is given by (3.3) then

$$\sum_{k\varepsilon I} \nu_k (S_k')^2 \leq B.$$

and B is independent of ν_k, $k \varepsilon I$. The set of indices I are chosen as $\{2,\ldots,n-1\}$, $\{1,\ldots,n\}$ or $\{1,\ldots,n-1\}$ to correspond to the end conditions i', ii' or iii', respectively.

Proof: Since

$$\sum_{k\varepsilon I} \nu_k (S_k')^2 \leq [S, S] \leq [f, f] \tag{3.6}$$

for any $f \varepsilon H$ satisfying the appropriate end conditions and the interpolation conditions $f(t_i) = y_i$, $i = 1,\ldots,n$. Thus, if we choose f to satisfy this condition and also $f'(t_i) = 0$ $i \varepsilon I$, it is clear that the right side of (3.6) is independent of ν_k, $k \varepsilon I$.

To be specific, for the end conditions i', we can choose

$$f(t) = \begin{cases} H_1(t)y_1 + (1-H_1(t))y_2 + h_3 D_1(t), & t\varepsilon[t_1,t_2] \\ H_i(t)y_i + (1-H_i(t))y_{i+1}, & t\varepsilon[t_i,t_{i+1}], i=2,\ldots,n-2 \\ H_{n-1}(t)y_{n-1} + [1-H_{n-1}(t)]y_n + h_{n-1}D_{n-1}(t), & \\ \quad t\varepsilon[t_{n-1},t_n] & \end{cases}$$

where $D_1(t) = \left[\frac{t-t_1}{h_1}\right]^3 - 2\left[\frac{t-t_1}{h_1}\right]^2 + \left[\frac{t-t_1}{h_1}\right]$,

$$(3.7)\quad H_i(t) = 2\left[\frac{t-t_i}{h_i}\right]^3 - 3\left[\frac{t-t_i}{h_i}\right]^2 + 1,\ i = 1,\dots,n-1,$$

$$D_{n-1}(t) = \left[\frac{t-t_{n-1}}{h_{n-1}}\right]^3 - \left[\frac{t-t_{n-1}}{h_{n-1}}\right]^2 .$$

Then

$$[f,f] = 2\sum_{i=1}^{n-1} \frac{(y_{i+1}-y_i)^2}{(h_i)^3} + 12\left[\frac{(y_1-y_2)y_1'}{h_1^{\,2}} + \frac{(y_{n-1}-y_n)y_n'}{(h_{n-1})^2}\right]$$

$$+ (y_1')^2\left[\frac{2}{h_1} + \nu_1\right] + (y_n')^2\left[\frac{2}{h_{n-1}} + \nu_n\right]$$

which is clearly independent of ν_k, $k = 2,\dots,n-1$.∎

<u>Theorem 3.5</u>. $[S_k']^2$, $k \in I$ is a decreasing function of ν_k (ν_i, $i \neq k$ fixed) such that

$$\lim_{\nu_k \to \infty} [S_k']^2 = 0$$

<u>Proof</u>: The fact that convergence to zero is obtained is an immediate consequence of the previous lemma. The fact that $[S_k']^2$ is a decreasing function is a result of Theorem 4.2 of the following section, where we prove that the matrix

$$\left(S_i' \frac{\partial S_i}{\partial \nu_j} \right) \qquad (i,j) \in I \times I$$

is negative semidefinite and consequently $\frac{\partial [S_k']^2}{\partial \nu_k} \leq 0$ for $k \in I$.■

<u>Theorem 3.6</u>. The curve

$$(X_\infty, Y_\infty) = \lim_{\nu_k, \nu_{k+1} \to \infty} (X_\nu, Y_\nu), \; k, \; k+1 \in I,$$

is a straight line segment between (x_k, y_k) and (x_{k+1}, y_{k+1}).

<u>Proof</u>: It is clear from Theorem 3.5 and the fact that X_ν and Y_ν are both piecewise cubic polynomials that for $t \in [t_k, t_{k+1}]$ the limiting function has the form

$$X_\infty(t) = x_k H_k(t) + (1-H_k(t)) x_{k+1}$$

$$Y_\infty(t) = y_k H_k(t) + (1-H_k(t)) y_{k+1}$$

where H_k is given by equation (3.7).

Therefore,

$$(X_\infty(t) - x_{k+1})(y_k - y_{k+1}) = (Y_\infty(t) - y_{k+1})(x_k - x_{k+1})$$

and so X_ν and Y_ν are linearly related.■

4. Computational Equations for ν-splines.

From Theorem 3.1 we can see that the ν-spline S is a cubic on each subinterval $[t_i, t_{i+1}]$, $i = 1,\ldots, n-1$. If $g(t) = t^3 - t^2$, we have that

$$S(t) = g\left(\frac{t_{i+1} - t}{h_i}\right)[y_{i+1} - y_i - h_i S_i']$$

$$- g\left(\frac{t - t_i}{h_i}\right)[y_{i+1} - y_i - h_i S_{i+1}']$$

$$+ y_i\left(\frac{t_{i+1} - t}{h_i}\right) + y_{i+1}\left(\frac{t - t_i}{h_i}\right)$$

on $[t_i, t_{i+1}]$.

Therefore,

$$(4.1) \quad S''(t_i+) = \frac{2}{h_i}\left[\frac{3(y_{i+1} - y_i)}{h_i} - (S_{i+1}' + 2S_i')\right]$$

$$(4.2) \quad S''(t_i-) = \frac{-2}{h_{i-1}}\left[\frac{3(y_i - y_{i-1})}{h_{i-1}} - (2S_i' + S_{i-1}')\right]$$

Now using Lemma 3.2 we have

$$\frac{2}{h_i}\left[\frac{3(y_{i+1} - y_i)}{h_i} - (S_{i+1}' + 2S_i')\right]$$

$$+ \frac{2}{h_{i-1}}\left[\frac{3(y_i - y_{i-1})}{h_{i-1}} - (2S_i' + S_{i-1}')\right]$$

$$= \nu_i S_i' \quad i = 2,\ldots,n-1$$

which implies

$$\frac{S'_{i-1}}{h_{i-1}} + S'_i\left[\frac{2(h_i + h_{i-1})}{h_i\, h_{i-1}} + \frac{\nu_i}{2}\right] + \frac{S'_{i+1}}{h_i}$$

$$= 3\left[\frac{(y_{i+1}-y_i)}{(h_i)^2} + \frac{(y_i-y_{i-1})}{(h_{i-1})^2}\right], \quad i = 2,\ldots,n-1.$$

If we let $\lambda_i = \dfrac{h_i}{h_i + h_{i-1}}$, $\mu_i = 1 - \lambda_i$; $i = 2,\ldots,n-1$

and multiply by $h_{i-1}\lambda_i$ we have

$$S'_{i-1}\lambda_i + S'_i(2 + \bar{\nu}_i) + S'_{i+1}\mu_i$$

$$= 3\left[\mu_i\left(\frac{y_{i+1}-y_i}{h_i}\right) + \lambda_i\left(\frac{y_i-y_{i-1}}{h_{i-1}}\right)\right] \equiv d_i, \quad i=2,\ldots, n-1,$$

where

$$\bar{\nu}_i = \frac{\nu_i(h_i h_{i-1})}{2(h_i + h_{i-1})}\ .$$

We can now incorporate the end conditions. For i' we have the n-2 equations

$$\begin{bmatrix} 2+\bar{\nu}_2 & \mu_2 & & & \\ \lambda_3 & 2+\bar{\nu}_3 & \mu_3 & & \\ & \cdot & \cdot & & \\ & & & \cdot & \mu_{n-1} \\ & & & \lambda_{n-1} & 2+\bar{\nu}_{n-1} \end{bmatrix} \begin{bmatrix} S'_2 \\ \vdots \\ \vdots \\ S'_{n-1} \end{bmatrix} = \begin{bmatrix} d_2-\lambda_2 y'_1 \\ d_3 \\ \vdots \\ d_{n-3} \\ d_{n-1}-\mu_{n-1}y'_n \end{bmatrix}$$

(4.3)

In order to invoke the ii' end conditions we can use (4.1) and (4.2) to obtain

$$\nu_1 S_1' - S''(t_1+) = \nu_1 S_1' + \frac{2}{h_1}\left[(2S_1' + S_2') - \frac{3(y_2 - y_1)}{h_1}\right]$$

and

$$\nu_n S_n' + S''(t_n-) = \nu_n S_n' + \frac{2}{h_{n-1}}\left[(2S_n' + S_{n-1}') - \frac{3(y_n - y_{n-1})}{h_{n-1}}\right]$$

Setting these quantities to zero, we have

$$S_1'[2 + \frac{h_1\nu_1}{2}] + S_2' = 3[\frac{y_2 - y_1}{h_1}]$$

$$S_n'[2 + \frac{h_{n-1}\nu_n}{2}] + S_{n-1}' = 3[\frac{y_n - y_{n-1}}{h_{n-1}}]$$

Therefore, if we let $\bar{\nu}_1 = \frac{h_1\nu_1}{2}$, $\bar{\nu}_n = \frac{h_{n-1}\nu_n}{2}$ we have

$$\begin{bmatrix} 2+\bar{\nu}_1 & 1 & & & \\ \lambda_2 & 2+\bar{\nu}_2 & \mu_2 & & \\ & \cdot & \cdot & \cdot & \\ & & \lambda_{n-1} & 2+\bar{\nu}_{n-1} & \mu_{n-1} \\ & & & 1 & 2+\bar{\nu}_n \end{bmatrix} \begin{bmatrix} S_1' \\ S_2' \\ \vdots \\ \\ S_n' \end{bmatrix} = \begin{bmatrix} 3[\frac{y_2-y_1}{h_1}] \\ d_2 \\ \vdots \\ d_{n-1} \\ 3[\frac{y_n-y_{n-1}}{h_{n-1}}] \end{bmatrix} \tag{4.4}$$

For the periodic end conditions we assume $y_n = y_1$ and since $S_n' = S_1'$ we need only solve for the first $n-1$ derivatives.

We can again use (4.1) and (4.2) to yield

$$(\nu_1 + \nu_n)S_1' + S''(t_n-) - S''(t_1+)$$

$$= (\nu_1 + \nu_n)S_1' + \frac{2}{h_{n-1}}[(2S_1' + S_{n-1}') - \frac{3(y_n - y_{n-1})}{h_{n-1}}]$$

$$+ \frac{2}{h_1}[(2S_1' + S_2') - \frac{3(y_2 - y_1)}{h_1}]$$

and setting this equation to zero we get

$$S_1'\left[2(\frac{h_1 + h_{n-1}}{h_1\, h_{n-1}}) + \frac{\nu_1 + \nu_n}{2}\right] + \frac{S_2'}{h_1} + \frac{S_{n-1}'}{h_{n-1}}$$

$$= 3[\frac{(y_n - y_{n-1})}{(h_{n-1})^2} + \frac{(y_2 - y_1)}{(h_1)^2}].$$

If we let $\mu_1 = \frac{h_{n-1}}{h_1 + h_{n-1}}$ $\lambda_1 = 1 - \mu_1$,

$\bar{\nu}_1 = \frac{(\nu_1 + \nu_n)}{2} \frac{h_1 h_{n-1}}{(h_1 + h_{n-1})}$ and multiply the previous equation by $h_1\mu_1$ we obtain

$$(4.5)\quad \begin{bmatrix} 2+\bar{\nu}_1 & \mu_1 & & & \lambda_1 \\ \lambda_2 & 2+\bar{\nu}_2 & \mu_2 & & \\ & \cdot & \cdot & \cdot & \\ & & & & \mu_{n-2} \\ \mu_{n-1} & & & \lambda_{n-1} & 2+\bar{\nu}_{n-1} \end{bmatrix} \begin{bmatrix} S_1' \\ \vdots \\ S_{n-1}' \end{bmatrix} = \begin{bmatrix} d_1 \\ \vdots \\ d_{n-1} \end{bmatrix}$$

where $d_1 = 3\left[\lambda_1 \frac{(y_n - y_1)}{h_{n-1}} + \mu_1 \frac{(y_2 - y_1)}{h_1}\right]$

Equations (4.3) and (4.4) can be solved using the standard techniques for tridiagonal systems. Equation (4.5) is slightly different but can be solved in a similar way [4].

The following lemma will be used to prove Theorem 4.2 which was referred to in Section 3.

Lemma 4.1. The coefficient matrices of equations (4.3) (4.4) and (4.5) are positive definite.

Proof: Let A be the coefficient matrix of (4.4). Then with $\lambda_{n+1} = 0$, $\lambda_n = 1$, $\mu_0 = 0$, and $\mu_1 = 1$, we have

$$2x^*Ax = \sum_{i=1}^{n} [2\overline{\nu}_i + 3 - \mu_{i-1} - \lambda_{i+1}]x_i^2$$

$$+ \sum_{i=1}^{n-1} [\mu_i + \lambda_{i+1}][x_i + x_{i+1}]^2$$

and since $0 \leqslant \lambda_i, \mu_i \leqslant 1$, $i = 1,\ldots,n$, it is clear that A is positive definite. A similar argument can be used for the other cases.■

Theorem 4.2. The matrix

$$\left(\frac{\partial s_i^2}{\partial \nu_j}\right) \qquad (i,j) \in I\mathrm{x}I$$

is negative semidefinite. The notation is that of Lemma 3.4.

Proof: Let A denote the coefficient matrix of (4.3), (4.4) or (4.5), S' the matrix with entries $s_{ij} = \delta_{ij} S'_i$, $(i,j) \in I \times I$ and $\frac{\partial S'}{\partial \nu}$ the matrix $\left(\frac{\partial S'_i}{\partial \nu_j}\right)$ $(i,j) \in I \times I$. By taking the partial with respect to $\bar{\nu}_j$, $j \in I$ of (4.3), (4.4) or (4.5) we find that

$$A\frac{\partial S'}{\partial \bar{\nu}} = - S' .$$

Therefore,

$$\left(\frac{\partial (S'_i)^2}{\partial \bar{\nu}_j}\right) (i,j) \in I \times I = \left(2S'_i \frac{\partial S'_i}{\partial \nu_j}\right), (i,j) \in I \times I$$

$$= 2S' \frac{\partial S'}{\partial \bar{\nu}} = -2(S')^* A^{-1}(S')$$

Since A is positive definite, so is A^{-1}. Consequently $-2(S')^* A^{-1}(S')$ is negative semidefinite and recalling that $\bar{\nu}_j$ is simply a constant multiple of ν_j, we obtain the desired result.

5. Examples.

All of the examples in this section were generated with a Tektronix 4010 interactive graphics terminal and a DEC PDP-10 timesharing computer.* The actual hard-

* The author wishes to thank Yavapai College, Prescott, Arizona for the use of their DEC PDP-10 Computer.

copy plots were made using a HP 7200A plotter.

Example 1. This example illustrates the effect of the tension for both ν-splines and splines in tension. Figure 1 contains the graphs of a spline in tension with periodic end conditions, interpolating the vertices of an equilateral triangle. The knots are equally spaced in the parameter domain [0,1]. The tension values are $\alpha = 0,1,2,4,8,16$. Figure 2 shows a similar behavior for ν-splines with type iii' end conditions. The data and knot-spacing is the same as in Figure 1 but the tension values are $\nu_1 = \nu_2 = \nu_3 = \nu_4 = \nu = 0,2,8,32,128,512$.

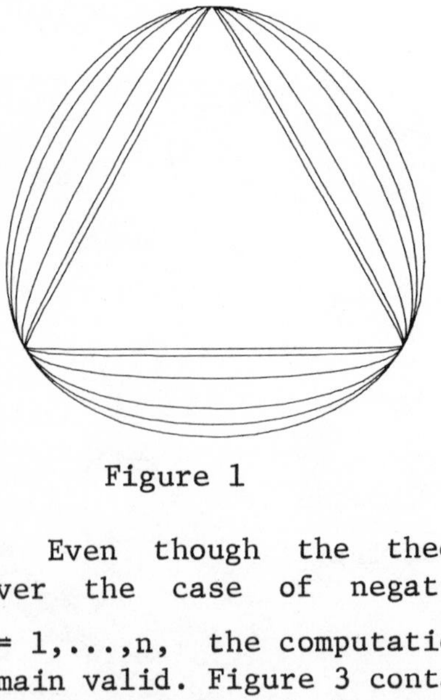

Figure 1

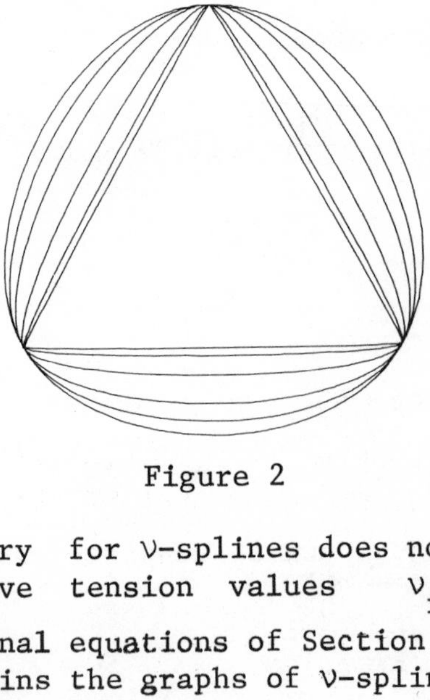

Figure 2

Even though the theory for ν-splines does not cover the case of negative tension values ν_i, $i = 1,\ldots,n$, the computational equations of Section 4 remain valid. Figure 3 contains the graphs of ν-spline similar to Figure 2, but with $\nu_1 = \nu_2 = \nu_3 = \nu_4 = \nu = -2, -8, -32, -128, -512$. This behavior is typical of ν-splines with negative tension values in that the curve first expands to a point where the directional derivatives at the knots reverse direction and loops appear. As the tension value is further decreased, the loops are eventually drawn out of the curve creating cusps at the interpolation points. We should point out that a negative value of α for the normal spline in tension does not exhibit this behavior, for α and $-\alpha$ generate precisely the same curve.

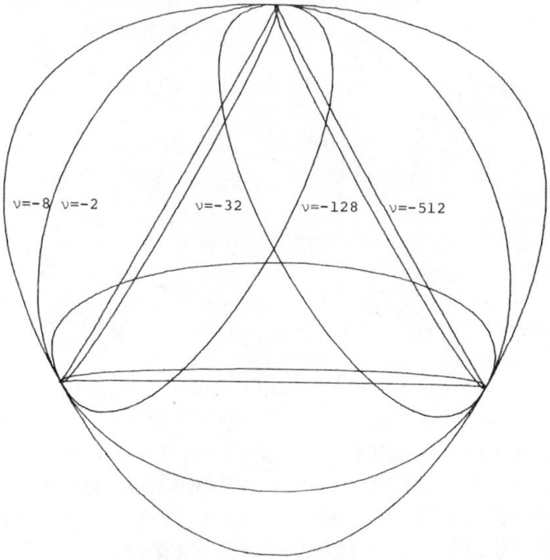

Figure 3

Example 2. This example illustrates one of the additional advantages that ν-splines have compared to the normal splines in tension in that tension can be applied selectively at each interpolation point. Figure 4 contains the graph of a spline in tension with natural end conditions and $\alpha = 0$ (i.e. a cubic interpolating spline with natural end conditions or equivalently a ν-spline with ii' end conditions and $\nu_i = 0$, $i = 1,\ldots,n$). The 14 points are labeled consecutively in a clockwise fashion beginning in the upper right hand corner. In order to put the desired corners into the curve by using a normal spline in tension it would be necessary to use $\alpha = \infty$ which would have uniform effect throughout the curve resulting in a polygonal line joining the data points. With the ν-spline it is possible to selectively apply varying values of tension at each of the knots yielding the curve in Figure 5.

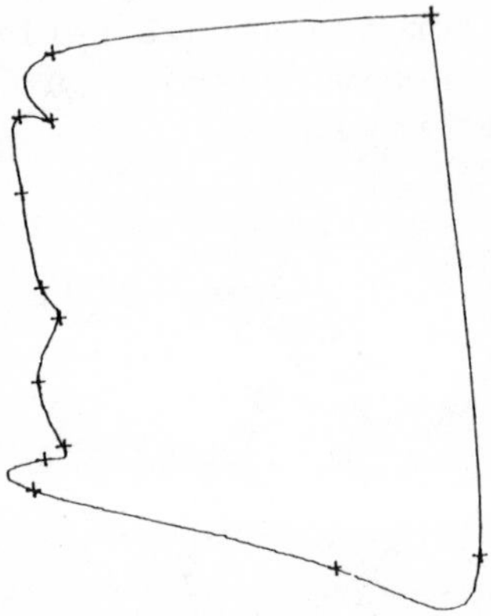

Figure 4

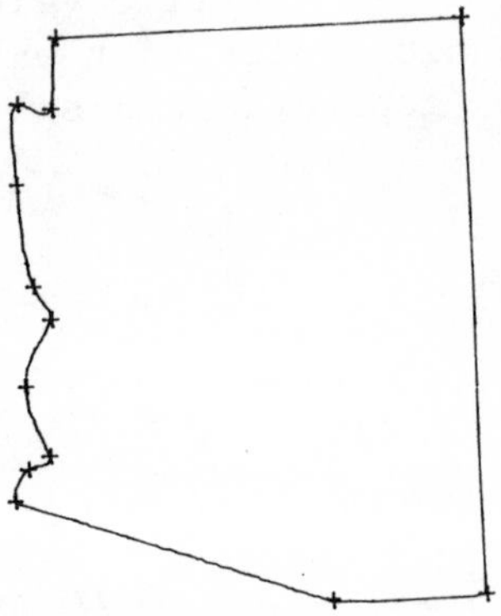

Figure 5

<u>Example 3</u>. This example illustrates the effect of type i' end conditions on ν-splines. There are five equally spaced interpolation points enumerated beginning at the left and proceeding in a counterclockwise fashion. The knots are equally spaced in the interval [0,1]. Figure 6 contains the graph of a ν-spline with increasing magnitude of a horizontal tangent vector at each of the end points. The actual $(x'(0), y'(0)) = 2^i\rho(p_1,p_2)(1,0)$, $(x'(1), y''(1)) = 2^i\rho(p_4,p_5)(-1,0)$, $i = 0,1,2,3,4$, where $\rho(p_i,p_j)$ represents the distance from p_i to p_j. Figure 7 shows the effect of the direction of the end tangent vectors. The respective tangent vectors are

$(x'(0), y'(0)) = 8(\cos(i\pi/4), \sin(i\pi/4))$,

$(x'(1), y'(1)) = 8(-\cos(i\pi/4), \sin(i\pi/4))$, $i=0,1,2,3,4$.

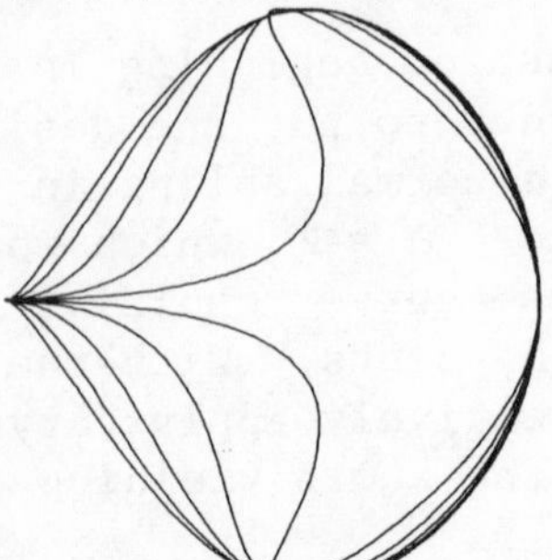

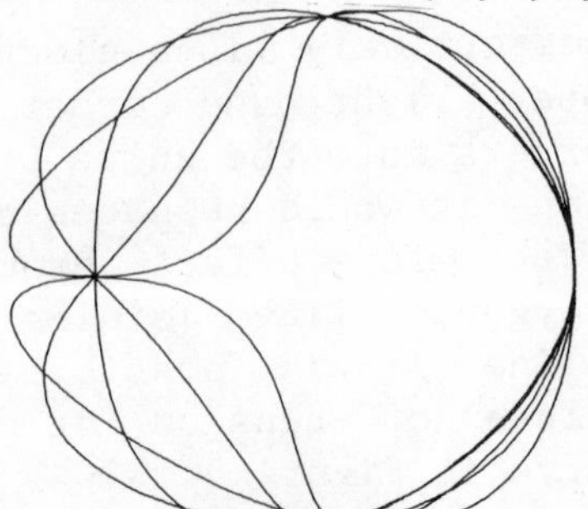

References

1. Cline, A.K., "Scalar- and Planar-Valued Curve Fitting Using Splines under Tension," Comm. ACM 17,4, 1974, pp. 218-220.

2. deBoor, C.R. and Lynch, R.E., "On Splines and Their Minimum Properties," J. Math. Mech. 15, 1966, pp. 953-969.

3. Golomb, M. and Weinberger, H.F., "Optimal Approximation and Error Bounds," R.E. Langer (ed.), "On Numerical Approximation", University of Wisconsin Press, Madison, 1959, pp. 117-190.

4. Nielson, G.M., "Computation of ν-splines," Technical Report NR 044-443-11, Dept. of Mathematics, Arizona State University, Tempe, Arizona, 1974.

5. Schweikert, D.G., "An Interpolation Curve Using a Spline in Tension, "J. Math. & Physics 45, 1966, pp. 312-317.

SMOOTH PARAMETRIC SURFACES

David Pilcher
Hercules, Inc.

1. Introduction

We shall concern ourselves with the problem of describing surfaces "in the large." Instead of subdividing a surface into parts or "patches", we shall investigate ways to treat it as a whole.

Very often it is possible to reduce the problem of describing a surface to one of describing appropriate curves. This reduces the complexity for it changes the mathematical problem from two variables to one. For example, we may illustrate the surface by displaying a family of curves formed by intersecting the surface with a set of parallel planes. The full mathematical description of the surface can be obtained by blending these curves [5] or by interpolating matching points on the various curves, etc. We shall, therefore, first consider some techniques for designing smooth curves. Insight gained here will aid in defining a general scheme for handling surfaces.

B-Spline Curves

A B-spline approximation to a curve often tends to be smoother than the usual polynomial spline approximation. We shall discuss why these approximations are so well-behaved.

Definition: An approximation $A(x)$ to the function $f(x)$ on $[a,b]$ is said to be variation-diminishing if it is exact for linear functions and if, for every line $\ell(x)$, the difference $A(x) - \ell(x)$ has no more variations in sign than the difference $f(x) - \ell(x)$.

It has been shown [8, p.9] that this smoothing property is preserved when such functions are used to to approximate a parametric curve.

Schoenberg [9] introduced the following spline approximation of degree k.

$$(1.1)\quad Sf(x) = S_{\Delta}^{k}f(x) = \sum_{j=-k}^{n-1} f(\xi_j)\, N_j(k), \quad a \leqslant x \leqslant b$$

where the set of knots $\Delta = \{a = x_0 < x_1 \leqslant x_2 \leqslant \ldots \leqslant x_{n-1} < x_n = b\}$ is extended by

$$(1.2)\quad x_{-k} = x_{-k+1} = \ldots = x_{-1} = a \quad \text{and}$$

$$x_{n+1} = x_{n+2} = \ldots x_{n+k} = b$$

The "nodes" ξ_j are defined by

$$(1.3)\quad \xi_j = \frac{x_{j+1} + \ldots + x_{j+k}}{k} \qquad (-k \leqslant j < n)$$

and the functions $N_j(x)$ are the normalized spline basis functions, or B-splines.

The $N_j(x)$ are non-negative and sum to one. Hence the curve will remain inside the convex hull of the data points $f(\xi_j)$.

Schoenberg's approximation suggests the vector analogue

$$(1.4) \qquad \vec{S}(t) = \sum_{j=-k}^{n-1} \vec{P}_j N_j(t)$$

as a design scheme. The curve will, of course, depend upon the choice of the knots Δ and its extension as well as the data set $\{\vec{P}_j\}$. The resulting parametric curve will be variation-diminishing and will have the convex hull property. Marsden [7, p.60] has shown that if the knots are evenly spaced, then the approximation is equivalent to Bernstein approximation on the intervals

$$(1.5) \quad \frac{(i-1)k}{n+k-1} \leqslant x \leqslant \frac{ik}{n+k-1} \qquad (0 \leqslant i \leqslant \frac{n+k-1}{k}).$$

This indicates that the Schoenberg approximation is a generalization of the familiar Bézier curve:

$$(1.6) \quad \vec{B}(t) = \sum_{n=0}^{N} \vec{f}_n \binom{N}{n} t^n (1-t)^{N-n}, \qquad t \in [0,1].$$

The B-spline curves of Gordon and Riesenfeld are a subset of these variation-diminishing curves. Likewise, after some effort [8], one can show that the B-spline curves of Coons fit in the same class.

These variation-diminishing curves have another property of interest here. Like the polynomial interpolating spline, the variation-diminishing spline of degree $2k - 1$ minimizes $\int_{t_0}^{t_n} [f^{(k)}]^2 dt$ under appropriate boundary and interpolation conditions.

<u>Lemma 1.1</u>. Given a data set $\{(x_i, y_i)\}_{i=0}^{n}$, let $f(x)$ satisfy

$$(1.7)\qquad f(x_i) = \sum_{j=i-2k+1}^{i-1} y_j N_j(x_i),$$

$f \in C^{k-1}[x_0,x_n]$, and $f^{(k)}$ piecewise continuous. Then the Schoenberg variation-diminishing spline $Sf(x)$ satisfies the inequality

$$(1.8)\qquad \int_{x_0}^{x_n} [Sf^{(k)}]^2 dx \leq \int_{x_0}^{x_n} [f^{(k)}]^2 dx$$

subject to appropriate end conditions.

Proof. The B-splines have limited support, so

$$(1.9)\qquad Sf(x_i) = \sum_{j=i-2k+1}^{i-1} y_j N_j(x_i) = y_i^*.$$

If one now considers $Sf(x)$ as a polynomial spline interpolating the data set $\{(x_i,y_i^*)\}$, the inequality follows immediately from the minimization property of polynomial splines. Q.E.D.

From this we may see that the cubic B-spline minimizes $\int_a^b [x''(t)]^2 dt$, the "linearized curvature", subject to appropriate boundary conditions, just as the cubic natural spline does.

2. Spline Under Tension

In the case of the B-spline curve we have sacrificed interpolation for greater smoothing capabilities. An alternate way of smoothing a curve is to use the spline under tension.

Intuitively one might eliminate extraneous loops or bumps in the interpolating spline curve by reducing its length. This suggests that the curve designed by a set of data $\{\vec{P}_i\}$ could be defined by seeking the curve $\vec{C}(t) \in C^2$ which minimizes

$$(2.1) \quad J(g) = \int_{t_0}^{t_n} [g'']^2 dt + \sigma^2 \int_{t_0}^{t_n} [g']^2 dt, \ \sigma > 0$$

for each coordinate function, subject to $\vec{C}(t_i) = \vec{P}_i$. The first term of the functional affects smoothness (as with the cubic spline) and the second term influences length. To see that the latter is true we note that for $\vec{f}(t) = [x(t),y(t)]$, using the Schwarz inequality,

$$(2.2) \text{Length} = \int_{t_0}^{t_n} \sqrt{\dot{x}^2+\dot{y}^2}\, dt \le \left[(t_n-t_0) \int_{t_0}^{t_n} (\dot{x}^2+\dot{y}^2) dt\right]^{\frac{1}{2}}.$$

Reduction of the length of the interpolating curve eliminates extraneous critical points. Schweikert [10] gave sufficient conditions for the interpolant to be void of such points. He suggested a function, called the spline under tension, which is a "blend" of the cubic spline and the piecewise linear interpolant. The function which minimizes $J(f)$ satisfies the Euler equation:

$$(2.3) \qquad f^{(4)}(x) - \sigma^2 f^{(2)}(x) = 0, \quad x \in [x_i, x_{i+1}].$$

The solution to this differential equation is

$$(2.4) \qquad f(x) = Ae^{-\sigma x} + Be^{\sigma x} + Cx + D;$$

A,B,C,D constants.

Demanding interpolation and second derivative continuity at each of the knots leads to a system of 4n-6 equations in 4n-4 unknowns. Two additional boundary conditions would complete the system.

Alternatively, we may specify that the function f satisfy $f''(x) - \sigma^2 f'(x)$. Cline [2] has used this approach of "blending" the cubic spline and linear spline interpolant and obtained the solution of (2.3) with uniform σ.

It has been shown [8, p.23] that it is possible to solve for the parameters $f''(x_i)$ when σ is allowed to vary over each subinterval. One obtains the linear system

$$\left[\frac{1}{h_{i-1}} - \frac{\sigma_{i-1}}{\sinh(\sigma_{i-1}h_{i-1})}\right]\frac{f''(x_{i-1})}{\sigma^2_{i-1}}$$

$$+\left[\frac{\cosh(\sigma_{i-1}h_{i-1})}{\sigma^2_{i-1}\sinh(\ {}^2_{i-1}h_{i-1})} - \frac{1}{(\sigma^2_{i-1}h_{i-1})}\right.$$

$$\left.+\frac{\cosh(\sigma_i h_i)}{\sigma_i^2\sin(\sigma_i h_i)} - \frac{1}{\sigma_i^2 h_i}\right] f''(x_i)$$

$$+\left[\frac{1}{h_i} - \frac{\sigma_i}{\sinh(\sigma_i h_i)}\right]\frac{f''(x_{i+1})}{\sigma_i^2} = \frac{y_{i+1}-y_i}{h_i} - \frac{y_i-y_{i-1}}{h_{i-1}}$$

$i = 2,3,\ldots,n-1.$

The spline under tension is very close to the cubic interpolating spline for small σ and approaches the piecewise linear interpolant for large σ. By adjusting the tension along the curve, a designer has great control over the shape of the curve. Unwanted bumps in a segment of the curve can be eliminated by reducing the length of that segment (increasing σ_i) and often loops can be removed. It is not true, however, that one can always remove an extraneous loop by increasing the tension. For example, consider the data set $\{(0,0),(0,2),(\frac{1}{10},1),(2,0)\}$ with initial slope of $-\frac{1}{2}$, where the curve traverses the points in the order listed.

Figure 1 shows an example of the spline under tension for various values of σ.

It is possible to establish a number of results corresponding to the well-known "integral relations" for polynomial splines [8]. We shall, however, include only the one of major interest to our discussion.

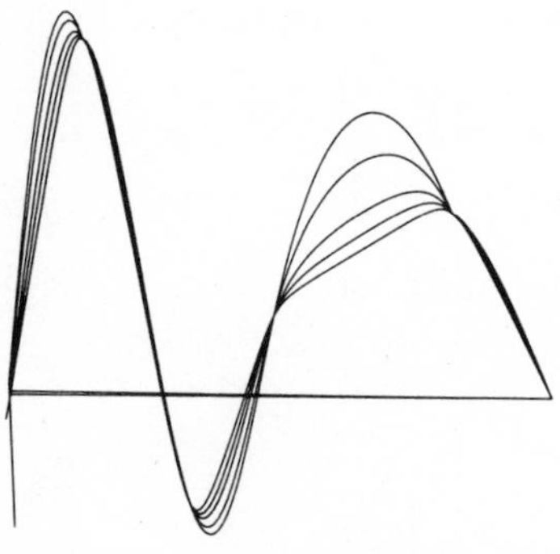

Figure 1

Theorem 2.1. Let $s(t)$ be the spline under tension with natural end conditions interpolating the data $\{(x_i,y_i)\}_{i=1}^n$. Let f be any interpolating function such that $f \in C^1$ and f'' is piecewise continuous. Then $J(s) \leq J(f)$ with equality if $s \equiv f$, where

$$J(f) = \int_{x_1}^{x_n} (f'')^2 dx + \sigma^2 \int_{x_1}^{x_n} (f')^2 dx.$$

Proof.

$$J(f) - J(s) = \int_{x_1}^{x_n} [(f''-s'')^2 + 2s''(f''-s'')]dx$$

$$+ \sigma^2 \int_{x_1}^{x_n} [(f'-s')^2 + 2s'(f'-s')]dx$$

$$= \int_{x_1}^{x_n} [(\varepsilon'')^2 + 2s''\varepsilon'' + \sigma^2((\varepsilon')^2 + 2s'\varepsilon')]dx$$

where $\varepsilon(x) = f(x) - s(x)$.

Integrating by parts, we obtain

$$\int_{x_1}^{x_n} s''\varepsilon''dx = \int_{x_1}^{x_n} \varepsilon s^{(4)}dx$$

and

$$\int_{x_1}^{x_n} s'\varepsilon'dx = -\int_{x_1}^{x_n} \varepsilon s''dx.$$

Since $s(t)$ satisfies the Euler equation $y^{(4)} - \sigma^2 y'' = 0$, we obtain

$$J(f) - J(s) = \int_{x_1}^{x_n} (\varepsilon'')^2 + \sigma^2(\varepsilon')^2 dx$$

(2.6)

$$+ 2\int_{x_1}^{x_n} \varepsilon(s^{(4)} - \sigma^2 s'')dx \geq 0.$$

If $J(f) = J(s)$, then

$$\int_{x_1}^{x_n} (\varepsilon'')^2 dx + \sigma^2 \int_{x_1}^{x_n} (\varepsilon')^2 dx = 0$$

which implies $\varepsilon(x) = f(x) - s(x) =$ a constant a.e. However $\varepsilon(x) \in C^1$ and $\varepsilon(x_1) = 0$, so $\varepsilon(x) \equiv 0$.

Q.E.D.

3. Tensor Products

We have illustrated that curves useful in the design process can be defined by demanding that they minimize certain functionals. We shall use this approach to define smooth surfaces.

For the initial design of parametric surfaces where the ability to alter easily the surface with a minimum of data manipulation is desired, the Coons spline seems, at present, to be the most convenient mathematical representation. This method is actually an extension of patching techniques.

Given a surface $\vec{f}(s,t)$ and/or a grid of points $\{\vec{P}_{ij}\}_{i,j=0}^{m,n}$, we construct the tensor product surface

$$(3.1)\quad A(s,t) = \sum_{i,j} \vec{P}_{ij} N_{i-c+1}(s) N_{j-d+1}(t)$$

$$0 \leqslant s \leqslant m, \qquad 0 \leqslant t \leqslant n.$$

The one variable B-spline curves have order c and d. For computational purposes we give the piecewise representation. Beginning at P_{00} we march along generating patches of surface. Each patch $A_{i,j}(s,t)$ is defined by

$$(3.2)\quad A_{i,j}(s,t) = \sum_{k=1}^{n} \sum_{j=1}^{m} \vec{\alpha}_{j,k} s^k t^j$$

$$0 \leqslant s \leqslant 1, \qquad 0 \leqslant t \leqslant 1$$

where

$$(3.3) \qquad \alpha_{j,k} = \sum_{\ell=1}^{m} \sum_{i=1}^{n} b_{k,i} c_{j,\ell} \vec{P}_{i\ell}.$$

$[b_{ij}]$ is the appropriate matrix for the (c-1) degree spline in s and $[c_{ij}]$ is the appropriate matrix for the (d-1) degree spline in t. Just as with the tensor product of polynomial splines, this tensor product minimizes

$$J_2(f) = \iint_R \left(\frac{\partial^4 f}{\partial x^2 \partial y^2}\right)^2 dx\, dy$$

subject to appropriate boundary conditions.

We consider now the problem of interpolation of data over a rectangular mesh with the tensor product of splines under tension $S(x,y)$. Suppose we are given two one-dimensional meshes over the rectangle $R \equiv [a,b] \times [c,d]$. This partitions R into a family of subrectangles $\{R_{ij}\}$ with vertices $\{P_{ij}\}$ $(i = 0,1,\ldots,n;\ j = 0,1,\ldots,m)$ where $P_{ij} = (x_i,y_j)$. We again impose the "natural" boundary conditions:

$$(3.4) \qquad \begin{aligned} &\frac{\partial^2}{\partial x^2} S(P_{ij}) = 0, \quad i = 0,n;\ j = 1,2\ldots,m-1 \\ &\frac{\partial^2}{\partial y^2} S(P_{ij}) = 0, \quad i = 1,2,\ldots,n-1;\ j = 0,m \\ &\frac{\partial^4}{\partial x^2 \partial y^2} S(P_{ij}) = 0, \quad i = 0,n;\ j = 0,m. \end{aligned}$$

Conditions (3.4) imply that

$$(3.5) \qquad \frac{\partial^2 S}{\partial n^2} = 0 \quad \text{on } \partial R.$$

We note that over each subrectangle R_{ij} the tensor product satisfies the partial differential equation

$$\frac{\partial^8 S}{\partial x^4 \partial y^4} - \sigma^4 \frac{\partial^4 S}{\partial x^2 \partial y^2} = 0. \tag{3.6}$$

Theorem 3.1. Let the rectangle $R \equiv [a,b]\times[c,d]$ be given along with a rectangular mesh with mesh points $\{(x_i,y_j)\}$ $(i = 0,1\ldots,n;\ j = 0,1\ldots,m)$. Also, let the set of real numbers $\{z_{ij}\}$ be given where z_{ij} is associated with (x_i,y_j). Of all functions $f(x,y)$ in $C^{2,2}[R]$ which interpolate the given data, the spline under tension $S(x,y)$ with "natural" end conditions minimizes

$$J_3(f) = \int_a^b \int_c^d \left[\frac{\partial^4 f}{\partial x^2 \partial y^2}\right]^2 + \sigma^4 \left[\frac{\partial^2 f}{\partial x \partial y}\right]^2 dxdy \tag{3.7}$$

Proof. Let $\varepsilon(x,y) = f(x,y) - S(x,y)$. Consider $J(f) - J(S)$ and integrate by parts using (3.5) and the fact that $\varepsilon(x,y) = 0$ on ∂R. Thus

$$J_3(f) - J_3(S) = \int_R \left\{\left[\frac{\partial^4 \varepsilon}{\partial x^2 \partial y^2}\right]^2 + \sigma^4 \left[\frac{\partial^2 \varepsilon}{\partial x \partial y}\right]^2\right\} dxdy + 2\int_R \left[\frac{\partial^8 S}{\partial x^4 \partial y^4} - \sigma^4 \frac{\partial^4 S}{\partial x^2 \partial y^2}\right] \varepsilon\, dxdy \tag{3.8}$$

Applying (3.5) to the third term, we obtain

$$J_3(f) - J_3(S) \geq 0. \tag{3.9}$$

Q.E.D.

The following figures show the tensor product of the spline under tension. The data set is the same in both cases. For Figure 2 the tension σ was 0.5. For Figure 3 it was 9.0. The change from the curving surface in Figure 2 to nearly piecewise linear one in Figure 3 indicates the usefulness of this function as a design tool.

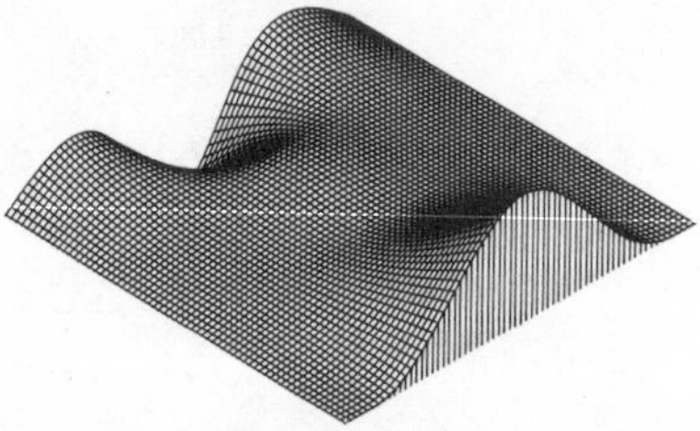

Figure 2

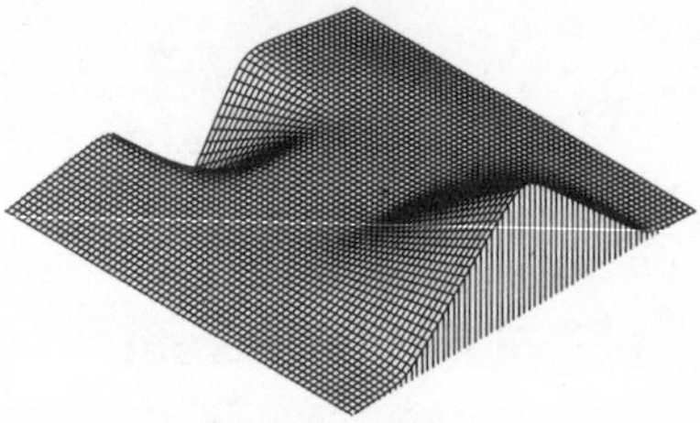

Figure 3

Figure 4 is a first cut of an auto body. Input data was given for only 6 lines running the length of the body and was rather sparse. Figure 5 shows a refinement of the design.

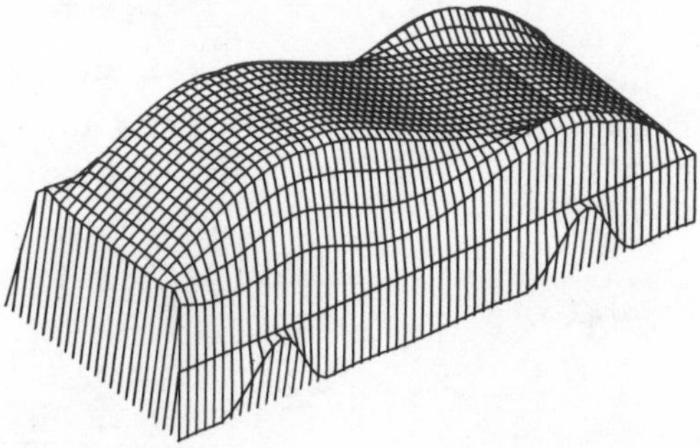

Figure 4

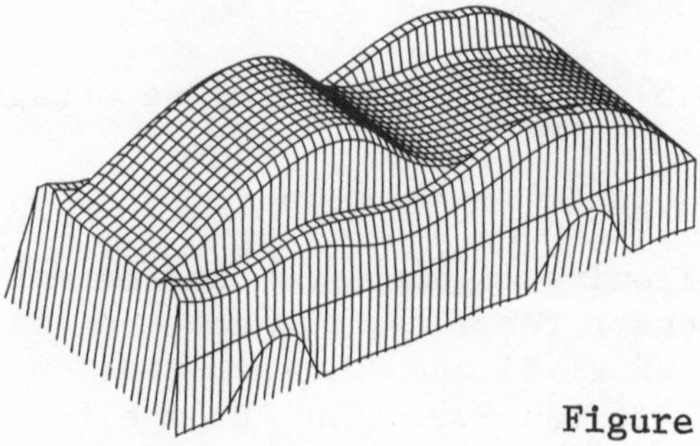

Figure 5

4. Fitting Random Data with an Elastic Skin

As with curves in the plane, we shall control the surface by selecting an interpolant which minimizes an appropriate functional. Experimentation with tensor products of splines indicate that one term of the functional should be $\int_\Omega \left[\frac{\partial^4 f}{\partial x^2 \partial y^2}\right]^2$. This term will influence the smoothness of the surface. To avoid unwanted undulations, a second part is added to influence the area. For functions of two variables defined over a region Ω, area is found by

$$A(f) = \int_\Omega \sqrt{(1 + f_x^2 + f_y^2)}\, dxdy.$$

From the Schwarz Inequality,

$$\begin{aligned} A(f) &\le \left[\int_\Omega dxdy\right]^{\frac{1}{2}} \left[\int_\Omega (1 + f_x^2 + f_y^2)\, dxdy\right]^{\frac{1}{2}} \\ (4.1) \qquad &\le k_1 \int_\Omega (f_x^2 + f_y^2) dxdy + k_2; \; k_1, k_2 \text{ constants.} \end{aligned}$$

The functional of interest is thus

$$(4.2) \quad J_4(f) = \int_\Omega \left(\left(\frac{\partial^4 f}{\partial x^2 \partial y^2}\right)^2 + \sigma^2 \left(\frac{\partial f}{\partial x}\right)^2 + \sigma^2 \left(\frac{\partial f}{\partial y}\right)^2 \right) dxdy.$$

Let

$$\frac{\partial^{m+n} f}{\partial x^m \partial y^n} = f_{m,n}.$$

To allow for arbitrary placement of data, we shall use the finite element method [11] to approximate the function $U(x,y)$ which minimizes $J_4(f)$ subject to

$$f(x_i, y_i) = z_i ,$$

$$f(x,y) = g(x,y) \quad \text{on the boundary of } \Omega.$$

The domain Ω is triangulated and an approximate solution $v(x,y)$ is determined from among those functions which have continuous first partial derivatives and for which $v_{2,2} \in L_2$ on each subregion. Possible interpolants include the blending function interpolants like those found in [1] as well as the polynomial interpolants appearing in engineering literature. The reader interested in polynomial interpolants will find [4,11] helpful. The linear systems which arise from the finite element method are rather large and so it is a distinct advantage to keep the number of parameters per triangle as small as possible. The form of the functional, $J_4(f)$, demands that the interpolant be in $C^3(\Omega)$. After one obtains such an interpolant, it is possible through use of an affine transformation to calculate $J_4(f)$ only on the standard triangle (vertices (0,0),(1,0), (1,1)) rather than over each triangle of the domain. Details of this are found in [8, p. 40]. For methods of triangulating the domain we refer the reader to George [4].

Modeling surfaces by minimizations of functionals such as $J_4(f)$ is practical with present computer capabilities. Engineers are having great success using the finite element method for solving problems which are mathematically equivalent to those discussed here. The techniques suggested allow one to build desirable physical properties into the mathematical model. Research has been carried out on high order interpolants associated with $J_4(f)$. To reduce the algebraic complexity of such interpolants, extensive use was made of REDUCE 2 [6], an algebraic programming system available at the University of Utah.

5. General Parametric Surface

Let $\vec{X} = \vec{X}(u,v)$ be a given surface and let $ds^2 = Edu^2 + 2Fdudv + Gdv^2$ be the linear element of $\vec{X}$, where

$$(5.1)\qquad \begin{aligned} E &= (\vec{X}_{1,0},\vec{X}_{1,0}) \\ F &= (\vec{X}_{1,0},\vec{X}_{0,1}) \\ G &= (\vec{X}_{0,1},\vec{X}_{0,1}); \end{aligned} \qquad (.,.) \text{ is the Euclidean inner product.}$$

The discriminant $EG - F^2$ we shall denote by D. The area of a region on the surface is

$$(5.2)\qquad A = \iint_R D\, dudv$$

where R is the set of points in the uv-plane corresponding to the region. Earlier discussions lead us to define

(5.3)
$$J_6(\vec{X}) = \iint_R \left\{ \sum_{i=1}^{3} (x^i_{2,2})^2 + \sigma^2 \sum_{\substack{i=1 \\ j<i}}^{3} (x^i_{1,0}x^j_{0,1} - x^i_{0,1}x^j_{1,0})^2 \right\} dudv.$$

The first term again affects smoothness and the second area. To determine a function $\vec{U}^*(u,v)$ approximating $\vec{U}(u,v)$, the function which minimizes J_6 subject to appropriate boundary conditions, we would need to solve a system of nonlinear equations. To avoid this situation we choose instead the functional

(5.4)

$$J_7(\vec{X}) = \int_R\int \left\{ \sum_{i=1}^{3} (x^i_{2,2})^2 + \sigma^2 (x^i_{0,1})^2 + \sigma^2 (x^i_{1,0})^2 \right\} dudv.$$

$$\vec{X} = [x^1(u,v), x^2(u,v), x^3(u,v)]$$

subject to interpolation of the data. This is strictly a component-wise approach.

References.

1. R.E. Barnhill and J.A. Gregory, *Blending Function Interpolation to Boundary Data on Triangles*, TR/14, Department of Mathematics, Brunel University, Uxbridge, England, 1972.

2. A.K. Cline, *Scalar- and- Planar Valued Curve Fitting Using Splines under Tension*, Comm. ACM 17, 4 pp. 218-220, 1974.

3. C.R. deBoor and R.E. Lynch, *On Splines and Their Minimum Properties*, J. Math. Mech. 15 (1966), 953-969.

4. J.A. George, *Computer Implementation of the Finite Element Method*, Ph.D. Thesis, Computer Science Department, Stanford University, 1971.

5. W.J. Gordon, *Spline-Blended Surface Interpolation Through Curve Networks*, J. Math. Mech. 18 (1969), 931-952.

6. A.C. Hearn, *REDUCE 2 Users Manual*, Computer Science Division, University of Utah, 1973.

7. M.J. Marsden, *An Identity for Spline Functions with Applications to Variation-Diminishing Spline Approximation*, J. Approx. Theory 3 (1970).

8. D.T. Pilcher, *Smooth Approximation of Parametric Curves and Surfaces*, Ph.D. Thesis, Mathematics Department, University of Utah, 1973.

9. I.J. Schoenberg, *On Spline Functions*, in "Inequalities", (Symposium at Wright-Patterson Air Force Base), Academic Press, New York, 1967, 255-291.

10. D.G. Schweikert, *An Interpolation Curve Using a Spline Under Tension*, J. Math and Physics, 45, (1966), 312-317.

11. M. Zlámal, *On the Finite Element Method*, Numer. Math. 12 (1968), 394-409.

THE SPACE CURVE AS A FOLDED EDGE

Ronald D. Resch
University of Utah

Since a folded edge can determine a space curve, this research focused on the question: given any space curve, can one develop a two dimensional score line such that its folding will produce the desired space curve as a folded edge?

The images on the following pages exhibit the use of a given space curve as a folded edge in an architectural model. The model was designed with the aid of the computer images. A numeric control tape, which determined the layout of the sheets to be developed, was used in the fabrication of the physical models.

Ephraim Cohen (now at Applicon Corp., Burlington, Mass.) was responsible for the mathematical definition and the computer programming of a folded, curved edge.

The research reported in this paper was directed by the author during 1972-73 under ARPA-IPT DOD Contract #F30602-70-C-0300.

References

1. Resch, R., "The Topological Design of Sculptural and Architectural Systems", AFIPS - CONFERENCE PROCEEDINGS, Vol. 42, NCC, 1973, 643-650.

2. Resch, R., "Portfolio of Shaded Computer Images", Proceedings of IEEE, Vol. 62 no. 4, April 1974, 496-502.

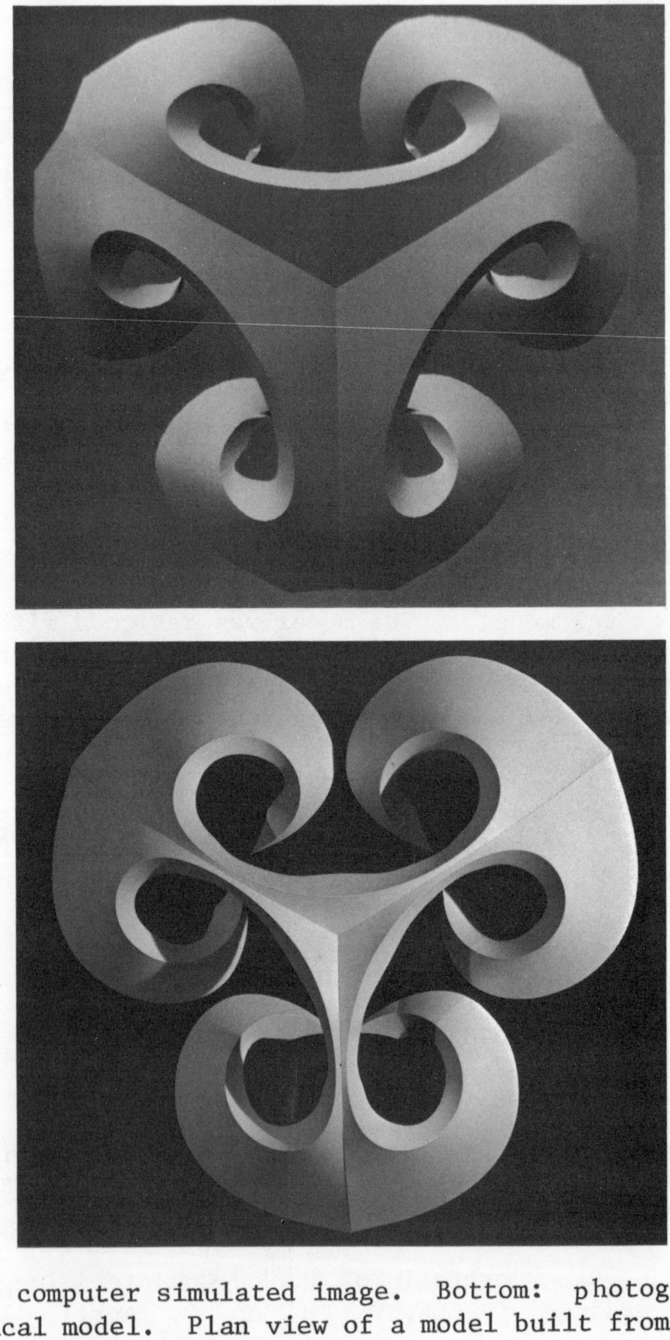

Top: computer simulated image. Bottom: photograph of physical model. Plan view of a model built from developable surfaces with folded edges.

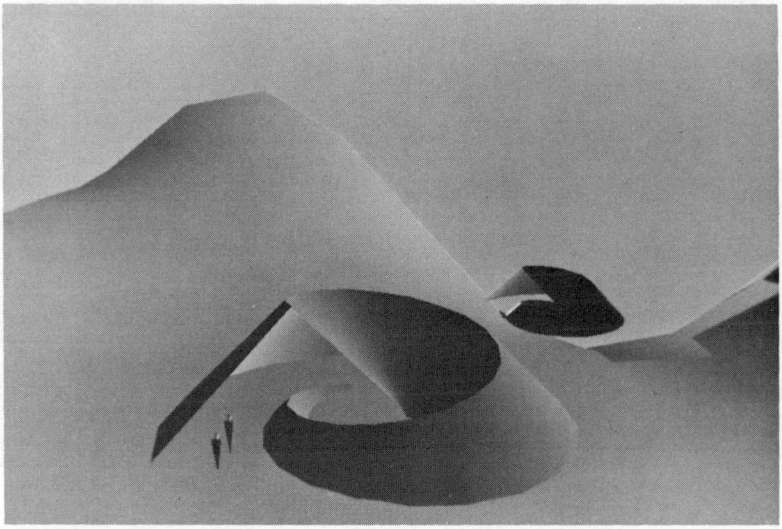

Top: computer simulated image. Bottom: photograph of physical model. Elevation and oblique views, respectively, of same structure.

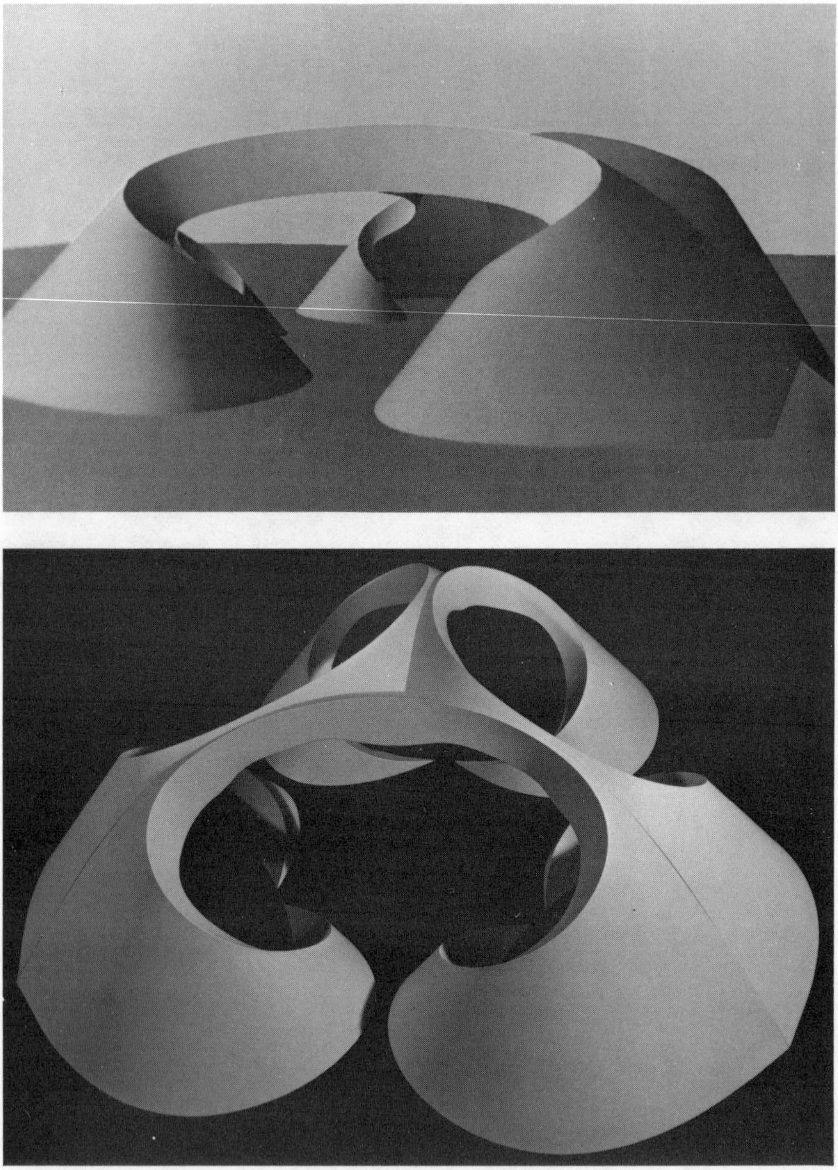

Top: computer simulated image of interior elevation view of a variation of the previous structure. Bottom: computer simulated image of suggested architectural structure.

interactive computer graphics application of the
PARAMETRIC BI-CUBIC SURFACE
to engineering design problems

by George J. Peters
McDonnell Douglas Automation Company
St. Louis, Missouri

1. INTRODUCTION

Engineering design has typically depended upon a great number of mathematical forms and techniques. It is most unusual to expect any one device or curve to serve more than one purpose. This paper concerns, however, just such a multipurpose device – one which may well turn out to be a panacea for engineering design.

The entity of interest here is the parametric cubic (PC) curve and its surface counterpart, the PC bi-cubic surface patch. The original theoretical analyses were set forth by Coons [1,2]* and Ferguson [3]; Forrest [4] expanded their efforts. Extensive batch computer development of the PC for structural design applications has been done by Douglas Aircraft Company and McDonnell Douglas Astronautics Company under the leadership of Eshleman and Meriwether [5].

McDonnell Douglas Automation Company, in conjunction with McDonnell Aircraft Company, has been pursuing another objective–complete marriage of the PC with a computer-aided design and drafting package. Basic work on this Company package, a completely interactive computer graphics (ICG) system for engineering design, is detailed by Lavick [6,7] and Martin [8].

In this paper, however, we focus on the mathematical techniques employed in PC work, especially with respect to the PC patch. Theoretical treatment later gives way to actual ICG design examples. These examples validate the applicability of the PC to engineering.

2. INVESTIGATIVE COMPUTER ENVIRONMENT

In the mathematical analyses following, many figures are presented which depict actual on-line computer communication between man and machine. The machine environment in which this communication was obtained is briefly described below.

Fig. 1 outlines the computer/terminal configuration satisfying computer-aided design/computer-aided manufacturing (CAD/CAM) requirements at McDonnell Douglas Corporation in St. Louis. Development of this CAD/CAM system has faithfully given prime consideration to problems of handling large on-line software systems and the definition and centralization of a geometric data base. The ability to provide a satisfactory time-sharing environment for computer-use economies has been an equally important consideration. Specific hardware used is an IBM Model 195 with 4-million bytes of main core storage. This is, of necessity, a large facility; it is

See References, page 43.

devoted to the application of automation techniques and data processing within a wide range of activities that share its resources and costs. For example, as can be seen in Fig. 1, a large multi-terminal information management system (IMS) as well as a general stream of batch processing (scheduled from another Model 195 computer) cohabit this configuration with CAD/CAM systems.

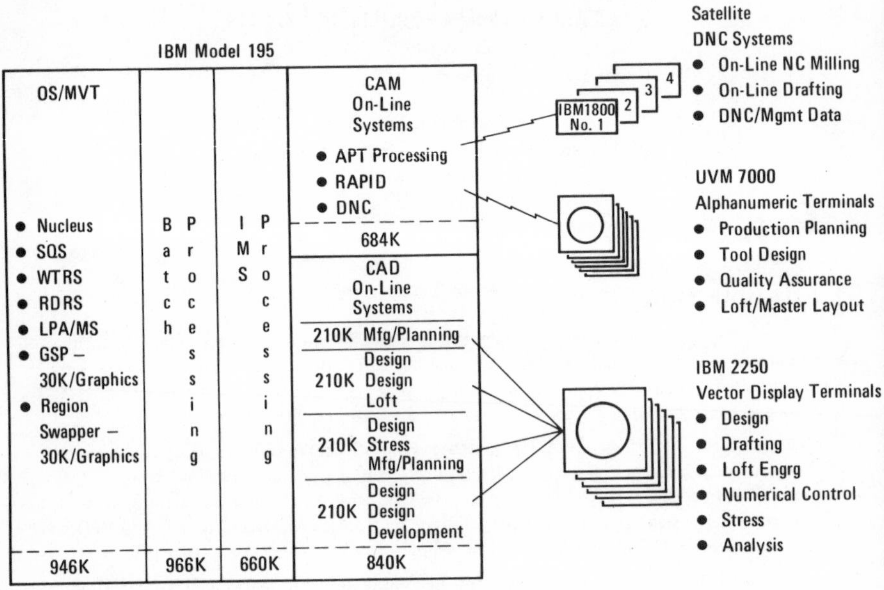

Fig. 1
Interactive CAD/CAM configuration
at McDonnell Douglas Corporation, St. Louis
(May 1973)

The CAD/CAM systems feature a mix of teleprocessing (phone-line-connected) terminals as well as locally-connected vector graphic display terminals. For CAM, the RAPID (Remote APT Processing via Interactive Devices) system includes thirteen alphanumeric terminals which support production planning, tool design, quality assurance and loft (including master layout) activities. These terminals are used for a variety of CAM functions such as APT (automatically programmed tools) part programming, debugging and data transmission to satellite IBM 1800 computers used in direct numerical control (DNC) for on-line machining or drafting. For CAD, ten IBM 2250 vector display (CRT) terminals are located in user project areas at distances up to 12,000 feet from the computer, which is believed to be the farthest remote interactive facility in the world.

Fig. 2 illustrates the layout of these terminals and their connection distances from the main frame computer. The philosophy and effectiveness of locating these types of devices in direct user areas are highlighted in [7] and [8]. One CRT, located in loft engineering, is used primarily for loft surface shape definition. Two CRTs are located in manufacturing production planning.

These are used in the graphics numerical control (GNC) process which involves retrieving an engineering drawing and then interactively directing the machine tool around the drawing to generate the APT part program. Six CRTs, located in engineering project areas, are dedicated to structural/mechanical design applications. Lastly, one CRT is devoted to the development and testing of new capabilities.

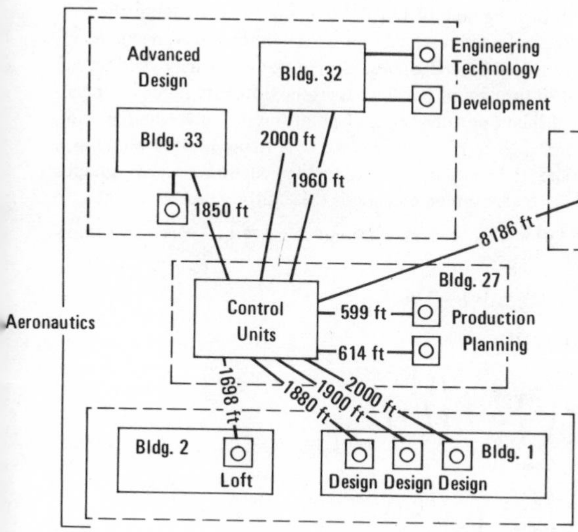

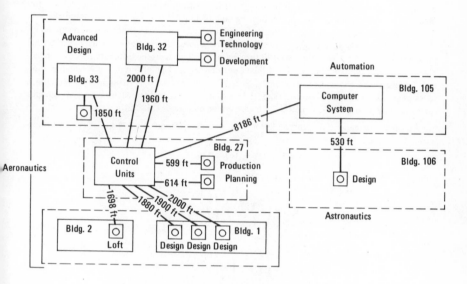

Fig. 2
Remote locations of on-line computer graphics terminals
at McDonnell Douglas Corporation, St. Louis (May 1973)

3. PARAMETRIC REPRESENTATION

Many reasons for using the parametric form of a curve vis-à-vis the nonparametric form are found in [4]. A few of these reasons are addressed below.

The use of the nonparametric form – in which the real space components are related such as $x = f(y)$ and $z = g(y)$ – is largely confined to planar curves. Aircraft and ship lofting use conic sections, cubics and higher order polynomials; lofting techniques for these curves are well established. To avoid some of the difficulties inherent in the nonparametric form, Newell [9] has classified the conic into 34 separate cases and Shelley [10], using a different approach, into three cases. By their very nature, conics cannot yield curves with points of inflection. Yet such curves often exist in aircraft shapes, for example, in duct contours.

The planar cubic in the nonparametric form arises mainly from the use of splines. The nonparametric spline is a two-dimensional curve. It is continuous in both first and second derivatives throughout its length, and is considered by aircraft and shipbuilding industries to give a smooth and fair curve. There is an inherent difficulty, however, in curve fitting with splines obtained from data having an implied discontinuity in the second derivative. While this is not too common with ships and aircraft, it is a frequent occurrence in other areas of mechanical design. An obvious example is the fillet radius joining two straight lines. In this case the spline tends to oscillate about the expected curve in an unacceptable manner unless appropriate end conditions are applied [11]. In addition, splines may be inconvenient when the deflections become large or the radius of the curvature becomes small.

The nonparametric curve form has several inherent drawbacks. A curve which is defined by tangent properties as well as points may well require an infinite slope. This can be avoided either by changing the coordinate axes or by using a different form of equation. However, either procedure is cumbersome. Curve segments must be bounded by defining the end points. But the tests to determine whether a point lies on the bounded segment can be elaborate and even ambiguous when the curve loops. In the case of two-dimensional curves, a given value of x may yield several values of y which must be tested. And in the case of twisted curves the difficulty is compounded. This complicates the computation for display, plotting, etc., of points on the curve; computation may involve evaluating square, cube and higher roots. If the curve is to be plotted either as a series of points or a series of straight lines, the computation required to generate a visually smooth curve could be prodigious. Parametric methods overcome many of these difficulties.

Consider the parametric representation of a general continuous curve in 3-space as a transformation of the form

$$x = f(u),\ y = g(u),\ z = h(u)$$

defined for u in the interval [a,b]. In vector notation

$$\overline{r(u)} = \begin{pmatrix} x \\ y \\ z \end{pmatrix} = \begin{pmatrix} f(u) \\ g(u) \\ h(u) \end{pmatrix},$$

then

$$\frac{d\bar{r}}{du} = \begin{pmatrix} dx/du \\ dy/du \\ dz/du \end{pmatrix} = \begin{pmatrix} f'(u) \\ g'(u) \\ h'(u) \end{pmatrix}$$

is the tangent vector. The real slopes of the curve are given by the ratios of the components of the tangent vector. For example,

$$\frac{dz}{dx} = (dz/du)/(dx/du) = \frac{h'(u)}{f'(u)} .$$

An infinite slope is specified by setting one component of the tangent vector to zero.

A parametric curve is bounded by two parametric values. The test for a point lying on the curve reduces to finding the parametric value defining the point and verifying that this value lies within the stated range. To compute points on the curve segment, a parametric value is substituted in two or three equations. And in the case of commonly used curves such as conics and cubics, these equations will be polynomials rather than equations involving roots. If the curve is twisted, it is clearly easier to substitute one value of a parameter in three equations and obtain x, y and z directly than to solve for points lying on the intersections of two surfaces, and then check that they lie on the specified portion of the curve. The parametric form of the curve is easily transformed by matrix multiplication into a curve of similar form, but different orientation or scale; that is to say, the mathematical form of the curve may be axis independent. Similar transforms on nonparametric curves are more difficult.

Hence, the parametric form is not only more general, but it is well suited to computation and display. In addition, we will see that this form has properties which are attractive for computer-aided design.

4. THE PARAMETRIC CUBIC SPACE CURVE

4.1 In Mathematical Form

The PC space curve is represented as:

$$V(u) = Au^3 + Bu^2 + Cu + D, \tag{1}$$

where V is defined as a general coordinate and stands for x, y or z. In matrix notation,

$$V(u) = (u^3\ u^2\ u\ 1)\,(A\ B\ C\ D)^T, \tag{2}$$

where T is the transpose of the row matrix. For convenience, the curve parameter u is defined to be in the region $0 \leqslant u \leqslant 1$. Eq. (1) is called the algebraic form of the PC since it is the usual polynomial representation of a function.

The parametric derivative is

$$\frac{dV}{du} = V'(u) = 3Au^2 + 2Bu + C, \tag{3}$$

or

$$\frac{dV}{du} = (3u^2\ 2u\ 1\ 0)\,(A\ B\ C\ D)^T.$$

Consider the following set of four equations obtained by setting u = 0 and u = 1 in eq. (1) and in eq. (3):

$$\begin{aligned} V(0) &= D \\ V(1) &= A+B+C+D \\ V'(0) &= C \\ V'(1) &= 3A+2B+C \end{aligned}$$

or

$$\begin{bmatrix} V(0) \\ V(1) \\ V'(0) \\ V'(1) \end{bmatrix} = \begin{bmatrix} 0 & 0 & 0 & 1 \\ 1 & 1 & 1 & 1 \\ 0 & 0 & 1 & 0 \\ 3 & 2 & 1 & 0 \end{bmatrix} \begin{bmatrix} A \\ B \\ C \\ D \end{bmatrix}. \tag{4}$$

Solving linear system (4) for the algebraic coefficients produces

$$(A\ B\ C\ D)^T = (M)\ [V(0)\ \ V(1)\ \ V'(0)\ \ V'(1)]^T, \tag{5}$$

where

$$M = \begin{bmatrix} 2 & -2 & 1 & 1 \\ -3 & 3 & -2 & -1 \\ 0 & 0 & 1 & 0 \\ 1 & 0 & 0 & 0 \end{bmatrix}. \tag{6}$$

Substituting eq. (5) into eq. (1), and rearranging, we obtain

$$V(u) = V(0)\,F_1(u) + V(1)\,F_2(u) + V'(0)\,F_3(u) + V'(1)\,F_4(u), \tag{7}$$

where

$$\begin{aligned} F_1(u) &= 2u^3 - 3u^2 + 1 \\ F_2(u) &= -2u^3 + 3u^2 \\ F_3(u) &= u^3 - 2u^2 + u \\ F_4(u) &= u^3 - u^2 \end{aligned} \tag{8}$$

Eq. (7) is called the geometric form of the PC curve. Eq. (8) defines the so-called "blending functions". These functions blend the quantities V(0), V(1), V′(0) and V′(1) to form a continuous curve satisfying the end conditions.

In matrix notation, we can write eq. (7) as

$$V(u) = (u^3\ u^2\ u\ 1)\,(M)\begin{bmatrix} V(0) \\ V(1) \\ V'(0) \\ V'(1) \end{bmatrix}. \qquad (9)$$

Note that we obtain the end position values and parametric derivative values of the curve by inspecting eq. (9). For this reason, the geometric form is sometimes preferred over the algebraic form of eq. (2).

After expanding eq. (9), we can totally represent the curve by

$$\begin{bmatrix} x(u) \\ y(u) \\ z(u) \end{bmatrix}^T = (u^3\ u^2\ u\ 1)\,(M)\begin{bmatrix} x(0) & y(0) & z(0) \\ x(1) & y(1) & z(1) \\ x'(0) & y'(0) & z'(0) \\ x'(1) & y'(1) & z'(1) \end{bmatrix}.$$

Fig. 3 depicts the correspondence between real x, y, z space and parametric space and, in addition, shows the parametric plot. It is most important to realize here that x, y and z usually can be related only through the parameter u.

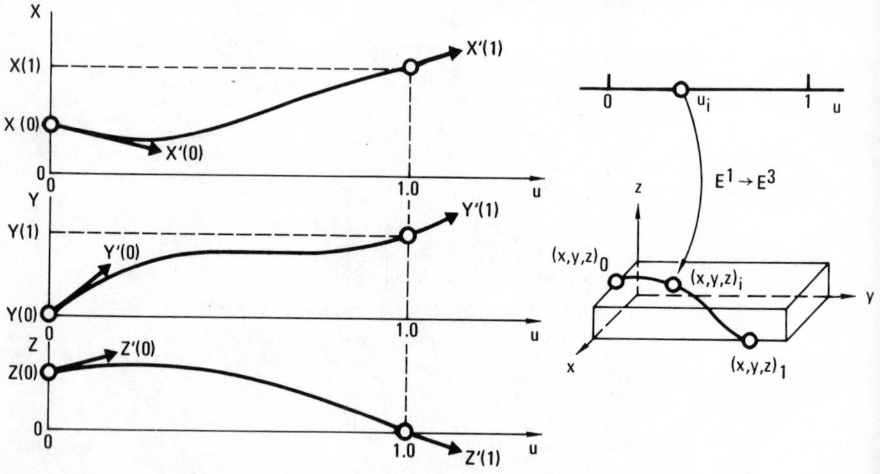

Algebraic Form

$$V(u) = Au^3 + Bu^2 + Cu + D$$

Geometric Form

$$V(u) = V(0)\,F_1(u) + V(1)\,F_2(u) + V'(0)\,F_3(u) + V'(1)\,F_4(u)$$

Fig. 3
Parametric cubic (PC) space curve in mathematical form

4.2 Creating a PC Curve

There are many ways to create a PC curve; however, each must provide sufficient data to determine the 12 coefficients implied by eq. (1) or by eq. (7), i.e., the four coefficients for each of x, y and z. From the numerical analysis viewpoint, three important considerations are:

- If only position data points are given, are the interior u values specified?
- If direction cosine data are given in addition to point data, be careful concerning the mathematical dependency of the real slope data.
- Are the given data planar or nonplanar (twisted)?

Two cases will now be considered:

CASE 1 – Consider 4 points (planar or twisted) with the interior u values specified, i.e., $0<u_1<u_2<1$. Using eq. (1) or eq. (7), we can obtain the unique PC by solving four linear simultaneous equations for each of the coordinates x, y and z.

CASE 2 – Consider 3 points with nonplanar direction cosines at the first and last point. Here we use the geometric form

$$V(u) = V(0)\,F_1(u) + V(1)\,F_2(u) + V'(0)\,F_3(u) + V'(1)\,F_4(u).$$

The three unknowns are the internal value of u corresponding to the middle point, and the parametric tangents V'(0) and V'(1). It is now necessary to relate the direction cosines to the parametric tangents. Consider the tangent vector

$$\overline{T} = \left(\frac{dx}{du}\ \frac{dy}{du}\ \frac{dz}{du}\right)^T;$$

then

$$S(u) = \|\overline{T}\|$$

is the norm or length of the tangent vector at point u defined by

$$\|\overline{T}\| = \sqrt{\left(\frac{dx}{du}\right)^2 + \left(\frac{dy}{du}\right)^2 + \left(\frac{dz}{du}\right)^2}.$$

Furthermore,

$$\frac{dx}{du} = S(u)a$$
$$\frac{dy}{du} = S(u)b \qquad (10)$$
$$\frac{dz}{du} = S(u)c$$

which relate the parametric tangents to the direction cosines a, b and c at the point of interest. Rewriting our system to be solved for the unique PC:

$$x(u) = x(0)F_1(u) + x(1)F_2(u) + S(0)\,a_oF_3(u) + S(1)a_1F_4(u)$$
$$y(u) = y(0)F_1(u) + y(1)F_2(u) + S(0)\,b_oF_3(u) + S(1)b_1F_4(u)$$
$$z(u) = z(0)F_1(u) + z(1)F_2(u) + S(0)\,c_oF_3(u) + S(1)c_1F_4(u).$$

These three nonlinear equations in the three unknowns can be solved very efficiently by N-dimensional Newton-Raphson [12], provided a judicious choice is made for the initial solution vector $[u\ S(0)\ S(1)]_o^T$. *Then, eq. (10) is used to obtain the parametric tangents. Finally, these tangents in conjunction with the given position data determine a unique PC. Note that since many curves can exhibit the same direction cosines at their end points, it is necessary to obtain the lengths of the tangent vectors to establish uniqueness.*

Fig. 4 shows some examples of PC creation at the CRT. These curves do not represent an over-conditioned situation; they were created by conjuring up the minimum data required to define a unique PC.

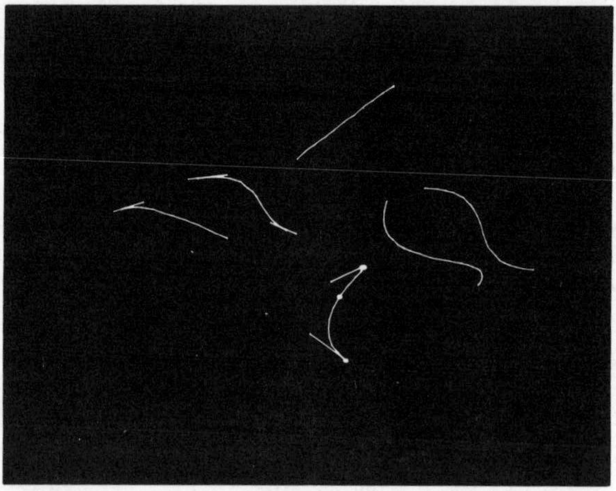

Fig. 4
Creating planar and nonplanar PC curves at the CRT

4.3 Testing for Planar/Twist PC

The "measure of twist" or torsion of a space curve is obtained by using Frenet's formulas, which are fundamental in the theory of space curves. Ref. [13] readily shows that torsion is defined by

$$\tau = \frac{(\dot{\bar{r}} \times \ddot{\bar{r}}) \cdot \dddot{\bar{r}}}{|\dot{\bar{r}} \times \ddot{\bar{r}}|^2} \quad , \tag{11}$$

where the expression

$$\bar{r} = [x(u)\ y(u)\ z(u)]^T \tag{12}$$

represents the position vector to any point on the curve and the dot above the vector signifies differentiation with respect to u. Note that a zero denominator in eq. (11) implies a straight-line PC. Therefore, assuming a nonzero denominator, the plane-curve or zero-torsion condition is represented by

$$(\dot{\bar{r}} \times \ddot{\bar{r}}) \cdot \dddot{\bar{r}} = 0. \tag{13}$$

Moreover, eq. (13) is the scalar triple product (or "box product") which can be expressed in determinant form as

$$\begin{vmatrix} \dot{x} & \dot{y} & \dot{z} \\ \ddot{x} & \ddot{y} & \ddot{z} \\ \dddot{x} & \dddot{y} & \dddot{z} \end{vmatrix} = 0. \tag{14}$$

Now using the algebraic form of the PC, taking the required parametric derivatives and substituting in eq. (14), we obtain

$$\begin{vmatrix} A_x & B_x & C_x \\ A_y & B_y & C_y \\ A_z & B_z & C_z \end{vmatrix} = 0. \tag{15}$$

Thus, to ensure no twist, the coefficients of the PC must satisfy (15). Observe that if A_x, A_y, and A_z are all zero, then the torsion is zero. This means, of course, that the "space curve" is a parametric quadratic; therefore, parametric quadratics can have no twist and thus are planar curves. Hence, the minimum power required for a parametric representation to be twisted is three, i.e., cubic. Also, if all the quadratic coefficients (B_x, B_y, B_z) or all the linear coefficients (C_x, C_y, C_z) are zero, then the curve is also planar.

4.4 Varying Tangent Vector Length

A powerful tool is afforded by parametric representation – that being the ability to drastically change the shape of the curve while maintaining the end direction cosine slopes. This is done by varying the tangent vector length, S, at the end points. For example,

$$\frac{dy}{dx} = \frac{dy/du}{dx/du} = \frac{K\ dy/du}{K\ dx/du}, \tag{16}$$

where K is an arbitrary constant. Note that it is very easy to handle an infinite slope for dy/dx; merely set dx/du equal to zero.

S-variation can be used as an ICG design tool to modify an existing PC, e.g., to clear an obstruction. Fig. 5 shows the effect of S-variation and indicates that unwanted kinks can occur if the arbitrary K factor identified above becomes too large.

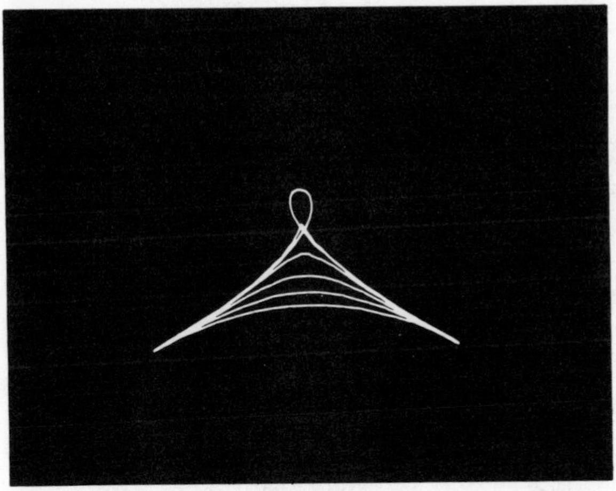

Fig. 5
Varying PC tangent vector length (S) affects curve shape

4.5 Determining Arc Length

In parametric form, PC arc length is expressed as

$$L = \int_{u_1}^{u_2} \sqrt{\dot{\bar{r}} \cdot \dot{\bar{r}}}\ du, \tag{17}$$

where $u_2 > u_1$ and $\bar{r}$ is obtained from eq. (12). Equation (17) can be reduced to

$$L = \int_{u_1}^{u_2} \sqrt{A_4u^4+A_3u^3+A_2u^2+A_1u+A_0}\ du, \tag{18}$$

where the A_i constants are defined in terms of the algebraic PC coefficients. Functionally, eq. (18) may be expressed as

$$L = \int_{u_1}^{u_2} f(u)\, du.$$

Using Gauss quadrature [14],

$$\int_{u_1}^{u_2} f(u)\, du = \sum_{i=1}^{N} w_i f(u_i),$$

where N is the number of points used, w_i are the weight values and u_i are the Gaussian abcissas. The Gaussian abcissas may be normalized to a more convenient interval $(0 \leqslant u_i \leqslant 1)$ by using the transformation

$$z = \frac{u - u_1}{u_2 - u_1}.$$

Then, L may be written

$$L = (u_2-u_1) \int_0^1 f[u_1+(u_2-u_1)z]\, dz,$$

or

$$L = (u_2-u_1) \sum_{i=1}^{N} w_i g(z_i),$$

where weights and abcissas are with respect to the new interval. For example, using N=9 with the weights and abcissas obtained from [15], the quadrature formula possesses a degree of precision of 2N–1, i.e., yields exact results if f(u) were a polynomial of the 17th order or less. The basic geometric properties of the PC, including arc length (N=9), are shown in Fig. 6.

4.6 Segmenting a PC Curve

Assume that we wish to define a new curve from u_1 to u_2 on the original curve in Fig. 7. Using the linear transformation

$$u = u_1 + t(u_2-u_1),$$

$$\frac{du}{dt} = u_2-u_1.$$

Then at t=0, $u=u_1$; and at t=1, $u=u_2$. Since V(u) = V[u(t)],

$$\frac{dV}{dt} = \frac{dV}{du}\frac{du}{dt}. \tag{19}$$

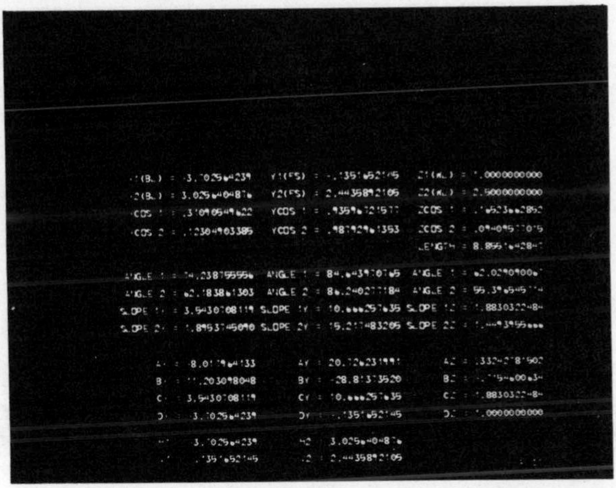

Fig. 6
Geometric properties of the PC

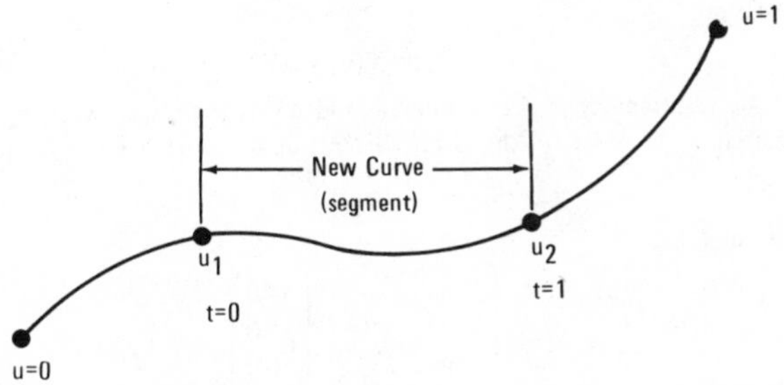

Fig. 7
Geometry for segmenting a PC curve

Using eq. (19) and denoting the new curve by v(t), the geometric coefficients of the segmented curve in terms of the given curve are

$$\begin{bmatrix} v(0) \\ v(1) \\ v'(0) \\ v'(1) \end{bmatrix} = \begin{bmatrix} V(u_1) \\ V(u_2) \\ (u_2-u_1)V'(u_1) \\ (u_2-u_1)V'(u_2) \end{bmatrix} . \qquad (20)$$

Several examples of segmenting a given PC curve are shown in Fig. 8.

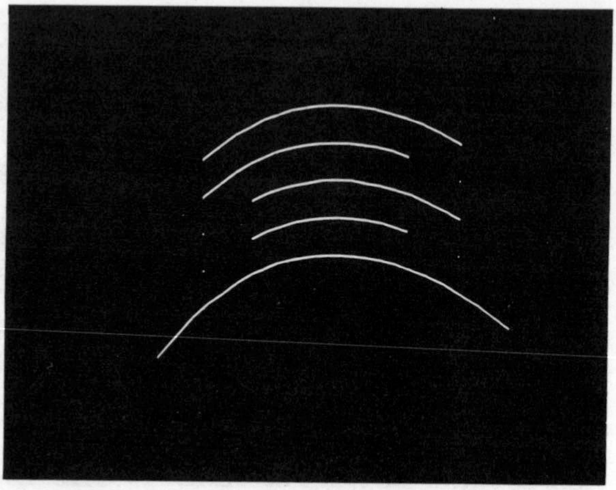

Fig. 8
Examples of segmenting a PC curve

4.7 Translating, Rotating and Scaling

Transformation operations on PCs are actually performed on their equations.

For **translation**:

$$v(u) = V(u) + \Delta V,$$

where v(u) is the resultant x, y or z coordinate and ΔV is the respective translation. In algebraic form, the translation is added to the D coefficient; in geometric form, it is added to both V(0) and V(1).

For **rotation**:

$$\begin{bmatrix} X(u) \\ Y(u) \\ Z(u) \end{bmatrix} = (A) \begin{bmatrix} x(u) \\ y(u) \\ z(u) \end{bmatrix}, \tag{21}$$

where A is the 3 x 3 rotation matrix. If the given PC is in geometric form, then

$$\begin{bmatrix} X(u) \\ Y(u) \\ Z(u) \end{bmatrix} = (A) \begin{bmatrix} x(0) & x(1) & x'(0) & x'(1) \\ y(0) & y(1) & y'(0) & y'(1) \\ z(0) & z(1) & z'(0) & z'(1) \end{bmatrix} (M)^T \begin{bmatrix} u^3 \\ u^2 \\ u \\ 1 \end{bmatrix}. \tag{22}$$

For **scaling**:

$$\begin{bmatrix} X(u) \\ Y(u) \\ Z(u) \end{bmatrix} = \begin{bmatrix} 1-k_1 & 0 & 0 \\ 0 & 1-k_2 & 0 \\ 0 & 0 & 1-k_3 \end{bmatrix} \begin{bmatrix} x_r \\ y_r \\ z_r \end{bmatrix} + \begin{bmatrix} k_1 & 0 & 0 \\ 0 & k_2 & 0 \\ 0 & 0 & k_3 \end{bmatrix} \begin{bmatrix} x(u) \\ y(u) \\ z(u) \end{bmatrix}, \tag{23}$$

where k_1, k_2 and k_3 are the scale factors for x, y and z respectively; and the subscript r signifies a reference point for scaling.

For equal scaling, sometimes called ratio, eq. (23) can be written

$$\begin{bmatrix} X(u) \\ Y(u) \\ Z(u) \end{bmatrix} = (1-k) \begin{bmatrix} x_r \\ y_r \\ z_r \end{bmatrix} + k \begin{bmatrix} x(u) \\ y(u) \\ z(u) \end{bmatrix},$$

where k is the common scale factor. Fig. 9 shows PC curve transformations.

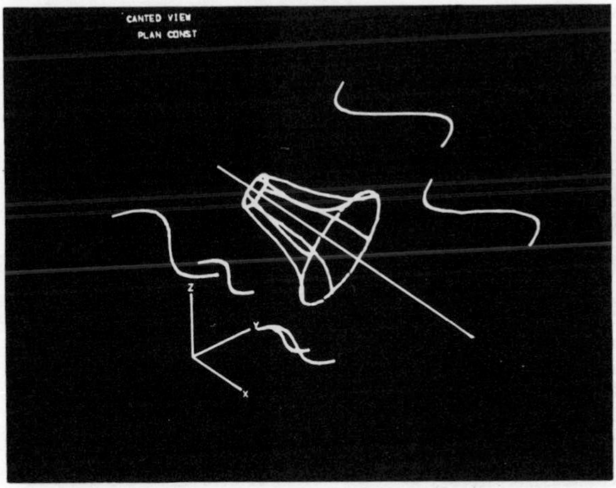

Fig. 9
Translating, rotating, and scaling PC curves

4.8 Intersecting

Two cases will be considered: the intersection of a plane with a PC curve and the intersection of two PC curves.

For the former case, let the plane be determined by the normal vector $\bar{N}$ and a point $\bar{p}_0$ in the plane; therefore, using the definition of a plane,

$$\bar{N} \cdot \overline{(p - p_0)} = 0,$$

or

$$N_x[x(u) - x_0] + N_y[y(u) - y_0] + N_z[z(u) - z(0)] = 0. \qquad (24)$$

Since each coordinate is a cubic in u, eq. (24) is a cubic equation which can be solved (either closed form or iteratively) for its real roots. Of course, the roots of interest are within the region $0 \leqslant u_i \leqslant 1$.

For the intersection of two PC curves, we can make the following realistic assumptions: (a) each PC is planar and (b) both curves are coplanar. At a point of intersection,

$$\overline{r_{pc_1}} = \overline{R_{pc_2}},$$

where $\bar{r}$ and $\bar{R}$ are the position vectors for curves 1 and 2 respectively at the intersection point. Therefore, since the problem is planar,

$$x(u) - X(w) = 0 \qquad 0 \leqslant u \leqslant 1,$$
$$y(u) - Y(w) = 0 \qquad 0 \leqslant w \leqslant 1.$$

Expanding the x component equation and using the algebraic form,

$$A_x u^3 + B_x u^2 + C_x u + D_x - (A_X w^3 + B_X w^2 + C_X w + D_X) = 0.$$

A similar equation can be written for y. Hence, the result is two nonlinear equations in two unknowns, u and w. Since a light pen detect can be made very close to the visible intersection on the CRT, Newton-Raphson becomes a very efficient servant for solving this problem.* Some CRT examples are shown in Fig. 10.

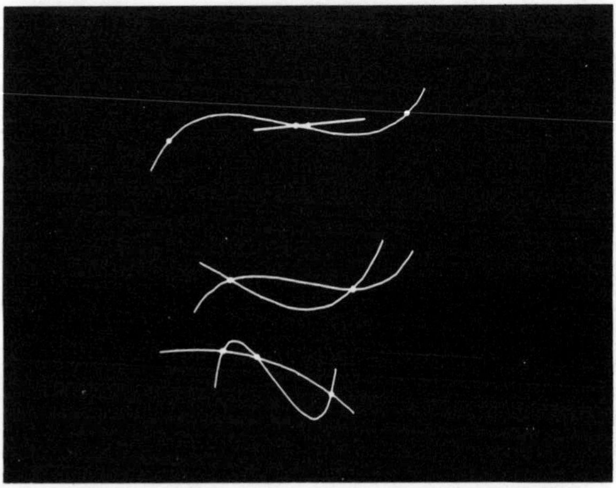

Fig. 10
Intersecting a PC with a plane or a PC

4.9 Converting an Arc to a PC

Using the geometry of Fig. 11 and assuming a unit radius, we can convert the ideal arc to an approximating PC expressed as

$$x(u) = (u^3\ u^2\ u\ 1)\,(M) \begin{bmatrix} \cos\phi \\ \cos\phi \\ 4(1-\cos\phi) \\ -4(1-\cos\phi) \end{bmatrix}, \tag{25}$$

and

$$y(u) = (u^3\ u^2\ u\ 1)\,(M) \begin{bmatrix} -\sin\phi \\ \sin\phi \\ 4(1-\cos\phi)/\tan\phi \\ 4(1-\cos\phi)/\tan\phi \end{bmatrix}, \tag{26}$$

where

$$\phi = \frac{\phi_2 - \phi_1}{2}\ .$$

According to Acton [12], Newton-Raphson is rather like the little girl in the nursery rhyme who had a curl in the middle of her forehead and "when she was good, she was very, very good; but when she was bad, she was horrid!"

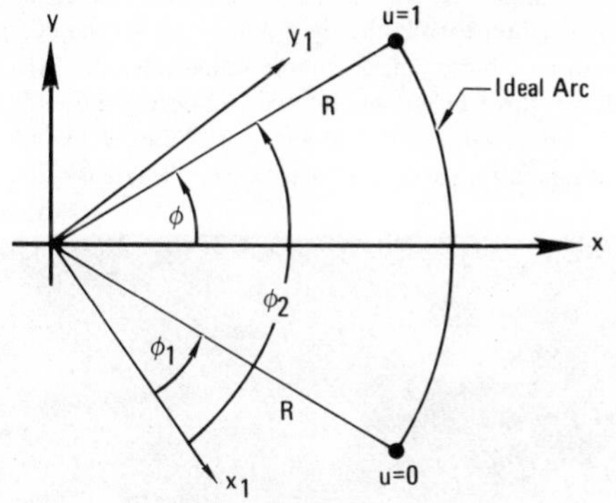

Fig. 11
Arc-to-PC conversion geometry

The question of accuracy naturally comes to mind. How good is the approximation? At any point within the range $0 \leqslant u \leqslant 1$,

$$r(u) = \sqrt{[x(u)]^2 + [y(u)]^2} ,$$

where r(u) is the distance from the origin to the PC. The error function is expressed by

$$\Delta R(u) = r(u) - R,$$

where R is the radius of the true arc; R=1 in eqs. (25) and (26). Normalizing with respect to the given radius yields

$$\frac{\Delta R(u)}{R} = \frac{r(u)}{R} - 1.$$

For a given ϕ, we must extremize $\Delta R(u)/R$; this then, will provide the worst error characterizing the fit. Therefore,

$$\frac{\Delta R}{R} = \underset{u \epsilon [0, 1]}{\text{ext}} \left[\frac{\Delta R(u)}{R} \right] ,$$

and the values of u are the extrema of

$$\frac{d}{du} [r(u)] = 0.$$

Then, differentiating:

$$x(u) \frac{dx}{du} + y(u) \frac{dy}{du} = 0, \tag{27}$$

which is a 5th order equation in u. By inspection of eqs. (25) and (26), there are three u values for which ΔR is zero; these values are 0, 0.5 and 1. In addition, these u's also satisfy eq. (27). Therefore, solving the resultant quadratic equation yields

$$u = \frac{1}{2} \pm \frac{1}{2} \sqrt{1 - 4(k_1/k_2)} , \tag{28}$$

where k_1 and k_2 are functions of only the given ϕ. Note that the extrema deviations are symmetrical with respect to u=0.5. Using the values from eq. (28) in eqs. (25) and (26), we can show that the error excursion about the true arc is always positive. Furthermore, these two values produce equal deviations.

Typical arc-to-PC examples are shown in Fig. 12 for radii of 20, 30, 40 and 50 inches. The left portion shows the original circles while the right portion shows the PC approximations. The number of PC curves are determined by keying in the desirable tolerance ΔR. Using ΔR=0.001 inch with the above radii produced three PC curves for the 180-degree subtended angle shown in the figure. However, with R=5 inches and the same tolerance, two PC curves would be created. Fig. 13 shows the maximum error obtained for various total arc angles (where $\theta = 2\phi$).

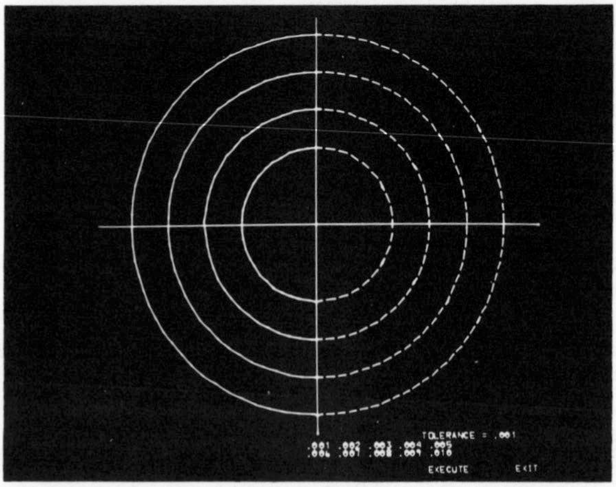

Fig. 12
Converting an arc or circle to a PC

θ (deg.)	$\frac{\Delta R}{R}$
10	5.0×10^{-10}
20	3.3×10^{-8}
30	3.7×10^{-7}
45	4.0×10^{-6}
60	2.4×10^{-5}
90	2.7×10^{-4}
120	1.5×10^{-3}
160	8.9×10^{-3}
180	1.5×10^{-2}

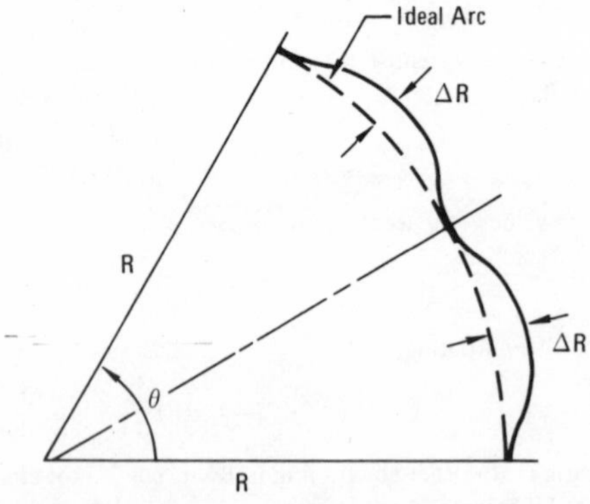

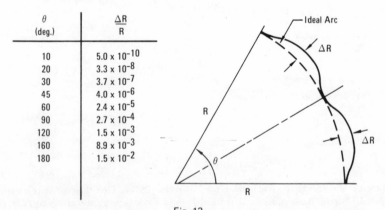

Fig. 13
Arc-to-PC conversion accuracy

Curves do not occur in isolation in the description of solid objects, but bound or lie on the surface regions which define these objects. Thus, the study of curves is a prerequisite to the study of surfaces. Therefore, having covered some of the features of the PC curve, it is now possible to discuss its surface extension, the PC patch.

5. THE PARAMETRIC BI-CUBIC SURFACE PATCH

5.1 In Mathematical Form

The general continuous surface in 3-space can be expressed as a transformation of the form

$$x = f(u,w)$$
$$y = g(u,w)$$
$$z = h(u,w),$$

whose domain is a set D in the uw plane. In particular, the PC bi-cubic surface patch is defined as

$$V(u,w) = (u^3\ u^2\ u\ 1)\,(M)\,(B)\,(M)^T \begin{bmatrix} w^3 \\ w^2 \\ w \\ 1 \end{bmatrix},$$

where (M) was defined in eq. (6) and

$$(B) = \begin{bmatrix} V_{00} & V_{01} & V_{00w} & V_{01w} \\ V_{10} & V_{11} & V_{10w} & V_{11w} \\ V_{00u} & V_{01u} & V_{00uw} & V_{01uw} \\ V_{10u} & V_{11u} & V_{10uw} & V_{11uw} \end{bmatrix}. \qquad (29)$$

The matrix B is called the boundary matrix since its elements are geometric properties of the boundaries of the surface patch. Fig. 14 summarizes the basic concepts of a patch.

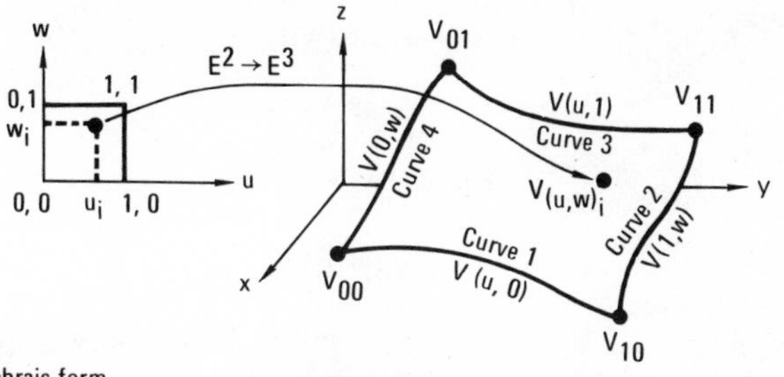

Algebraic form

$$V(u,w) = [u^3\ u^2\ u\ 1]\,[S] \begin{bmatrix} w^3 \\ w^2 \\ w \\ 1 \end{bmatrix}$$

$[S] = [M]\,[B]\,[M]^T$ = Algebraic Form of Patch Coefficients

Geometric form

$$V(u,w) = [u^3\ u^2\ u\ 1]\,[M] \underbrace{\begin{bmatrix} V_{00} & V_{01} & V_{00w} & V_{01w} \\ V_{10} & V_{11} & V_{10w} & V_{11w} \\ V_{00u} & V_{01u} & V_{00uw} & V_{01uw} \\ V_{10u} & V_{11u} & V_{10uw} & V_{11uw} \end{bmatrix}}_{[B]} [M]^T \begin{bmatrix} w^3 \\ w^2 \\ w \\ 1 \end{bmatrix}$$

[B] = Geometric Form of Patch Coefficients

Fig. 14
PC patch mathematical form

It is important to understand the notation in eq. (29). The number subscripts refer to values of the parametric variables u and w at the corner points, while the letter subscripts indicate the derivative with respect to that parametric variable. For example

$$V_{01} = [V(u,w)]_{\substack{u=0\\w=1}} = V(0,1) \quad \text{point data,}$$

$$V_{10w} = \left[\frac{\partial V(u,w)}{\partial w}\right]_{\substack{u=1\\w=0}} = V(1,0)_w \quad \text{rate data,}$$

$$V_{11uw} = \left[\frac{\partial^2 V(u,w)}{\partial u\,\partial w}\right]_{\substack{u=1\\w=1}} = V(1,1)_{uw} \quad \text{twist data.}$$

Recall that V stands for x, y or z. There is a B matrix for each coordinate. Using a more compact matrix notation,

$$V(u,w) = [F(u)]\ (B)\ [F(w)]^T,$$

where

$$[F(u)] = (u^3\ u^2\ u\ 1)\,(M)$$

and

$$[F(w)] = (w^3\ w^2\ w\ 1)\,(M)$$

are the blending functions defined in eq. (8).

Computing expense is minimized by the use of another form:

$$V(u,w) = (U)\,(S)\,(W)^T, \tag{30}$$

where

$$(U) = (u^3\ u^2\ u\ 1)\,,$$
$$(W) = (w^3\ w^2\ w\ 1)\,,$$

and

$$(S) = (M)\,(B)\,(M)^T. \tag{31}$$

Analogous to the PC curve, the terms "geometric" and "algebraic" form also apply to the PC patch coefficients. Boundary matrix (B) of eq. (29) is the geometric form, while the surface matrix (S) is called the algebraic form.

Equation (29) now requires more attention since it embodies the individual geometric character of any surface patch. Note that the first and second rows are the PC boundary curves for u=0 and u=1 respectively; while the first and second columns are the curves for w=0 and w=1 respectively. Following Herzog [16], eq. (29) can be divided into four 2 x 2 partitions:

$$(B) = \left(\begin{array}{c|c} P & R_w \\ \hline R_u & T \end{array}\right). \tag{32}$$

The partition P contains the position data of the four end or corner points. Partitions R_u and R_w contain parametric rates which are related to the real slopes or tangents at the corner points. The interior character of the patch is controlled by the twist or cross-derivative partition, T. It should be emphasized that the richness of information contained in matrix (B) is readily combined and manipulated by the computer.

From a terminology point of view, the terms "surface" and "patch" are used interchangeably. However, in a more general sense, surface is the superset since a surface can contain one or more patches.

5.2 Creating a PC Patch

As with the PC curve, there are many ways to create a PC patch; however, each approach must provide sufficient data to determine the 48 coefficients implied by eq. (29) or eq. (31), i.e., 16 coefficients for each of x, y and z. Three specific cases will now be considered.

CASE 1 – Consider a grid of 16 points (planar or twisted) with uw values not specified in advance. Fig. 15 shows a rough outline of the desired boundary curves through the border points. An estimate of the uw values for other than the corner points can be obtained by using a ratio of line segments to get a value between 0 and 1. Then using the algebraic form of the patch in eq. (30)

$$(u^3\ u^2\ u\ 1)\,(S)\begin{bmatrix} w^3 \\ w^2 \\ w \\ 1 \end{bmatrix} = V(u,w),$$

and expanding this

$$(u^3w^3)\,s_{11} + (u^3w^2)\,s_{12} + (u^3w)\,s_{13} + (u^3)\,s_{14} + (u^2w^3)\,s_{21} + \cdots$$
$$+ (uw^3)\,s_{31} + \cdots + (w^3)\,s_{41} + \cdots + s_{44} = V(u,w)$$

or

$$(C)\,\overline{(p)} = \overline{(b)}. \qquad (33)$$

Hence, the result is a linear simultaneous system of equations whose unknowns are the elements of (S). Specifically, (C) is a 16 x 16 matrix of uw products; $\overline{(p)}$ is a 16 x 1 vector of the unknown (S) elements; and $\overline{(b)}$ is a 16 x 1 vector of the given data points. Note that the solution to eq. (33) provides three S matrices – one for each of the coordinates x, y and z. The Gauss-Jordan elimination technique with maximum pivot strategy [17] readily handles this problem. Fig. 16 depicts a resultant patch created at the CRT.

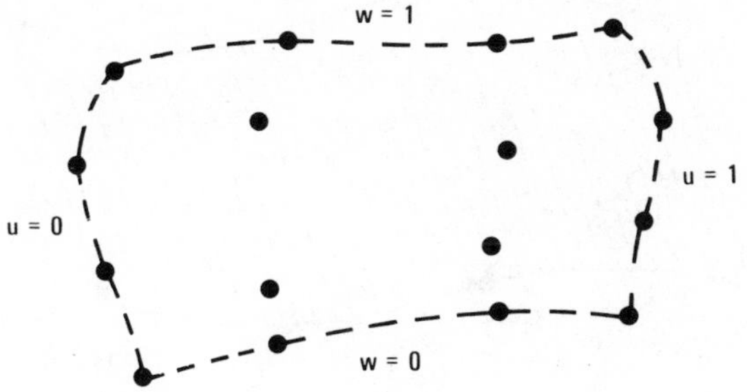

Fig. 15
Geometry for creating a PC patch, Case 1

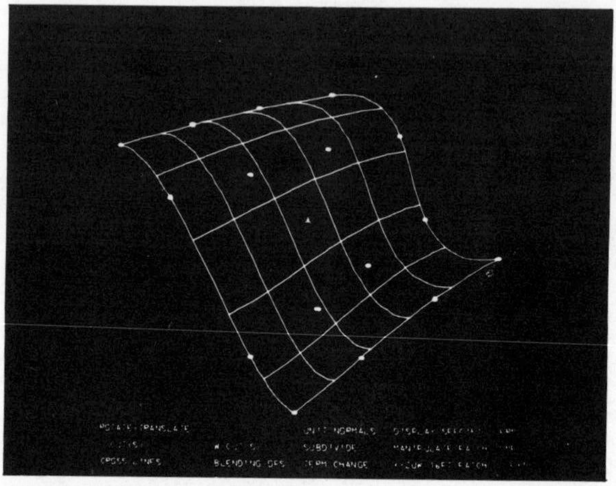

Fig. 16
PC patch defined by 16 points

CASE 2 – Consider two PC curves (planar or twisted). Create a ruled surface patch between them (refer to Fig. 17). Assume that the surface is to be ruled in w; therefore, curves 1 and 2 are f(u). It can be shown that the general point on the patch is given by

$$V(u,w) = V_1(u) + w[V_2(u) - V_1(u)]\,; \quad 0 \leqslant w \leqslant 1, \tag{34}$$

where the subscripts refer to curves 1 or 2. Since the parametric derivative and cross derivative can easily be obtained from eq. (34), all the elements of the (B) matrix are known.

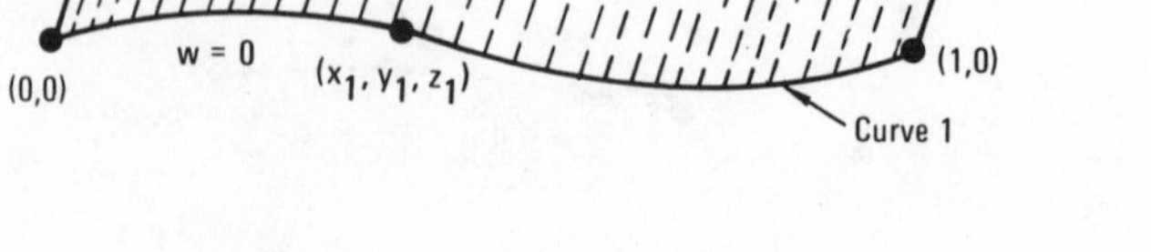

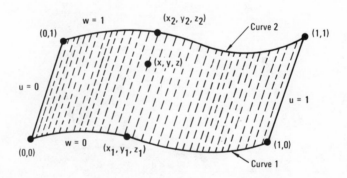

Fig. 17
Geometry for creating a PC patch, Case 2

CASE 3 – Consider four connected PC curves (planar or twisted). See Fig. 18. This case is the classic Coons patch with zero twist elements in the (B) matrix. The patch is completely defined by the four given boundary curves.

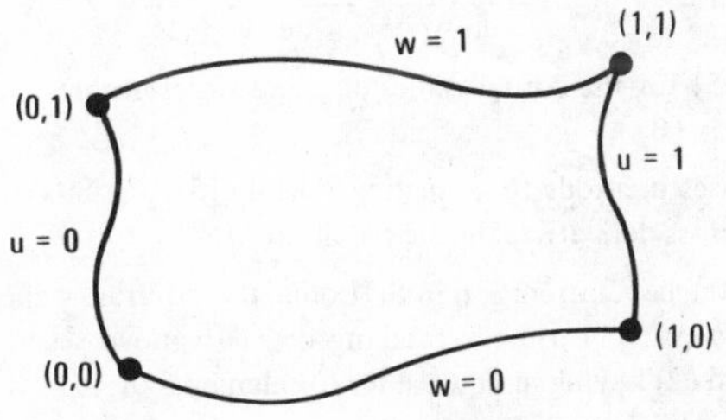

Fig. 18
Geometry for creating a PC patch, Case 3

Fig. 19 shows planar and nonplanar ruled patches and Coons patches.

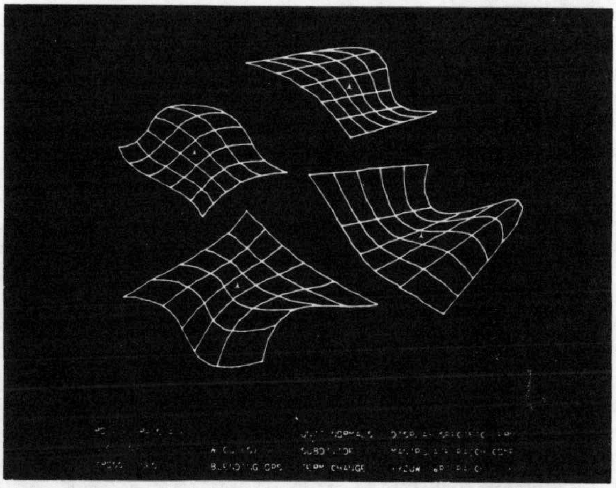

Fig. 19
PC ruled patches and Coons patches

5.3 Determining Cross-Derivatives

The cross-derivative elements of the boundary matrix are essential to the PC patch system. They not only provide higher accuracy in fitting given data, but they also permit adjustment of the surface normal slope along a boundary. Therefore, they have practical significance.

The following questions now come to mind: How are the cross-derivatives originally determined? Is there a general equation for them? There is no general rule. Each surface has its own characteristic interior shape; many times this is dictated by the designer. For example, if a ruled surface is desired, using eq. (34) yields

$$\frac{\partial^2 V(u,w)}{\partial u \partial w} = \frac{dV_2(u)}{du} - \frac{dV_1(u)}{du}, \tag{35}$$

and evaluating eq. (35) for the corner values of u and w determines the four numbers to be placed in partition T of matrix (B).

Ref. [16] discusses methods for adjusting T while [5] presents some excellent pictures showing the effect of the cross-derivatives on the patch interior.

At McDonnell Douglas Corporation in St. Louis, the interior of the patch can also be modified interactively in two ways: (1) using a tracking cross to move selected defining points to other desirable locations and (2) keying in new values for elements of T.

5.4 Determining the Normal Vector

For a smooth surface in 3-space, the normal vector at a point is

$$\bar{N} = \bar{r}_u \times \bar{r}_w = \left[\frac{\partial \bar{r}(u,w)}{\partial u}\right] \times \left[\frac{\partial \bar{r}(u,w)}{\partial w}\right], \tag{36}$$

or using the Jacobian notation,

$$\bar{N} = \left[\frac{\partial(y,z)}{\partial(u,w)}\ \frac{\partial(z,x)}{\partial(u,w)}\ \frac{\partial(x,y)}{\partial(u,w)}\right]^T .$$

The typical patch has four boundary curves and $\bar{N}$ is easily computed. However, three-sided (octant of a sphere) and even two-sided patches do exist, i.e., the length of a boundary curve can be zero. For these cases, the Jacobian is singular and the usual normal is not defined at the degenerate point. The coding of the computer program that computes the coefficients in matrix array for the surface normals recognizes the degenerate curve and performs the appropriate vector arithmetic on the two curves that actually intersect at the point. The form of this matrix array is the same as the standard four-sided patch. Fig. 20 shows the surface normal vectors on a PC patch.

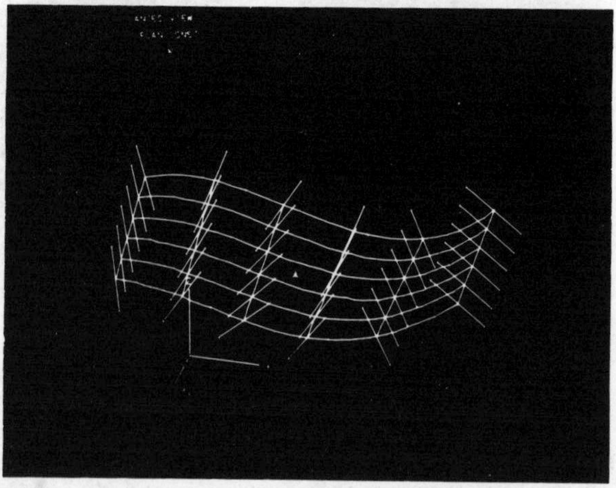

Fig. 20
Surface normal vectors on a PC patch

5.5 Testing for Planar/Nonplanar Patch

Sometimes it is necessary to know whether a given patch is planar or nonplanar, for example, in blending operations. Rather than just "plugging in" uw values and determining whether the associated x, y, z points lie in a plane – certainly somewhat laborious and definitely not rigorous – consider the following analysis which is an extension of the technique suggested by Martin [18].

Using the definition of a plane

$$\overline{n(0,0)} \cdot \overline{[r(u,w) - r(0,0)]} = 0, \tag{37}$$

where $\overline{n(0,0)}$ is a vector in the direction of the patch normal at (0,0), $\overline{r(u,w)}$ is the position vector to a general (u,w), and $\overline{r(0,0)}$ is the position vector to the point (0,0). If eq. (37) is true for all u,w within the interval [0,1], then the patch is planar. Expanding the above equation

$$n_x(0,0)x(u,w) + n_y(0,0)y(u,w) + n_z(0,0)z(u,w) = n_x(0.0)x(0,0) + n_y(0,0)y(0,0) + n_z(0,0)z(0,0). \tag{38}$$

Note that the right hand side of eq. (38) is a constant:

$$K(0,0) = \overline{n(0,0)} \cdot \overline{r(0,0)}\,.$$

Now witness

$$\int_0^1 \int_0^1 \overline{n(0,0)} \cdot \overline{r(u,w)}\, du\, dw = \int_0^1 \int_0^1 K(0,0)\, du\, dw$$

or

$$n_x(0,0) \int_0^1 \int_0^1 x(u,w)\, du\, dw + n_y(0,0) \int_0^1 \int_0^1 y(u,w)\, du\, dw + n_z(0,0) \int_0^1 \int_0^1 z(u,w)\, du\, dw = K(0,0). \tag{39}$$

We can see that if the above integration can be performed, then the constraint conditions for planarity will be independent of u,w explicitly. Recall from eq. (30) that the general patch coordinate is

$$V(u,w) = (U)\,(S)\,(W)^T,$$

which can also be written

$$V(u,w) = \sum_{i=1}^{4} \sum_{j=1}^{4} s_{ij}\, u^{4-i} w^{4-j}.$$

Hence,

$$\int_0^1 \int_0^1 V(u,w)\, du\, dw = \sum_{i=1}^{4} \sum_{j=1}^{4} \frac{s_{ij}}{(5-i)(5-j)},$$

and when this result is used in eq. (39)

$$n_x(0,0) \sum_{i=1}^{4} \sum_{j=1}^{4} \frac{s_{ijx}}{(5-i)(5-j)} + n_y(0,0) \sum_{i=1}^{4} \sum_{j=1}^{4} \frac{s_{ijy}}{(5-i)(5-j)} + n_z(0,0) \sum_{i=1}^{4} \sum_{j=1}^{4} \frac{s_{ijz}}{(5-i)(5-j)} - K(0,0) = 0. \tag{40}$$

If the coefficients of the patch satisfy eq. (40), then the patch is planar.

5.6 Geometric Properties

The parametric form of the surface lends itself very nicely to computation of geometric properties since explicit points do not have to be computed.

Consider the determination of surface area

$$dA = \|\overline{N}(u,w)\| \, du \, dw = f_1(u,w) \, du \, dw,$$

where $\overline{N}$ is from eq. (36) and dA is the scalar element of area. Hence

$$A = \int_0^1 \int_0^1 f_1(u,w) \, du \, dw.$$

Using Gauss quadrature

$$A = \sum_{j=1}^{N} \sum_{i=1}^{N} g_i h_j f_1(u_j,w_i), \qquad (41)$$

where g_i and h_j are the weight values associated with the specific N-point formula.

For the volume of a closed region, it can be shown [19] that

$$dv = \frac{1}{3} [\overline{r}(u,w) \cdot \overline{N}(u,w)] \, du \, dw = f_2(u,w) \, du \, dw,$$

where $\overline{r}$ and $\overline{N}$ are the position vector and normal vector, respectively, and dv is the scalar element of volume. Therefore,

$$v = \int_0^1 \int_0^1 f_2(u,w) \, du \, dw,$$

and again, quadrature can be used as in eq. (41).

As for PC arc length, N = 9 is used to compute both surface area and volume. Other desirable properties such as moments of inertia, center-of-gravity, and principal axes information are also obtainable.

5.7 Creating a Patch from a Given Patch

Three techniques will now be presented whereby a new patch can be designed which has geometric properties similar to a given patch

Subdividing/Extending – Consider the sketch in Fig. 21. We wish to create patch P_2 from P_1 with the indicated new corner points determined by u_1, u_2, w_1 and w_2. The (B) matrix for P_2 is obtained as follows: For position and parametric slope data, the PC segmentation principles of eq. (20) are employed, e.g.,

$$[V(0,0)]_{P_2} = [V(u_1,w_1)]_{P_1}$$

and

$$[V(0,0)_u]_{P_2} = (u_2-u_1)\,[V(u_1,w_1)_u]_{P_1}.$$

The corner cross-derivatives for P_2 are obtained by evaluating the partial derivatives of P_1 at the given subdivide points, e.g.,

$$[V(1,1)_{uw}]_{P_2} = \left\{ \left[\frac{\partial^2 V(u,w)}{\partial u \partial w} \right]_{P_1} \right\}_{\substack{u=u_2 \\ w=w_2}}$$

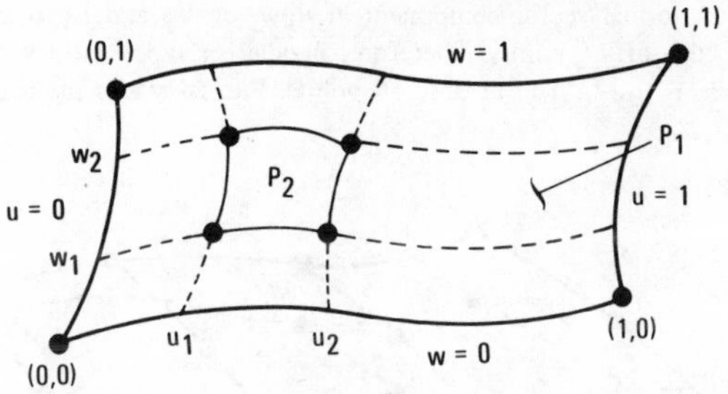

Fig. 21
Geometry for creating a patch by subdividing a given patch

Therefore, the entire geometric form for P_2 can be easily obtained. As a point of interest, the patch can be extended beyond its original borders; however, this is not advisable since extrapolation is dangerous (at least, large extrapolation). Fig. 22 shows several examples of the subdivide/extend capability.

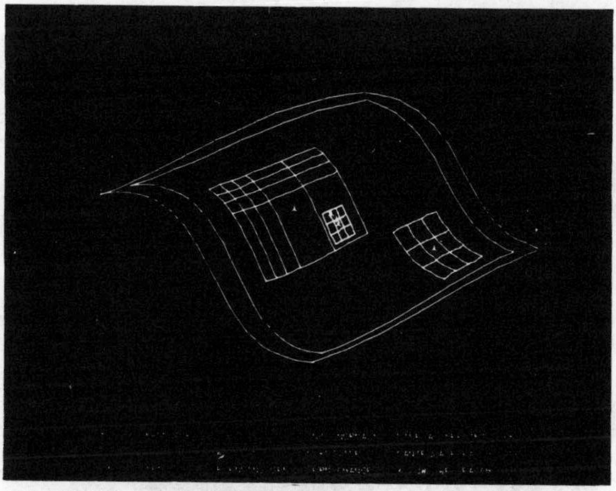

Fig. 22
PC patch subdivision or extension

Offsetting – Given a patch P_1, create an offset patch P_2 governed by some rule (see Fig. 23). Select 16 convenient points, e.g.,

$$(u_i, w_i) \qquad u,w = 0, 1/3, 2/3, 1;$$

then the offset points can be generated by

$$[V(u,w)]_{P_2} = [V(u,w)]_{P_1} + [n_V(u,w)]_{P_1} \, L_V(u,w),$$

where n_V is the unit normal vector component at u_i, w_i on P_1 and $L_V(u,w)$ is the law or rule which will produce the offset points. Therefore, parallel or tapered thickness surfaces can be created. Of course, P_2 is truly offset at only 16 points. Fig. 24 shows the offset capability for a constant value of L_V.

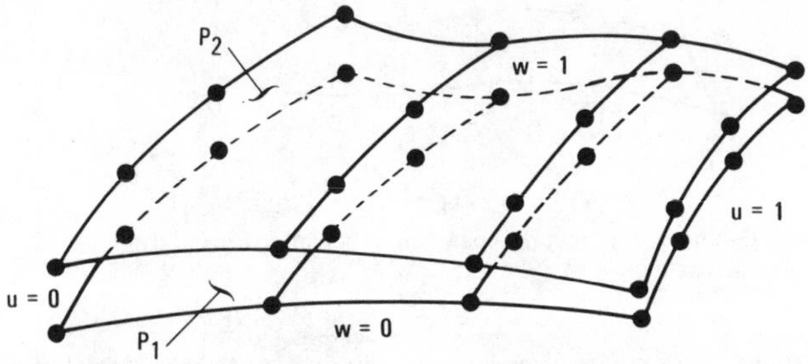

Fig. 23
Geometry for creating a patch by offsetting a given patch

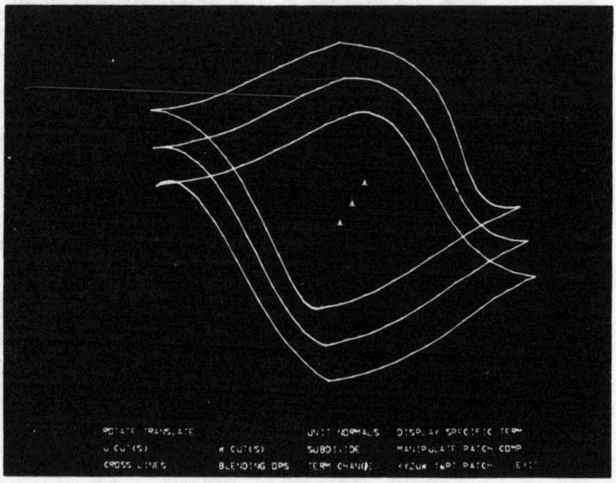

Fig. 24
PC patch offsetting

Translating, Rotating and Scaling – Transformation operations on the PC patch are very similar to those already discussed for the PC curve in eqs. (21), (22) and (23). Again the operations are performed on equations, not just data points. Suffice it to say that for translation in algebraic form, ΔV is added to the s_{44} element of the (S) matrix; while in geometric form, ΔV is added to each element of the P partition of the (B) matrix in eq. (32). Rotation and scaling are similar. Fig 25 shows the transformation operations on a PC patch.

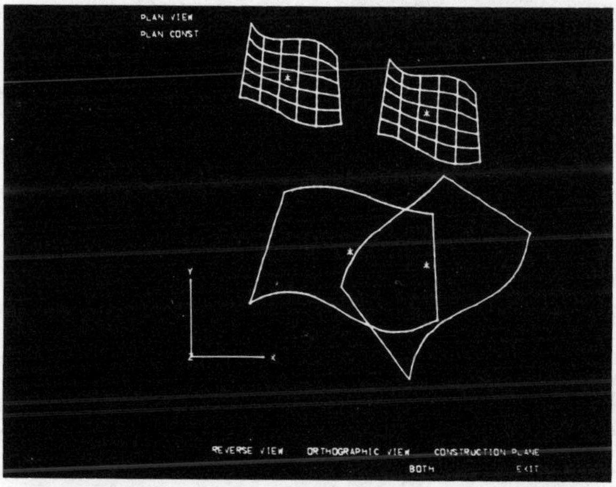

Fig. 25
PC patch translation and rotation

5.8 Blending Patches

Three specific cases will be discussed. These are: (1) blending at a common border, (2) blending between two nonadjacent patches, and (3) blending a given patch to the borders of another patch.

Blending at a Common Border – Consider patches P_1 and P_2 in Fig. 26. We wish to blend the two patches such that $C^{(0)}$ and $C^{(1)}$ continuity exist across the common boundary.

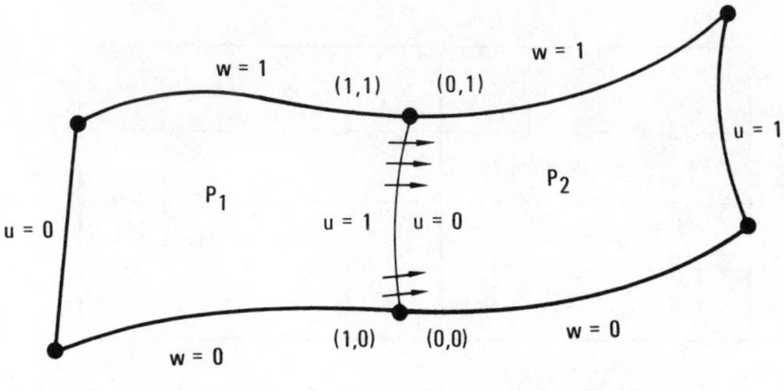

Fig. 26
Geometry for blending at a common border

But before proceeding, we must first discuss a most important consideration: the slopes across the boundary curve of a PC patch. Indeed, a powerful feature of the patch is that slopes across a boundary curve can be expressed as an actual equation by merely inspecting the geometric form in eq. (29). The equation of the parametric slopes in the u direction along the u=1 curve of P_1 is

$$\left[\frac{\partial V(u,w)}{\partial u}\right]_{u=1} \equiv (1,w)_u$$

$$= F_1(w)V_{10u} + F_2(w)V_{11u} + F_3(w)V_{10uw} + F_4(w)V_{11uw}.$$

Note that the cross-derivatives affect the slopes all along the boundary except at w=0 and w=1, where F_3 and F_4 are both zero.

As pointed out in eq. (16), multiplying all the parametric slopes by a constant k just scales up or down on the real space slope vector, i.e., direction cosine data are not changed. Hence, with respect to the form of the (B) matrix, the blending operations for the sample sketch are

$$(u{=}0, \text{row } 1)_{P_2} = (u{=}1, \text{row } 2)_{P_1} \qquad C^{(0)} \text{ continuity,}$$

and

$$(u{=}0, \text{row } 3)_{P_2} = k(u{=}1, \text{row } 4)_{P_1} \qquad C^{(1)} \text{ continuity.}$$

Therefore, adjacent patches have position and slope continuity only if common position rows (or columns) are identical and if common slope rows (or columns) are multiples of each other. Graphically, the elements of interest in the (B) matrices for both patches of the sample are as shown in Fig. 27. Figs. 28, 29 and 30 show the blending operation sequence for adjacent patches. Fig. 28 shows the obvious slope discontinuity at the common border prior to blending; Fig. 29 shows the slope continuity after blending. Fig. 30 depicts the blended patches from another view. The bottom patch lies completely in the xy plane while the top patch is truly three-dimensional, i.e., has depth (z) values.

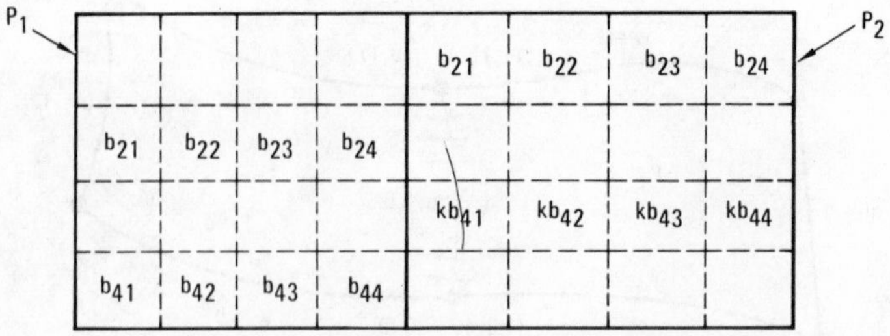

Fig. 27
Boundary (B) matrices elements of interest
for patches blended at a common border

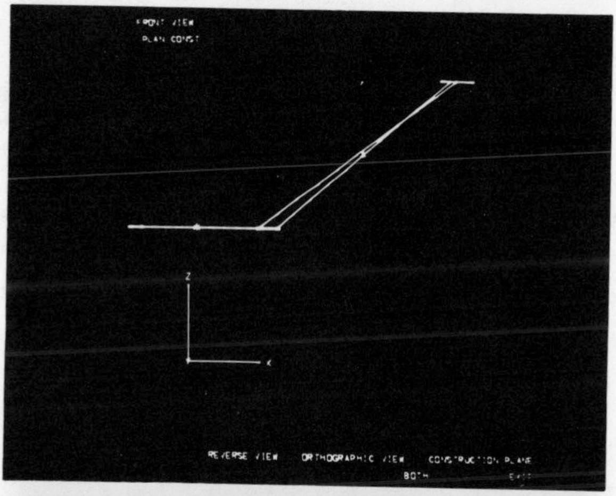

Fig. 28
Blending PC patches at a common border, slope discontinuity prior to blending

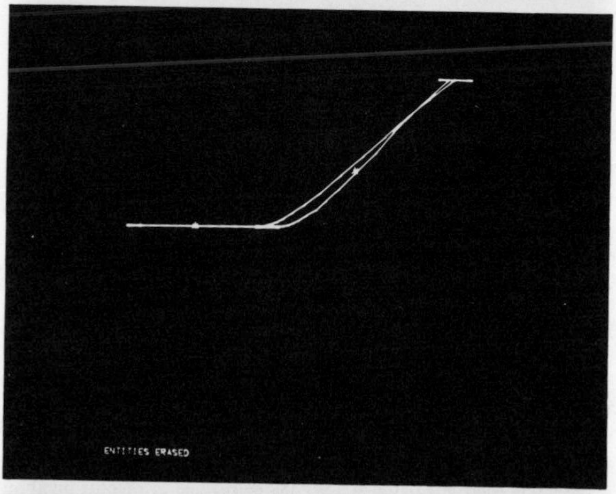

Fig. 29
Blending PC patches at a common border, slope continuity after blending

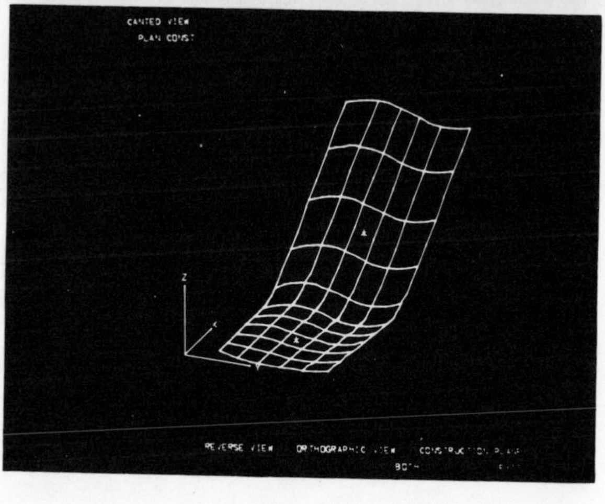

Fig. 30
Blending PC patches at a common border, bottom patch in X-Y plane

Blending Between Two Nonadjacent Patches – This case is characterized by the sketch in Fig. 31. Patch P_3 is to be created such that it manifests $C^{(0)}$ and $C^{(1)}$ continuity with patches P_1 and P_2 at the respective common borders. The technique applied here is the same as that used in the previous section on blending at a common border (page 27), that is

$$(u{=}0,\ \text{row } 1)_{P_3} = (u{=}1,\ \text{row } 2)_{P_1}, \tag{42}$$

$$(u{=}1,\ \text{row } 2)_{P_3} = (u{=}0,\ \text{row } 1)_{P_2}, \tag{43}$$

$$(u{=}0,\ \text{row } 3)_{P_3} = k_1(u{=}1,\ \text{row } 4)_{P_1},\ \text{and} \tag{44}$$

$$(u{=}1,\ \text{row } 4)_{P_3} = k_2(u{=}0,\ \text{row } 3)_{P_2}. \tag{45}$$

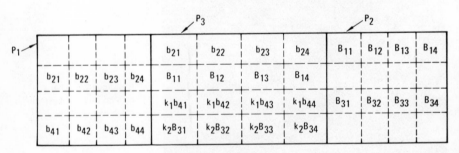

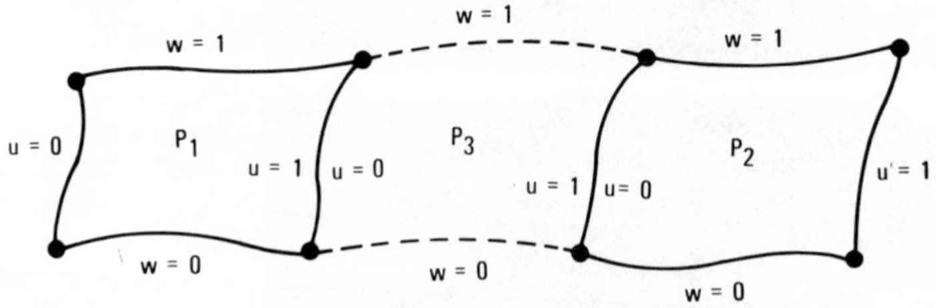

Fig. 31
Geometry for blending between two nonadjacent patches

Equations (42) and (43) guarantee $C^{(0)}$ continuity while (44) and (45) guarantee $C^{(1)}$ continuity. Graphically, the elements of interest in the boundary matrices are as shown in Fig. 32. Figs. 33 and 34 show a patch blended between two nonadjacent patches. In both of these figures, the patch on the left is ruled and in the xy plane while the right patch is a 90 degree surface of revolution about the y axis.

P_1				P_3				P_2			
				b_{21}	b_{22}	b_{23}	b_{24}	B_{11}	B_{12}	B_{13}	B_{14}
b_{21}	b_{22}	b_{23}	b_{24}	B_{11}	B_{12}	B_{13}	B_{14}				
				k_1b_{41}	k_1b_{42}	k_1b_{43}	k_1b_{44}	B_{31}	B_{32}	B_{33}	B_{34}
b_{41}	b_{42}	b_{43}	b_{44}	k_2B_{31}	k_2B_{32}	k_2B_{33}	k_2B_{34}				

Fig. 32
Boundary (B) matrices elements of interest
for blending between two nonadjacent patches

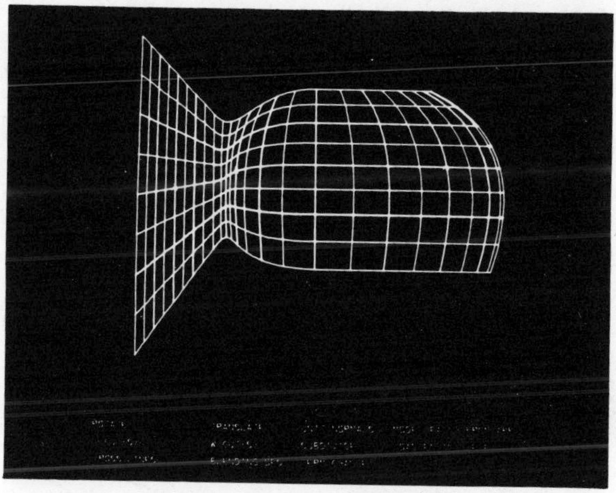

Fig. 33
Blending a PC patch between two nonadjacent patches, plan view

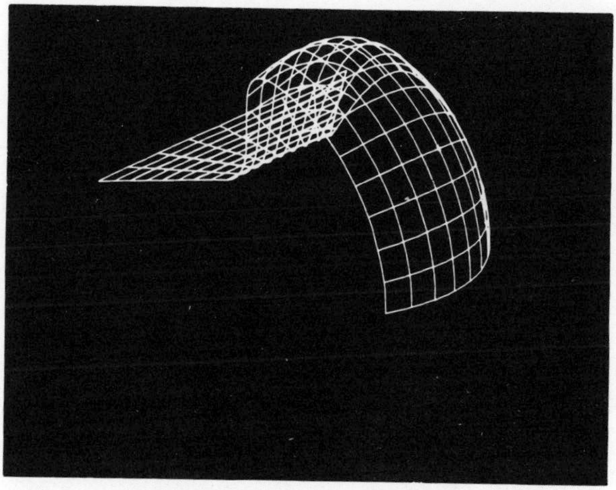

Fig. 34
Blending a PC patch between two nonadjacent patches, trimetric view

Blending a Patch to the Borders of Another Patch – Consider Fig. 35. The objective is to blend P_2 into the borders of P_1. This will be accomplished by creating eight blending patches indicated by the dashed lines. Note that the boundary curves of P_2 are constant parameter values on P_1; hence this is a special case. Again, the key to this operation is the relationship between the parametric tangents when a PC is segmented. Referring to Fig. 36 and using eq. (19) from the section on segmenting a PC curve, it can be shown that

$$\left(\frac{dV}{dt}\right)_{t=0} = \left(\frac{u_2-u_1}{u_1}\right)\left(\frac{dV}{dv}\right)_{v=1},$$

and

$$\left(\frac{dV}{dt}\right)_{t=1} = \left(\frac{u_2-u_1}{1-u_2}\right)\left(\frac{dV}{ds}\right)_{s=0}.$$

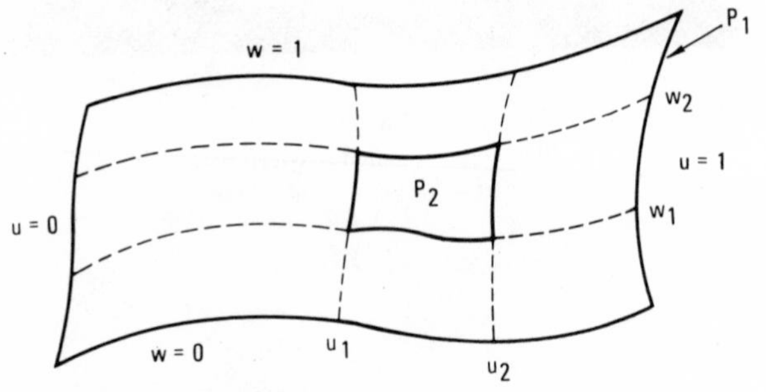

Fig.35
Geometry for blending to the borders of another patch, special case

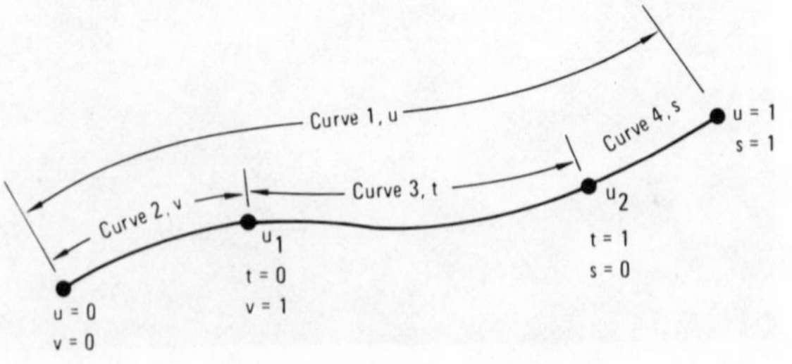

Fig. 36
Geometry for segmenting a PC curve as applied to blending patches

Now, applying the ideas of previous sections on blending (page 30), we can show that the elements of interest in the (B) matrices are as shown in Fig. 37. This format conveniently combines matrix information with uw values. The blank entries are dictated by surrounding patches. A.L. Eshleman of Douglas Aircraft Company, who originated this technique, calls these blank spaces "freedom elements" since they can be arbitrary if there are no surrounding patches. The ratio values

$$r_1 = \frac{w_1}{w_2 - w_1}$$

$$r_2 = \frac{1 - w_2}{w_2 - w_1}$$

$$r_3 = \frac{u_1}{u_2 - u_1}$$

$$r_4 = \frac{1 - u_2}{u_2 - u_1}$$

guarantee $C^{(1)}$ continuity across the boundaries. Fig. 38 shows a surface generated by the "blend eight" operation.

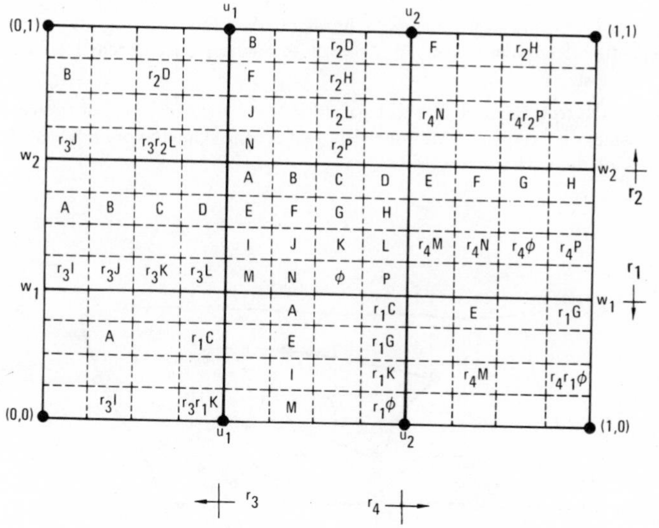

Fig. 37
Boundary (B) matrices elements of interest
for blending a patch to the borders of another patch

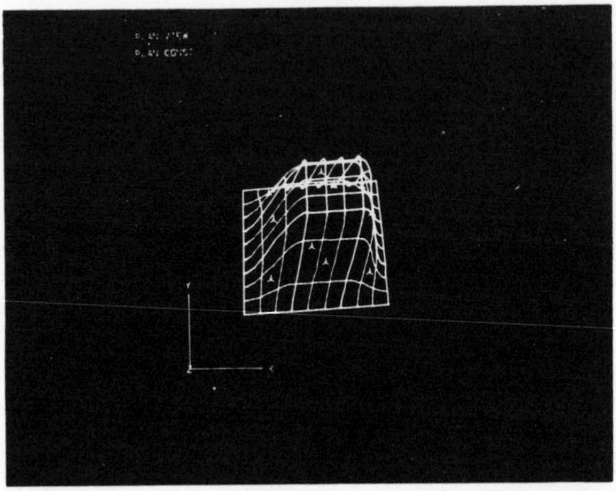

Fig. 38
Blending a PC patch to the borders of another patch

The general "blend eight" case can be pictured as shown in Fig. 39. This case has been implemented and it involves eight ratios, which of course reduce to four for the special case described previously.

If the patch to be blended, P_2, is planar, then both patches can be rotated such that P_2 is in a principal plane, e.g., xy plane; this effectively reduces the computations involved. After blending, the patches are rotated back.

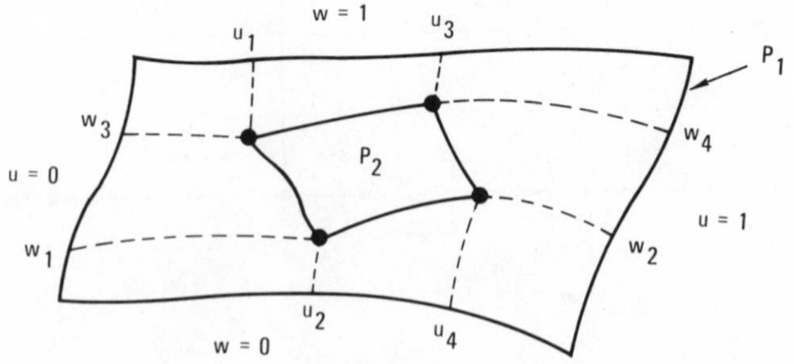

Fig. 39
Geometry for blending to the borders
of another patch, general case

5.9 Intersecting a Patch with a Plane

Consider the sketch in Fig. 40. In order to generate "cut points" to be fitted later by PC curves, witness

$$\Delta w = w_2 - w_1 \qquad w_2 > w_1,$$

where w_1 and w_2 are obtained by intersecting a boundary curve or curves with the plane. One of the values for w_1 or w_2 is not necessarily 0 or 1 since a plane could intersect only one boundary curve. Let

$$p = \frac{w - w_1}{w_2 - w_1} \qquad 0 \leq p \leq 1,$$

hence,

$$w = w_1 + p\,\Delta w.$$

For p=p*,

$$w^* = w_1 + p^*\,\Delta w$$

and u = u* (along the line w=w*) is produced by cutting w* with the plane. Hence, the point on the patch surface V (u*, w*) is easily computed. The points produced in this fashion are then fitted with a PC curve(s) to a given tolerance. The point of interest here is that we produce—not a

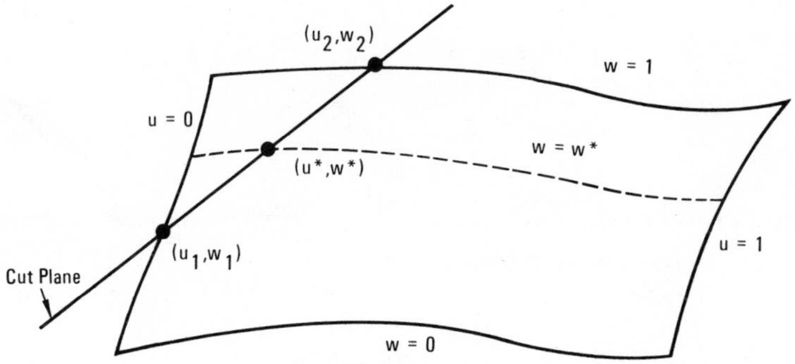

Fig. 40
Geometry for intersecting a patch with a plane

string of discrete data points–but actual continuous curves. Fig. 41 shows the intersection of a compound curvature patch by a family of planes. The solid lines are the resultant intersection curves while the dashed lines are constant uw lines used for display.

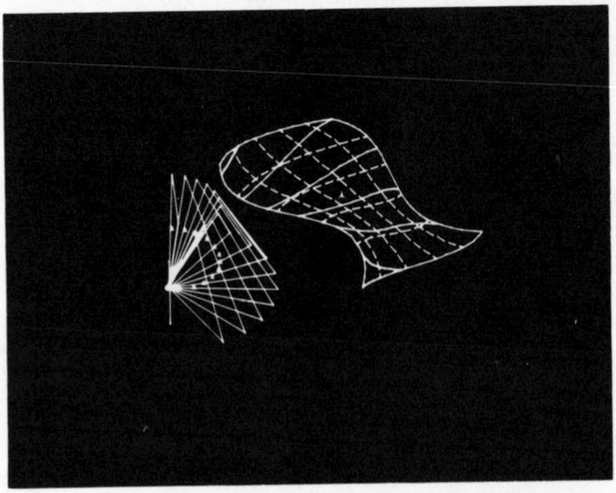

Fig. 41
Intersecting a PC patch with a plane

6. ENGINEERING DESIGN APPLICATIONS

The following typical design problems and their solutions validate the claim that the PC patch is a realistic, efficient, and accurate device for CAD interactive graphics.

6.1 Surface Modification to Incorporate a Hinge Line

The problem statement is depicted in Fig. 42 where the two end points of the hinge line lie on the surface of the body of revolution (e.g., radome or nose cone). The local neighborhood of the surface near the hinge is to be modified. The solution is shown in Fig. 43 where the blending patches are created by using the principles previously described. Fig. 44 shows a plane cut through the hinge line while Fig. 45 shows the edge view of the cut plane.

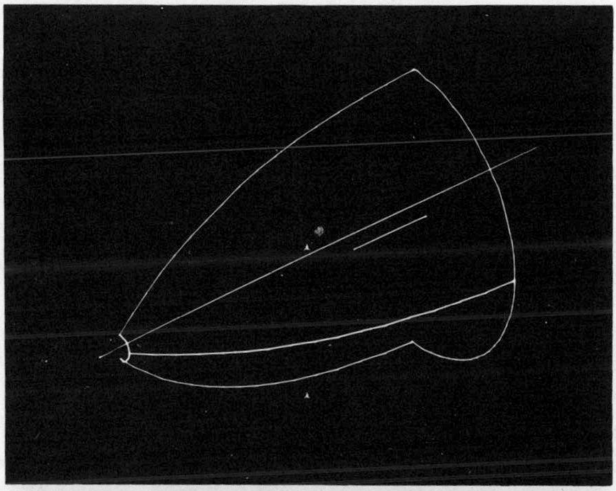

Fig. 42
Surface modification to include straight hinge line-problem statement

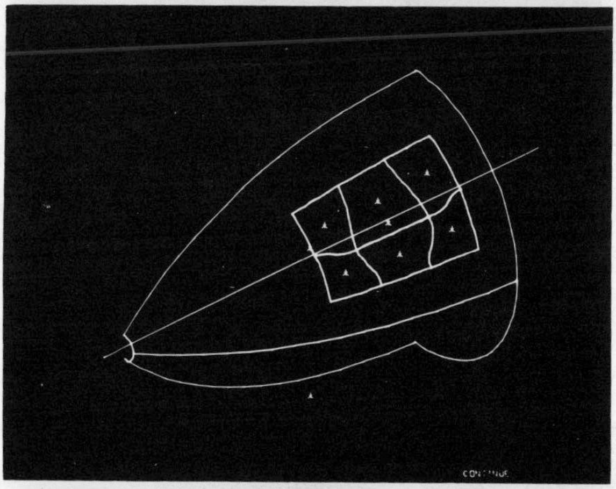

Fig. 43
Surface modification - solution showing blending patches

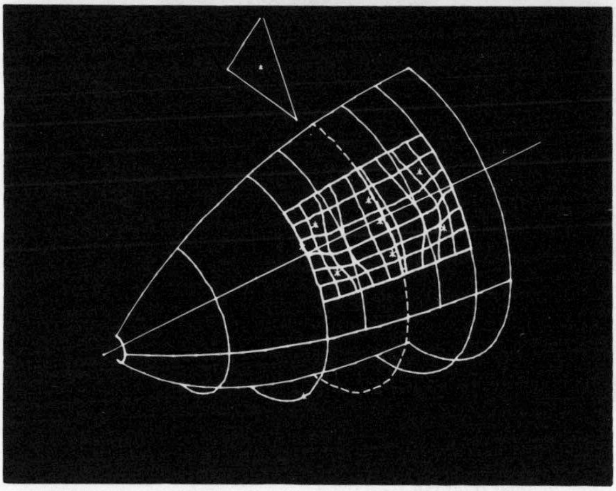

Fig. 44
Surface modification - plane cut through hinge line

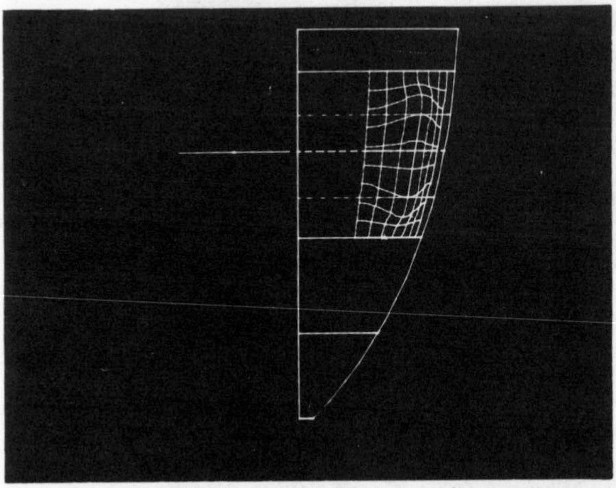

Fig. 45
Surface modification - edge view of cut plane

6.2 Engine Inlet Duct

The problem is to design an inlet duct in which plane cuts normal to the air flow center-of-gravity satisfy aerodynamic and propulsion requirements. It should be noted that typical duct contours possess points of inflection. Of course, this presents no difficulty for the PC. Fig. 46 shows the duct cut by a plane and the resultant closed and continuous PC curve lying on the surface. Fig. 47 shows the edge view of the plane.

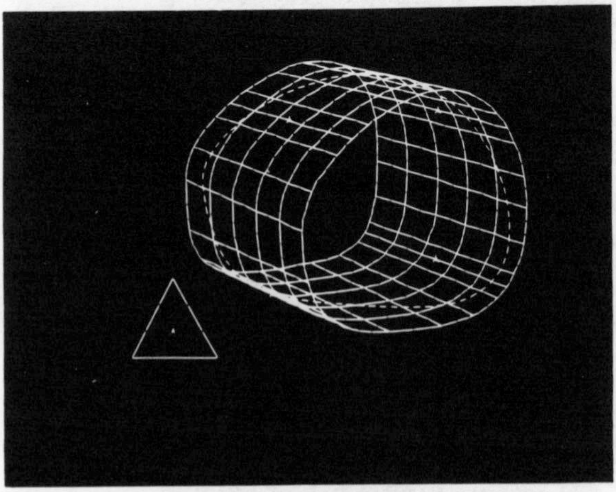

Fig. 46
Engine inlet duct cut by a plane

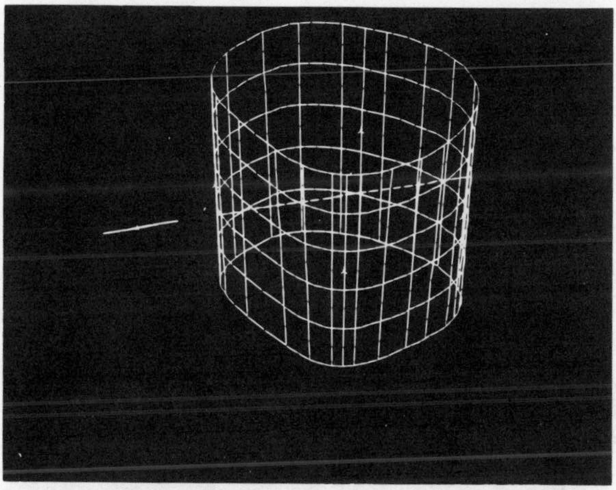

Fig. 47
Engine inlet duct—edge view of cut plane

6.3 Creation of Bolt Holes for Access Door

The problem here is to construct two bolt holes at a specified location on a surface. The solution employs PC surface subdivision and patch revision through blending. Fig. 48 shows the "bossed areas" blended into the original surface.

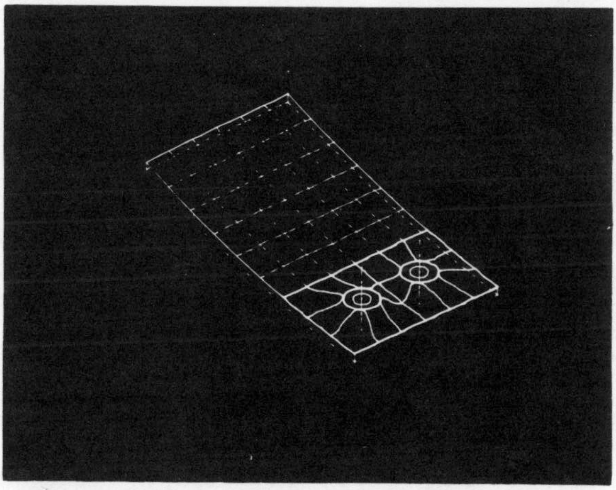

Fig. 48
Creation of bolt holes for access door

6.4 Thermal Insulation Tile for Re-Entry Vehicle

The problem is to create a parallel or thick surface. The solution involves specifying the desired thickness and using the offset capability on the given patch. Fig. 49 shows the designed tile.

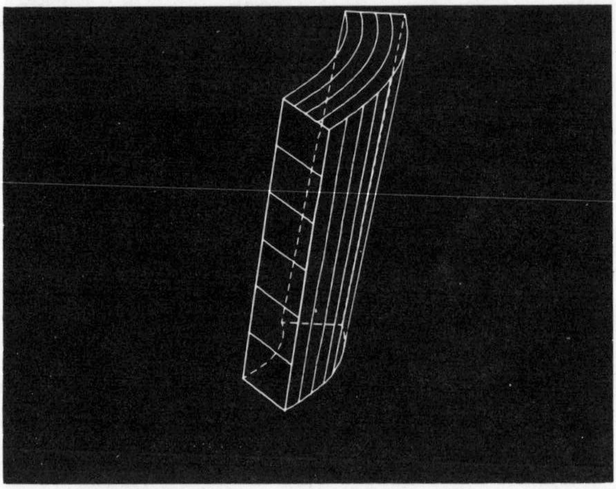

Fig. 49
Thermal insulation tile for re-entry vehicle

6.5 Stress Analysis

The success of the discrete or finite element method in solving practical structural mechanics problems has led to its increased use in other disciplines of engineering mechanics. In large part, the success of the method has been the result of its ability to represent the geometric irregularities so often present in actual hardware. Ironically, most efforts to improve the method have ignored the representation of the initial geometry and have focused on improving the representation of the deformed geometry (analysis variables). This has led to many new plate and shell discrete elements whose accuracy decreases sharply for structures with initially curved boundaries. The number of straight-sided quadrilateral and/or triangular elements needed to accurately solve an elliptic-plate problem is significantly higher than that required for a square plate. This behavior is directly related to the poor approximation of the curved plate boundary with straight-sided discrete elements.

Ref. [20] provides several excellent examples of the above behavior associated with a higher order triangular discrete element. To avoid the situation, it is enough to return to the basic strength of the discrete element method and improve the representation of the initial geometry. Parametric discrete elements, specifically PC representation, provide this improved modeling for both the deformed and undeformed geometry.

Fig. 50A shows a pseudo-elastic picture obtained by computing the principal strain differences, fitting them with PC surface patches over each element and slicing these surfaces with equally spaced planes. The spacing of the cutting planes is proportional to the fringe constant of the photoelastic material (Homalite 100), and hence they should produce the same "fringe" pattern as the photoelastic test results depicted in Fig. 50B. How close the parametric discrete element solution comes to this condition can be seen in the overlay shown in Fig. 50C. These rather remarkable figures were obtained through the courtesy of Stanton [21].

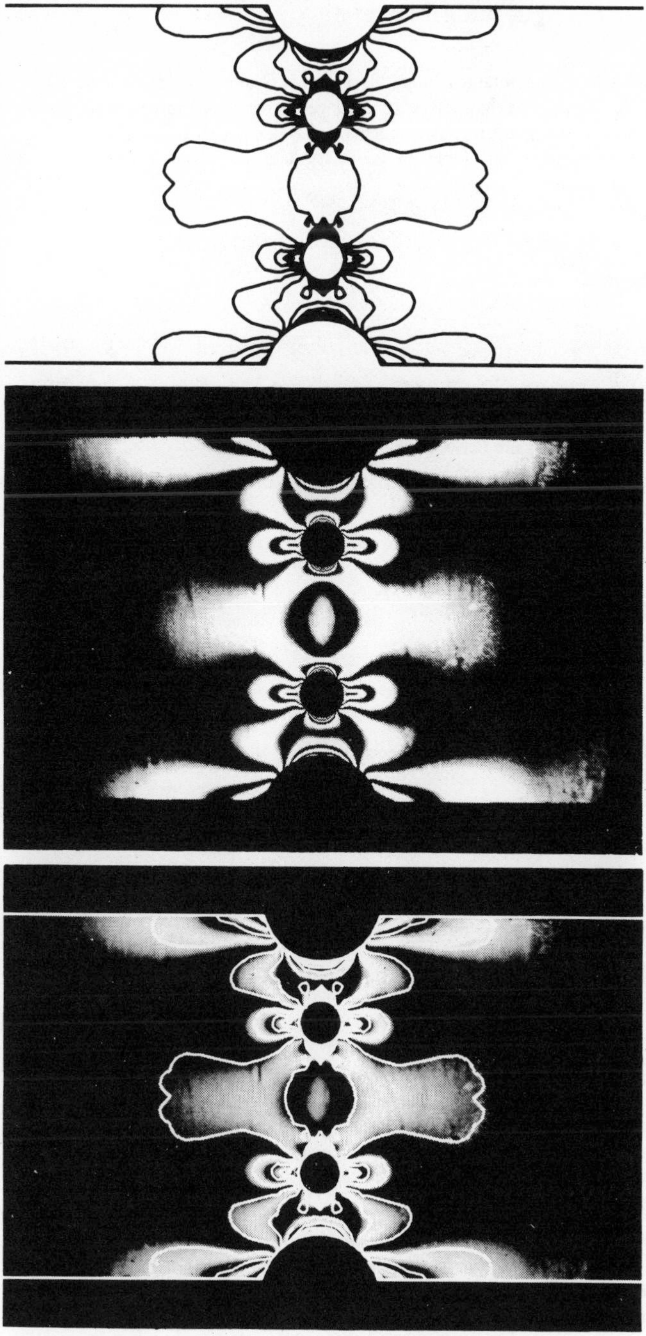

A
Plan view isogram of principal strain differences

B
Photoelastic test results

C
Overlay of photoelastic results and parametric solution

Fig. 50
Specimen stress analysis

Although these results were not obtained interactively, an ICG implementation is obviously desirable, since a change in the patches that define the plate geometry would automatically create a new discrete element model for analysis. Also, much of the existing software developed for surface representation can be used to automate the geometry data for discrete element analysis and to plot the stress and displacement results.

7. CONCLUSIONS

This paper has discussed the implementation of the PC curve and surface patch from the following aspects: the desirability of the parametric representation, the computer system environment, the mathematical formulations, and ICG engineering design problems.

Some of the features of this design device which make it an unusually attractive candidate for computer-aided design are:

- All curves and surfaces are used in a single form (the PC curves are a subset of PC surfaces).
- Planar or twisted data can easily be handled.
- Infinite slopes require no special handling.
- Points of inflection are readily accommodated.
- Rotation, translation, and scaling are done on equations.
- Arc length, surface area, volume, etc. are computed directly without computing explicit points.
- Coordinates of end points of curves and corner points of patches are used directly as coefficients of curves in the PC equation, thus providing an aid to the identification of surface patches and connectivity to other patches.
- Cross-derivative coefficients alter the shape of the surface without affecting the boundary PC curves.
- Patches are bounded by four space curves. However, curves may be of zero length, i.e., 2-sided or 3-sided patches are possible.
- Two or more patches can be matched identically along one boundary of an adjacent patch.
- There exists a one-to-one mapping for analysis results; i.e., stress, strain, temperature, pressure, etc. distributions can be obtained.

Parametric cubic curves and patches form a realistic, flexible surface system suitable for describing most engineering shapes. It should be emphasized that the designer's geometric inputs at the CRT are transformed into actual surface mathematics in such a way that the mathematics are completely hidden from him unless he requests their display. Hence, the experienced designer is free to concentrate on attaining the solution to his defined problem or indeed, to create the definition of his problem.

REFERENCES

[1] S.A. Coons, "Surfaces for Computer-Aided Design of Space Figures," M.I.T. ESL Memorandum 9442-M-139, January 1964.

[2] S.A. Coons, "Surfaces for Computer-Aided Design of Space Forms," Project MAC, Massachusetts Institute of Technology 1967.

[3] J.C. Ferguson, "Multi-variable Curve Interpolation," The Boeing Company, Document D2-22504, July 1963.

[4] A.R. Forrest, "Curves and Surfaces for Computer-Aided Design," Doctoral thesis, University of Cambridge, 1968.

[5] A.L. Eshleman and H.D. Meriwether, "Graphic Applications to Aerospace Structural Design Problems, "SHARE Annual Design Automation Workshop, Los Angeles, 1967.

[6] J.J. Lavick, "Design Philosophies for a Man-Machine Engineering Environment, "McDonnell Douglas Automation Report No. 6045, 1967.

[7] J.J. Lavick, "Computer-Aided Design at McDonnell Douglas," International Symposium (CG 70), Brunel University, Uxbridge, England, April 1970.

[8] J.J. Lavick and G.L. Martin, "Modern Techniques in Design," 1972 CAD/CAM Conference, Society of Manufacturing Engineers, Atlanta, Georgia, February 1972.

[9] A. Newell, "A General Discussion of the Use of Conic Equations to Define Curved Surfaces," The Boeing Company, Document D2-4398, March 1960.

[10] J.H. Shelley, "The Development of Curved Surfaces for Aero-Design," Gloster Aircraft Co., Ltd., 1947.

[11] J.H. Ahlberg, E.N. Nilson, and J.L. Walsh, *The Theory of Splines and their Application,* Academic Press, 1967.

[12] F. Acton, *Numerical Methods that Work,* Harper and Row, New York, 1970.

[13] L. Brand, *Vector and Tensor Analysis,* John Wiley and Sons, New York, 1947.

[14] F.B. Hildebrand, *Introduction to Numerical Analysis,* McGraw-Hill, New York, 1956.

[15] *Handbook of Mathematical Formulas,* U.S. Government Printing Office, Washington, D.C., 1970.

[16] B. Herzog and G. Valle, "Interactive Control of Surface Patches," International Symposium (CG 70), Brunel University, Uxbridge, England, April, 1970.

[17] R.H. Pennington, *Introductory Computer Methods and Numerical Analysis,* Macmillan Company, Toronto, 1970.

[18] S.L. Martin, Informal notes, presently at Stanford University, formerly with Douglas Aircraft, Long Beach, California.

[19] R.C. Buck, *Advanced Calculus,* McGraw-Hill, New York, 1956.

[20] M.W. Chernuka, G.R. Cowper, G.M. Lindberg, and M.D. Olson, "Application of the High Precision Triangular Plate-Bending Element to Problems With Curved Boundaries," NAE Aeronautical Reports LR-529, National Research Council of Canada, October 1969.

[21] E.L. Stanton and E.L. Palacol, "Anisotropic Parametric Plate Discrete Elements," International Journal for Numerical Methods in Engineering, Volume 6, 1973.

ACKNOWLEDGEMENTS

I would like to express my gratitude to several people: Richard C. Rolph for his vast experience in lofting techniques and programming which made easier the implementation of the PC in the Computer-Aided Design and Drafting package; Gerard L. Gilsinn for many helpful mathematical discussions and for programming assistance relative to the PC; Arthur L. Eshleman and Harry D. Meriwether for introducing me to the PC and providing the batch programs which formed the kernel of ICG surface development in St. Louis; and Jerry J. Lavick and Billy K. Winters for a managerial insight that recognized this design technique's potential.

In addition, I offer my appreciation to the entire Computer-Aided Design and Drafting team, both computer programmers and engineers, for excellent achievement over a period of several years in providing an interactive engineering design capability.

Also, special recognition is due various people too numerous to name in the Graphics Communications and in the Duplicating Services activities of McDonnell Aircraft Company. And lastly, for his patient reading of drafts and for his invaluable advice on final changes in text, illustration and format, I am indebted to an able editor–William C. Praeger, McDonnell Douglas Automation Company.

MAN MACHINE COMMUNICATION IN THREE DIMENSIONS+

Martin E. Newell
University of Utah

1. Introduction.

Computer Aided Geometric Design tends to focus attention on techniques for convenient mathematical description of objects. Attention is paid to the problem of how to manipulate models, e.g. Bézier's introduction of control points as a means of controlling shape was a very important contribution [2].

However, what good is a Bézier control point if you have no convenient means for moving it, or for evaluating the effect of that move? Anyone who has worked with Bézier or B-spline patches [7] will know that a screen full of parametric lines mixed up with control meshes can be very confusing.

This paper sets out to survey some of the techniques now available, both hardware and software, for 3-D communication with a computer. The paper concentrates more on recent and/or unusual developments in this field, with the accent on developments at the University of Utah during the past few years.

Communications with a computer can be categorized two ways: input and output. Some examples of input and output devices will be reviewed followed by some possible combinations forming design systems either existing or under development.

2. Input Devices.

There is now in existence an extensive family of devices to facilitate input of information to a

+Supported by DARPA contract DAHC 15-73-C-0363.

computer. These range from the humble teletype to machines such as the Twinklebox [3]. The relevance of devices considered suitable for 3-D work will be discussed.

The teletype and like devices, workhorses of man-machine communication, are almost too ubiquitous to warrant mentioning. However, it is worth noting that some sophisticated and versatile 3-D design systems have been developed in which the teletype was the principal input device, for example, Armit's Multipatch and Multiobject systems [1]. However, the success of such systems is more a tribute to the careful design of structured command languages than to the suitability of the teletype for such functions.

Some of the better known graphical input devices include tablet, light-pen, tracker ball, joystick and shaft encoder. The first three of these provide for input of position information in 2-D, whereas the others provide for input of orientation information in 3-D. Various software techniques for adding the missing facilities needed for 3-D work have been used, such as working with three or more 2-D projections of a 3-D object. However, such techniques have always been less than ideal.

Motivated by the need for direct 3-D position input, a number of devices have been developed, some more successful than others. These include the spark pen, marketed by Science Accessories Corporation, 3-wire wand, and Twinklebox.

The spark pen, as the name implies, consists of a hand held stylus which produces small electrical sparks. These generate acoustic wave fronts which are detected by three orthogonally mounted strip microphones. Strip microphones are mounted on long tubes and are sensitive to sound along their entire length. At the time each spark is generated, a counter is started. The counter is read as the wave front is detected at each microphone, thereby determining the time taken for the wave front to reach each microphone. Knowing the speed of sound, the position of the spark can be determined.

The 3-wire wand employs three shaft encoders mounted at the vertices of a triangle on the ceiling. Each shaft encoder is fitted with a spring loaded pulley, around which a wire is wrapped. The three wires are joined together on a hand grip. By maintaining a measure of the lengths of the three wires, the computer can determine the position of the hand grip.

Although the spark pen and 3-wire wand both provide direct 3-D position input, neither of them provides the position of more than one point, although a multipen spark pen would be feasible for a limited number of pens. These devices have even more severe limitations though - care must be taken to avoid obstructing the signals, either the sound waves or the wires. With these thoughts in mind the Twinklebox was developed by Robert Burton.

The Twinklebox is a device for sensing the positions of one or more small light sources. This is done using four scanners, one at each corner of the ceiling. Each scanner consists of a rotating disc around the edge of which radial slots have been cut, see Fig. 1. The axis of each disc points towards the centre of the room. Consider positioning your eye behind a disc. As a slot passes your eye you see a planar slice through the room. If you were looking for a small light source, you would only see it when your eye, the slot, and the light source were all in the same plane.

In the Twinklebox your eye is replaced by a photomultiplier which outputs a pulse when it sees a light. Two photomultipliers are used with each disc, subtending a right angle at the centre of the disc, thereby giving two planes on which the light must lie. The four scanners therefore give eight planes to which a best fit point is found. Since only three planes are needed to define the position of a point, the system is highly redundant, thereby allowing up to five scanners to be obscured without ill effect. The positions of multiple points are determined by turning lights on one at a time - hence the name Twinklebox.

The Twinklebox as it presently exists is not entirely satisfactory. This is not due to any shortcoming of the fundamental concept, but largely a result of the significant mechanical content of the device, which has caused accuracy problems. Also, four 17" discs with slots around the periphery, rotating at 3600 r.p.m., make a fairly efficient siren. Finally the necessity for working in near darkness is less than ideal. For these reasons, several solid state devices are under investigation in the hope of removing some or all of these objections. All these devices operate by determining angles of incidence of light on detectors, and using multiple detectors.

3. Output Devices.

There are many more techniques available for graphical output than for input. Almost all available devices produce images on 2-D surfaces, the impression of 3-D being produced by various illusions.

Among the better known output devices are various types of plotters and cathode ray tubes with vector generators, including storage tubes. The thing all these devices have in common is that they are used to produce line drawings, in which edges and discontinuities in objects are drawn as lines. Other lines sometimes used are section lines, or constant parameter lines in the case of parametric surfaces. Various techniques can be used to improve the effectiveness of line drawn displays. These include depth modulation, stereo pairs, hidden line removal and real time motion.

Depth modulation refers to the technique of indicating depth with intensity. Objects far away are drawn dimmer than those near the eye. This very simple technique can make a significant contribution to depth perception, removing ambiguities associated with line drawings.

Stereo pairs normally require special viewing apparatus, but provide a good impression of depth, for those who can use it. It normally takes twice as long and twice the drawing area to produce such pictures, which may or may not cause problems depending on the hardware used. Hidden line removal has the disadvantage that the removal of hidden lines by computer is still a relatively slow process. However, it does have the significant advantage that no special purpose hardware or viewing apparatus is needed.

Real time motion can give a very good impression of depth, especially when combined with depth modulation and/or stereo pairs. A small dedicated computer can maintain a reasonable image update rate to give the impression of motion, although if really smooth motion with thousands of lines is required then special purpose hardware is needed. Such hardware is now commercially available at a cost which makes it available to a much wider range of users than was the case a few years ago.

Perhaps the most ambitious device yet developed for improving the effectiveness of line drawing displays is the Head Mounted Display, developed by Ivan Sutherland [9]. This combines depth modulation, stereo pairs and real time motion. The device consists of two 1" cathode ray tubes mounted one on either side of a cap worn by the user. A system of lenses and half-silvered mirrors brings the images on the two tubes to the user's eyes. The system as described, together with a real time line drawing system, provides a wide angle stereo viewer with depth modulation and real time motion. The head mounted display at the University of Utah goes one step further. The display system is connected via a system of levers, pulleys, and shaft encoders back to the computer which is controlling the generation of images. This enables the computer to know the position and attitude of the user's head at all times and the images displayed can be made to appear as an object in front of the user which remains stationary even when he moves his head.

One is led to ask what is the point of a system which lets the user walk around the object, as opposed to one where the object rotates in front of the user? There are two main differences: 1) a system which produces a 3-D image of a stationary object can be used together with a 3-D input device which uses the same coordinate system in order to close the interactive loop. Such combinations of devices will be described in Section 4. 2) The head mounted system gives effectively 360° field of view, which allows one to work on a small detail of an object while maintaining a good appreciation for its relation to the whole.

The obvious next development after line drawings was shaded pictures where TV-like images of objects are produced. Techniques for the production of shaded pictures have been under development for a number of years. Two approaches have received considerable attention - scan line methods and priority methods. In scan line methods, a fact made use of is that the picture will be displayed on a device having a finite number of scan lines. The visible surface problem is solved on each scan line, and the picture can be displayed as it is being computed. Hardware, developed by Gary Watkins [10], has been built using this approach and can produce real time pictures (30 frames per second) of scenes containing up to 2000 edges. Such hardware is now commercially available, although the cost is relatively high.

The other approach, referred to as priority methods, attempts to establish a priority list of objects. An object is defined to have a lower priority than another if it does not obscure any part of the other. The first real-time visible surface hardware, developed by Bob Schumacker et al. [8] at General Electric, used priority to determine which of a number of potentially visible surfaces was actually visible at a given point on the screen. Another use of priority lists, developed by Newell et al [6], involves the use of a frame buffer, a device for digitally storing one frame of information. Objects are written to the frame buffer in reverse priority order, nearer objects overwriting further objects thus solving the visible surface problem.

Frame buffers have other uses in image generation. Even if you cannot compute an image in 1/30 second, a frame buffer allows you to view it on a refreshed display, possibly a standard TV monitor providing the buffer can be read at video rate. Also a frame buffer allows the production of video recordings via a video disc, an alternative to using movie film for animation. Even if the final product is to be on film, video recordings allow a quick-look at animated sequences when the sequence cannot be produced in real time.

A relatively recent addition to the range of 3-D output devices is the foam cutter [5]. This is essentially a small three-axis milling machine capable of cutting styro-foam at high speed. With such devices we can get away from trying to give the illusion of three dimensionality by actually making a model of the object under consideration. The principal disadvantages of this device are its speed in terms of both set up time and cutting time, and the restrictions on the shapes that it can cut. For example, a three-axis machine cannot cut anything with an overhang making it necessary to cut such objects with separate cuts or in separate parts. However, in cases where these drawbacks are not important the foam cutter can give hitherto unattainable reality.

4. Design Systems.

Apart from the fairly standard assemblies of CRTs, plotters, tablets, etc., there are a number of configurations using some of the less usual devices which promise to have significant advantages. Some of these configurations already exist or are under construction.

Systems based on the head mounted display (HMD) tend to fire the imagination more than some others. In order that the HMD can develop its full potential, a real time line drawing system is necessary. However, the HMD is merely two CRTs specially mounted, and so there is no fundamental reason why it should not be used with a real time shaded picture system. The system of levers used with the HMD at the University of Utah is a little cumbersome and restricts movement to a fairly small volume. All that is needed in order to determine head position and orientation is the positions of three points on the head. This could be achieved using three spark pens, or three lights sensed by the Twinklebox. In order that it should be possible to interact with the object being viewed, some form of 3-D input device is necessary, such as a spark pen, 3-wire wand or again the Twinklebox. Here, the HMD allows something that is not practical with other displays. It is possible to reach out into the image and 'touch' various points on the image. The problem of correlating the input position with a point on the object can be done by using the windowing hardware which is a part of the real time image generating system. If a small window is set around the input point and the object is drawn once, then anything that appears in the window must be near the wand.

A design system dealing with B-spline surfaces and using the above ideas is currently under development at Utah.

Another rather more conventional system is also under development at Utah. This is based on a PDP-11/45 system. As proposed, the PDP-11 will have attached to it a real-time line drawing system and a frame buffer. The line drawing system will be used not only to produce line drawings, but will be capable of carrying out a number of the more commonly needed functions found in processing three dimensional information. These include matrix multiplication and the ability to clip polygons with an arbitrary number of edges. The frame buffer will be configured so as to be accessible from the PDP-11 as 128K of high speed store. Thus, when not used for refreshing a TV monitor, the frame buffer will give a large memory expansion to the PDP-11 for storing data structures or whatever else seems appropriate. The whole system will be connected to the ARPA Network as a host. For interaction, the system will initially have a teletype and tablet. Hard copy listings and drawings will be obtained by using existing facilities. It is proposed to connect the head mounted display to this system, using a derivative of the Twinklebox for determining head position and for 3-D input. When operational, this system will provide facilities for working interactively with line drawings, and for producing direct-view shaded pictures.

5. Conclusions.

Three dimensional man-machine communication has not yet lived up to its rich promise. This is due to a number of causes. Among these are, in the opinion of this author, such things as:

i) Inadequate liaison between the people with problems and those with potential solutions.

ii) A failure on the part of many people working in the field to appreciate what is difficult and what is not difficult about 3-D interaction. People who think that all systems should be structured with picture data structure and object data structure, all made out of richly pointered ring structures are destined to be disillusioned. On the other hand, to view 3-D interaction as a simple extension of 2-D work, and to believe that all the special hardware needed is a storage tube is a gross oversimplification. Yet it is surprising how many people seem to hold one or other of these extreme views.

iii) The cost of special purpose hardware is high, which is a major reason for the popularity of relatively inexpensive storage tube terminals. Equipment of advanced capability will always be more expensive than more standard devices. However, if the cost trend of the last five years continues, and there is evidence to show that it will, then the expense of such devices really will cease to be a major issue.

iv) Lack of properly integrated systems of hardware, software, and application. All too often one has to make do with unsuitable facilities. For example, manipulating 3-D objects with a teletype, trying to work interactively with a heavily loaded time-sharing system, or trying to design a heavily constrained object with a system having too many degrees of freedom. Some of the more successful design systems have resulted from an effort to solve only a limited class of problems. A free form patch based system can be a positive hindrance in trying to design a ship hull. The type of parameters needed are things like length, breadth, position of maximum breadth etc. However, such a system would not be suitable for designing a car body, for example.

In spite of these problems, three dimensional man machine interaction is a fast growing field, and will continue to be so, spurred on by the increasing number of beneficial applications and by the promise of greater rewards. This paper has described some devices and techniques which, it is believed, will contribute to a better understanding of what is possible and what is needed to improve man machine communications in three dimensions.

REFERENCES

1. Armit, A. P. "Multipatch and Multiobject Design Systems" Proc. Royal Society, London 321, 1971, 235-242.

2. Bézier, P. "Numerical Control-Mathematics and Applications" (translated by A. R. Forrest) London, John Wiley & Sons, 1972.

3. Burton, R. P. "Real-time Measurement of Multiple Three Dimensional Positions" University of Utah Comp. Sci. Technical Report UTEC-CSc-72-122 Salt Lake City, Utah, June 1973.

4. Coons, S. A. "Surfaces for Computer-Aided Design of Space Forms" Project MAC, MIT, 1964. Revised to MAC-TR-41, 1967.

5. Lang, C.A. "A Three Dimensional Model Making Machine" Proceedings of Prolemat 73, April 1973.

6. Newell, M. E., Newell, R. G., Sancha, T. L. "A Solution to the Hidden Surface Problem" ACM Conference Proceedings, 1972, Vol. 1, 443-450.

7. Riesenfeld, R. F. "Applications of B-Spline Approximation to Geometric Problems of Computer-Aided Design" University of Utah Comp. Sci. Technical Report UTEC-CSc-73-126 Salt Lake City, Utah, March 1973.

8. Schumaker, R., Brand, B., Gilliland, M., Sharp, W. "Study for Applying Computer Generated Images to Visual Simulation" General Electric Technical Information Series R69ELS-110, Dec. 1969.

9. Sutherland, I. E. "A Head-Mounted Three-Dimensional Display" AFIPS Conference Proceedings 1968. Vol. 33, 757-764.

10. Watkins, G. S. "A Real-Time Visible Surface Algorithm" University of Utah Comp. Sci. Technical Report UTEC-CSc-70-101 Salt Lake City, Utah, June 1970.

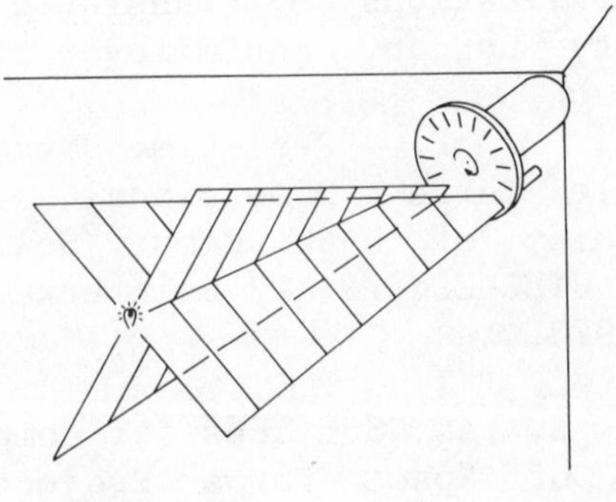

Figure 1. Scanner

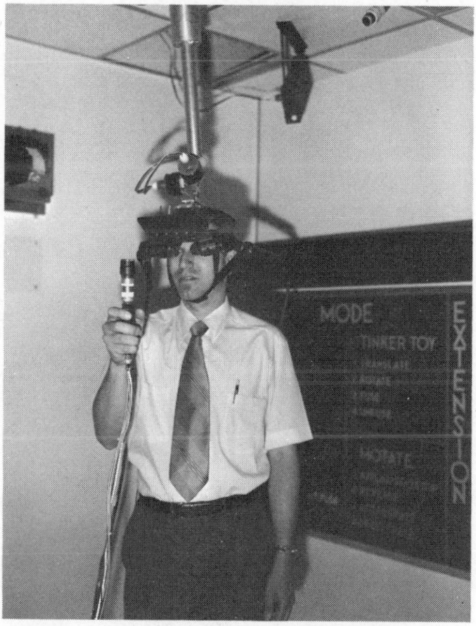

Figure 2. Head Mounted Display

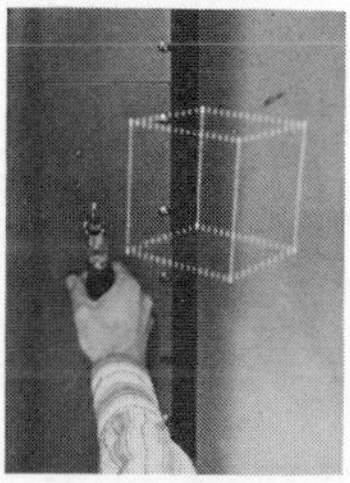

(a)

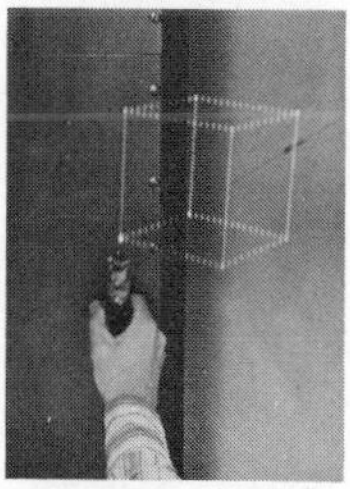

(b)

Figure 3. Goblet

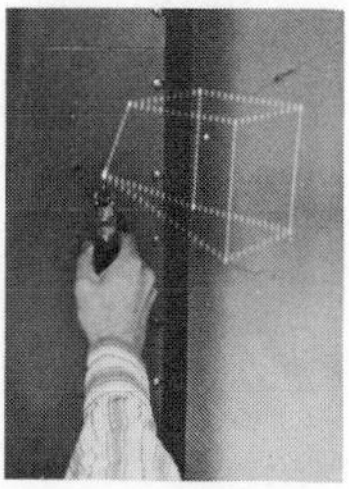

(c)

(d)

Figure 4
3-Wire Wand

A CLASS OF LOCAL INTERPOLATING SPLINES

Edwin Catmull
Raphael Rom

University of Utah

1. INTRODUCTION

In this paper we present a general class of splines. We shall show that some known splines are special cases of these splines. Of particular interest, however, is the subclass of these splines that is local and interpolating.

The spline will be presented in a parametric form:

$$\mathbf{F}(s) = [x_1(s),\ x_2(s),\ .\ .\ .]$$

For the purpose of the mathematics it is only necessary to consider one component, say $x(s)$, since the others are treated in the same way.

For the purpose of this paper we use the following terminology:

(i) Defining points: a set of ordered data points p_i that are evenly spaced in s. In our examples we shall usually use two dimensions.

(ii) Spline: A piecewise function with preset properties of continuity and differentiability.

(iii) Interpolating spline: a spline that passes through its defining points.

(iv) Approximating splines: a spline that may not pass

This work was supported by the Advanced Research Projects Agency of the Department of Defence under contract number DAHC15-73-C-0363.

through its defining points.

(v) Local spline: a spline that changes in a finite interval when one of its defining points is changed.

(vi) Cardinal function: a function that is 1 at some knot, 0 at all other knots and can be anything in between the other knots. It satisfies $F_i(s_j)=\delta_{ij}$.

2. THE MODEL

Consider two functions of s: $x_1(s)$ and $x_2(s)$. The average function $F(s)=(x_1(s)+x_2(s))/2$ is a function that for each s passes midway between the two given functions. We may also assign different weights and have

$$F(s)=(w_1x_1(s)+w_2x_2(s))/(w_1+w_2)$$

thus emphasizing the effect of one function over the other. This is merely a weighted average of x_1 and x_2. Finally this can be extended to make w a function of s thus varying the weight on the x's as we vary s. Also the number of functions can be increased and the model of the spline will then be

$$F(s)=\sum x_i(s)\,w_i(s)/\sum w_i(s) \tag{1}$$

The $w_i(s)/\sum w_i(s)$ are often called blending functions.

It should be emphasized at this point that in the model defined by equation (1), functions are blended together rather than the defining points as in other interpolating schemes.

If $w_i(s)$ is zero outside some given interval of s then $x_i(s)$ has an effect only in that interval. In other words, $x_i(s)$ has only a local effect on $F(s)$. Note that the differentiability of $F(s)$ is determined by the minimum differentiability of $x_i(s)$ and $w_i(s)$.

Consider the following case: Let $x_i(s)$ be any function interpolating the points p_i through s_{i+k}, and let $w_i(s)$ be zero outside (s_{i-1}, s_{i+k+1}). The function $F(s)$ defined in equation (1) will thus be an interpolating function. Intuitively, this says that if all of the functions that have an effect at a point, pass through the point, then the average of the functions will pass through the point.

In general, the points p_j are pairs (x_j, y_j) and in the parametric space we can, without loss of generality, place $s_j = j$.

A polynomial of degree k that passs through k+1 given points will be used as $x(s)$. In general it will not pass through the other points. If the width of the interval in which $w_i(s)$ is non zero is less than or equal to k+2 then $x_i(s)$ will not affect $F(s)$ outside the interpolation interval. This means that $F(s)$ will be an interpolating function. On the other hand if the width of $w_i(s)$ is greater than k+2 then $x_i(s)$ will have an effect on the curve outside the interpolation interval. $F(s)$ will then be an approximating function.

One example is the B-spline where the polynomials are of degree 0 $[x_i(s) = P_i]$ and $w_i(s) = N_{i,k}(s)$ the B-spline basis function. Since $\sum N_{i,k}(s) = 1$ then $F(s) = \sum P_i N_{i,k}(s)$. For cubic B-splines the width of $N_{i,3}(s)$ is 4 which is greater than the degree of the polynomial+2. Therefore the B-spline is approximating.

3. BLENDING FUNCTIONS

Since the blending functions presented above are, as of now, completely arbitrary we impose some constraints in order to make them easier to use. We shall deal only with blending functions that are zero outside of some given interval. Also we require that $\sum w_i(s)$ does not vanish for any s. We shall normalize

$w_i(s)$ so that $\sum w_i(s)=1$ for all s. In addition, since it is most likely to choose $x_i(s)$ as polynomials which are infinitely differentiable, $F(s)$ inherits the differentiability of $w(s)$. Thus a differentiability constraint must also be imposed on these blending functions.

1. A blending function already used for approximating splines is the B-spline basis function. It has been used for blending together points (constant functions) to get an approximating spline. We have extended its use to blend functions together. There are several ways of generating the basis function [6].

2. Another function that was tried was a sort of tapered end window with more control over the differentiability (see figure 3). This is an even function that is zero for $|t| \geq t_1$ (see figure 1) and the part of the function between $t_{1/2}$ and t_1 is skew symmetric about $t_{1/2}$. This latter portion was generated using Bézier curves [3,5] for the set of points spaced as indicated in figure 1. (crosses mark the points) By virtue of

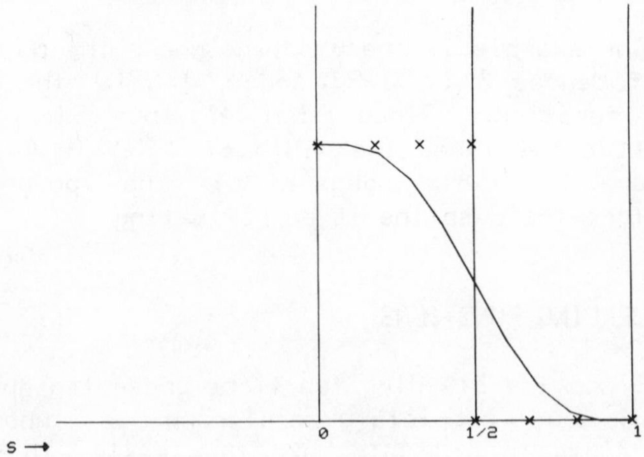

Figure 1

a property of Bézier curves, the differentiability of the function depends linearly upon the number of points. The example in Figure 1 will yield a curve of differentiability 3.

3. The previous two blending functions are piecewise polynomials. In general we might make a blending function out of pieces of polynomials where the ends of the pieces have continuity and differentiability constraints.

4. CALCULATING CARDINAL FUNCTIONS

If in equation (1) we assume $x_i(s)$ to be polynomials of degree k then this equation can be reduced to a much simpler form:

$$F(s) = \sum_j p_j C_{jk}(s) \tag{2}$$

where the $C_{jk}(s)$ are cardinal blending functions and j is the knot to which the cardinal function and the point belong and each $C_{jk}(s)$ is a shifted version of $C_{0,k}(s)$. $C_{0,k}(s)$ is a function of both the degree k of the polynomials and the blending function $w(s)$:

$$C_{0,k}(s) = \sum_{i=0}^{k} \left[\prod_{\substack{j=i-k \\ j \neq 0}}^{i} (s/j+1) \right] w(s+i) \tag{3}$$

In essence we see that for a polynomial case our cardinal functions are a blend of Lagrange polynomials. When calculating $C_{0,k}(s)$, $w(s)$ should be centered about k/2.

We have thus shown a way of creating sets of cardinal functions that are non-zero in a finite interval and the differentiability of which can be easily controlled. This result enables us to reduce the computation when creating interpolating splines.

5. EXAMPLES

To demonstrate this class of splines we have chosen to blend polynomials using both the B-spline and Bézier curves as blending functions. Our parameters are:

1. Differentiability
2. Degree of polynomials to be blended
3. The localness of the spline (which determines whether it interpolates or approximates)
4. Type of blending function (B-spline or Bézier curve)

To demonstrate the functions we are using a two dimensional case $F(s)=[X(s),Y(s)]$

Figure 2 shows a B-spline blending function with differentiability 1. The vertical lines represent the knots' coordinates. Figure 3 shows a Bézier curve type blending function with differentiability 2 and width 4. We have already shown that the blending together of polynomials is equivalent to blending points with a corresponding cardinal function. If the blending function of figure 2 is to be applied to polynomials of degree 1 (i.e. the straight lines passing through adjoining points) then the corresponding cardinal function is shown in figure 4.

The blending function of figure 4 when applied to the points yield the spline of figure 5. Figure 6 shows a cardinal function made for polynomials of degree 2 using B-spline blending functions of differentiability 2. Figure 7 shows the resulting spline.

6. EXTENSIONS

By taking the cartesian cross product of two splines one can get a bivariate surface that interpolates a grid of points.

As an example, we can find the coefficients of bicubic patches that interpolate a grid of points. The cardinal function of figure 4 is a combination of the B-spline basis function of differentiability 1 and linear functions, which yields a cubic.

The formulation for a surface patch using that cardinal function can be shown to be:

$$[s^3\ s^2\ s\ 1]\ M \begin{bmatrix} P_{11} & P_{12} & P_{13} & P_{14} \\ P_{21} & P_{22} & P_{23} & P_{24} \\ P_{31} & P_{32} & P_{33} & P_{34} \\ P_{41} & P_{42} & P_{43} & P_{44} \end{bmatrix} M^T\ [t^3\ t^2\ t\ 1]^T$$

$$\text{where } M=1/2 \begin{bmatrix} -1 & 3 & -3 & 1 \\ 2 & -5 & 4 & -1 \\ -1 & 0 & 1 & 0 \\ 0 & 2 & 0 & 0 \end{bmatrix}$$

and P_{ij} are point values. The patch interpolates the middle four points. Adjoining patches have continuity of the first derivative. This can be compared with other methods for generating bicubic patches in [1,2,4].

7. CONCLUSION

We have presented a class of splines in equation (1) that has some useful characteristics for design purposes because it is local and interpolating. We think this spline bears further investigation on its properties.

REFERENCES

[1] Bézier, P. "Mathematical and Practical Possibilities of UNISURF." These proceedings.

[2] Coons, S. A. "Surfaces for Computer-Aided Design of Space Forms." Project MAC, MIT, 1964. Revised to MAC-TR--41, 1967.

[3] Forrest, A. R. "Interactive Interpolation and Approximation by Bézier Polynomials." Computer Journal, Vol. 15 (1972), pp. 71-79.

[4] Forrest, A. R. "On Coons and Other Methods for the Representation of Curved Surfaces." Computer Graphics and Image Processing (1972) pp. 341-359.

[5] Gordon, W. J. and Riesenfeld, R. F. "Bernstein-Bézier Methods for the Computer-Aided Design of Free-Form Curves and Surfaces." JACM (April 1974)

[6] Gordon, W. J. and Riesenfeld, R. F. "B-Spline Curves and Surfaces." These proceedings.

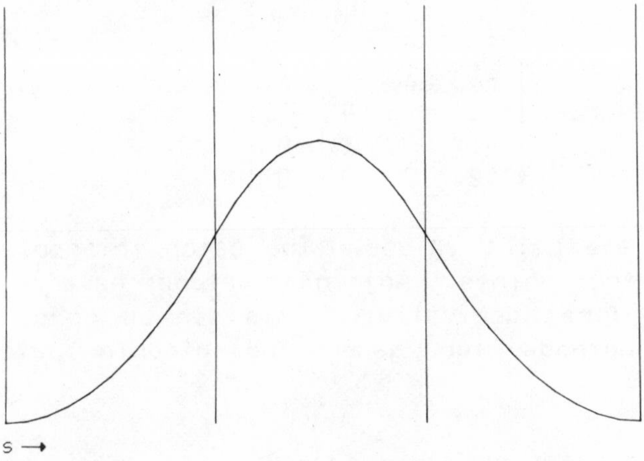

INTERVAL WIDTH=3, DIFFERENTIABILITY=1, TYPE: B-SPLINE

Figure 2

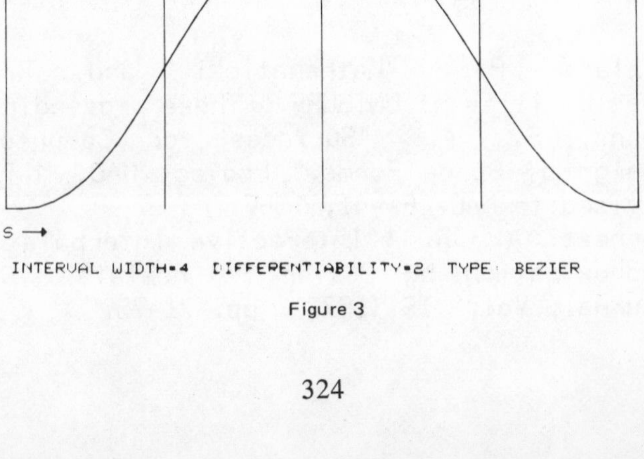

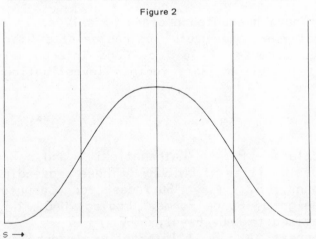

INTERVAL WIDTH=4 DIFFERENTIABILITY=2, TYPE: BEZIER

Figure 3

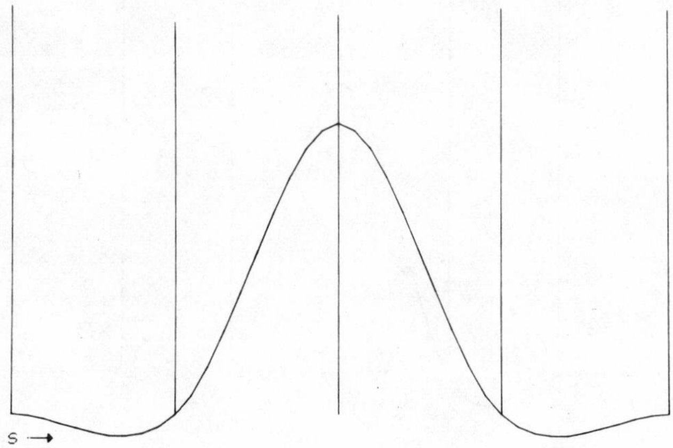

INTERVAL WIDTH=4, DIFFERENTIABILITY=1, TYPE B-SPLINE
DEGREE OF POLYNOMIAL FOR CARDINAL FUNCTION IS 1

Figure 4

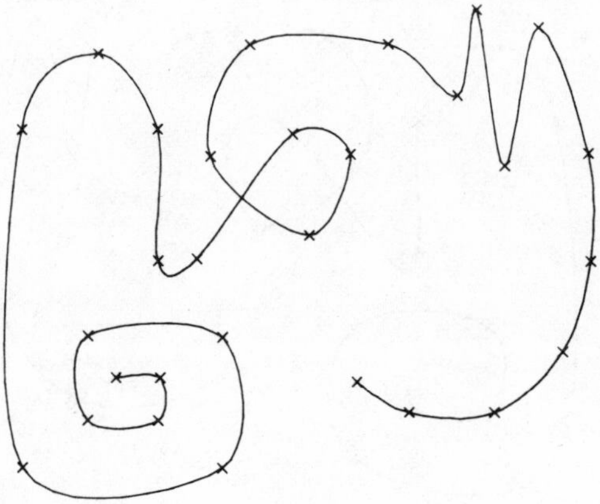

DEGREE OF POLYNOMIAL FOR CARDINAL IS 1
DIFFERENTIABILITY=1, TYPE B-SPLINE
WIDTH OF BLENDING FUNCTION=4

Figure 5

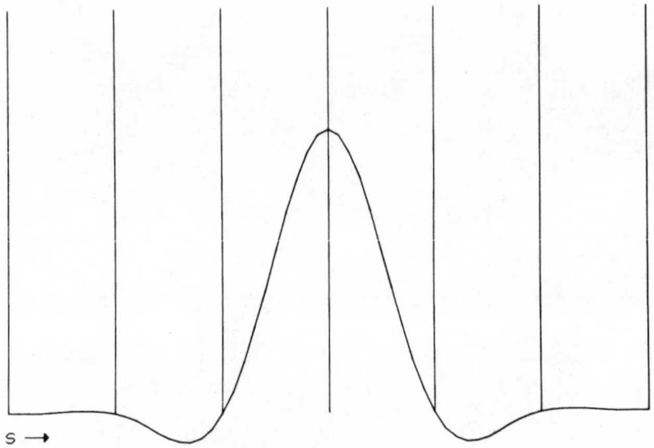

INTERVAL WIDTH=6, DIFFERENTIABILITY=2, TYPE: B-SPLINE
DEGREE OF POLYNOMIAL FOR CARDINAL FUNCTION IS 2

Figure 6

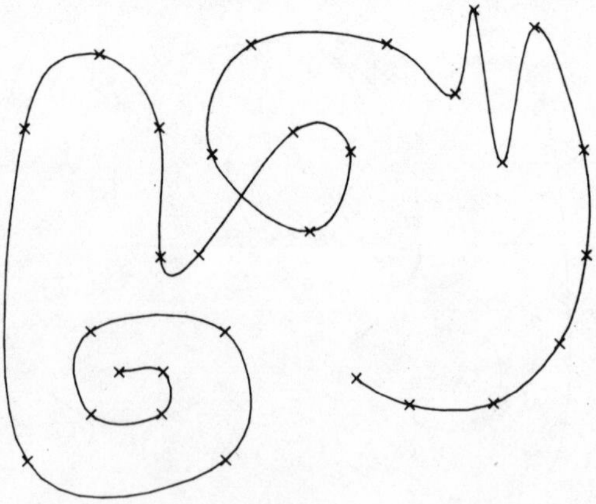

DEGREE OF POLYNOMIAL FOR CARDINAL IS 2
DIFFERENTIABILITY=2, TYPE: B-SPLINE
WIDTH OF BLENDING FUNCTION=6

Figure 7